Full Color on Every Page!

Microsoft® Word 97 Simplified™

IDG's 3-D Visual™ Series

IDG BOOKS

From maranGraphics™

IDG Books Worldwide, Inc.
An International Data Group Company
Foster City, CA • Indianapolis • Chicago • Dallas

Microsoft® Word 97 Simplified™

Published by
IDG Books Worldwide, Inc.
An International Data Group Company
919 E. Hillsdale Blvd., Suite 400
Foster City, CA 94404

Library of Congress Catalog Card No.: 97-070364
ISBN: 0-7645-6011-5

Printed in the United States of America
10 9 8

XX/XX/XX/XX/XX

Distributed in the United States by IDG Books Worldwide, Inc.

Distributed by Macmillan Canada for Canada; by Contemporanea de Ediciones for Venezuela; by Distribuidora Cuspide for Argentina; by CITEC for Brazil; by Ediciones ZETA S.C.R. Ltda. for Peru; by Editorial Limusa SA for Mexico; by Transworld Publishers Limited in the United Kingdom and Europe; by Academic Bookshop for Egypt; by Levant Distributors S.A.R.L. for Lebanon; by Al Jassim for Saudi Arabia; by Simron Pty. Ltd. for South Africa; by Pustak Mahal for India; by The Computer Bookshop for India; by Toppan Company Ltd. for Japan; by Addison Wesley Publishing Company for Korea; by Longman Singapore Publishers Ltd. for Singapore, Malaysia, Thailand, and Indonesia; by Unalis Corporation for Taiwan; by WS Computer Publishing Company, Inc. for the Philippines; by WoodsLane Pty. Ltd. for Australia; by WoodsLane Enterprises Ltd. for New Zealand. Authorized Sales Agent: Anthony Rudkin Associates for the Middle East and North Africa.

For general information on IDG Books Worldwide's books in the U.S., please call our Consumer Customer Service department at 800-762-2974. For reseller information, including discounts and premium sales, please call our Reseller Customer Service department at 800-434-3422.

For information on where to purchase IDG Books Worldwide's books outside the U.S., please contact our International Sales department at 415-655-3172 or fax 415-655-3295.

For information on foreign language translations, please contact our Foreign & Subsidiary Rights department at 415-655-3021 or fax 415-655-3281.

For sales inquiries and special prices for bulk quantities, please contact our Sales department at 415-655-3200 or write to the address above.

For information on using IDG Books Worldwide's books in the classroom or for ordering examination copies, please contact our Educational Sales department at 800-434-2086 or fax 817-251-8174.

For press review copies, author interviews, or other publicity information, please contact our Public Relations department at 415-655-3000 or fax 415-655-3299.

For authorization to photocopy items for corporate, personal, or educational use, please contact Copyright Clearance Center, 222 Rosewood Drive, Danvers, MA 01923, or fax 508-750-4470.

Trademark Acknowledgments

maranGraphics Inc. has attempted to include trademark information for products, services and companies referred to in this guide. Although maranGraphics Inc. has made reasonable efforts in gathering this information, it cannot guarantee its accuracy.

All brand names and product names used in this book are trade names, service marks, trademarks, or registered trademarks of their respective owners. IDG Books Worldwide is not associated with any product or vendor mentioned in this book.

FOR PURPOSES OF ILLUSTRATING THE CONCEPTS AND TECHNIQUES DESCRIBED IN THIS BOOK, THE AUTHOR HAS CREATED VARIOUS NAMES, COMPANY NAMES, MAILING ADDRESSES, E-MAIL ADDRESSES AND PHONE NUMBERS, ALL OF WHICH ARE FICTITIOUS. ANY RESEMBLANCE OF THESE FICTITIOUS NAMES, COMPANY NAMES, MAILING ADDRESSES, E-MAIL ADDRESSES AND PHONE NUMBERS TO ANY ACTUAL PERSON, COMPANY AND/OR ORGANIZATION IS UNINTENTIONAL AND PURELY COINCIDENTAL.

The animated characters are the copyright of maranGraphics, Inc.

U.S. Corporate Sales
Contact maranGraphics at (800) 469-6616 or Fax (905) 890-9434.

U.S. Trade Sales
Contact IDG Books at (800) 434-3422 or (415) 655-3000.

Welcome to the world of IDG Books Worldwide.

IDG Books Worldwide, Inc., is a subsidiary of International Data Group, the world's largest publisher of computer-related information and the leading global provider of information services on information technology. IDG was founded more than 25 years ago and now employs more than 8,500 people worldwide. IDG publishes more than 270 computer publications in over 75 countries (see listing below). More than 90 million people read one or more IDG publications each month.

Launched in 1990, IDG Books Worldwide is today the #1 publisher of best-selling computer books in the United States. We are proud to have received eight awards from the Computer Press Association in recognition of editorial excellence and three from Computer Currents' First Annual Readers' Choice Awards. Our best-selling ...For Dummies® series has more than 25 million copies in print with translations in 30 languages. IDG Books Worldwide, through a joint venture with IDG's Hi-Tech Beijing, became the first U.S. publisher to publish a computer book in the People's Republic of China. In record time, IDG Books Worldwide has become the first choice for millions of readers around the world who want to learn how to better manage their businesses.

Our mission is simple: Every one of our books is designed to bring extra value and skill-building instructions to the reader. Our books are written by experts who understand and care about our readers. The knowledge base of our editorial staff comes from years of experience in publishing, education, and journalism - experience which we use to produce books for the '90s. In short, we care about books, so we attract the best people. We devote special attention to details such as audience, interior design, use of icons, and illustrations. And because we use an efficient process of authoring, editing, and desktop publishing our books electronically, we can spend more time ensuring superior content and spend less time on the technicalities of making books.

You can count on our commitment to deliver high-quality books at competitive prices on topics you want to read about. At IDG Books Worldwide, we continue in the IDG tradition of delivering quality for more than 25 years. You'll find no better book on a subject than one from IDG Books Worldwide.

John Kilcullen
President and CEO
IDG Books Worldwide, Inc.

IDG Books Worldwide, Inc., is a subsidiary of International Data Group, the world's largest publisher of computer-related information and the leading global provider of information services on information technology. International Data Group publishes over 276 computer publications in over 75 countries. Ninety million people read one or more International Data Group publications each month. International Data Group's publications include: Argentina: Annuario de Informatica, Computerworld Argentina, PC World Argentina; Australia: Australian Macworld, Client/Server Journal, Computer Living, Computerworld, Computerworld 100, Digital News, IT Casebook, Network World, On-line World Australia, PC World, Publishing Essentials, Reseller, WebMaster; Austria: Computerwelt Osterreich, Networks Austria, PC Tip; Belarus: PC World Belarus; Belgium: Data News; Brazil: Annuário de Informática, Computerworld Brazil, Connections, Super Game Power, Macworld, PC Player, PC World Brazil, Publish Brazil, Reseller News; Bulgaria: Computerworld Bulgaria, Networkworld/Bulgaria, PC & MacWorld Bulgaria; Canada: CIO Canada, Client/Server World, ComputerWorld Canada, InfoCanada, Network World Canada; Chile: Computerworld Chile, PC World Chile; Colombia: Computerworld Colombia, PC World Colombia; Costa Rica: PC World Centro America; The Czech and Slovak Republics: Computerworld Czechoslovakia, Elektronika Czechoslovakia, Macworld Czech Republic, PC World Czechoslovakia; Denmark: Communications World, Computerworld Danmark, Macworld Danmark, PC Privat Danmark, PC World Danmark, PC World Danmark Supplements, TECH World; Dominican Republic: PC World Republica Dominicana; Ecuador: PC World Ecuador; Egypt: Computerworld Middle East, PC World Middle East; El Salvador: PC World Centro America; Finland: MikroPC, Tietoverkko, Tietoviikko; France: Distributique, Golden, Hebdo-Distributique, Info PC, Le Guide du Monde Informatique, Le Monde Informatique, Reseaux & Telecoms; Germany: Computer Partner, Computerwoche, Computerwoche Extra, Computerwoche Focus, I/M Information Management, Macwelt, PC Welt; Greece: GamePro, Multimedia World; Guatemala: PC World Centro America; Honduras: PC World Centro America; Hong Kong: Computerworld Hong Kong, PCWorld Hong Kong, Publish in Asia; Hungary: ABCD CD-ROM, Computerworld Szamitastechnika, PC & Mac World Hungary, PC-X Magazine; Iceland: Tolvuheimur/PC World Island; India: Information Systems Computerworld, PC World India, Publish in Asia; Indonesia: InfoKomputer PC World, Komputek Computerworld, Publish in Asia; Ireland: ComputerScope, PC Live!; Israel: People & Computers; Italy: Computerworld Italia, Computerworld Italia Special Editions, Macworld Italia, Networking Italia, PC Shopping, PC World Italia, PC World/Walt Disney; Japan: DTP World, HP Open World Japan, Macworld Japan, Nikkei Personal Computing, Open World Japan, OS/2 World Japan, SunWorld Japan, Windows World Japan; Kenya: East African Computer News; Korea: Hi-Tech Information/Computerworld, Macworld Korea, PC World Korea; Macedonia: PC World Macedonia; Malaysia: Computerworld Malaysia, PC World Malaysia, Publish in Asia; Mexico: Computerworld Mexico, Macworld, PC World Mexico; Myanmar: PC World Myanmar; Netherlands: Computer! Totaal, LAN Magazine, LanWorld Buyers Guide, Macworld, Net Magazine, Totaal! Beurskrant; New Zealand: Absolute Beginner's Guide, Computer Buyer, Computer Industry Directory, Computerworld New Zealand, MTB, Network World, PC World New Zealand; Nicaragua: PC World Centro America; Nigeria: PC World Nigeria; Norway: Computerworld Norge, Computerworld Privat (Datamagasinet), CW Rapport Norge, IDG's KURSGUIDE, Macworld Norge, Multimediaworld, PC World Ekspress, PC World Nettverk, PC World Norge, PC World's Produktguide, Windows World Spesial; Pakistan: Computerworld Pakistan, PC World Pakistan; Panama: PC World Panama; P. R. of China: China Computer Users, China Computerworld, China Infoworld, China Telecom World Weekly, Computer & Communication, Electronic Design China, Electronics Today, Electronics Weekly, Game Camp, Game Soft, Network World China, PC World China, Popular Computer Weekly, Software Weekly, Software World, Telecom World; Peru: Computerworld Peru, PC World Profesional Peru, PC World Peru; Poland: Computerworld Poland, Computerworld Special Report, Macworld, Networld, PC World Komputer; Philippines: Computerworld Philippines, PC World Philippines, Publish in Asia; Portugal: Cerebro/PC World, Computerworld/Correio Informático, Dealer World Portugal, Mac*In/PC*In, Multimedia World Portugal; Puerto Rico: PC World Puerto Rico; Romania: Computerworld Romania, PC World Romania, Telecom Romania; Russia: Computerworld Russia, Mir PK, Sety; Singapore: Computerworld Singapore, PC World Singapore, Publish in Asia; Slovenia: MONITOR; South Africa: Computing S.A., InfoWorld S.A., Network World S.A., Software World; Spain: Computerworld Espa-a, COMUNICACIONES WORLD, Dealer World, Macworld Espa-a, PC World Espa-a; Sweden: CAP&Design, Computer Sweden, Corporate Computing, MacWorld, Maxi Data, MikroDatorn, Nätverk & Kommunikation, PC/Aktiv, PC World, Windows World; Switzerland: Computerworld Schweiz, Macworld Schweiz, PCtip; Taiwan: Computerworld Taiwan, Macworld Taiwan, PC World Taiwan, Publish Taiwan, Windows World; Thailand: Thai Computerworld, Publish in Asia; Turkey: Computerworld Turkiye, MACWORLD Turkiye, PC WORLD Turkiye; Ukraine: Computerworld Kiev, Computers & Software, Multimedia World Ukraine, PC World Ukraine; United Kingdom: Acorn User, Amiga Action, Amiga Computing, Appletalk, Computing, GamePro, Macworld, Network News, Parents and Computers, PC Advisor, PC Home, PSX Pro UK, The WEB; United States: Cable in the Classroom, CD Review, CIO Magazine, Computerworld, Computerworld Client/Server Journal, Digital Video Magazine, DOS World, Federal Computer Week, GamePro, InfoWorld, I-Way, JavaWorld, Macworld, Multimedia World, Netscape World Online, Network World, PC Entertainment, PC World, Publish, SunWorld Online, SWATPro Magazine, Video Event, WebMaster; Uruguay: PC World Uruguay; Venezuela: Computerworld Venezuela, PC World Venezuela; and Vietnam: PC World Vietnam.

Every maranGraphics book represents the extraordinary vision and commitment of a unique family: the Maran family of Toronto, Canada.

Back Row (from left to right): *Sherry Maran, Rob Maran, Richard Maran, Maxine Maran, Jill Maran.*
Front Row (from left to right): *Judy Maran, Ruth Maran.*

Richard Maran is the company founder and its inspirational leader. He developed maranGraphics' proprietary communication technology called "visual grammar." This book is built on that technology—empowering readers with the easiest and quickest way to learn about computers.

Ruth Maran is the Author and Architect—a role Richard established that now bears Ruth's distinctive touch. She creates the words and visual structure that are the basis for the books.

Judy Maran is the Project Coordinator. She works with Ruth, Richard and the highly talented maranGraphics illustrators, designers and editors to transform Ruth's material into its final form.

Rob Maran is the Technical and Production Specialist. He makes sure the state-of-the-art technology used to create these books always performs as it should.

Sherry Maran manages the Reception, Order Desk and any number of areas that require immediate attention and a helping hand.

Jill Maran is a jack-of-all-trades and dynamo who fills in anywhere she's needed anytime she's back from university.

Maxine Maran is the Business Manager and family sage. She maintains order in the business and family—and keeps everything running smoothly.

Oh, and three other family members are seated on the sofa. These graphic disk characters help make it fun and easy to learn about computers. They're part of the extended maranGraphics family.

Credits

Author & Architect:
Ruth Maran

Copy Development & Screen Captures:
Alison MacAlpine
Brad Hilderley

Project Coordinator:
Judy Maran

Editors:
Wanda Lawrie
Karen Derrah

Layout Designers:
Christie Van Duin
Tamara Poliquin

Illustrations & Screens:
Chris K.C. Leung
Russell Marini
Ben Lee
Jeff Jones

Indexer:
Kelleigh Wing

Post Production:
Robert Maran

Acknowledgments

Thanks to the dedicated staff of maranGraphics, including Karen Derrah, Francisco Ferreira, Brad Hilderley, Jeff Jones, Wanda Lawrie, Ben Lee, Peter Lejcar, Chris K.C. Leung, Alison MacAlpine, Michael W. M[ac]Donald, Jill Maran, Judy Maran, Maxine Maran, Robert Maran, Sherry Maran, Russ Marini, Tamara Poliquin, Christie Van Duin, Paul Whitehead and Kelleigh Wing.

Finally, to Richard Maran who originated the easy-to-use graphic format of this guide. Thank you for your inspiration and guidance.

TABLE OF CONTENTS

CHAPTER 1

GETTING STARTED

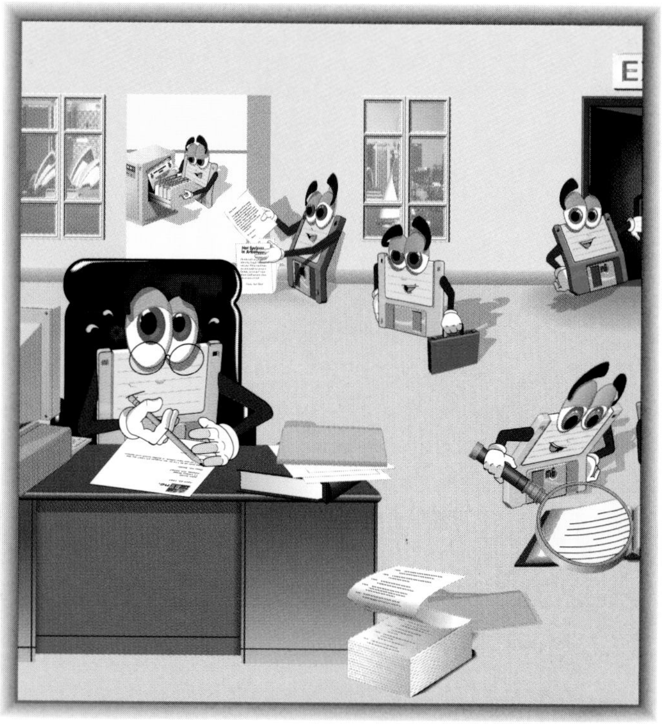

CHAPTER 2

SAVE AND OPEN YOUR DOCUMENTS

CHAPTER 3

CHANGE DOCUMENT DISPLAY

CHAPTER 4

EDIT YOUR DOCUMENTS

TABLE OF CONTENTS

CHAPTER 5

FORMAT TEXT

CHAPTER 6

FORMAT PAGES

CHAPTER 7

PRINT YOUR DOCUMENTS

CHAPTER 8

WORK WITH MULTIPLE DOCUMENTS

TABLE OF CONTENTS

CHAPTER 9

WORK WITH TABLES

CHAPTER 10

WORK WITH GRAPHICS

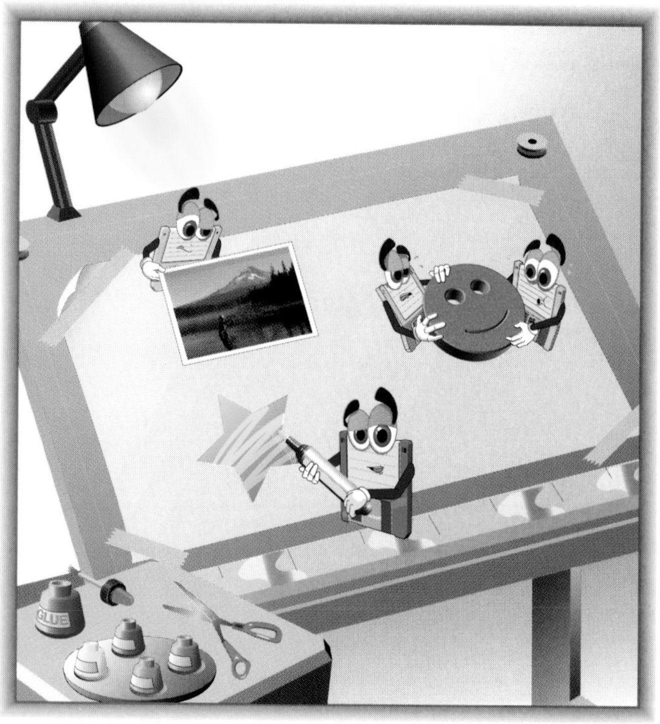

CHAPTER 11

MAIL MERGE

CHAPTER 12

WORD AND THE INTERNET

WORD 97
Microsoft Word - Document1
File Edit View Insert Format Tools Table Window Help
100%
Normal
Arial
12
Ln 1
REC TRK EXT WPH

CHAPTER 1

GETTING STARTED

Do you want to begin using Microsoft Word 97? This chapter will help you get started.

INTRODUCTION

Word lets you produce professional-looking documents quickly and efficiently.

maranGraphics
Our First Annual COMPANY PICNIC
101 Reasons to Save The Earth
Illustration

You can use Word to create letters, reports, manuals, newsletters and brochures.

Editing

Word offers many features that help you work with text in a document. You can easily edit text, rearrange paragraphs and check for spelling mistakes.

There is a 10th 13th anniversary High School Reunion on August 8, 9 and 10 at Woodblock High School. We all hope to see you
for more information.
Susan Hughes

Formatting

You can easily change the appearance of a document. You can add page numbers, center text and use various fonts in a document.

Save the World Inc.
NEWSLETTER - JUNE 1997
1

Printing

You can produce a paper copy of a Word document. Word lets you see on the screen exactly what the printed document will look like.

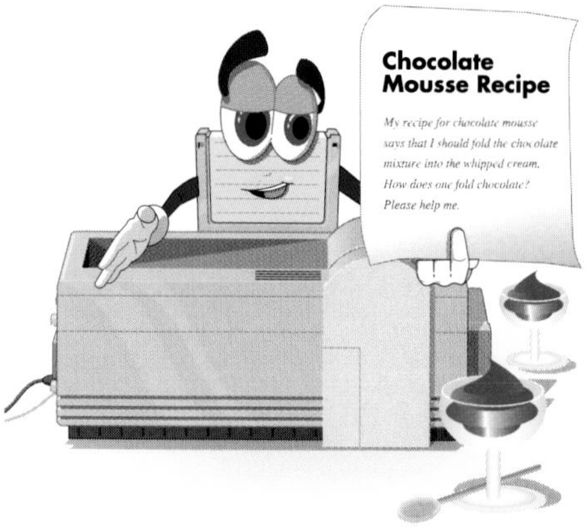
Chocolate Mousse Recipe
My recipe for chocolate mousse says that I should fold the chocolate mixture into the whipped cream. How does one fold chocolate? Please help me.

Tables

You can create tables to neatly display information in your document. Word lets you draw a table on the screen as you would draw a table with a pen and paper.

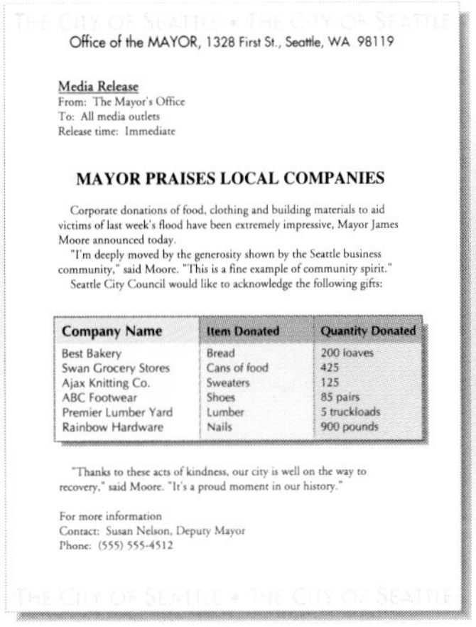
THE CITY OF SEATTLE • THE CITY OF SEATTLE

Office of the MAYOR, 1328 First St., Seattle, WA 98119

Media Release
From: The Mayor's Office
To: All media outlets
Release time: Immediate

MAYOR PRAISES LOCAL COMPANIES

Corporate donations of food, clothing and building materials to aid victims of last week's flood have been extremely impressive, Mayor James Moore announced today.

"I'm deeply moved by the generosity shown by the Seattle business community," said Moore. "This is a fine example of community spirit."

Seattle City Council would like to acknowledge the following gifts:

Company Name	Item Donated	Quantity Donated
Best Bakery	Bread	200 loaves
Swan Grocery Stores	Cans of food	425
Ajax Knitting Co.	Sweaters	125
ABC Footwear	Shoes	85 pairs
Premier Lumber Yard	Lumber	5 truckloads
Rainbow Hardware	Nails	900 pounds

"Thanks to these acts of kindness, our city is well on the way to recovery," said Moore. "It's a proud moment in our history."

For more information
Contact: Susan Nelson, Deputy Mayor
Phone: (555) 555-4512

THE CITY OF SEATTLE • THE CITY OF SEATTLE

Graphics

Word comes with many types of graphics that you can use to enhance the appearance of your documents.

Fishing Guide

When was the last time you heard someone boast about the trophy largemouth bass they reeled in on their last fishing outing? Have you always wanted to go fishing but didn't know where to start? Whether you assume this popular sport is as easy as finding a pond and plopping yourself down with a line, or whether you are intimidated by the large array of rods, reels, baits, lures and fish, these few basic guidelines will help you get started.

The choices in the world of fishing are enormous. Do you want to fish for fun, for trophy or for supper? Are you looking for a particular type of fish or for the most convenient location? Are you handy with a boat or more comfortable sticking to shore?

No matter what your preferences are, try to choose a quiet location in the cool still of the early morning or evening. Make sure you are aware of the weather forecast before you set out so you can dress appropriately. Remember that temperatures are often cooler by the water, with different wind factors. Don't be discouraged by light rain since some of the best fishing can be done in the rain! And don't forget to pack plenty to eat for an enjoyable outing.

Some good guides to fishing spots in your area can be obtained from local tourism information.

Mail Merge

You can quickly produce personalized letters and mailing labels for each person on a mailing list.

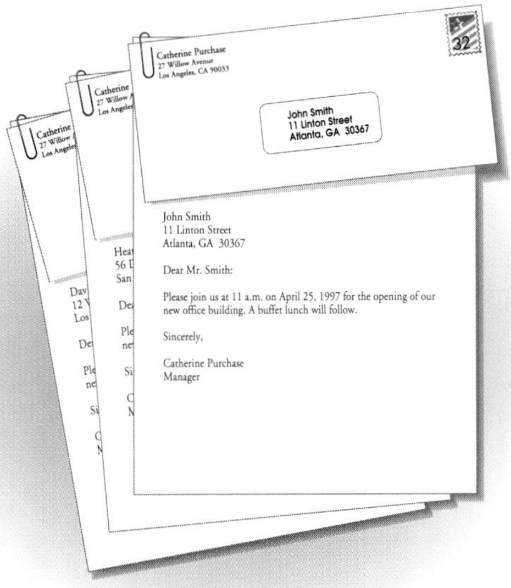
Catherine Purchase
27 Willow Avenue
Los Angeles, CA 90033

John Smith
11 Linton Street
Atlanta, GA 30367

John Smith
11 Linton Street
Atlanta, GA 30367

Dear Mr. Smith:

Please join us at 11 a.m. on April 25, 1997 for the opening of our new office building. A buffet lunch will follow.

Sincerely,

Catherine Purchase
Manager

The Internet

You can make documents you create available on the company intranet or the World Wide Web. Word offers many features that help you take advantage of the Internet.

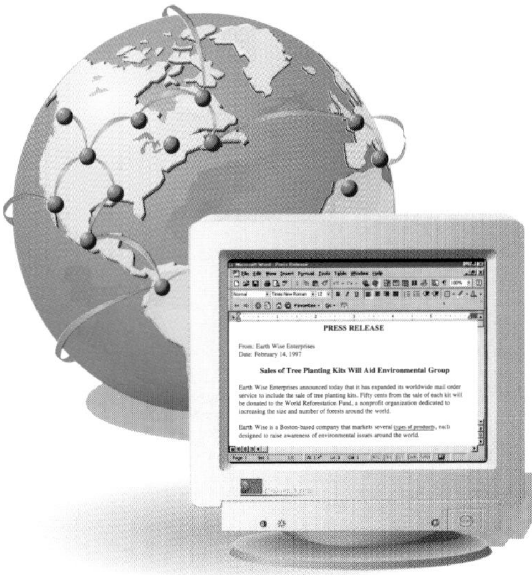
PRESS RELEASE
Sales of Tree Planting Kits Will Aid Environmental Group

USING THE MOUSE

A mouse is a hand-held device that lets you select and move items on your screen.

Holding the Mouse

Resting your hand on the mouse, use your thumb and two rightmost fingers to move the mouse on your desk. Use your two remaining fingers to press the mouse buttons.

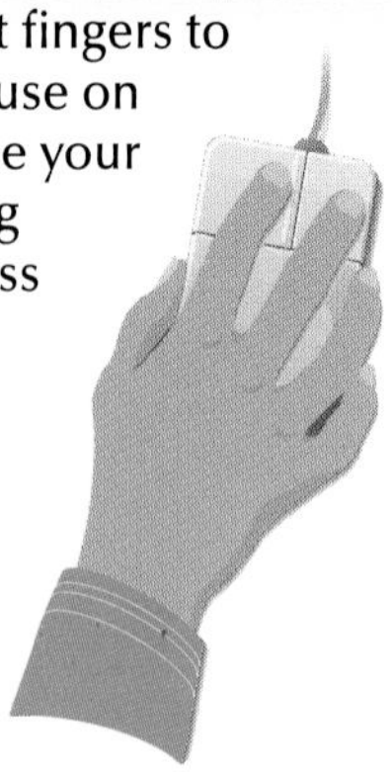

Moving the Mouse

When you move the mouse on your desk, the mouse pointer on the screen moves in the same direction.

The mouse pointer assumes different shapes (examples: ↖ or I), depending on its location on the screen and the task you are performing.

Cleaning the Mouse

A ball under the mouse senses movement. You should occasionally remove and clean this ball to ensure smooth motion of the mouse.

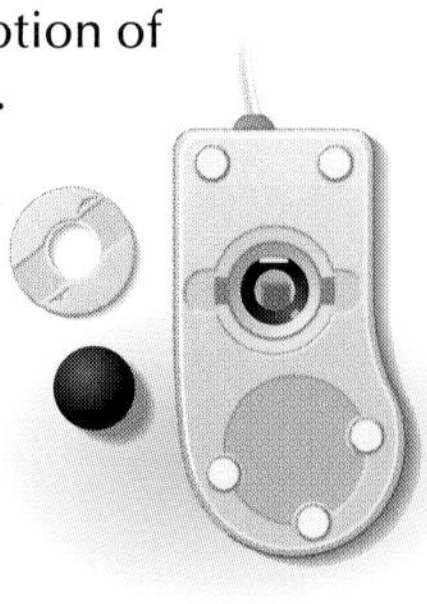

MOUSE ACTIONS

Click

Press and release the left mouse button.

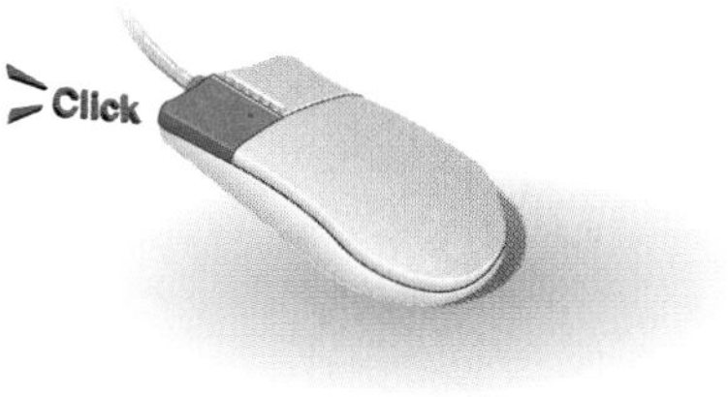

Double-Click

Quickly press and release the left mouse button twice.

Drag and Drop

Move the mouse pointer ( ) over an object on your screen and then press and hold down the left mouse button. Still holding down the mouse button, move the mouse to where you want to place the object and then release the mouse button.

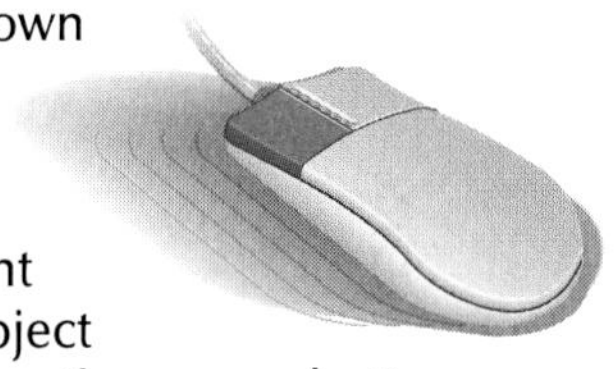

MICROSOFT INTELLIMOUSE

The new Microsoft IntelliMouse has a wheel between the left and right mouse buttons. Moving this wheel lets you quickly scroll through information on the screen.

You can also zoom in or out with the Microsoft IntelliMouse by holding down Ctrl on your keyboard as you move the wheel.

START WORD

When you start Word, a blank document appears. You can type text into this document.

START WORD

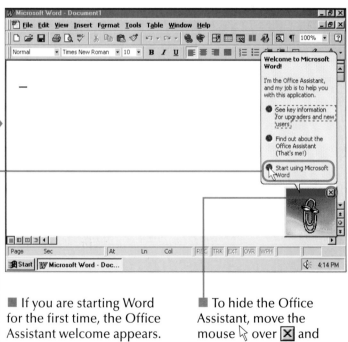

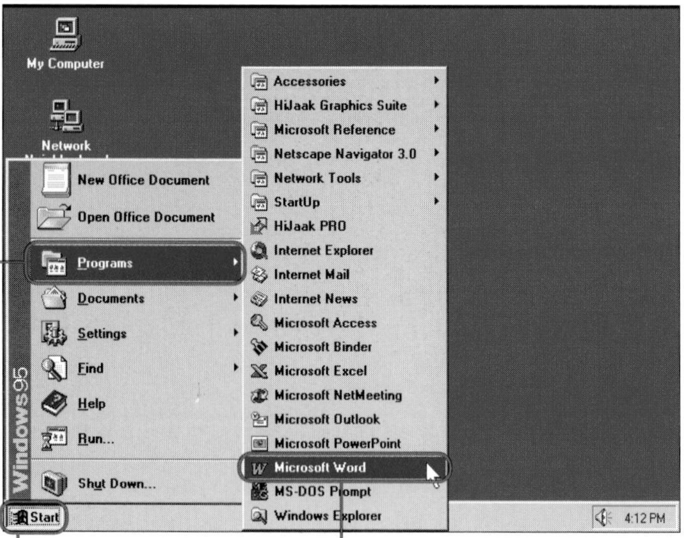

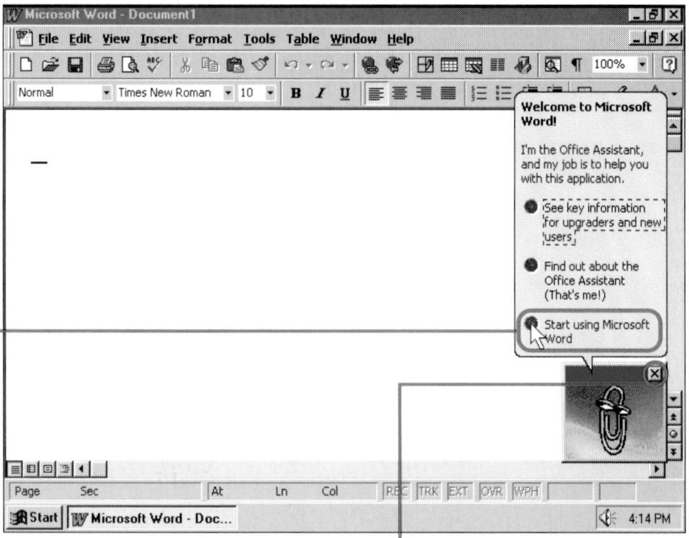

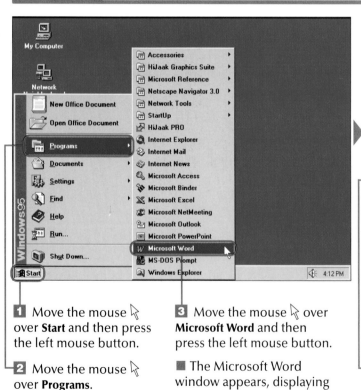

1 Move the mouse over **Start** and then press the left mouse button.

2 Move the mouse over **Programs**.

3 Move the mouse over **Microsoft Word** and then press the left mouse button.

■ The Microsoft Word window appears, displaying a blank document.

■ If you are starting Word for the first time, the Office Assistant welcome appears.

4 To start using Word, move the mouse over this option and then press the left mouse button.

■ To hide the Office Assistant, move the mouse over ☒ and then press the left mouse button.

Note: For more information on the Office Assistant, refer to page 16.

THE WORD SCREEN

Toolbars

Contain buttons to help you quickly select commonly used commands.

Ruler

Allows you to change margin and tab settings for your document.

Insertion Point

The flashing line on your screen that indicates where the text you type will appear.

Status Bar

Displays information about the area of the document displayed on your screen and the position of the insertion point.

Page 1

The page displayed on your screen.

Sec 1

The section of the document displayed on your screen.

1/1

The page displayed on the screen and the total number of pages in the document.

At 1″

The distance from the top of the page to the insertion point.

Ln 1

The number of lines from the top of the page to the insertion point.

Col 1

The number of characters from the left margin to the insertion point, including spaces.

ENTER TEXT

ENTER TEXT

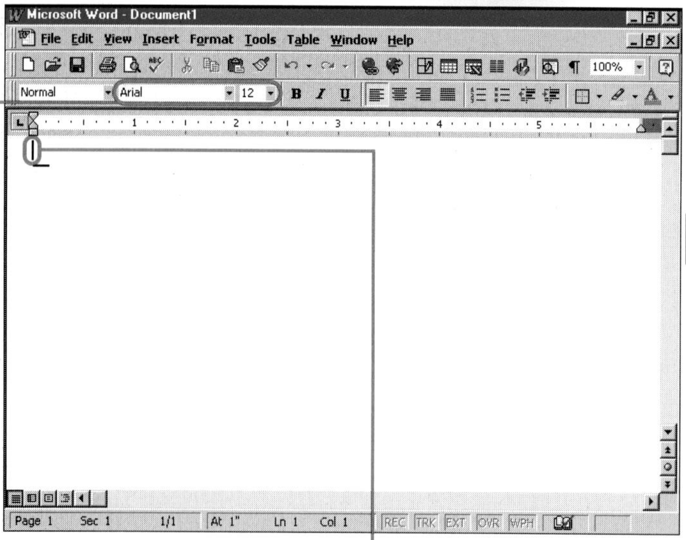

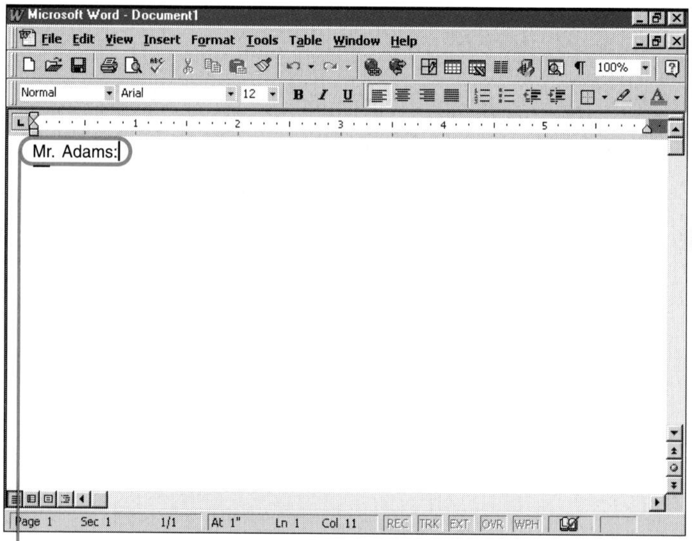

■ In this book, the design and size of text were changed to make the document easier to read. To change the design and size of text, refer to pages 74 and 75.

■ The flashing line on your screen, called the **insertion point**, indicates where the text you type will appear.

1 Type the first line of text.

2 To start a new paragraph, press **Enter** on your keyboard twice.

Can I enter symbols that are not available on my keyboard?

If you type one of the following sets of characters, Word will instantly replace the characters with a symbol. This lets you quickly enter symbols that are not available on your keyboard. To add other symbols to your document, refer to page 82.

(c)	©
(r)	®
(tm)	TM
:(	☹
:)	☺
:l	😐
<--	←
-->	→
<==	🡐
==>	🡒
<=>	⇔

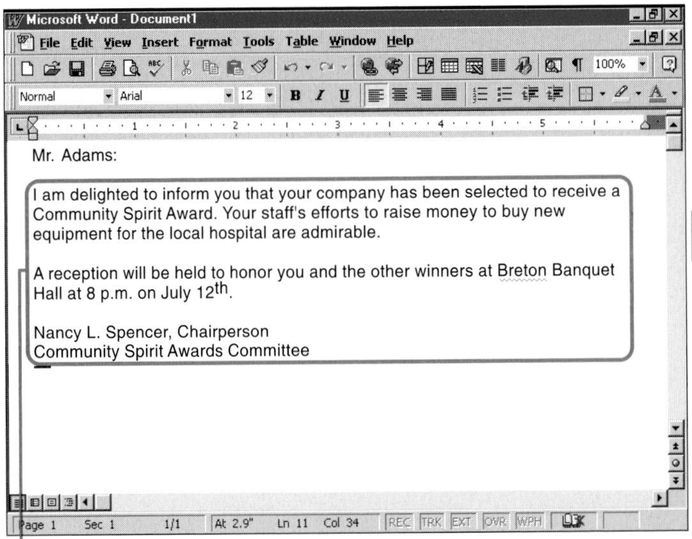
Microsoft Word - Document1
Mr. Adams:
I am delighted to inform you that your company has been selected to receive a Community Spirit Award. Your staff's efforts to raise money to buy new equipment for the local hospital are admirable.
A reception will be held to honor you and the other winners at Breton Banquet Hall at 8 p.m. on July 12th.
Nancy L. Spencer, Chairperson
Community Spirit Awards Committee

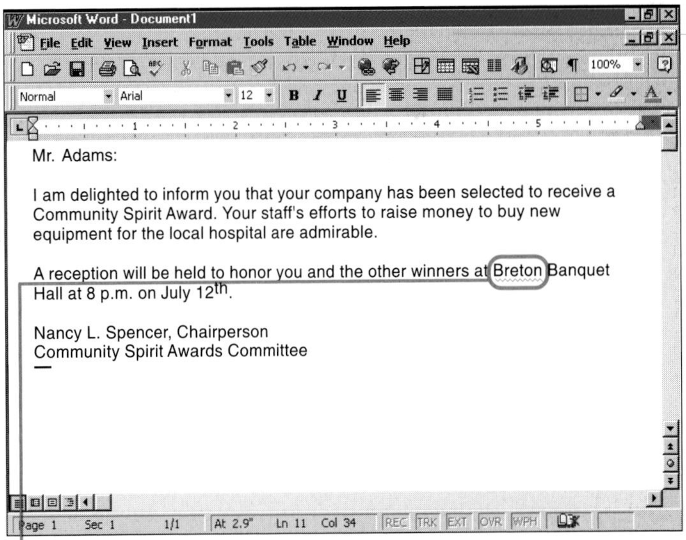
Microsoft Word - Document1
Mr. Adams:
I am delighted to inform you that your company has been selected to receive a Community Spirit Award. Your staff's efforts to raise money to buy new equipment for the local hospital are admirable.
A reception will be held to honor you and the other winners at Breton Banquet Hall at 8 p.m. on July 12th.
Nancy L. Spencer, Chairperson
Community Spirit Awards Committee

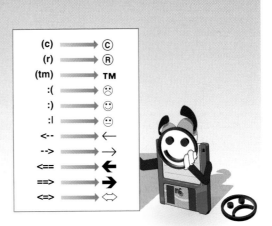

3 Type the remaining text.

■ When you reach the end of a line, Word automatically wraps the text to the next line. You only need to press **Enter** when you want to start a new line or paragraph.

■ Word automatically underlines misspelled words in red and grammar mistakes in green. The red and green underlines will not appear when you print your document.

Note: To correct spelling and grammar errors, refer to page 56.

SELECT TEXT

Before performing many tasks in Word, you must select the text you want to work with. Selected text appears highlighted on your screen.
admirable

SELECT TEXT

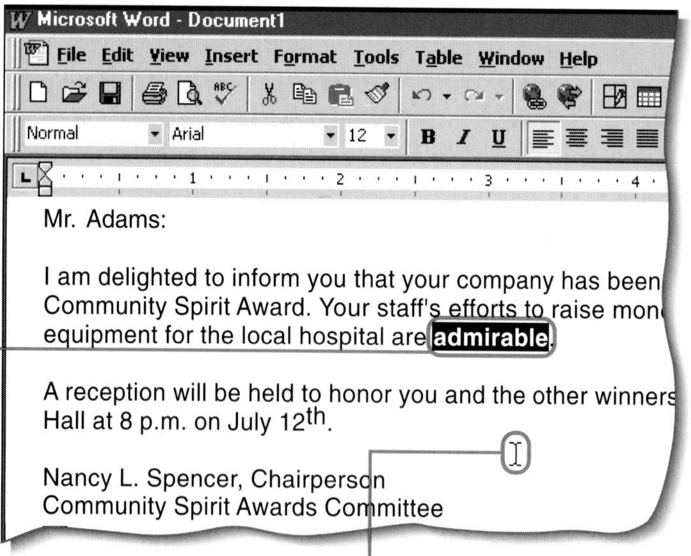

SELECT A WORD

1 Move the mouse I anywhere over the word you want to select and then quickly press the left mouse button twice.

■ To deselect text, move the mouse I outside the selected area and then press the left mouse button.

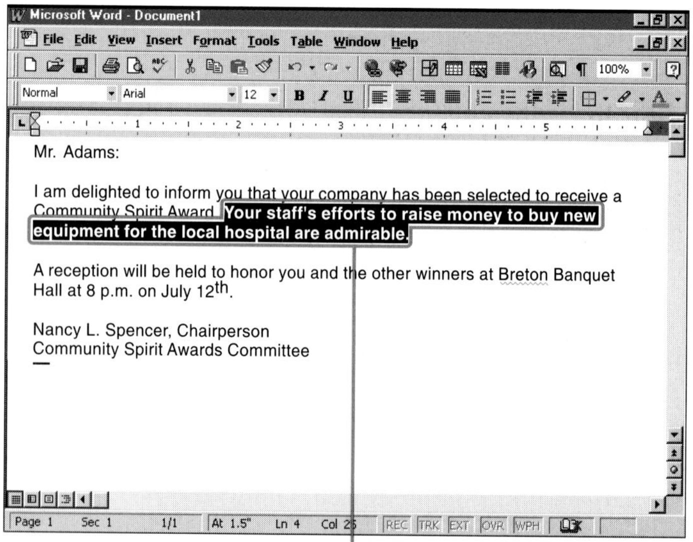

SELECT A SENTENCE

1 Press and hold down **Ctrl** on your keyboard.

2 Still holding down **Ctrl**, move the mouse I anywhere over the sentence you want to select and then press the left mouse button. Then release **Ctrl**.

How do I select all the text in my document?

To quickly select all the text in your document, press and hold down **Ctrl** and then press **A** on your keyboard. Then release both keys.

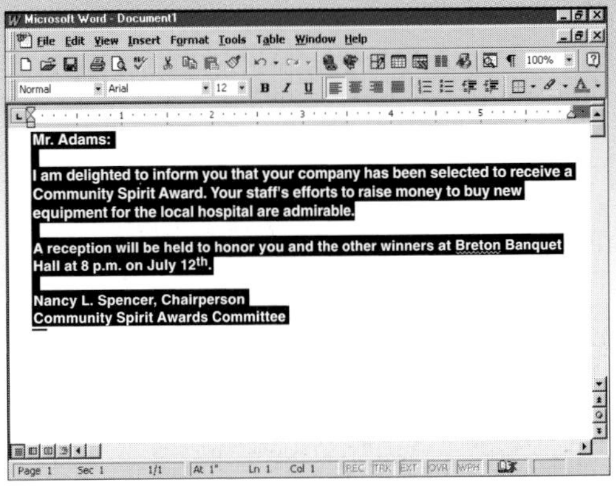

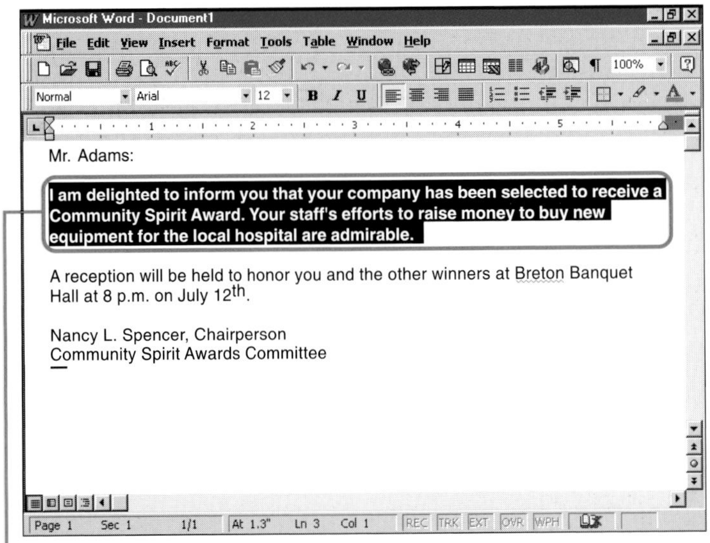
Microsoft Word - Document1
File Edit View Insert Format Tools Table Window Help
Mr. Adams:
I am delighted to inform you that your company has been selected to receive a Community Spirit Award. Your staff's efforts to raise money to buy new equipment for the local hospital are admirable.
A reception will be held to honor you and the other winners at Breton Banquet Hall at 8 p.m. on July 12th.
Nancy L. Spencer, Chairperson
Community Spirit Awards Committee

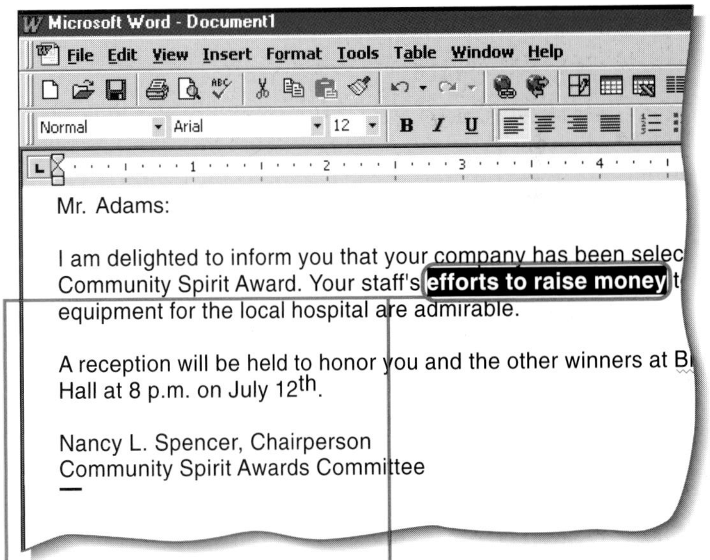
Microsoft Word - Document1
File Edit View Insert Format Tools Table Window Help
Mr. Adams:
efforts to raise money

SELECT A PARAGRAPH

1 Move the mouse I anywhere over the paragraph you want to select and then quickly press the left mouse button **three** times.

SELECT ANY AMOUNT OF TEXT

1 Move the mouse I over the first word you want to select.

2 Press and hold down the left mouse button as you move the mouse I over the text you want to select. Then release the mouse button.

MOVE THROUGH A DOCUMENT

You can easily move to another location in your document.

If you create a long document, your computer screen cannot display all the text at the same time. You must scroll up or down to view and edit other parts of the document.

MOVE THE INSERTION POINT

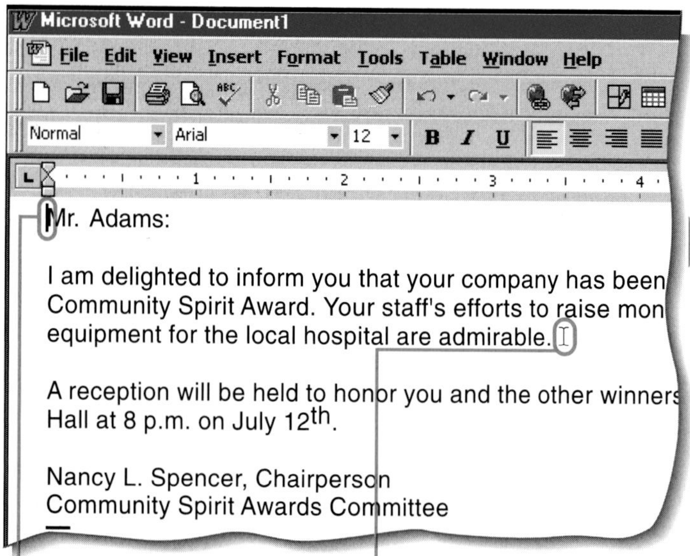

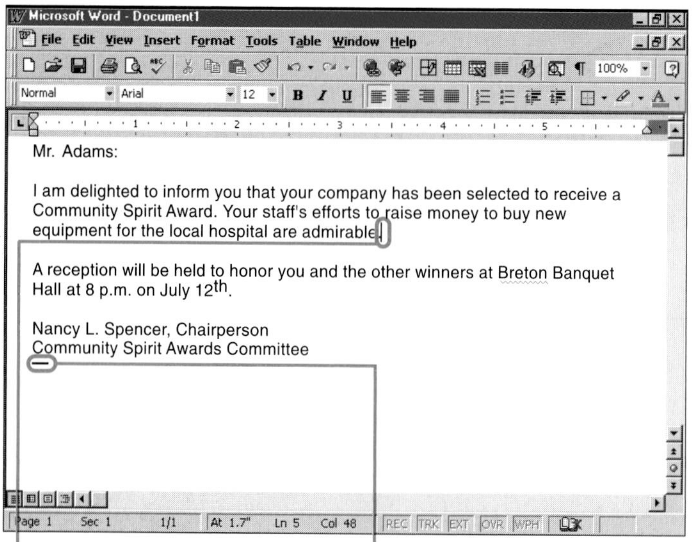

■ The flashing line on the screen, called the **insertion point**, indicates where the text you type will appear.

1 Move the mouse I to where you want to place the insertion point and then press the left mouse button.

■ The insertion point appears in the new location.

Note: You can also press ↑, ↓, ← or → on your keyboard to move the insertion point one line or character in any direction.

■ You cannot move the insertion point below the horizontal line displayed on the screen. To move this line, position the insertion point after the last character in the document and then press Enter several times.

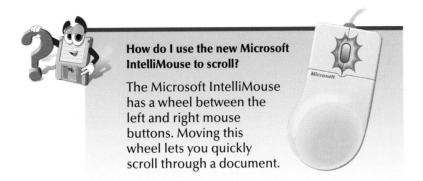

How do I use the new Microsoft IntelliMouse to scroll?

The Microsoft IntelliMouse has a wheel between the left and right mouse buttons. Moving this wheel lets you quickly scroll through a document.

Microsoft

SCROLL UP OR DOWN

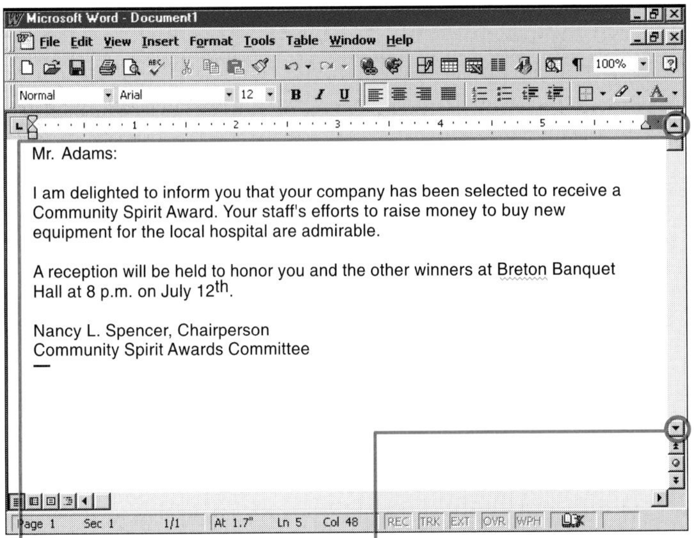
Microsoft Word - Document1
File Edit View Insert Format Tools Table Window Help
Mr. Adams:
I am delighted to inform you that your company has been selected to receive a Community Spirit Award. Your staff's efforts to raise money to buy new equipment for the local hospital are admirable.
A reception will be held to honor you and the other winners at Breton Banquet Hall at 8 p.m. on July 12th.
Nancy L. Spencer, Chairperson
Community Spirit Awards Committee
Page 1 Sec 1 1/1 At 1.7" Ln 5 Col 48

■ To scroll up one line, move the mouse over ▲ and then press the left mouse button.

■ To scroll down one line, move the mouse over ▼ and then press the left mouse button.

SCROLL TO ANY POSITION

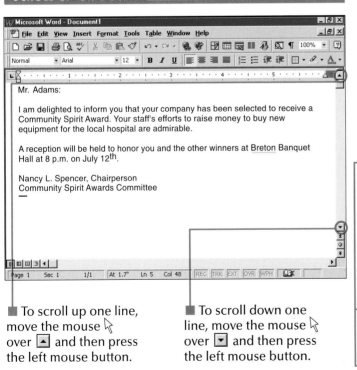

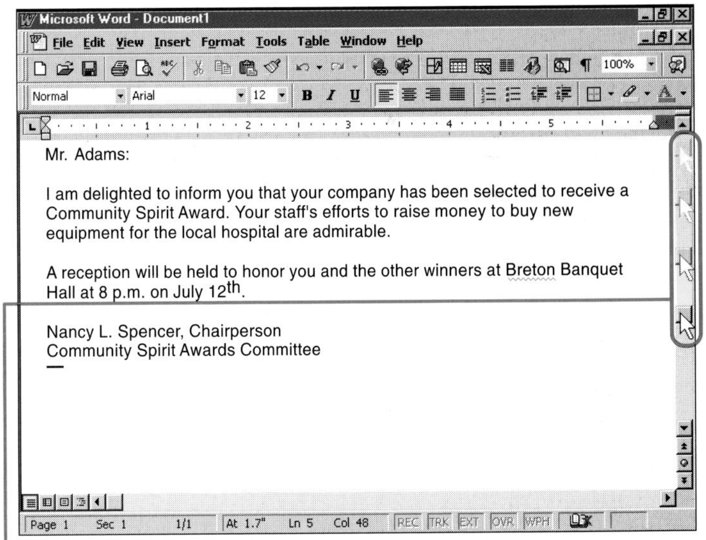
Microsoft Word - Document1
File Edit View Insert Format Tools Table Window Help
Mr. Adams:
I am delighted to inform you that your company has been selected to receive a Community Spirit Award. Your staff's efforts to raise money to buy new equipment for the local hospital are admirable.
A reception will be held to honor you and the other winners at Breton Banquet Hall at 8 p.m. on July 12th.
Nancy L. Spencer, Chairperson
Community Spirit Awards Committee
Page 1 Sec 1 1/1 At 1.7" Ln 5 Col 48

1 To quickly scroll through your document, move the mouse over the scroll box.

2 Press and hold down the left mouse button and then move the mouse up or down the scroll bar. Then release the mouse button.

■ The location of the scroll box indicates which part of the document you are viewing. To view the middle of the document, move the scroll box halfway down the scroll bar.

GETTING HELP

If you do not know how to perform a task you can ask the Office Assistant for help.
MANUAL
User's Manual

GETTING HELP

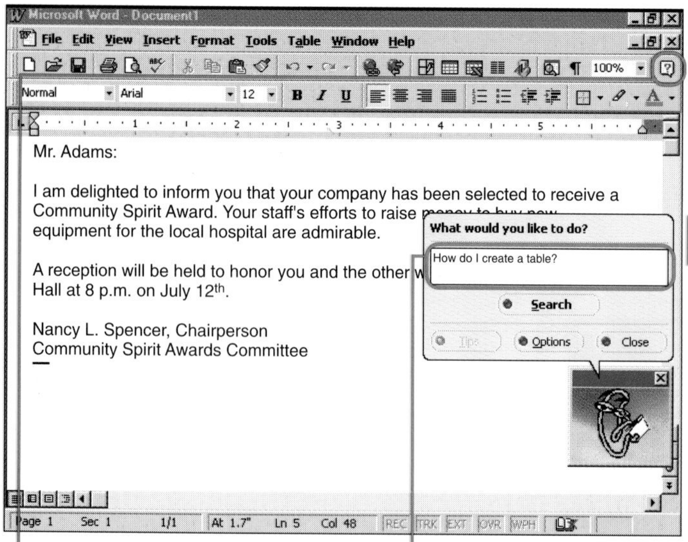
Microsoft Word - Document1
File Edit View Insert Format Tools Table Window Help
Normal
Arial
12
100%
Mr. Adams:
I am delighted to inform you that your company has been selected to receive a Community Spirit Award. Your staff's efforts to raise
equipment for the local hospital are admirable.
A reception will be held to honor you and the other
Hall at 8 p.m. on July 12th.
Nancy L. Spencer, Chairperson
Community Spirit Awards Committee
What would you like to do?
How do I create a table?
Search
Tips
Options
Close
Page 1
Sec 1
1/1
At 1.7"
Ln 5
Col 48
REC
TRK
EXT
OVR
WPH

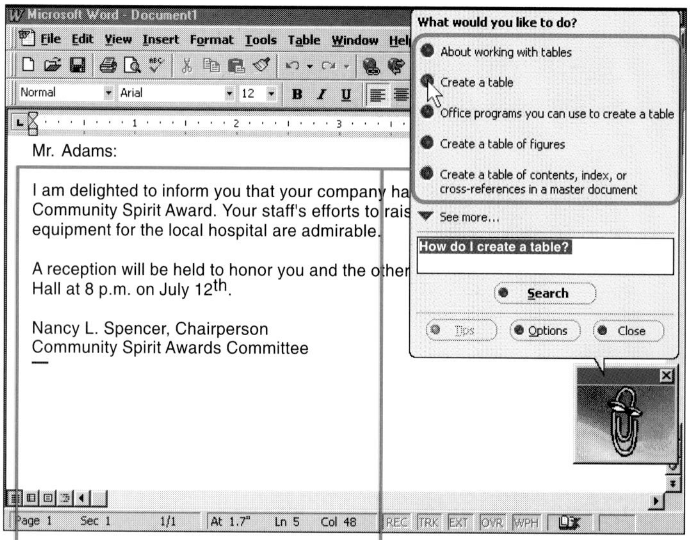
Microsoft Word - Document1
File Edit View Insert Format Tools Table Window Help
Normal
Arial
12
What would you like to do?
About working with tables
Create a table
Office programs you can use to create a table
Create a table of figures
Create a table of contents, index, or cross-references in a master document
See more...
How do I create a table?
Search
Tips
Options
Close
Mr. Adams:
I am delighted to inform you that your company ha
Community Spirit Award. Your staff's efforts to rais
equipment for the local hospital are admirable.
A reception will be held to honor you and the other
Hall at 8 p.m. on July 12th.
Nancy L. Spencer, Chairperson
Community Spirit Awards Committee
Page 1
Sec 1
1/1
At 1.7"
Ln 5
Col 48
REC
TRK
EXT
OVR
WPH

1 To display the Office Assistant, move the mouse over [?] and then press the left mouse button.

2 Type the question you want to ask and then press **Enter** on your keyboard.

■ The Office Assistant displays a list of help topics that relate to the question you asked.

Note: If you do not see a help topic of interest, try rephrasing your question. Type the new question and then press **Enter** *on your keyboard.*

3 Move the mouse over the help topic you want information on and then press the left mouse button.

How do I display the name of a toolbar button?

To display the name of a toolbar button, move the mouse over the button. After a few seconds, the name of the button appears.

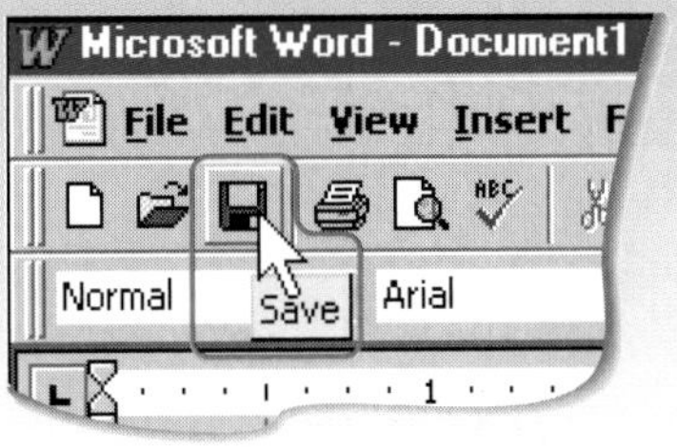
Microsoft Word - Document1
File Edit View Insert F
Normal
Save
Arial

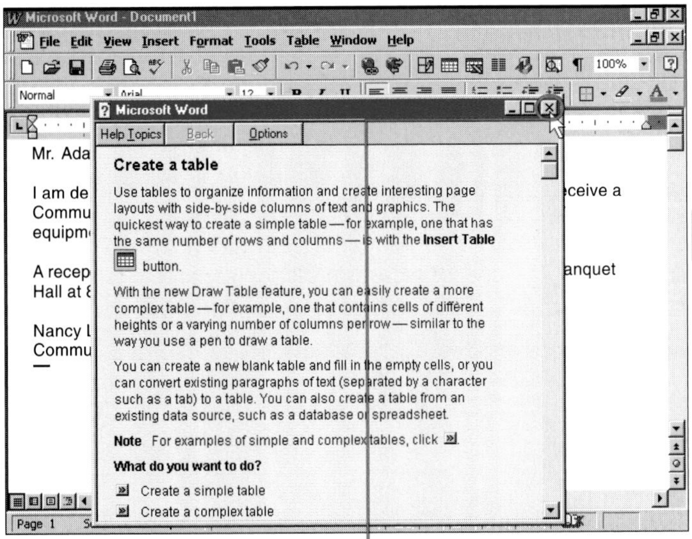
Microsoft Word - Document1
File Edit View Insert Format Tools Table Window Help
Microsoft Word
Help Topics
Back
Options
Create a table
Use tables to organize information and create interesting page layouts with side-by-side columns of text and graphics. The quickest way to create a simple table — for example, one that has the same number of rows and columns — is with the Insert Table button.
With the new Draw Table feature, you can easily create a more complex table — for example, one that contains cells of different heights or a varying number of columns per row — similar to the way you use a pen to draw a table.
You can create a new blank table and fill in the empty cells, or you can convert existing paragraphs of text (separated by a character such as a tab) to a table. You can also create a table from an existing data source, such as a database or spreadsheet.
Note For examples of simple and complex tables, click
What do you want to do?
Create a simple table
Create a complex table

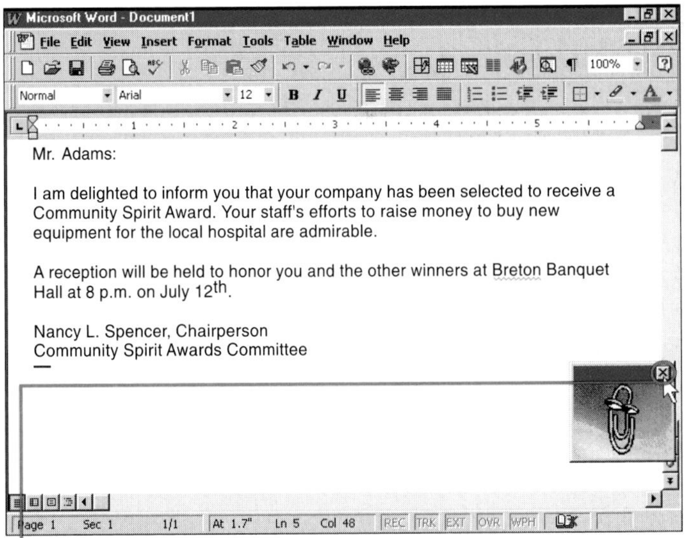
Microsoft Word - Document1
File Edit View Insert Format Tools Table Window Help
Normal
Arial
12
Mr. Adams:
I am delighted to inform you that your company has been selected to receive a Community Spirit Award. Your staff's efforts to raise money to buy new equipment for the local hospital are admirable.
A reception will be held to honor you and the other winners at Breton Banquet Hall at 8 p.m. on July 12th.
Nancy L. Spencer, Chairperson
Community Spirit Awards Committee
Page 1 Sec 1 1/1 At 1.7" Ln 5 Col 48

■ The Help window appears, displaying information about the topic you selected.

4 When you finish reading the information, move the mouse over [X] and then press the left mouse button to close the Help window.

5 To hide the Office Assistant, move the mouse over [X] and then press the left mouse button.

Dear Susan,
See you soon,
Nancy
next year. We've heard there
are some lovely hot springs in
the state, but we don't know
Thanks, Mark Court

CHAPTER 2

SAVE AND OPEN YOUR DOCUMENTS

How do I save and close my documents? How can I find a document if I do not remember its name? Learn how to manage your Word documents in this chapter.

SAVE A DOCUMENT

You should save your document to store it for future use. This lets you later retrieve the document for reviewing or editing.

SAVE A DOCUMENT

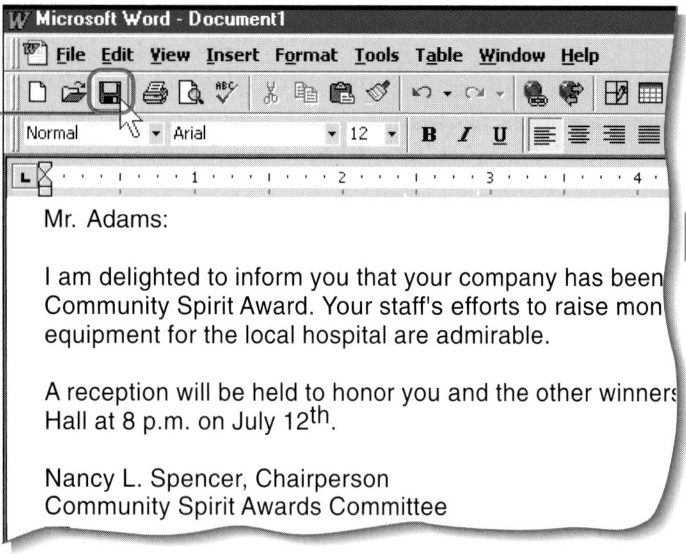

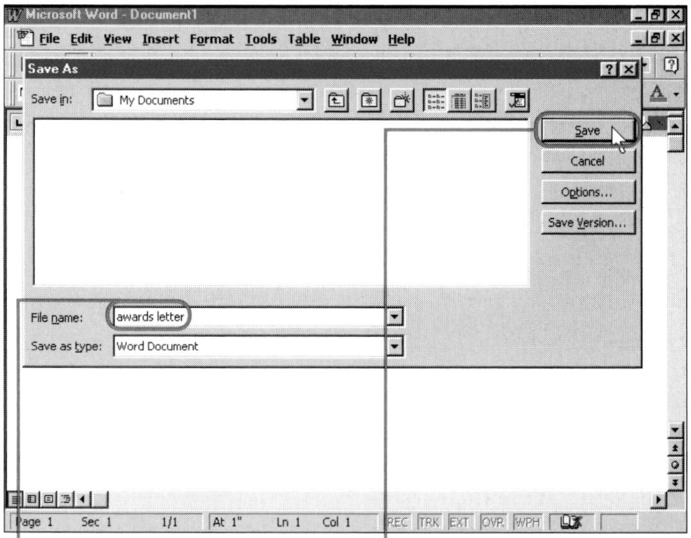

1 Move the mouse over 💾 and then press the left mouse button.

■ The **Save As** dialog box appears.

Note: If you previously saved the document, the ***Save As*** *dialog box will not appear since you have already named the document.*

2 Type a name for the document.

Note: You can use up to 255 characters to name a document.

3 Move the mouse over **Save** and then press the left mouse button.

Before you make major changes to a document, save the document with a different name. This gives you two copies of the document— the original document and a document with all the changes.
Letter
Revised Letter

SAVE A DOCUMENT WITH A NEW NAME

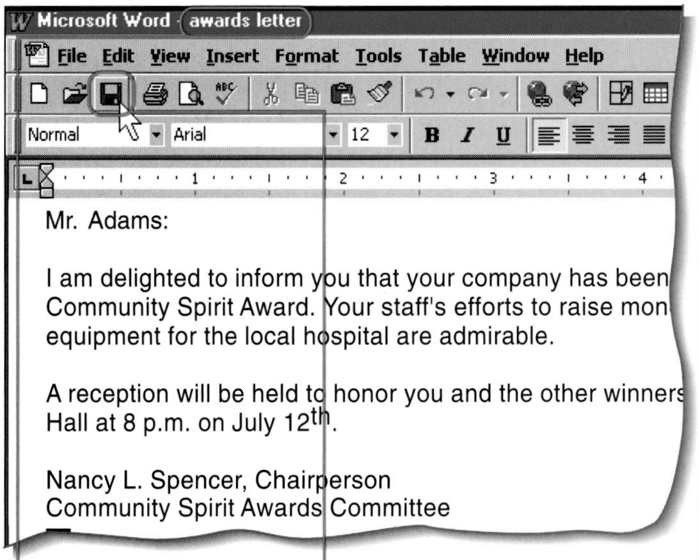

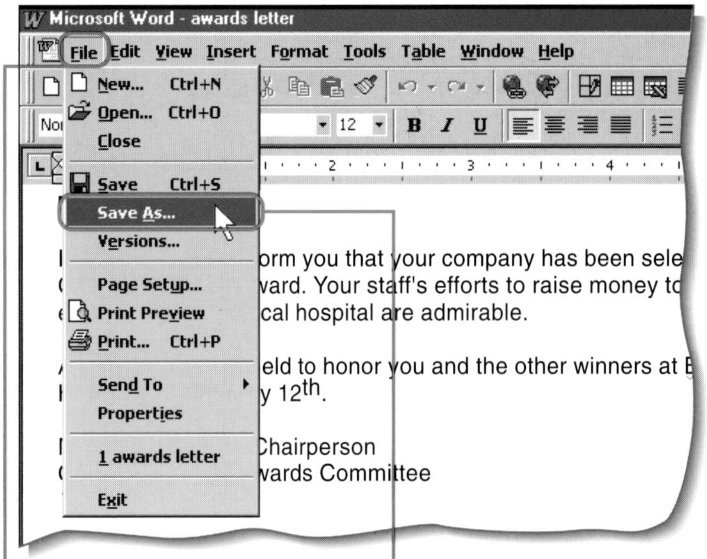

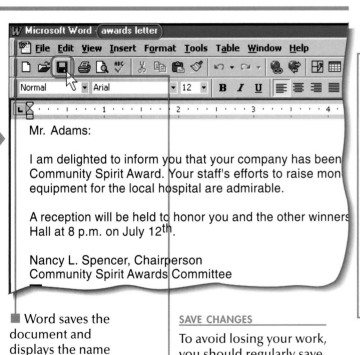

■ Word saves the document and displays the name at the top of the screen.

SAVE CHANGES

To avoid losing your work, you should regularly save changes you make to the document.

1 Move the mouse over the Save button and then press the left mouse button.

1 Move the mouse over **File** and then press the left mouse button.

2 Move the mouse over **Save As** and then press the left mouse button.

3 Perform steps 2 and 3 on page 20.

CLOSE A DOCUMENT

When you finish working with a document, you can close the document to remove it from your screen.

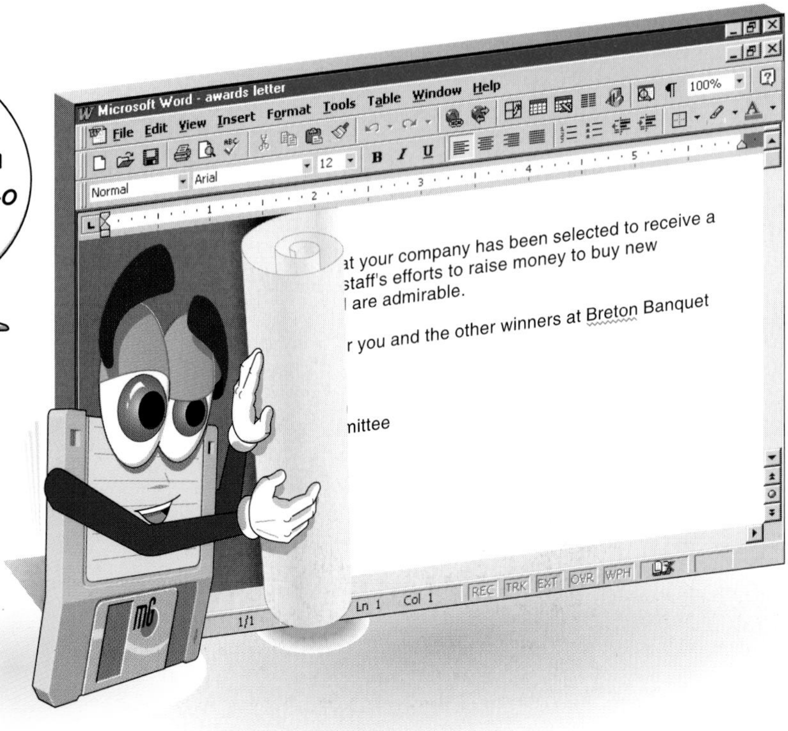

When you close a document, you do not exit the Word program. You can continue to work on other Word documents.

CLOSE A DOCUMENT

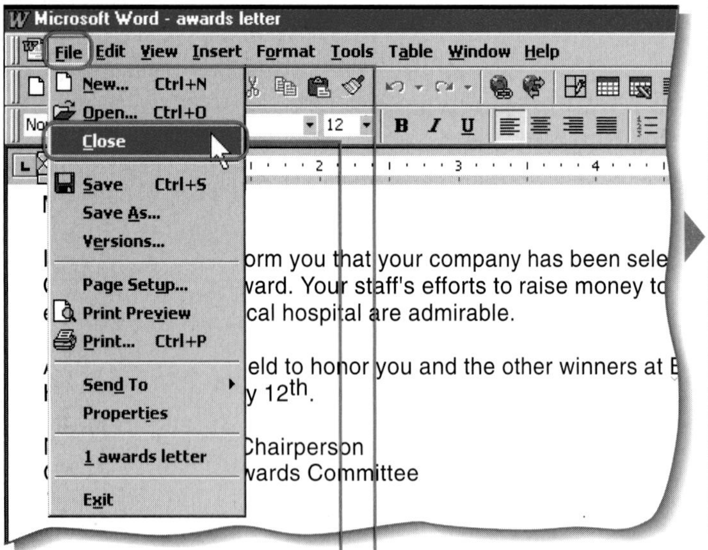

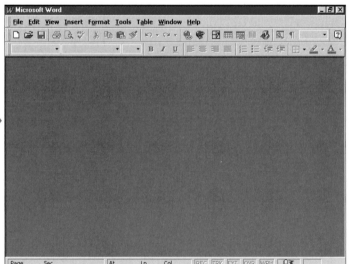

■ To save the document displayed on your screen before closing, refer to page 20.

1 To close the document, move the mouse over **File** and then press the left mouse button.

2 Move the mouse over **Close** and then press the left mouse button.

■ Word removes the document from your screen.

■ If you had more than one document open, the second last document you worked on would appear on the screen.

EXIT WORD

When you finish using Word, you can exit the program.
EXIT
mG

You should always exit all programs before turning off your computer.

EXIT WORD

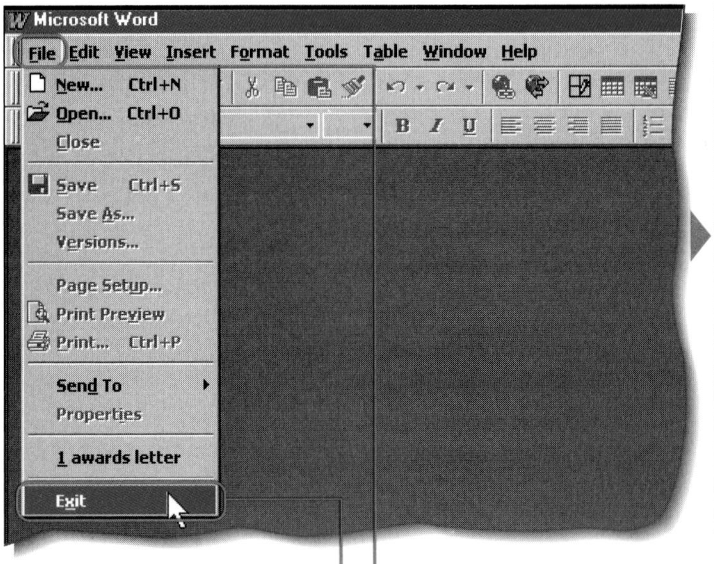

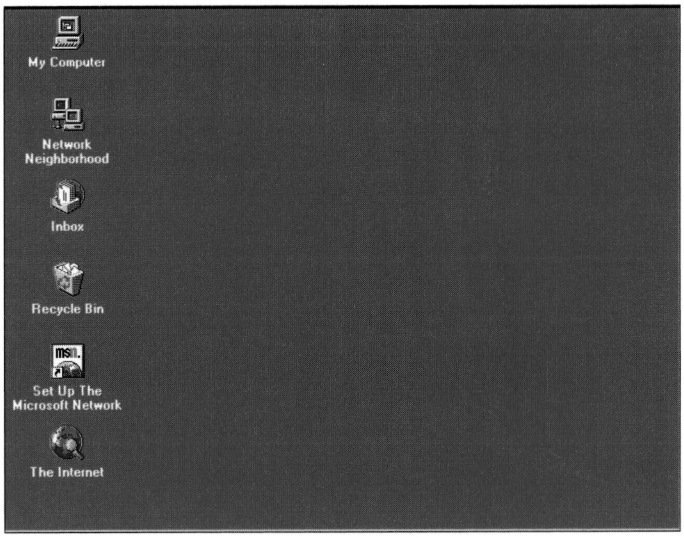

■ Save all open documents before exiting Word. To save a document, refer to page 20.

1 Move the mouse over **File** and then press the left mouse button.

2 Move the mouse over **Exit** and then press the left mouse button.

■ The Word window disappears from the screen.

Note: To restart Word, refer to page 8.

OPEN A DOCUMENT

You can open a saved document and display it on your screen. This allows you to review and make changes to your document.

OPEN A DOCUMENT

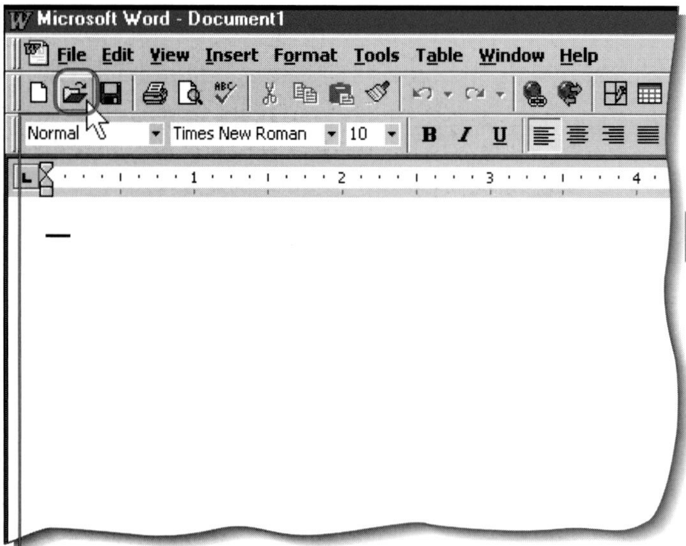

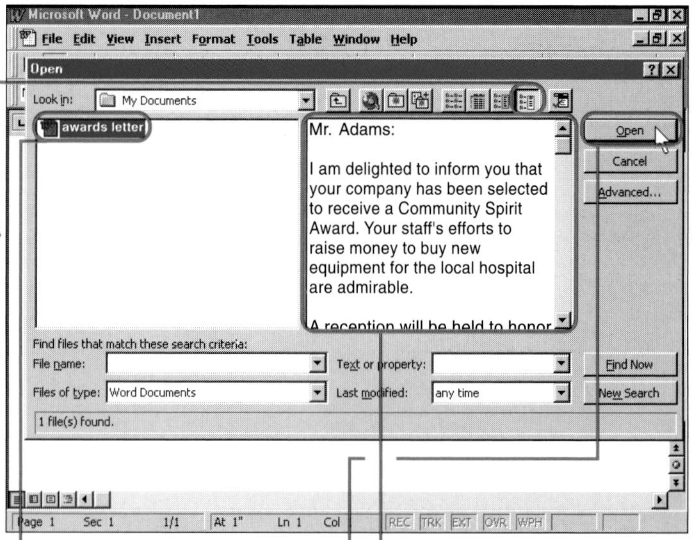

1 Move the mouse ↖ over 📂 and then press the left mouse button.

■ The **Open** dialog box appears.

2 Move the mouse ↖ over the name of the document you want to open and then press the left mouse button.

3 To see the contents of the document, move the mouse ↖ over ▤ and then press the left mouse button.

■ This area displays the contents of the document.

4 To open the document, move the mouse ↖ over **Open** and then press the left mouse button.

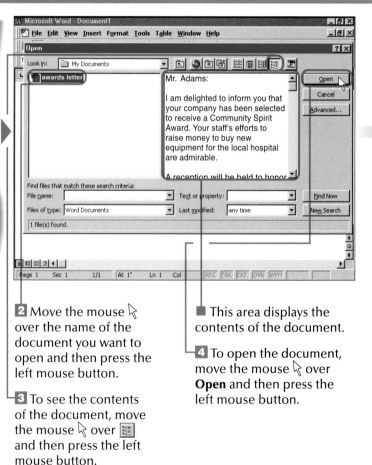

Word remembers the names of the last four documents you worked with. You can quickly open any of these documents.
Letter

QUICKLY OPEN A DOCUMENT

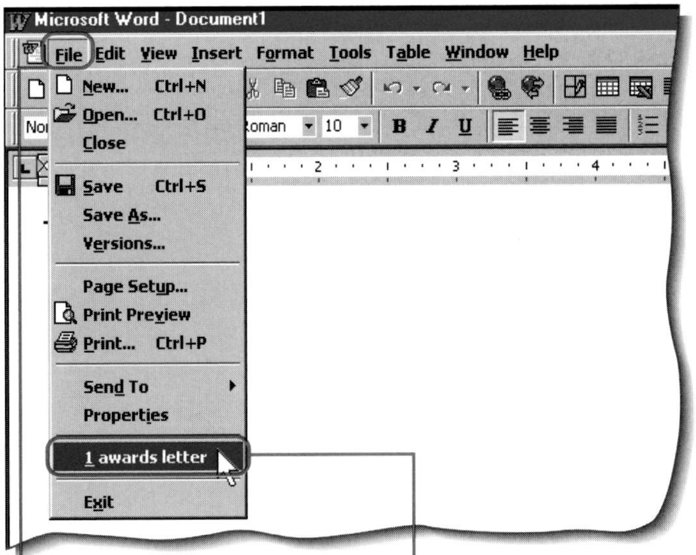

1 Move the mouse over **File** and then press the left mouse button.

2 Move the mouse over the name of the document you want to open and then press the left mouse button.

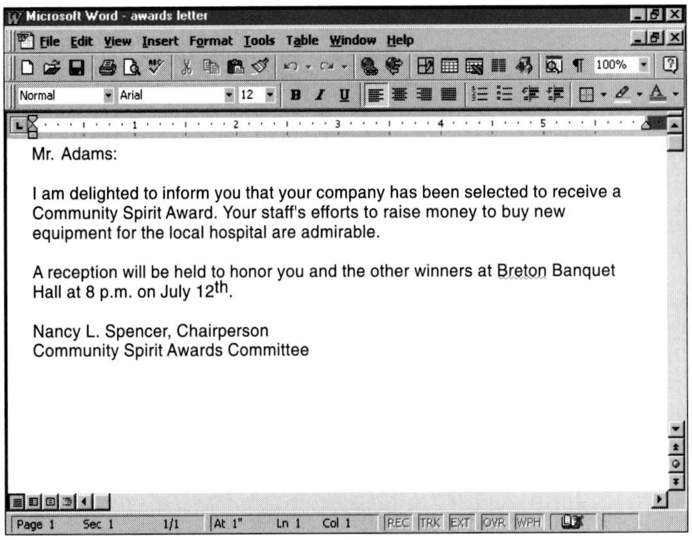

■ Word opens the document and displays it on the screen. You can now review and make changes to the document.

FIND A DOCUMENT

If you cannot remember the name or location of a document you want to open, you can have Word search for the document.
INVITATION

FIND A DOCUMENT

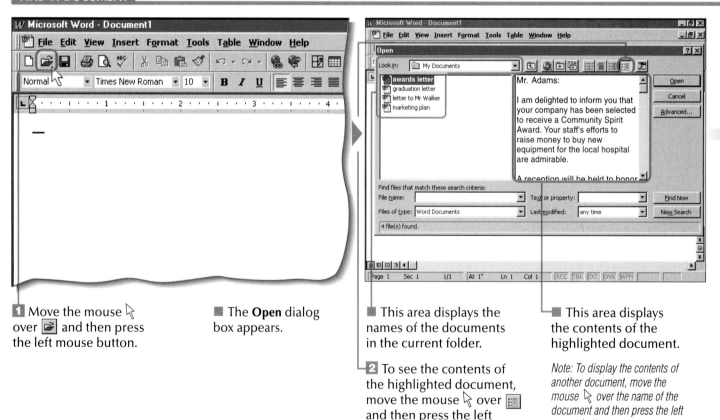

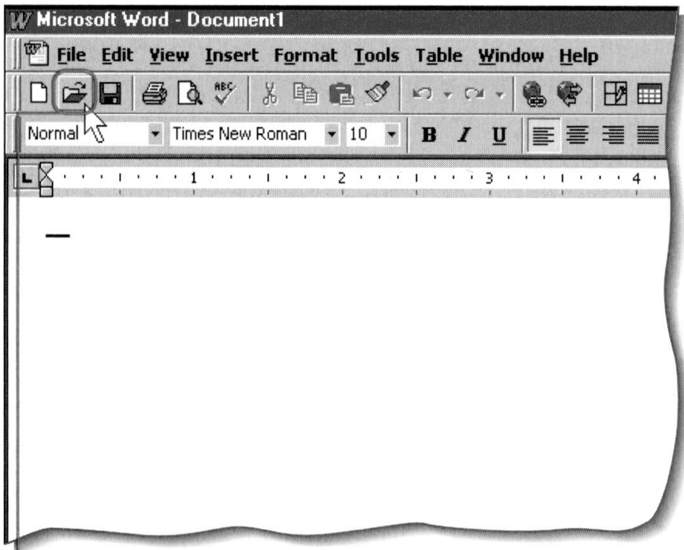

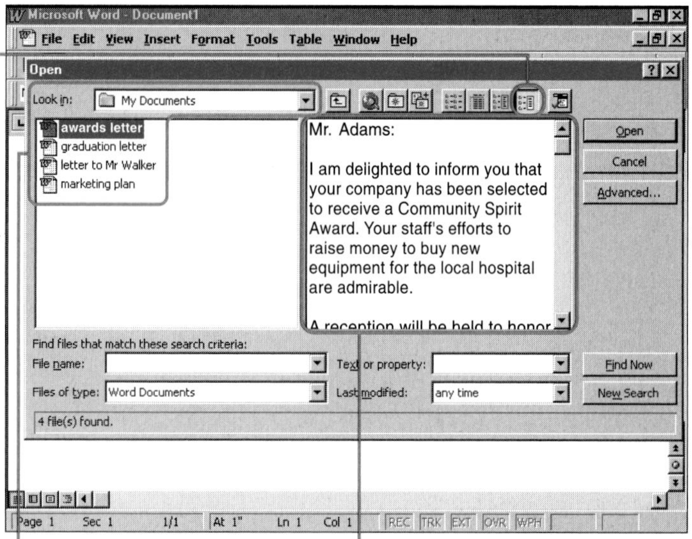

1 Move the mouse over and then press the left mouse button.

■ The **Open** dialog box appears.

■ This area displays the names of the documents in the current folder.

2 To see the contents of the highlighted document, move the mouse over and then press the left mouse button.

■ This area displays the contents of the highlighted document.

Note: To display the contents of another document, move the mouse over the name of the document and then press the left mouse button.

Can Word find a document if I know only part of the document name?

Word will find all the documents with names that contain the text you specify. For example, searching for **letter** will find **letter to Susan**, **graduation letter** and **my letter**.

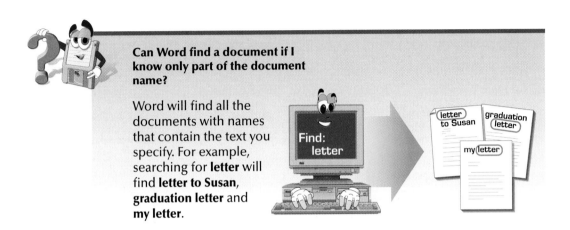

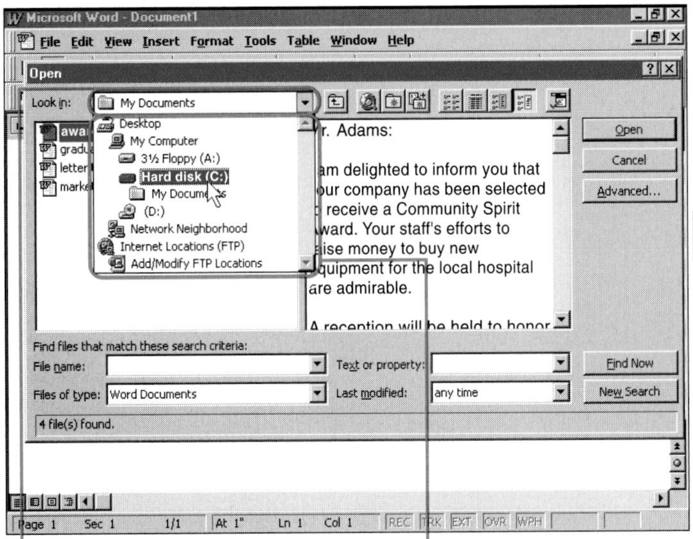

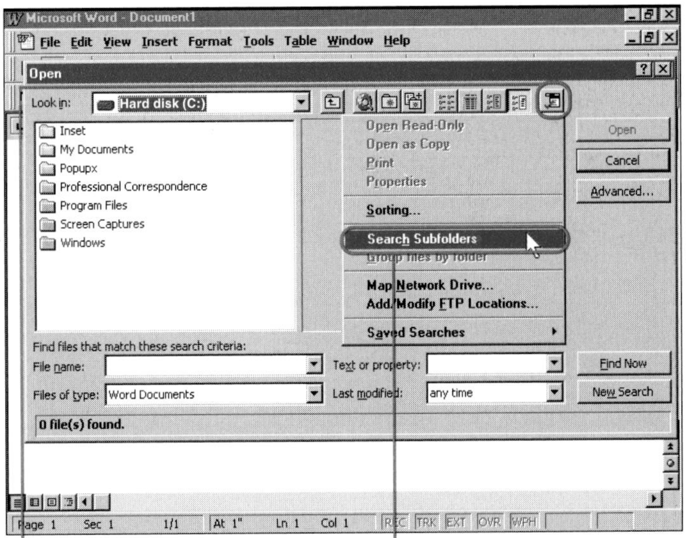

3 To specify where you want Word to search for the document, move the mouse over this area and then press the left mouse button.

4 Move the mouse over the location you want to search and then press the left mouse button.

5 To search the contents of all the folders in the location you selected, move the mouse over the icon and then press the left mouse button.

6 Move the mouse over **Search Subfolders** and then press the left mouse button.

CONTINUED

FIND A DOCUMENT

FIND A DOCUMENT (CONTINUED)

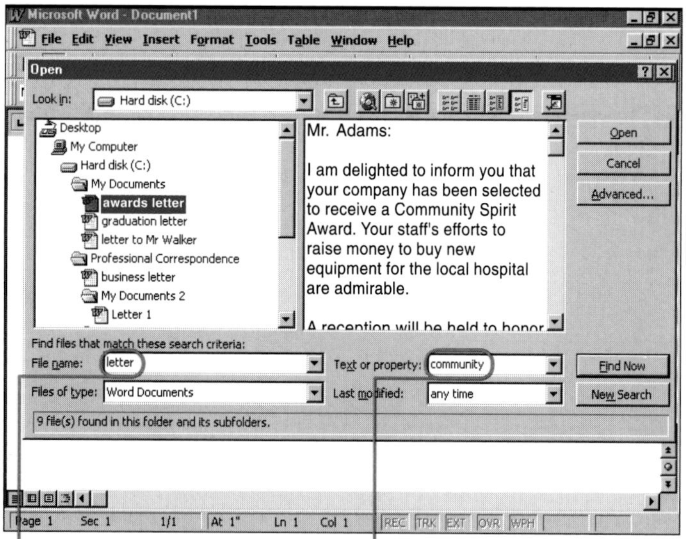

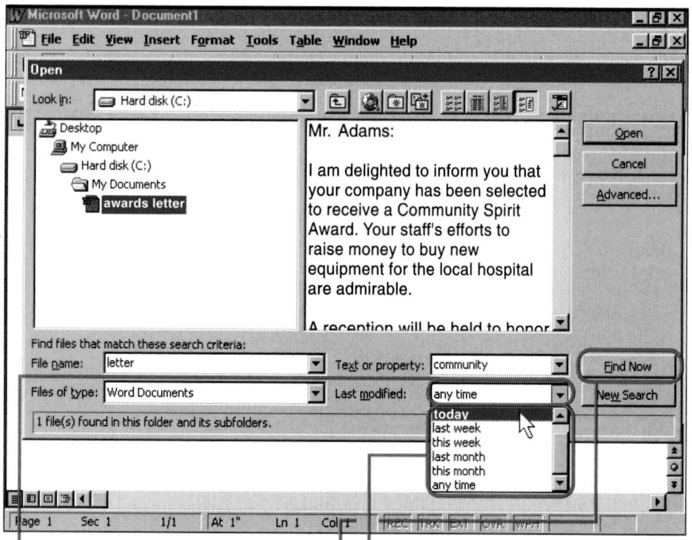

7 If you know part or all of the name of the document, move the mouse I over this area and then press the left mouse button. Then type the name.

8 If you know a word or phrase in the document, move the mouse I over this area and then press the left mouse button. Then type the word or phrase.

9 If you know when you last saved the document, move the mouse ↖ over this area and then press the left mouse button.

10 Move the mouse ↖ over the appropriate time period and then press the left mouse button.

11 To complete the search, move the mouse ↖ over **Find Now** and then press the left mouse button.

How can Word help me find a document?

There are many ways you can search for a document.

By document name **By contents** **By date**

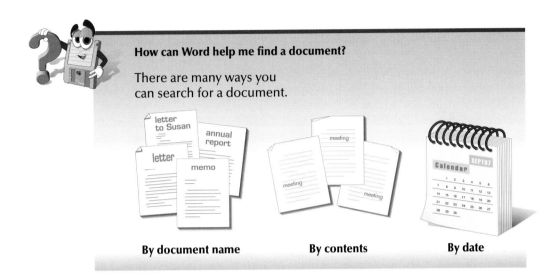

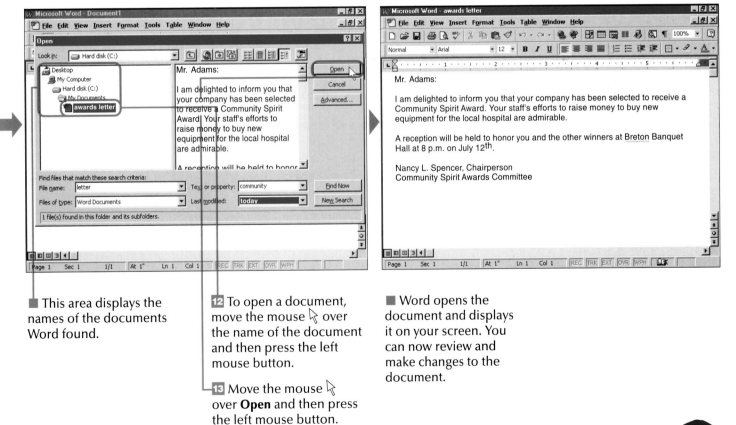

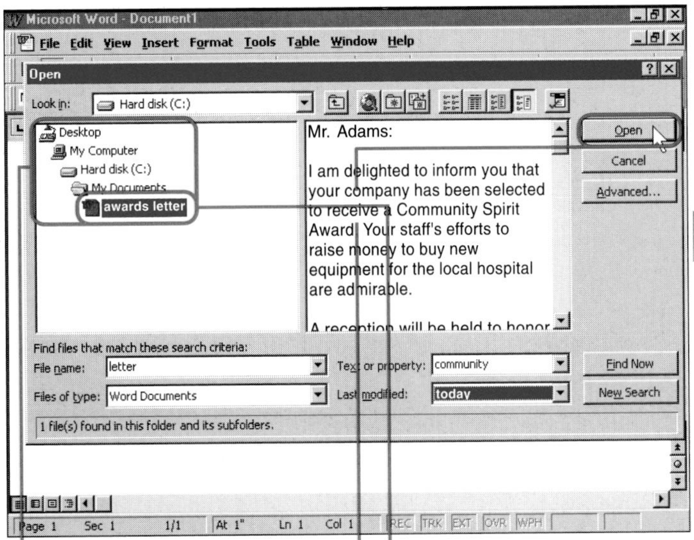

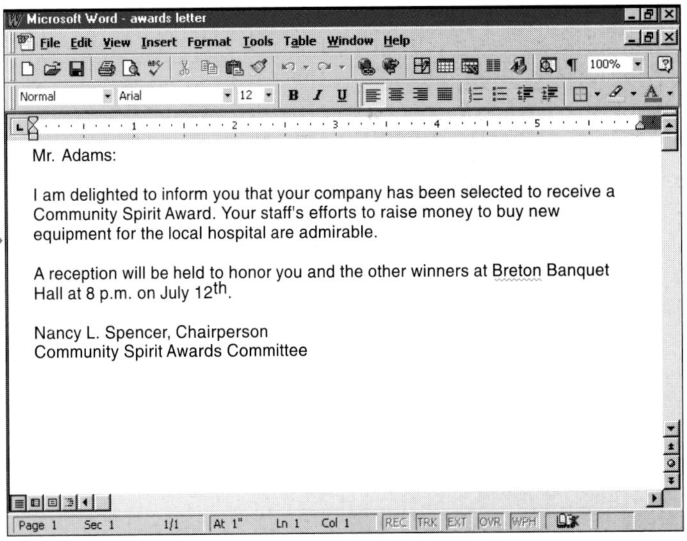

■ This area displays the names of the documents Word found.

12 To open a document, move the mouse over the name of the document and then press the left mouse button.

13 Move the mouse over **Open** and then press the left mouse button.

■ Word opens the document and displays it on your screen. You can now review and make changes to the document.

Microsoft Word - Document1
File Edit View Insert Format Tools Table Window Help
100%
Normal
Arial
12
B I U

CHAPTER 3

CHANGE DOCUMENT DISPLAY

Can I change the appearance of my Word screen? This chapter will teach you how to customize your screen to suit your needs.

CHANGE THE VIEW

Word offers four different ways to display your document. You can choose the view that best suits your needs.

CHANGE THE VIEW

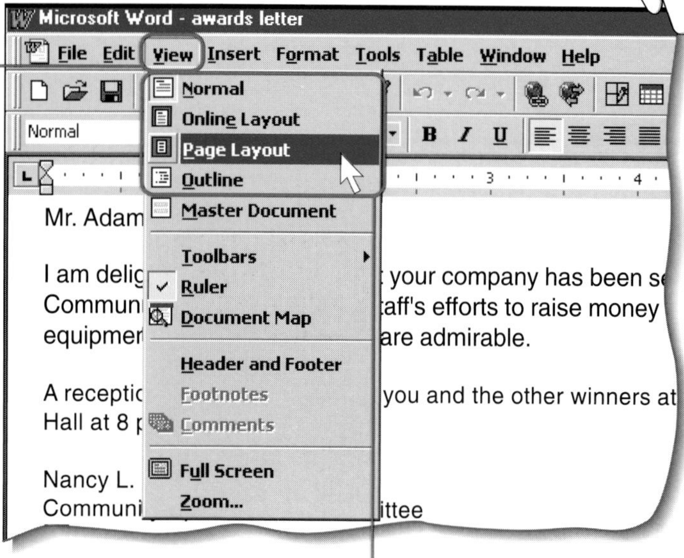

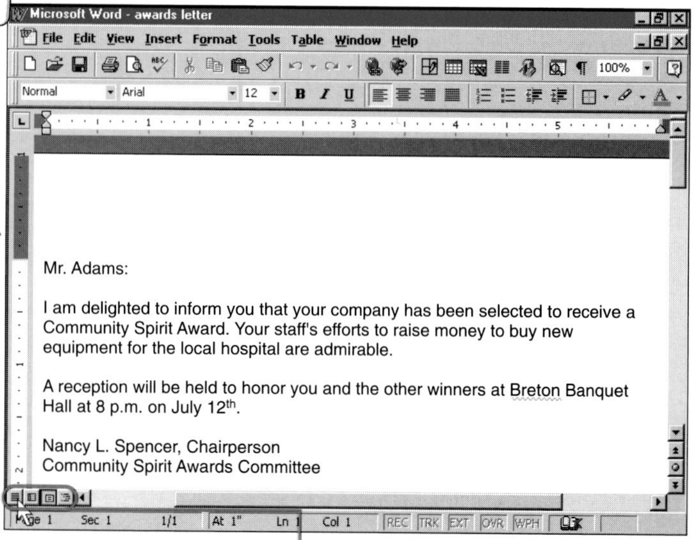

When you first start Word, the document appears in the Normal view.

1 To change the view, move the mouse over **View** and then press the left mouse button.

2 Move the mouse over the view you want to use and then press the left mouse button.

■ The document appears in the new view.

QUICKLY CHANGE THE VIEW

1 To quickly change the view, move the mouse over one of the following options and then press the left mouse button.

- Normal
- Online Layout
- Page Layout
- Outline

THE FOUR VIEWS

Normal View

This view simplifies the document so you can quickly enter, edit and format text. The Normal view does not display top or bottom margins, headers, footers or page numbers.

Outline View

This view helps you review and work with the structure of a document. You can focus on the main headings by hiding the remaining text.

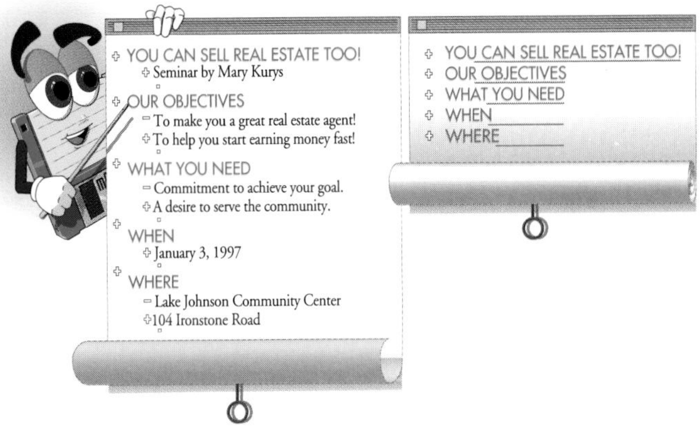
YOU CAN SELL REAL ESTATE TOO!
Seminar by Mary Kurys
OUR OBJECTIVES
To make you a great real estate agent!
To help you start earning money fast!
WHAT YOU NEED
Commitment to achieve your goal.
A desire to serve the community.
WHEN
January 3, 1997
WHERE
Lake Johnson Community Center
104 Ironstone Road
YOU CAN SELL REAL ESTATE TOO!
OUR OBJECTIVES
WHAT YOU NEED
WHEN
WHERE

Page Layout View

This view displays the document as it will appear on a printed page. The Page Layout view displays top and bottom margins, headers, footers and page numbers.

Online Layout View

This view displays documents so they are easy to read on the screen. The Online Layout view displays a document map, which lets you move quickly to specific locations in your document.

BLACK TEARS
ACT I
Scene i - Introduction to London Society
Scene ii - The Thames Family: The Toast of London
Scene iii - The Thames Family: The Real Story
ACT II
Scene i - The Prince's Gala
Scene ii -After the Gala

ZOOM IN OR OUT

Word lets you enlarge or reduce the display of text on your screen.

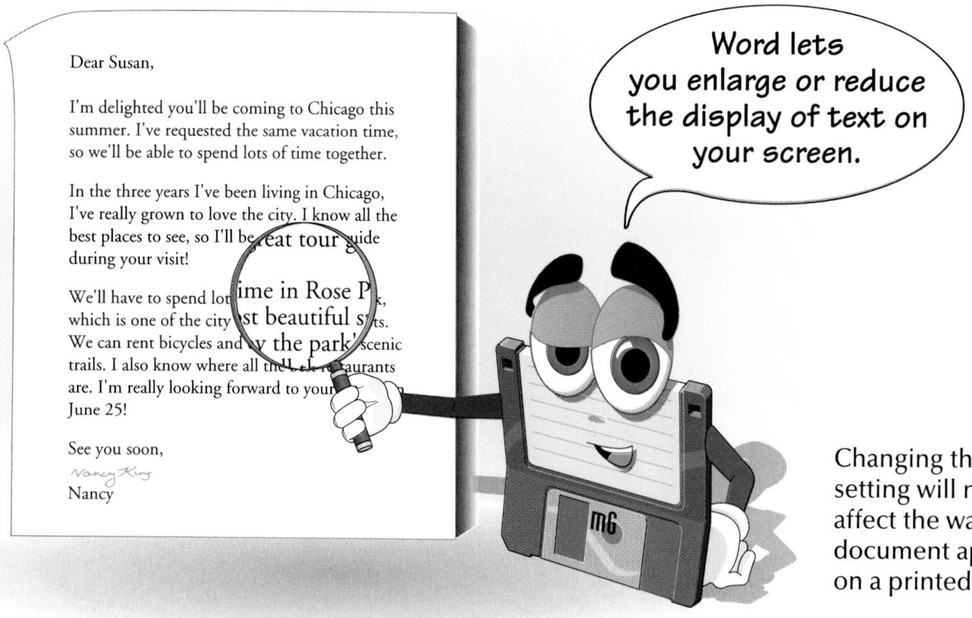

Changing the zoom setting will not affect the way the document appears on a printed page.

ZOOM IN OR OUT

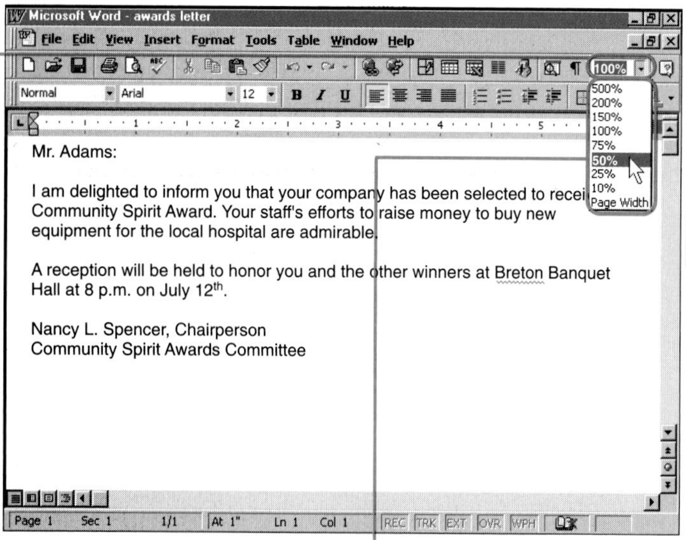

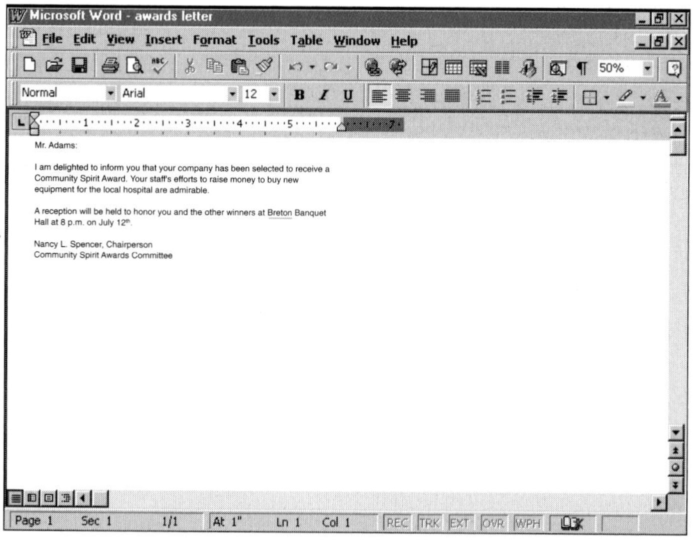

■ When you first start Word, the document appears in the 100% zoom setting.

1 To display a list of zoom settings, move the mouse over ▼ in this area and then press the left mouse button.

2 Move the mouse over the setting you want to use and then press the left mouse button.

■ The document appears in the new zoom setting. You can edit your document as usual.

■ To return to the normal zoom setting, repeat steps 1 and 2, selecting 100% in step 2.

DISPLAY OR HIDE THE RULER

You can use the ruler to position text on a page. You can display or hide the ruler at any time.
Dear Susan,
I'm delighted you'll be coming to Chicago this summer. I've requested the same vacation time, so we'll be able to spend lots of time together.
In the three years I've been living in Chicago, I've really grown to love the city. I know all the best places to see, so I'll be a great tour guide during your visit!
See you soon,
Nancy

When you first start Word, the ruler is displayed on your screen. Hiding the ruler provides a larger and less cluttered working area.

DISPLAY OR HIDE THE RULER

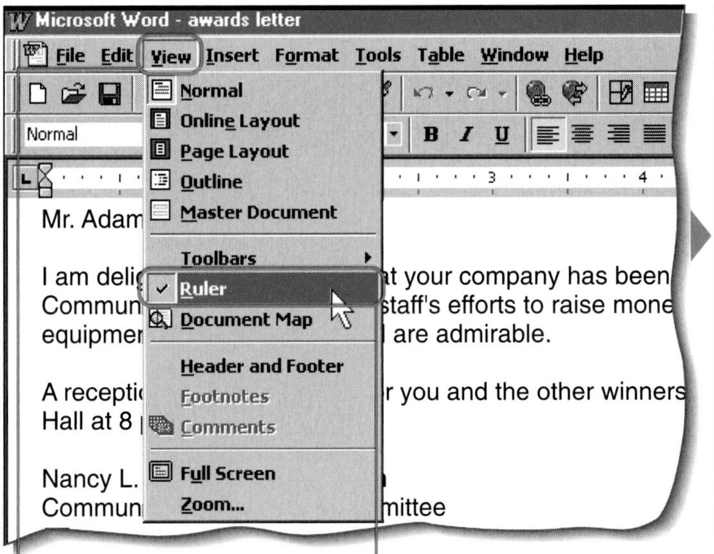
Microsoft Word - awards letter
File Edit View Insert Format Tools Table Window Help
Normal
Online Layout
Page Layout
Outline
Master Document
Toolbars
Ruler
Document Map
Header and Footer
Footnotes
Comments
Full Screen
Zoom...

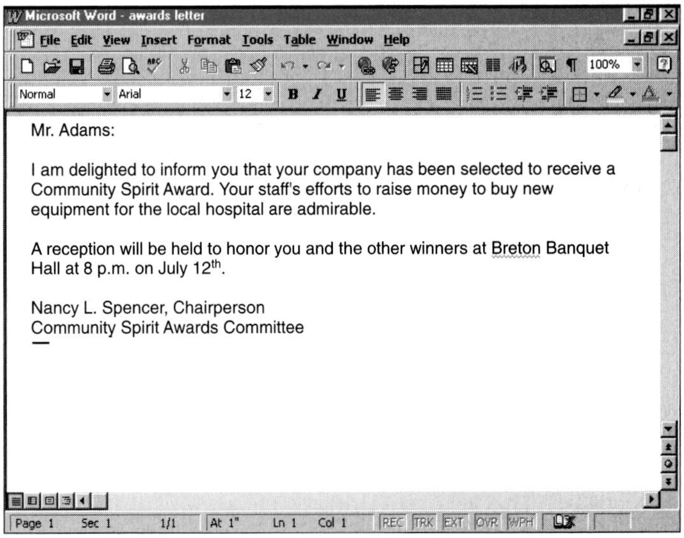
Microsoft Word - awards letter
File Edit View Insert Format Tools Table Window Help
Mr. Adams:
I am delighted to inform you that your company has been selected to receive a Community Spirit Award. Your staff's efforts to raise money to buy new equipment for the local hospital are admirable.
A reception will be held to honor you and the other winners at Breton Banquet Hall at 8 p.m. on July 12th.
Nancy L. Spencer, Chairperson
Community Spirit Awards Committee

1 To display or hide the ruler, move the mouse over **View** and then press the left mouse button.

2 Move the mouse over **Ruler** and then press the left mouse button. A check mark (✓) beside **Ruler** tells you the ruler is currently displayed.

■ Word displays or hides the ruler.

DISPLAY OR HIDE TOOLBARS

Word offers several toolbars that you can hide or display at any time. Each toolbar contains buttons that help you quickly perform common tasks.

DISPLAY OR HIDE TOOLBARS

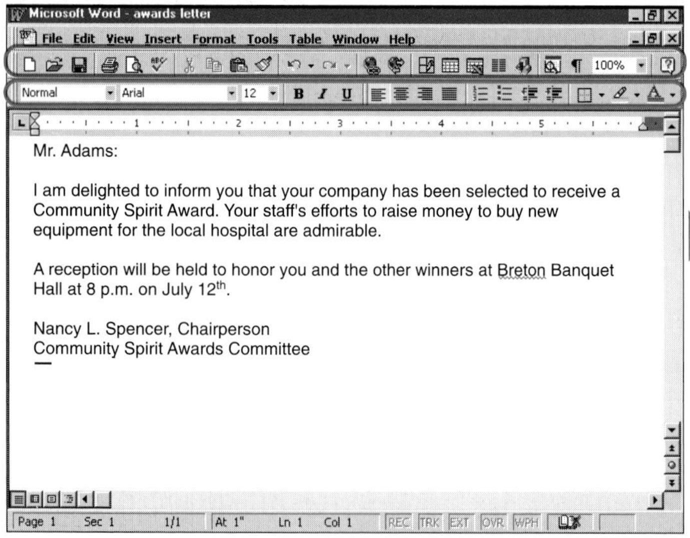

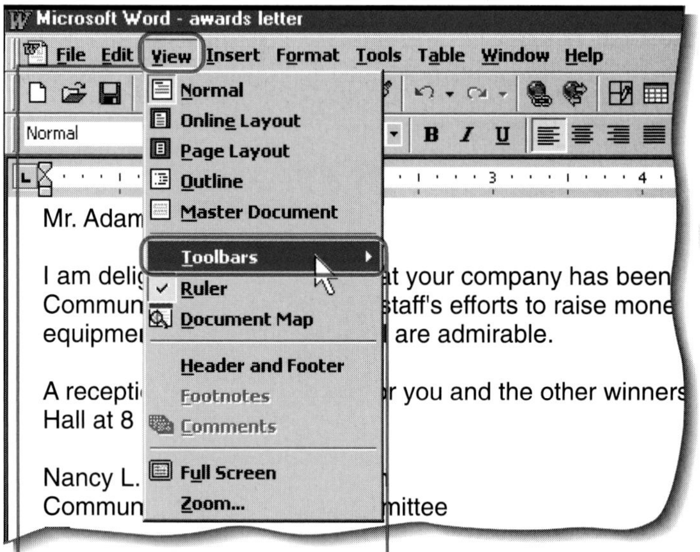

When you first start Word, the Standard and Formatting toolbars appear on the screen.

Standard toolbar

Formatting toolbar

1 To display or hide a toolbar, move the mouse over **View** and then press the left mouse button.

2 Move the mouse over **Toolbars**.

Why would I want to hide a toolbar?

A screen displaying fewer toolbars provides a larger and less cluttered working area.

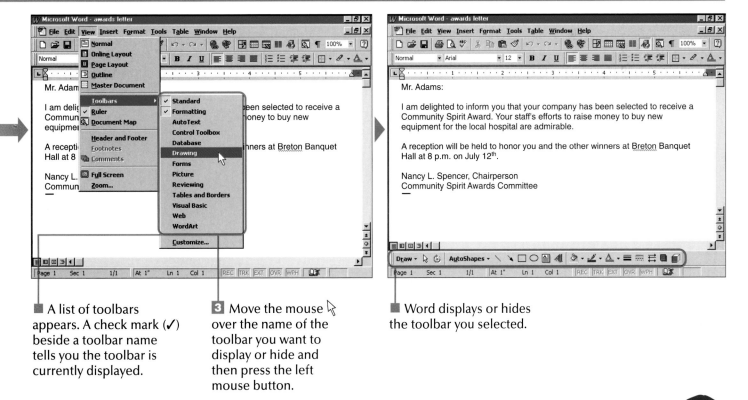

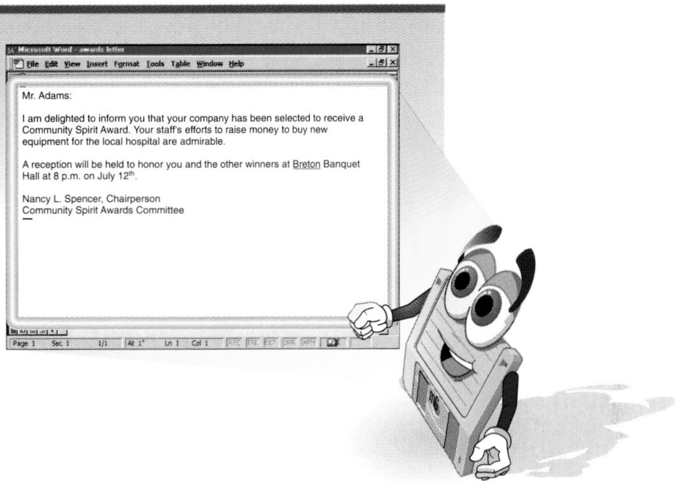
Microsoft Word - awards letter
Mr. Adams:
I am delighted to inform you that your company has been selected to receive a Community Spirit Award. Your staff's efforts to raise money to buy new equipment for the local hospital are admirable.
A reception will be held to honor you and the other winners at Breton Banquet Hall at 8 p.m. on July 12th.
Nancy L. Spencer, Chairperson
Community Spirit Awards Committee

Microsoft Word - awards letter
File Edit View Insert Format Tools Table Window Help
Normal
Online Layout
Page Layout
Outline
Master Document
Toolbars
Ruler
Document Map
Header and Footer
Footnotes
Comments
Full Screen
Zoom...
Standard
Formatting
AutoText
Control Toolbox
Database
Drawing
Forms
Picture
Reviewing
Tables and Borders
Visual Basic
Web
WordArt
Customize...

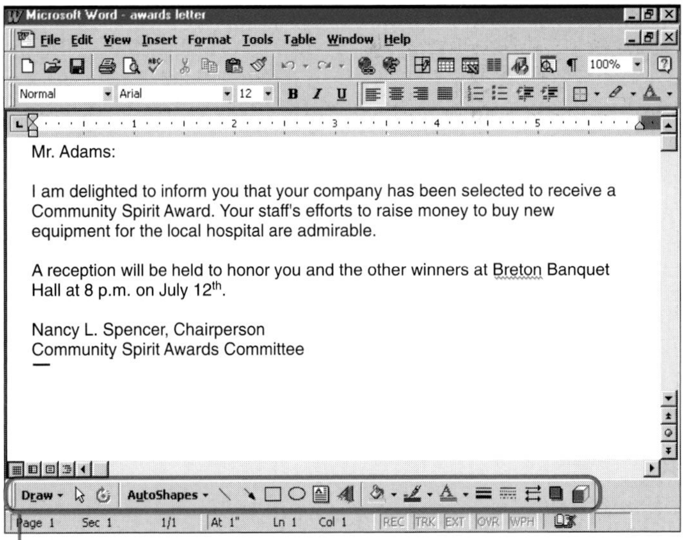
Microsoft Word - awards letter
File Edit View Insert Format Tools Table Window Help
Mr. Adams:
I am delighted to inform you that your company has been selected to receive a Community Spirit Award. Your staff's efforts to raise money to buy new equipment for the local hospital are admirable.
A reception will be held to honor you and the other winners at Breton Banquet Hall at 8 p.m. on July 12th.
Nancy L. Spencer, Chairperson
Community Spirit Awards Committee
Draw
AutoShapes

■ A list of toolbars appears. A check mark (✓) beside a toolbar name tells you the toolbar is currently displayed.

3 Move the mouse over the name of the toolbar you want to display or hide and then press the left mouse button.

■ Word displays or hides the toolbar you selected.

USING THE DOCUMENT MAP

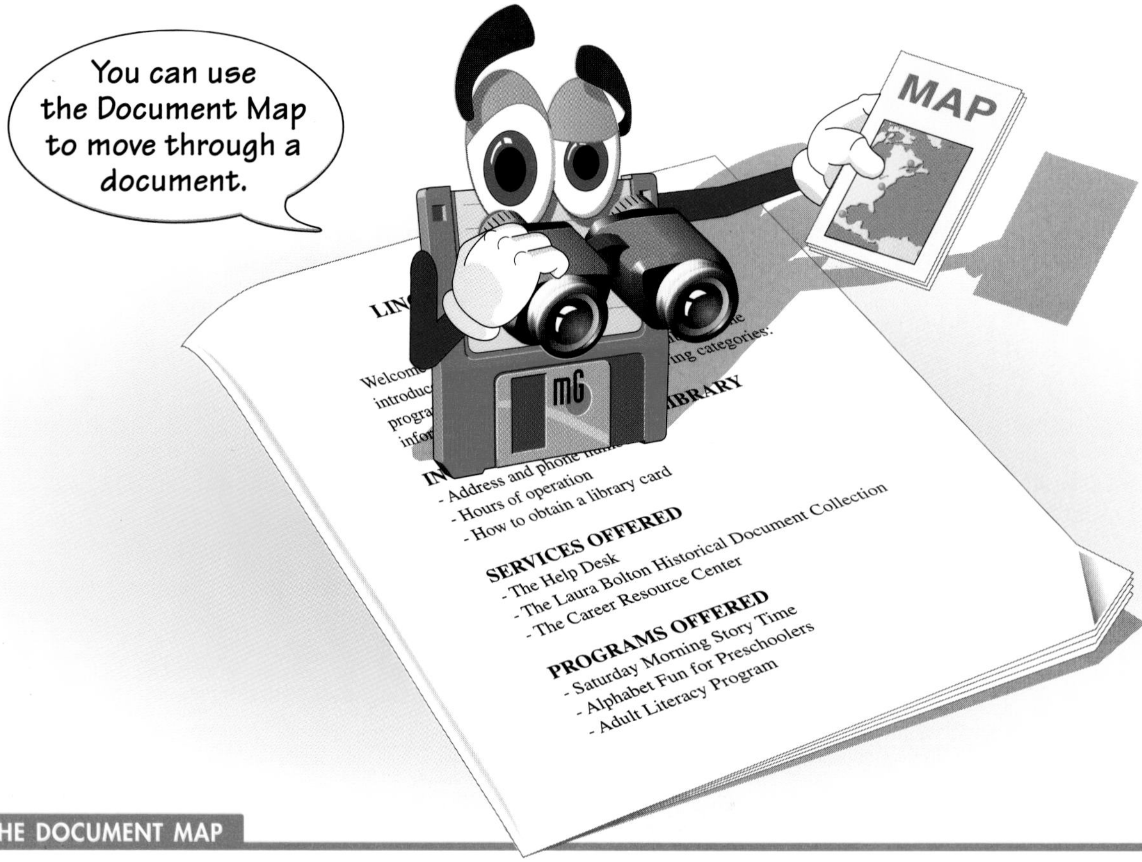

USING THE DOCUMENT MAP

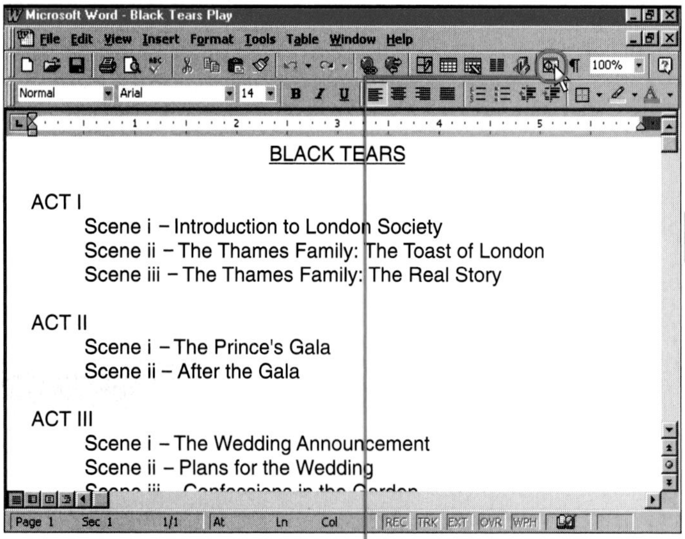

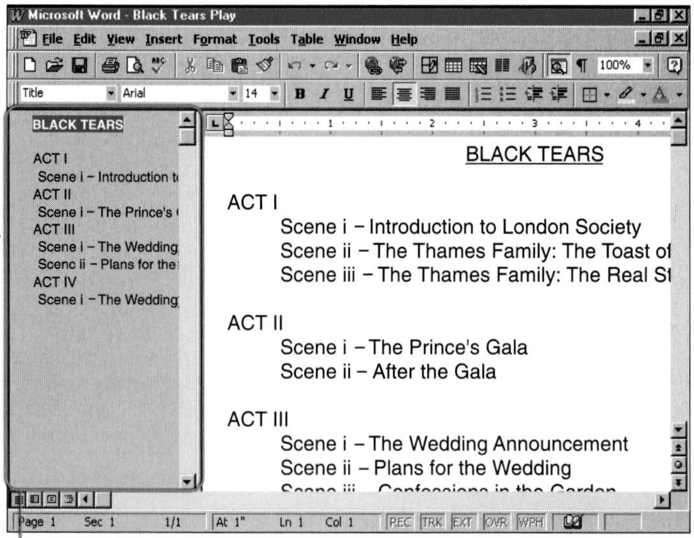

■ For this example, a new document was created.

1 To display the Document Map, move the mouse over and then press the left mouse button.

■ The Document Map appears and shows the main headings in your document.

Note: If Word does not find any headings in your document, the Document Map is blank.

Can I use the Document Map in any view?

You can use the Document Map in the Normal, Online Layout, Page Layout and Outline views. For information on the four views, refer to page 32.

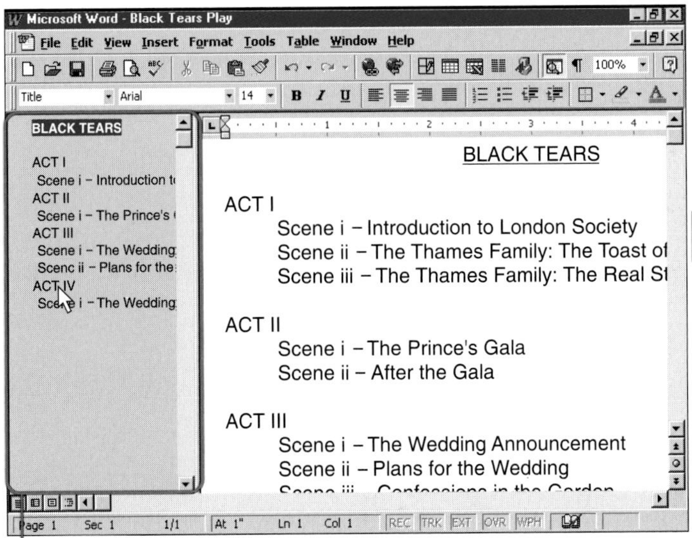

2 To instantly jump to a heading in your document, move the mouse over the heading in the Document Map and then press the left mouse button.

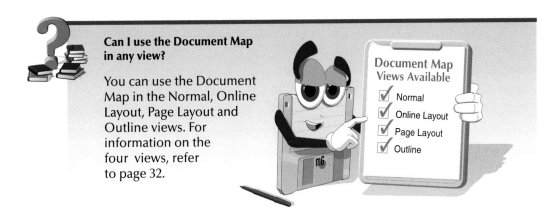

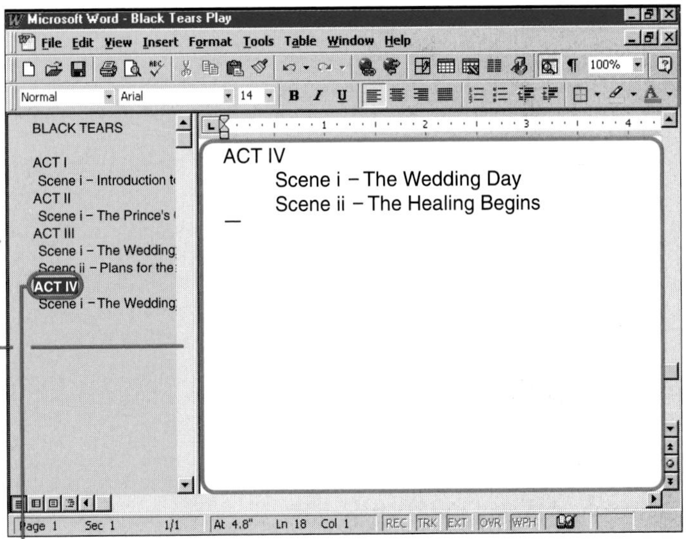

■ Word highlights the heading you selected to indicate your location in the document.

■ This area displays the area of the document you selected.

■ To hide the Document Map, repeat step 1.

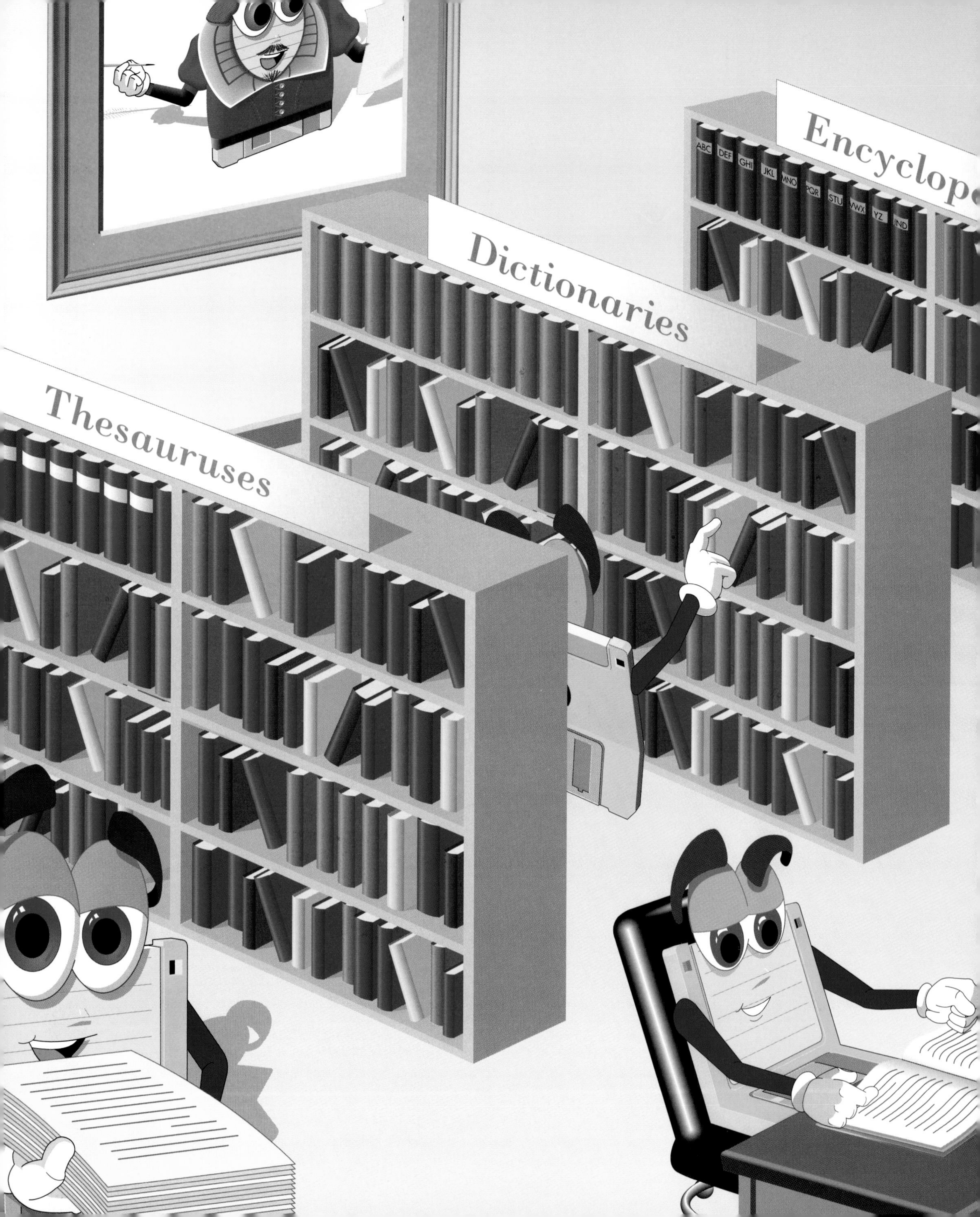
Encyclop
ABC
DEF
GHI
JKL
MNO
PQR
STU
VWX
YZ
IND
Dictionaries
Thesauruses

CHAPTER 4

EDIT YOUR DOCUMENTS

Wondering how to edit the text in your documents quickly and efficiently? Learn many timesaving techniques, including moving and copying text, creating AutoText and using the Thesaurus.

INSERT TEXT

Dear Susan:
School
Trafalgar High celebrates its 50th anniversary this year. We will be celebrating on September 11th with an Open House, followed by a buffet dinner.
Please bring your school photos and memorabilia for our display table.
Best regards,
Becky Flynn
Ink
You can easily add new text to your document. The existing text will move to make room for the text you add.

INSERT CHARACTERS

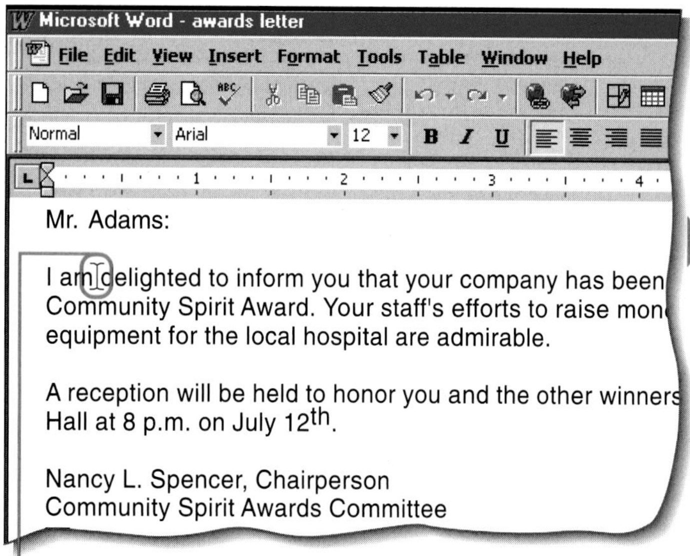
Microsoft Word - awards letter
File Edit View Insert Format Tools Table Window Help
Normal
Arial
12
Mr. Adams:
I am delighted to inform you that your company has been
Community Spirit Award. Your staff's efforts to raise mon
equipment for the local hospital are admirable.
A reception will be held to honor you and the other winners
Hall at 8 p.m. on July 12th.
Nancy L. Spencer, Chairperson
Community Spirit Awards Committee

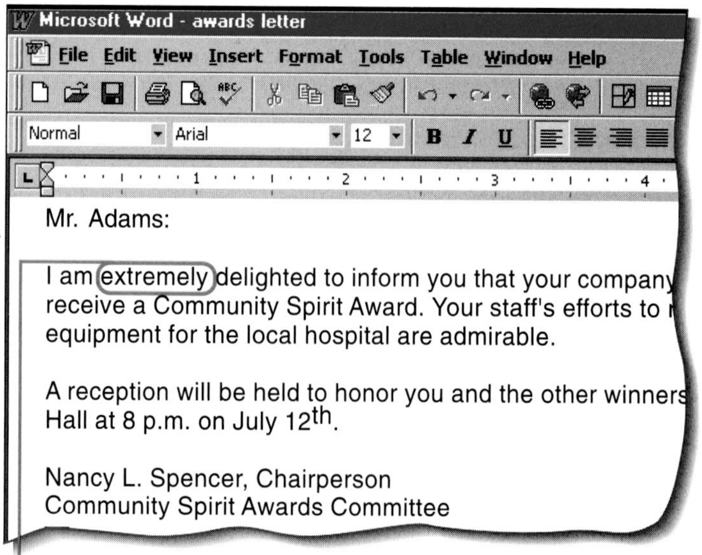
Microsoft Word - awards letter
File Edit View Insert Format Tools Table Window Help
Normal
Arial
12
Mr. Adams:
I am extremely delighted to inform you that your company
receive a Community Spirit Award. Your staff's efforts to
equipment for the local hospital are admirable.
A reception will be held to honor you and the other winners
Hall at 8 p.m. on July 12th.
Nancy L. Spencer, Chairperson
Community Spirit Awards Committee

1 Move the mouse I to where you want to insert the new text and then press the left mouse button.

2 Type the text you want to insert. To insert a blank space, press the **Spacebar**.

■ The words to the right of the new text move forward.

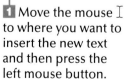

How do I insert symbols into my document?

Word will automatically replace specific characters you type with symbols. This lets you quickly enter symbols that are not available on your keyboard.

Type	Symbol
(c)	©
(r)	®
(tm)	™
:(	☹
:)	☺
:l	😐
<--	←
-->	→
<==	⬅
==>	➔
<=>	⇔

Note: For more information on inserting symbols, refer to page 82.

INSERT A BLANK LINE

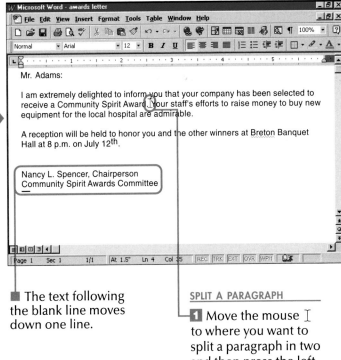

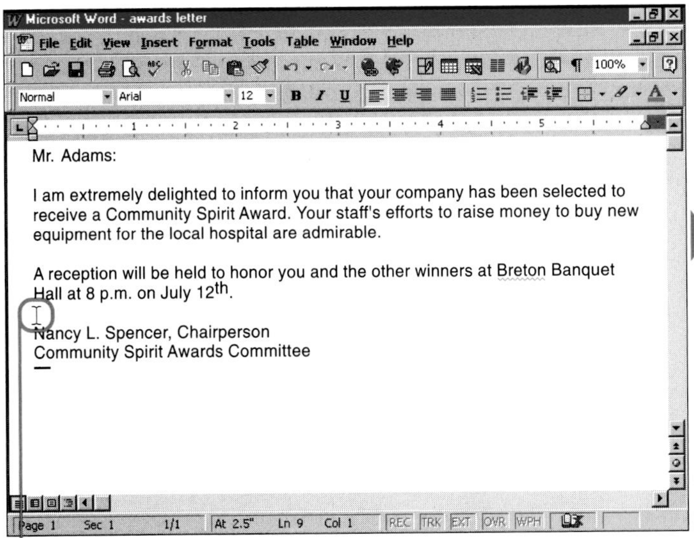
Microsoft Word - awards letter
Mr. Adams:
I am extremely delighted to inform you that your company has been selected to receive a Community Spirit Award. Your staff's efforts to raise money to buy new equipment for the local hospital are admirable.
A reception will be held to honor you and the other winners at Breton Banquet Hall at 8 p.m. on July 12th.
Nancy L. Spencer, Chairperson
Community Spirit Awards Committee

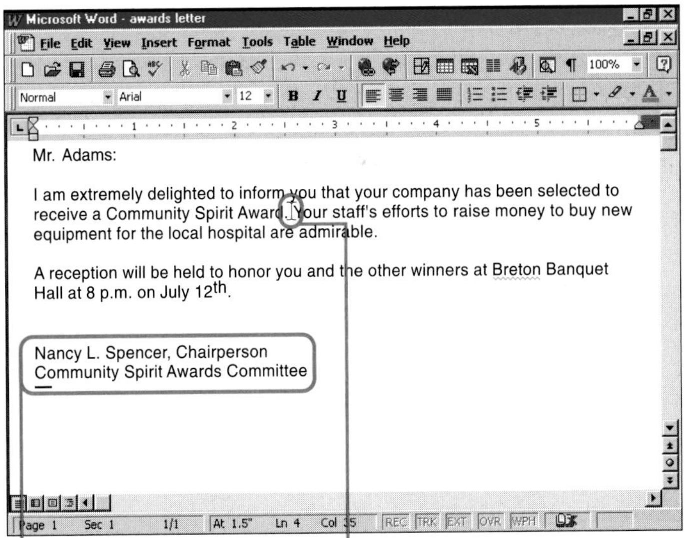
Microsoft Word - awards letter
Mr. Adams:
I am extremely delighted to inform you that your company has been selected to receive a Community Spirit Award. Your staff's efforts to raise money to buy new equipment for the local hospital are admirable.
A reception will be held to honor you and the other winners at Breton Banquet Hall at 8 p.m. on July 12th.
Nancy L. Spencer, Chairperson
Community Spirit Awards Committee

1 Move the mouse I to where you want to insert a blank line and then press the left mouse button.

2 Press **Enter** on your keyboard to insert the blank line.

■ The text following the blank line moves down one line.

SPLIT A PARAGRAPH

1 Move the mouse I to where you want to split a paragraph in two and then press the left mouse button.

2 Press **Enter** on your keyboard twice.

DELETE TEXT

You can easily remove text you no longer need. The remaining text moves to fill any empty spaces.
Dear Susan,
I'm delighted you'll be coming to Chicago this summer. I've requested the same vacation time, so we'll be able to spend lots of time together.
Nancy

DELETE CHARACTERS

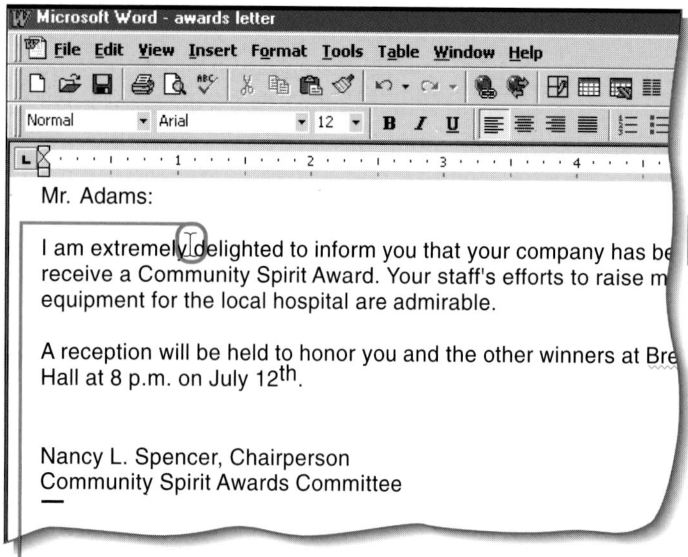

Microsoft Word - awards letter
File Edit View Insert Format Tools Table Window Help
Normal
Arial
12
Mr. Adams:
I am extremely delighted to inform you that your company has be
receive a Community Spirit Award. Your staff's efforts to raise m
equipment for the local hospital are admirable.
A reception will be held to honor you and the other winners at Bre
Hall at 8 p.m. on July 12th.
Nancy L. Spencer, Chairperson
Community Spirit Awards Committee

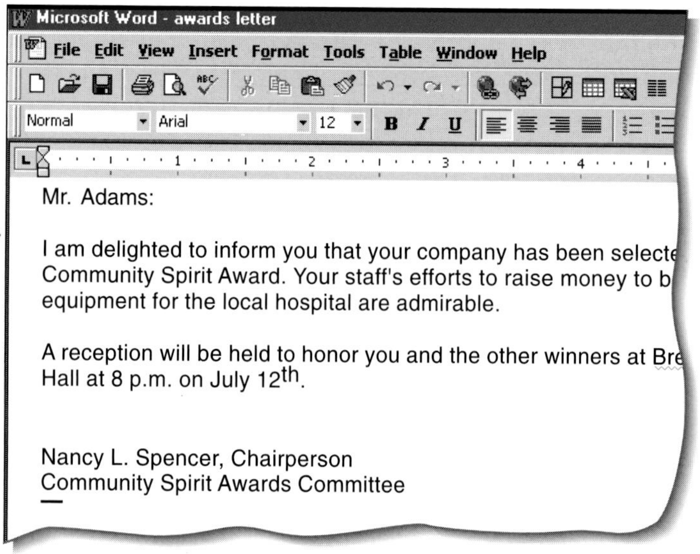

Microsoft Word - awards letter
File Edit View Insert Format Tools Table Window Help
Normal
Arial
12
Mr. Adams:
I am delighted to inform you that your company has been selecte
Community Spirit Award. Your staff's efforts to raise money to b
equipment for the local hospital are admirable.
A reception will be held to honor you and the other winners at Bre
Hall at 8 p.m. on July 12th.
Nancy L. Spencer, Chairperson
Community Spirit Awards Committee

1 Move the mouse I to the **right** of the first character you want to delete and then press the left mouse button.

2 Press ←Backspace on your keyboard once for each character or space you want to delete.

■ You can also use Delete on your keyboard to remove characters. Move the mouse I to the **left** of the first character you want to remove and then press the left mouse button. Press Delete once for each character or space you want to remove.

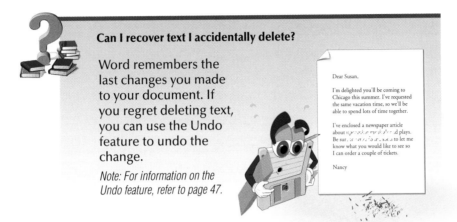

Can I recover text I accidentally delete?

Word remembers the last changes you made to your document. If you regret deleting text, you can use the Undo feature to undo the change.

Note: For information on the Undo feature, refer to page 47.

Dear Susan,
I'm delighted you'll be coming to Chicago this summer. I've requested the same vacation time, so we'll be able to spend lots of time together.
I've enclosed a newspaper article
know what you would like to see so I can order a couple of tickets.
Nancy

DELETE A BLANK LINE

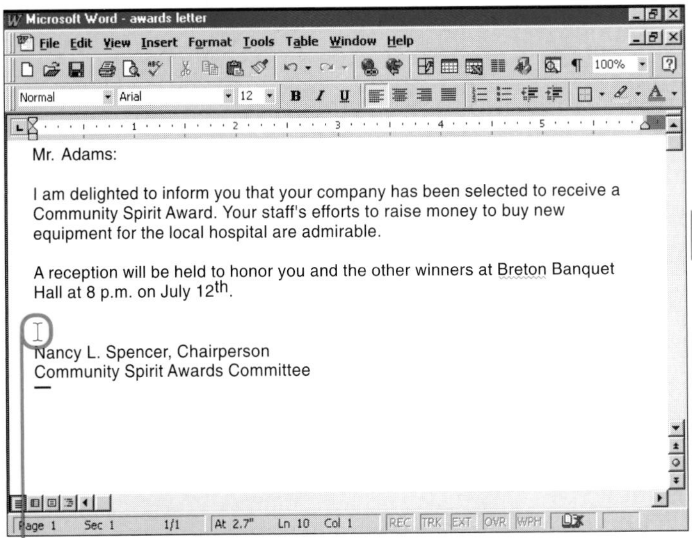

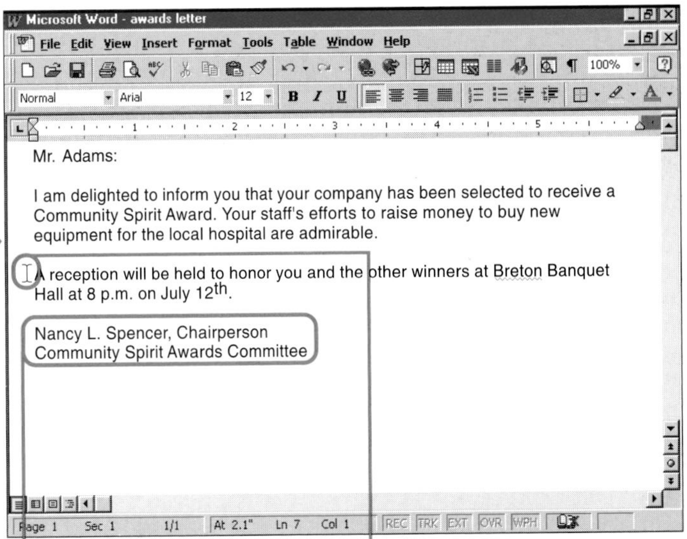

1 Move the mouse I to the beginning of the blank line you want to delete and then press the left mouse button.

2 Press Backspace on your keyboard to remove the blank line.

■ The text following the blank line moves up one line.

JOIN TWO PARAGRAPHS

1 Move the mouse I to the left of the first character in the second paragraph and then press the left mouse button.

2 Press Backspace on your keyboard until the paragraphs are joined.

DELETE TEXT

You can quickly delete text you have selected.
Dear Susan,
I've enclosed a newspaper article about upcoming musicals.
Be sure to write to me soon to let me know what you would like to see so I can order a couple of tickets.
Nancy

DELETE SELECTED TEXT

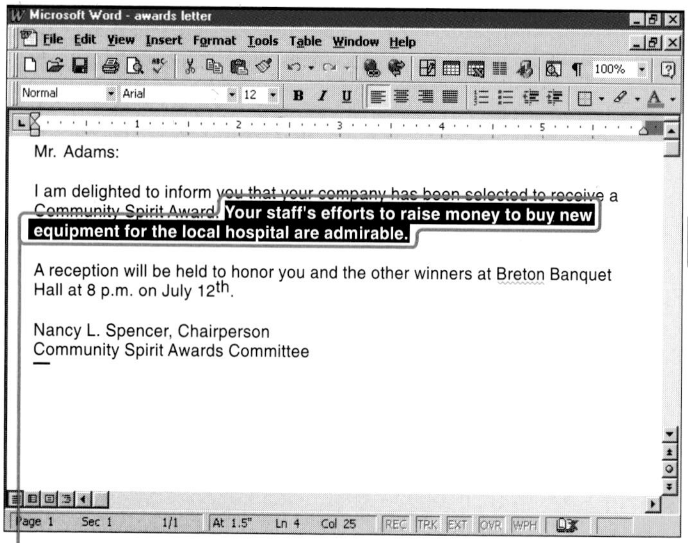
Microsoft Word - awards letter
Mr. Adams:
I am delighted to inform you that your company has been selected to receive a Community Spirit Award. Your staff's efforts to raise money to buy new equipment for the local hospital are admirable.
A reception will be held to honor you and the other winners at Breton Banquet Hall at 8 p.m. on July 12th.
Nancy L. Spencer, Chairperson
Community Spirit Awards Committee

1 Select the text you want to delete. To select text, refer to page 12.

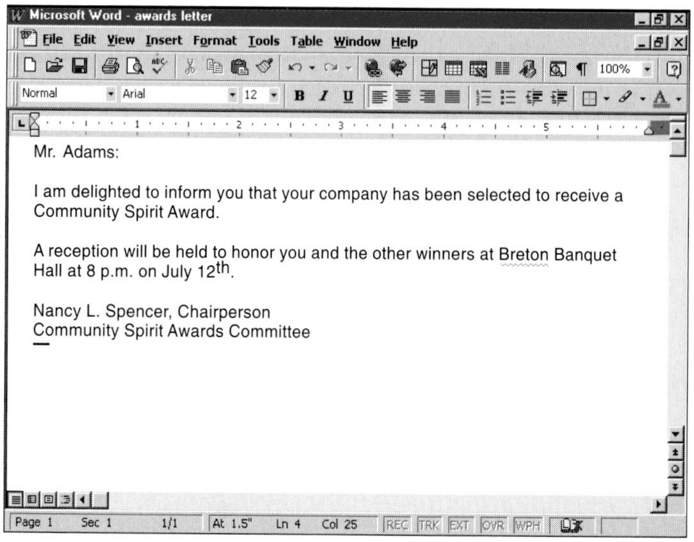
Microsoft Word - awards letter
Mr. Adams:
I am delighted to inform you that your company has been selected to receive a Community Spirit Award.
A reception will be held to honor you and the other winners at Breton Banquet Hall at 8 p.m. on July 12th.
Nancy L. Spencer, Chairperson
Community Spirit Awards Committee

2 Press **Delete** on your keyboard to remove the text.

UNDO LAST CHANGE

Word remembers the last changes you made to your document. If you regret these changes, you can cancel them by using the Undo feature.
enclosed

UNDO LAST CHANGE

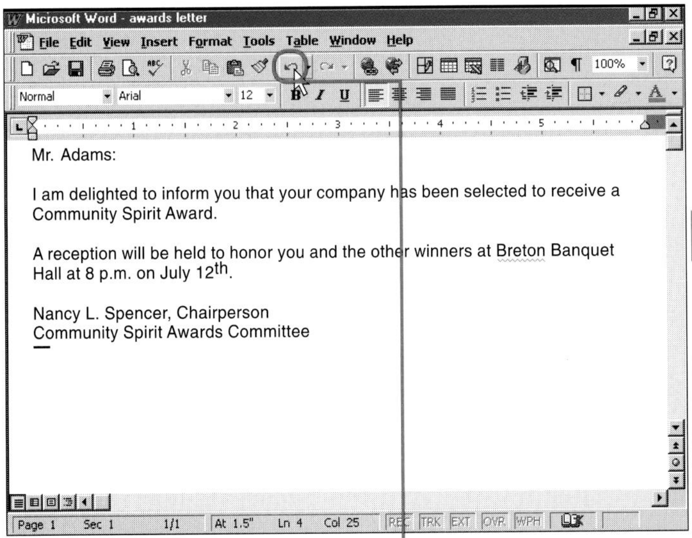

The Undo feature can cancel your last editing and formatting changes.

1 To undo your last change, move the mouse over ↶ and then press the left mouse button.

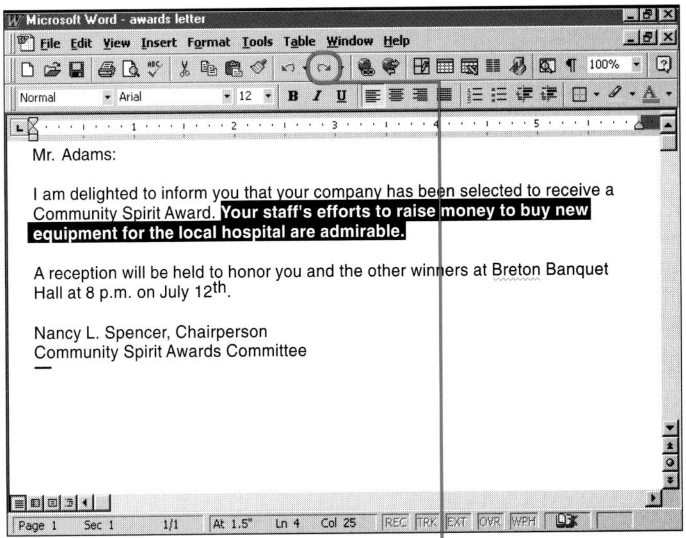

■ Word cancels the last change you made to your document.

■ You can repeat step 1 to cancel previous changes you made.

■ To reverse the results of using the Undo feature, move the mouse over ↷ and then press the left mouse button.

MOVE TEXT

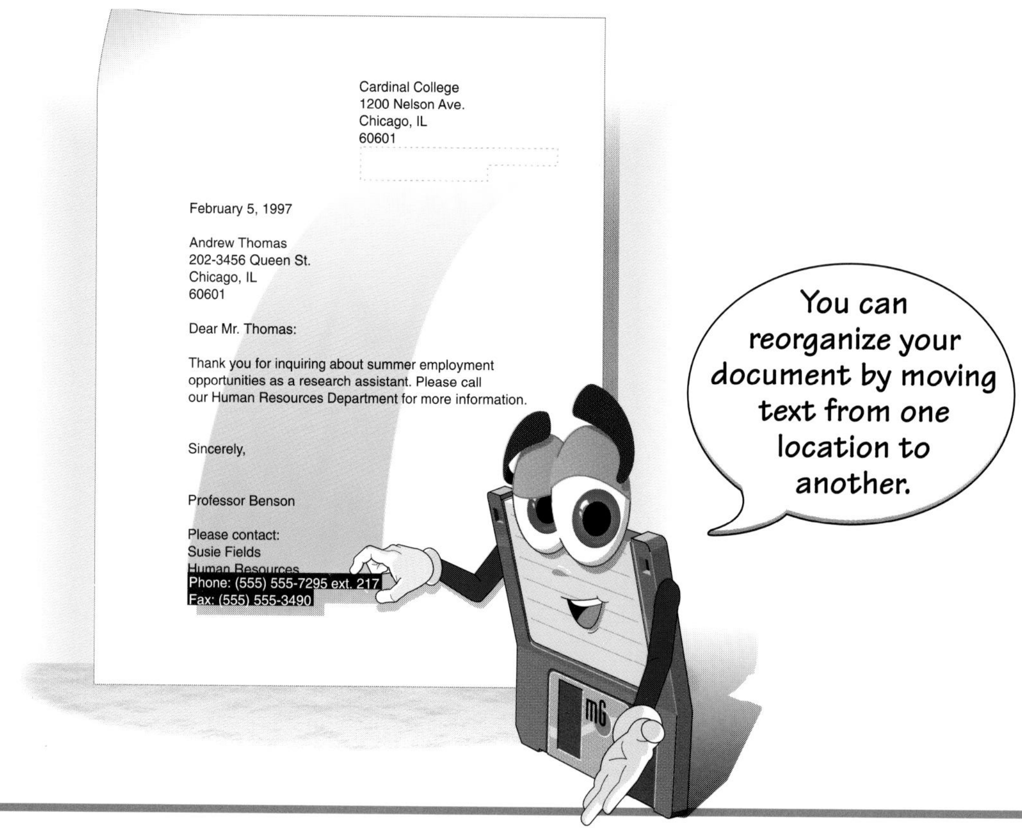
Cardinal College
1200 Nelson Ave.
Chicago, IL
60601
February 5, 1997
Andrew Thomas
202-3456 Queen St.
Chicago, IL
60601
Dear Mr. Thomas:
Thank you for inquiring about summer employment opportunities as a research assistant. Please call our Human Resources Department for more information.
Sincerely,
Professor Benson
Please contact:
Susie Fields
Phone: (555) 555-7295 ext. 217
Fax: (555) 555-3490
You can reorganize your document by moving text from one location to another.

MOVE TEXT

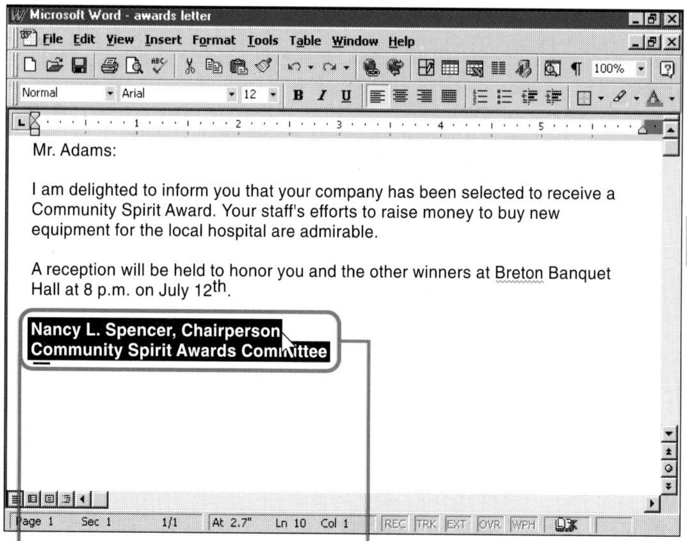
Microsoft Word - awards letter
File Edit View Insert Format Tools Table Window Help
Mr. Adams:
I am delighted to inform you that your company has been selected to receive a Community Spirit Award. Your staff's efforts to raise money to buy new equipment for the local hospital are admirable.
A reception will be held to honor you and the other winners at Breton Banquet Hall at 8 p.m. on July 12th.
Nancy L. Spencer, Chairperson
Community Spirit Awards Committee

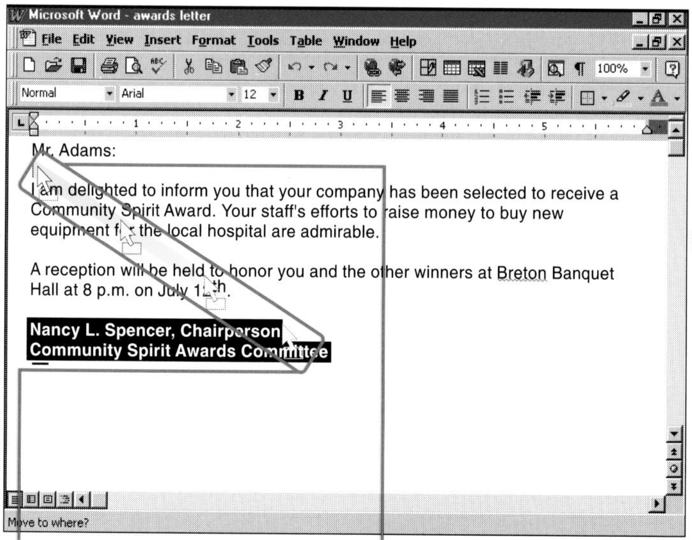
Microsoft Word - awards letter
File Edit View Insert Format Tools Table Window Help
Mr. Adams:
Nancy L. Spencer, Chairperson
Community Spirit Awards Committee
Move to where?

1 Select the text you want to move. To select text, refer to page 12.

2 Move the mouse I anywhere over the selected text (I changes to ↖).

3 Press and hold down the left mouse button as you move the mouse to where you want to place the text.

■ The text will appear where you position the dotted insertion point on your screen.

Can moving text help me edit my document?

Moving text lets you easily try out different ways of organizing the text in a document. You can find the most effective structure for your document by experimenting with different placements of sentences and paragraphs.

The Use of Symbols in "The Hero"

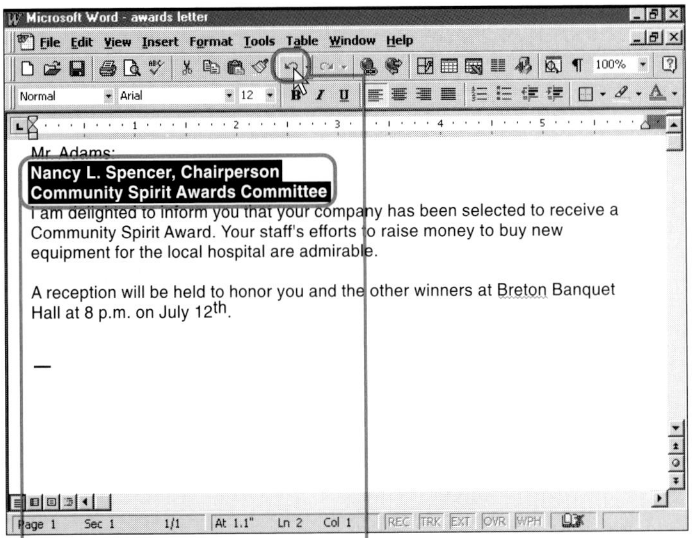
Microsoft Word - awards letter
Mr. Adams:
Nancy L. Spencer, Chairperson
Community Spirit Awards Committee
I am delighted to inform you that your company has been selected to receive a Community Spirit Award. Your staff's efforts to raise money to buy new equipment for the local hospital are admirable.
A reception will be held to honor you and the other winners at Breton Banquet Hall at 8 p.m. on July 12th.

4 Release the left mouse button and the text moves to the new location.

UNDO MOVE

1 To immediately move the text back, move the mouse over the Undo button and then press the left mouse button.

MOVE TEXT USING TOOLBAR BUTTONS

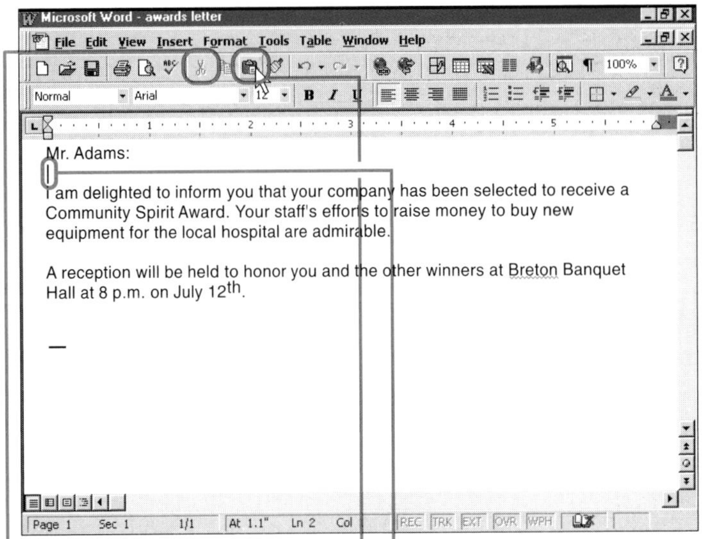
Microsoft Word - awards letter
Mr. Adams:
I am delighted to inform you that your company has been selected to receive a Community Spirit Award. Your staff's efforts to raise money to buy new equipment for the local hospital are admirable.
A reception will be held to honor you and the other winners at Breton Banquet Hall at 8 p.m. on July 12th.

1 Select the text you want to move.

2 Move the mouse over the Cut button and then press the left mouse button. The text you selected disappears from the screen.

3 Move the mouse I to where you want to place the text and then press the left mouse button.

4 Move the mouse over the Paste button and then press the left mouse button. The text appears in the new location.

COPY TEXT

You can place a copy of text in a different location in your document. This will save you time since you do not have to retype the text.
Cardinal College
1200 Nelson Ave.
Chicago, IL
60601
February 5, 1997
Andrew Thomas
202-3456 Queen St.
Chicago, IL
60601
Dear Mr. Thomas:
Thank you for inquiring about summer employment opportunities as a research assistant. Please send your résumé and three writing samples to our human resources address below.
Sincerely,
Professor Benson
Please contact:
Human Resources
Attention: Susie Fields
Cardinal College
1200 Nelson Ave.
Chicago, IL
60601

COPY TEXT

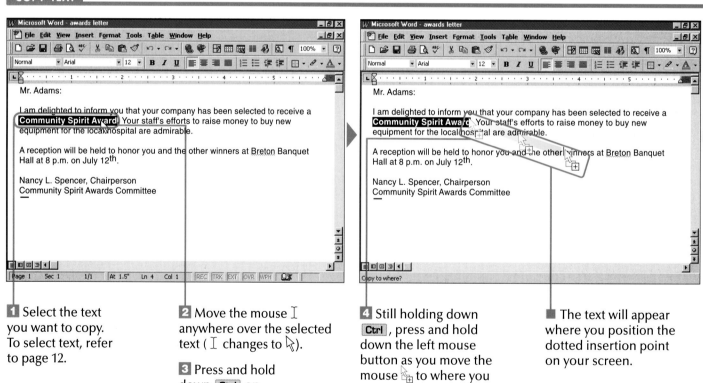

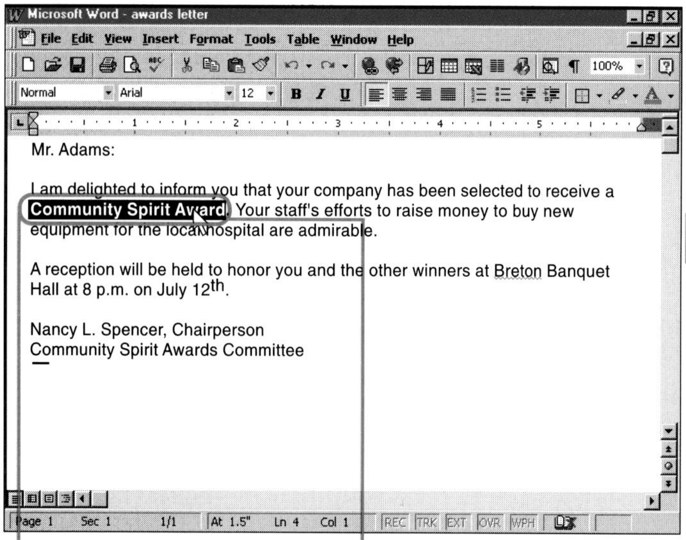
Microsoft Word - awards letter
File Edit View Insert Format Tools Table Window Help
Mr. Adams:
I am delighted to inform you that your company has been selected to receive a Community Spirit Award. Your staff's efforts to raise money to buy new equipment for the local hospital are admirable.
A reception will be held to honor you and the other winners at Breton Banquet Hall at 8 p.m. on July 12th.
Nancy L. Spencer, Chairperson
Community Spirit Awards Committee
Page 1 Sec 1 1/1 At 1.5" Ln 4 Col 1

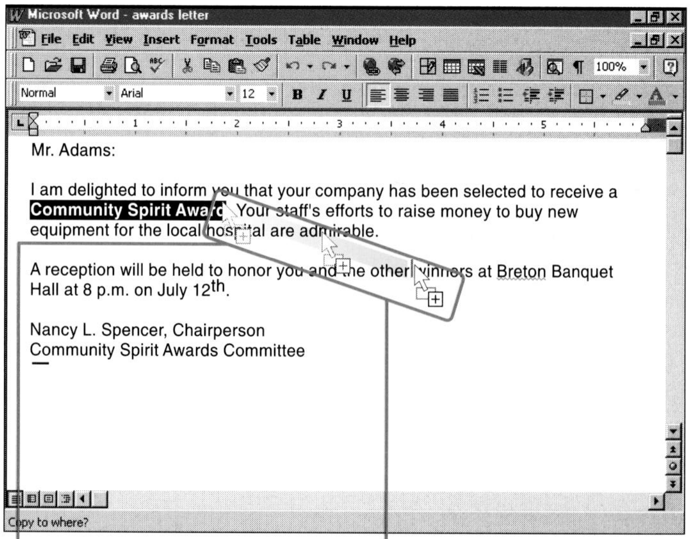
Microsoft Word - awards letter
File Edit View Insert Format Tools Table Window Help
Mr. Adams:
Nancy L. Spencer, Chairperson
Community Spirit Awards Committee
Copy to where?

1 Select the text you want to copy. To select text, refer to page 12.

2 Move the mouse I anywhere over the selected text (I changes to ↖).

3 Press and hold down Ctrl on your keyboard.

4 Still holding down Ctrl, press and hold down the left mouse button as you move the mouse to where you want to place the copy.

■ The text will appear where you position the dotted insertion point on your screen.

How can copying text help me edit my document?

If you plan to make major changes to a paragraph, you may want to copy the paragraph before you begin. This gives you two copies of the paragraph—the original paragraph and a paragraph with all the changes.

There is a 10th anniversary High School Reunion on August 8, 9 and 10 at **Woodblock** High School. We all hope to see you there. **Contact Susan Hughes** for more information.

There is an 11th anniversary High School Reunion on August 8, 9 and 10 at **Brown** High School. We all hope to see you there. **Call Bob Maki** for more information.

COPY TEXT USING TOOLBAR BUTTONS

5 Release the left mouse button and then release **Ctrl**.

■ A copy of the text appears in the new location.

UNDO COPY

1 To immediately remove the copy, move the mouse ⤢ over 🔙 and then press the left mouse button.

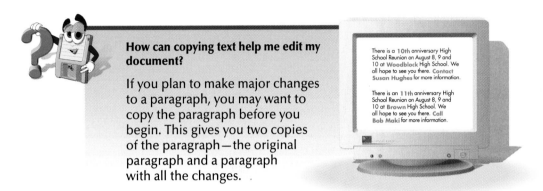

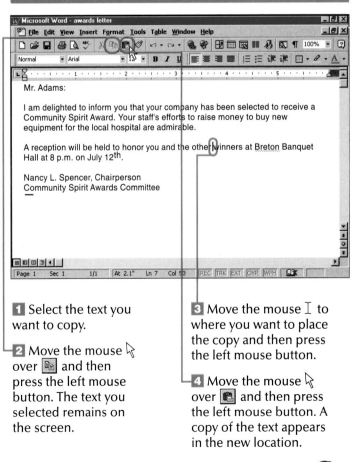

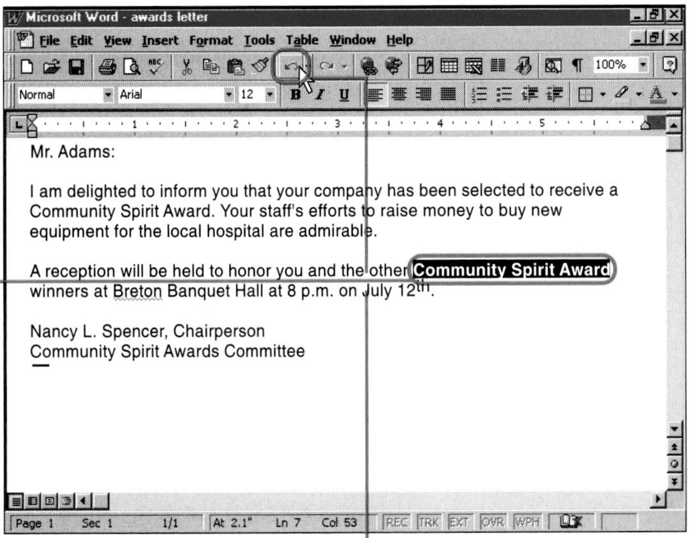

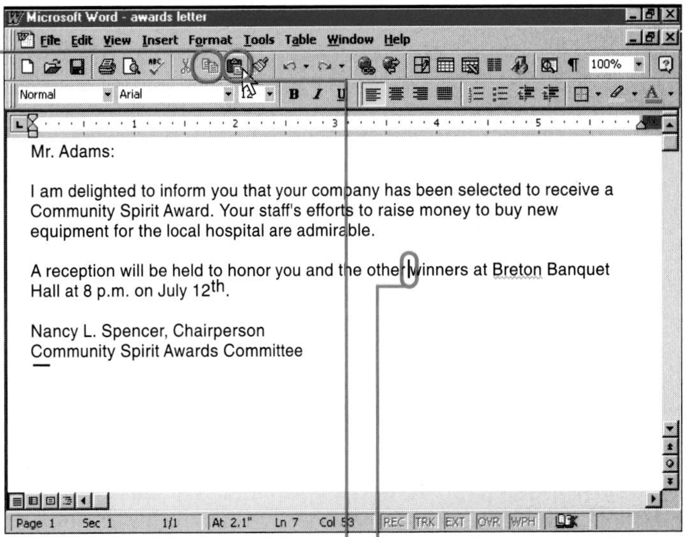

1 Select the text you want to copy.

2 Move the mouse ⤢ over 🖹 and then press the left mouse button. The text you selected remains on the screen.

3 Move the mouse I to where you want to place the copy and then press the left mouse button.

4 Move the mouse ⤢ over 🖹 and then press the left mouse button. A copy of the text appears in the new location.

FIND TEXT

FIND TEXT

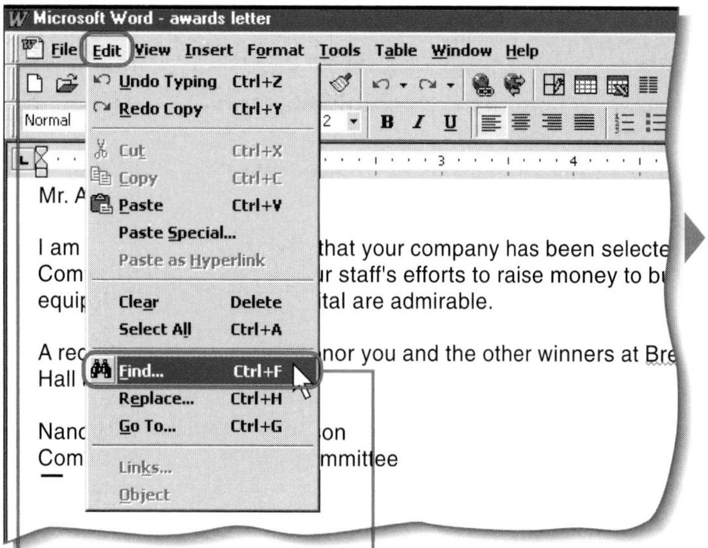

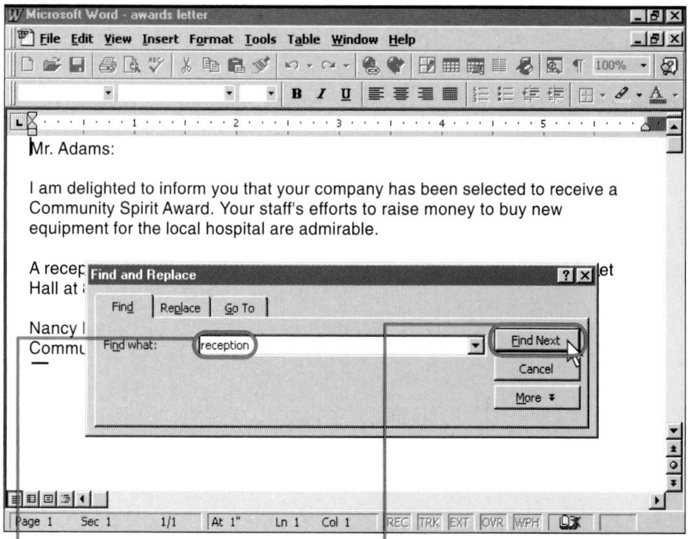

1 Move the mouse over **Edit** and then press the left mouse button.

2 Move the mouse over **Find** and then press the left mouse button.

■ The **Find and Replace** dialog box appears.

3 Type the text you want to find.

4 To start the search, move the mouse over **Find Next** and then press the left mouse button.

Can I search for part of a word?

When you search for text in your document, Word will find the text even if it is part of a larger word. For example, if you search for **place**, Word will also find **place**s, **place**ment and common**place**.

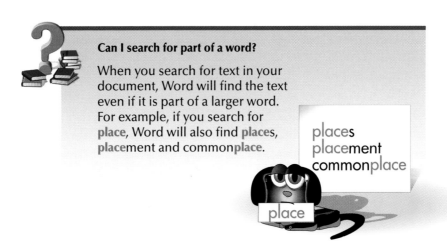

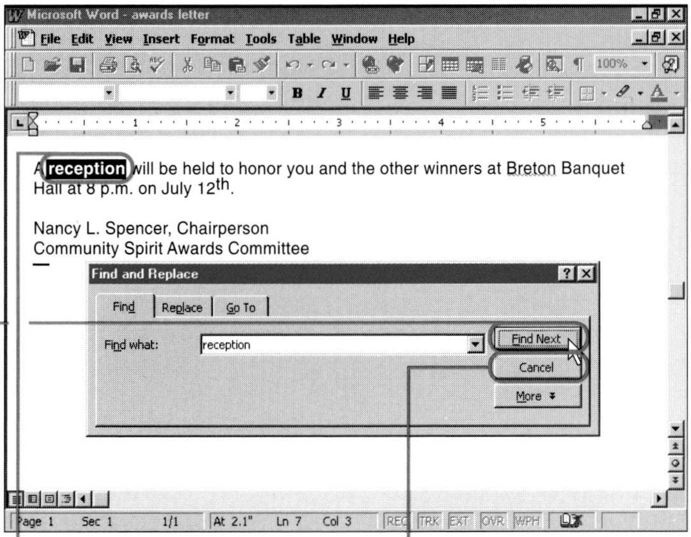

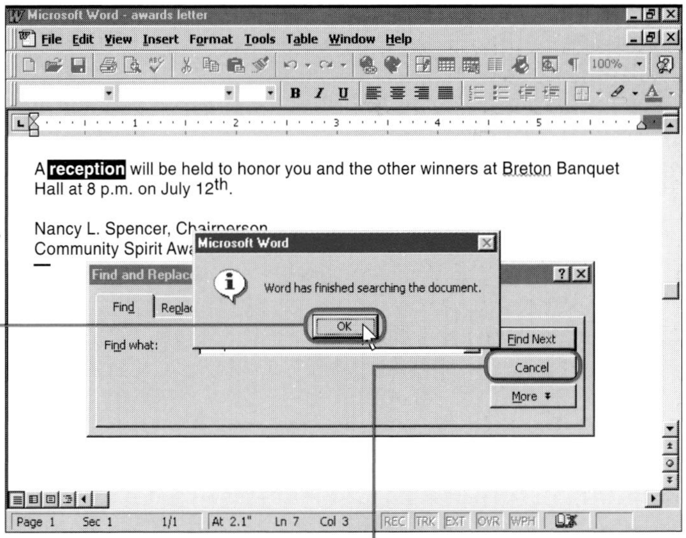

■ Word highlights the first matching word it finds.

5 To find the next matching word, move the mouse over **Find Next** and then press the left mouse button.

■ You can end the search at any time. To end the search, move the mouse over **Cancel** and then press the left mouse button.

6 Repeat step 5 until a dialog box appears, telling you the search is complete.

7 To close the dialog box, move the mouse over **OK** and then press the left mouse button.

8 To close the **Find and Replace** dialog box, move the mouse over **Cancel** and then press the left mouse button.

REPLACE TEXT

REPLACE TEXT

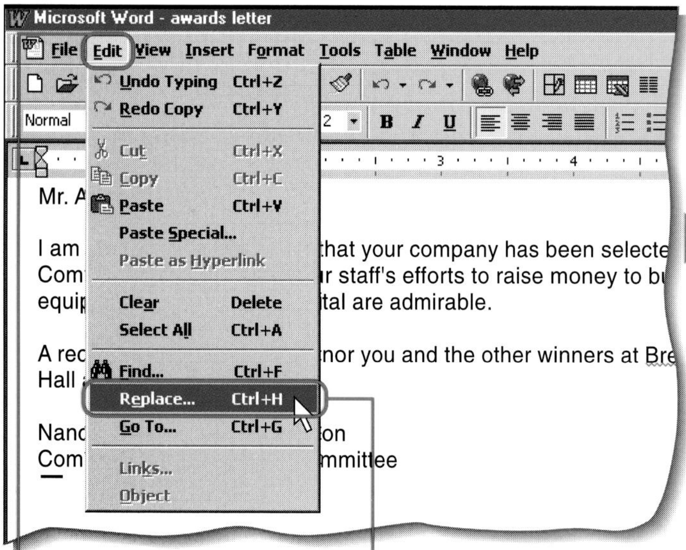

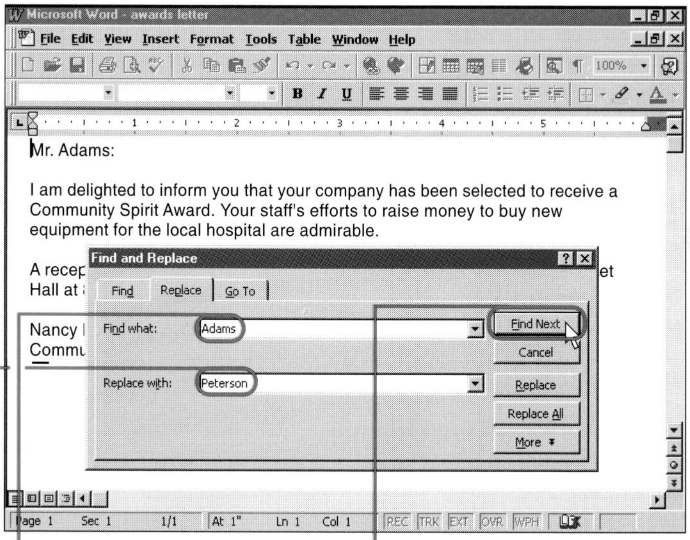

1 Move the mouse over **Edit** and then press the left mouse button.

2 Move the mouse over **Replace** and then press the left mouse button.

■ The **Find and Replace** dialog box appears.

3 Type the text you want to replace with new text.

4 Press Tab on your keyboard to move to the **Replace with** box. Then type the new text.

5 To start the search, move the mouse over **Find Next** and then press the left mouse button.

Can I use the Replace feature to enter text more quickly?

The Replace feature is useful if you have to type a long word or phrase (example: University of Massachusetts) many times in a document. You can type a short form of the word or phrase (example: UM) throughout your document and then have Word replace the short form with the full word or phrase.

I attend the University of Massachusetts. The University of Massachusetts is located in Amherst. I work in the University of Massachusetts bookstore.
U
M

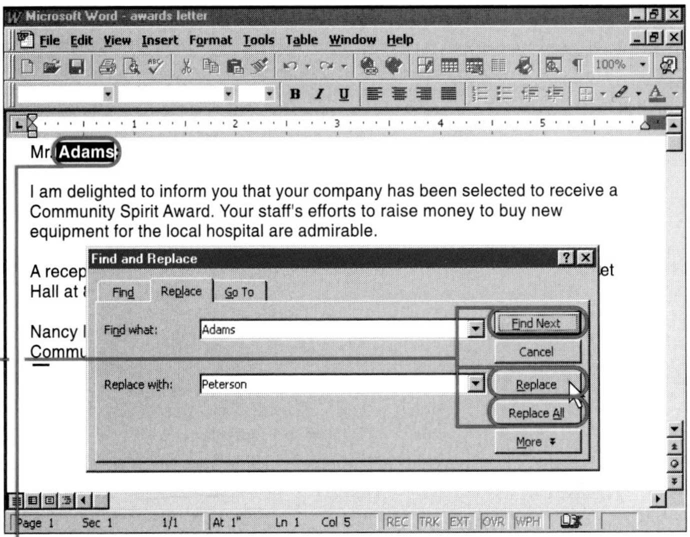
Microsoft Word - awards letter
Mr. Adams:
I am delighted to inform you that your company has been selected to receive a Community Spirit Award. Your staff's efforts to raise money to buy new equipment for the local hospital are admirable.
Find and Replace
Find
Replace
Go To
Find what:
Adams
Replace with:
Peterson
Find Next
Cancel
Replace
Replace All
More

■ Word highlights the first matching word it finds.

6 Move the mouse over one of these options and then press the left mouse button.

Find Next - Ignore the word.

Replace - Replace the word.

Replace All - Replace the word and all other matching words in the document.

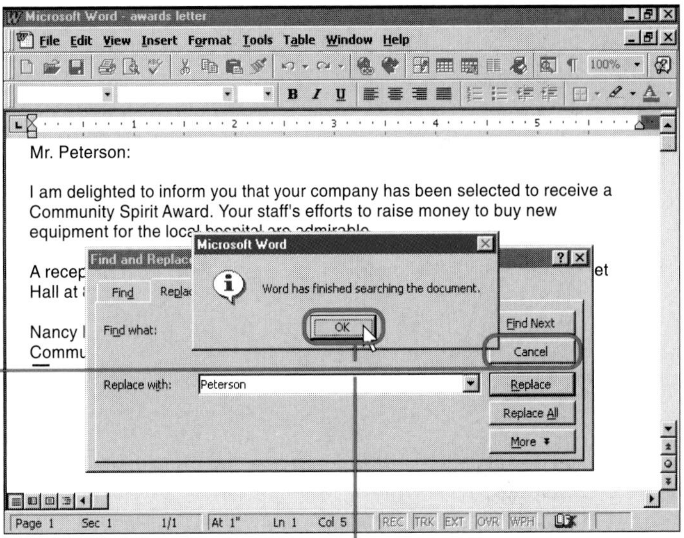
Microsoft Word - awards letter
Mr. Peterson:
I am delighted to inform you that your company has been selected to receive a Community Spirit Award. Your staff's efforts to raise money to buy new
Microsoft Word
Word has finished searching the document.
OK
Find Next
Cancel
Replace with:
Peterson
Replace
Replace All
More

■ In this example, Word replaces the text and searches for the next matching word.

■ You can end the search at any time. To end the search, move the mouse over **Cancel** or **Close** and then press the left mouse button.

7 Repeat step 6 until a dialog box appears, telling you the search is complete.

8 To close the dialog box, move the mouse over **OK** and then press the left mouse button.

CHECK SPELLING AND GRAMMAR

Word automatically checks your document for spelling and grammar errors as you type. You can easily correct these errors.
Word Dictionary

CORRECT AN ERROR

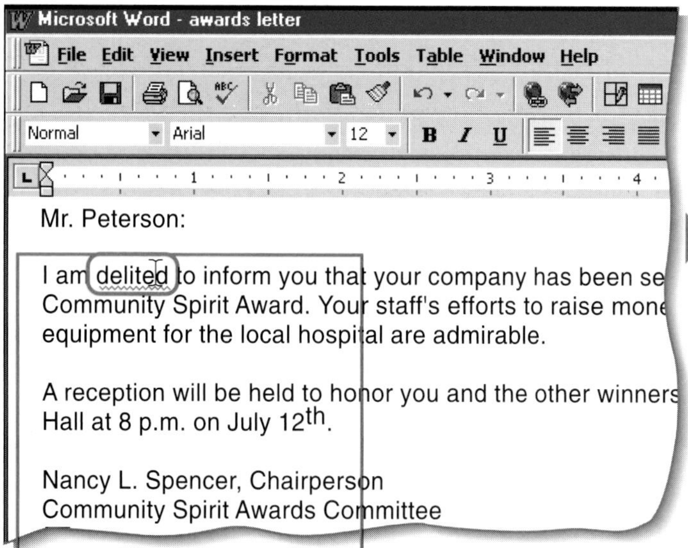

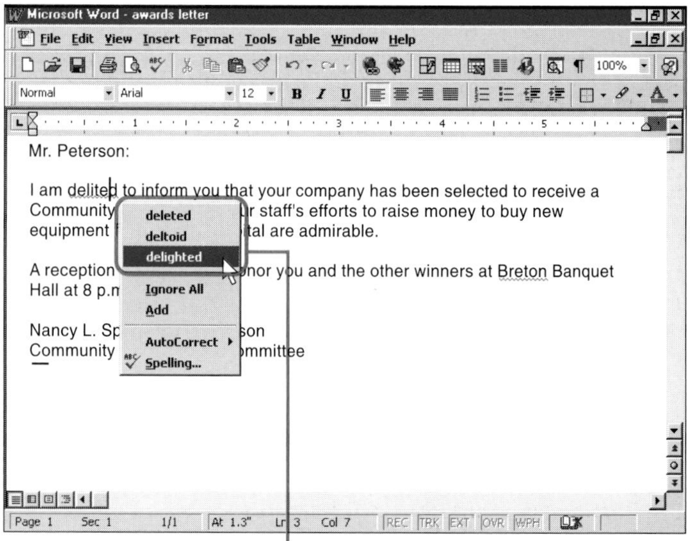

■ For this example, the spelling of **delighted** was changed to **delited**.

■ Word underlines misspelled words in red and grammar mistakes in green.

1 To correct an error, move the mouse I over the error and then press the **right** mouse button.

■ A menu appears with suggestions to correct the error.

■ If Word does not display a suggestion you want to use, move the mouse ↖ outside the menu and then press the left mouse button to hide the menu.

2 To select one of the suggestions, move the mouse ↖ over the suggestion and then press the left mouse button.

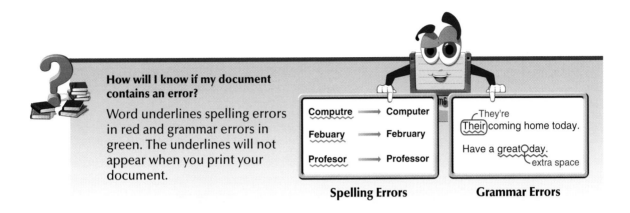

How will I know if my document contains an error?

Word underlines spelling errors in red and grammar errors in green. The underlines will not appear when you print your document.

Computre → Computer
Febuary → February
Profesor → Professor
They're
Their coming home today.
Have a great day.
extra space

Spelling Errors **Grammar Errors**

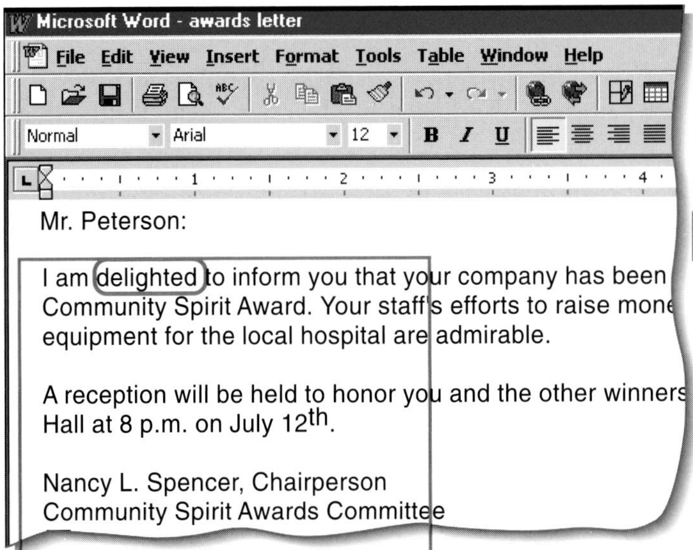
Microsoft Word - awards letter
File Edit View Insert Format Tools Table Window Help
Normal Arial 12
Mr. Peterson:
I am delighted to inform you that your company has been
Community Spirit Award. Your staff's efforts to raise mone
equipment for the local hospital are admirable.
A reception will be held to honor you and the other winners
Hall at 8 p.m. on July 12th.
Nancy L. Spencer, Chairperson
Community Spirit Awards Committee

■ The suggestion you selected replaces the error in your document.

■ The red or green underline disappears.

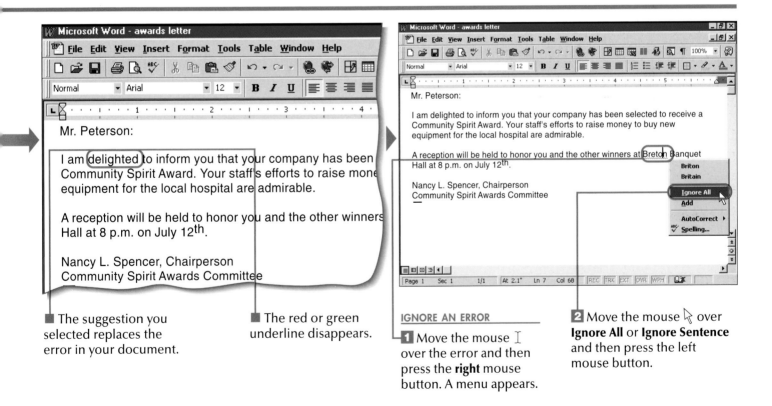

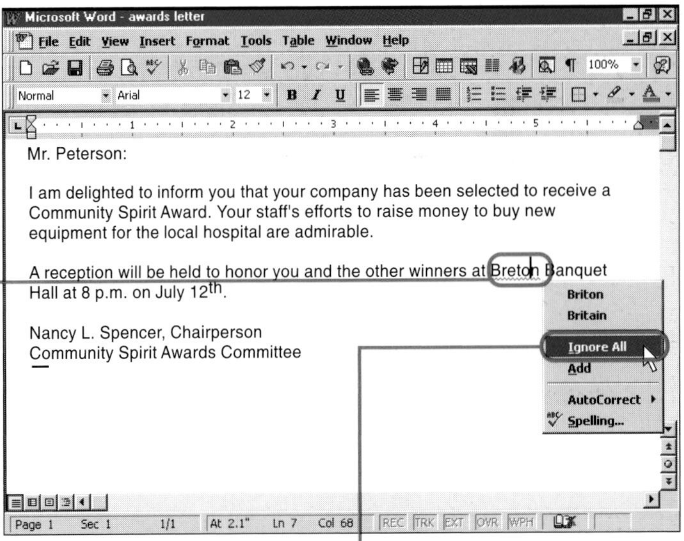
Microsoft Word - awards letter
File Edit View Insert Format Tools Table Window Help
Mr. Peterson:
I am delighted to inform you that your company has been selected to receive a
Community Spirit Award. Your staff's efforts to raise money to buy new
equipment for the local hospital are admirable.
A reception will be held to honor you and the other winners at Breton Banquet
Hall at 8 p.m. on July 12th.
Nancy L. Spencer, Chairperson
Community Spirit Awards Committee
Briton
Britain
Ignore All
Add
AutoCorrect
Spelling...

IGNORE AN ERROR

1 Move the mouse over the error and then press the **right** mouse button. A menu appears.

2 Move the mouse over **Ignore All** or **Ignore Sentence** and then press the left mouse button.

CHECK SPELLING AND GRAMMAR

When you finish typing your document, you can find and correct all spelling and grammar errors at once.
spelling error
wether
Suggestions
weather
wetter
whether
wither
grammar error
I did not buy no books.
I did not buy any books.

Word automatically underlines misspelled words in red and grammar mistakes in green. The red and green underlines will not appear when you print your document.

CORRECT ENTIRE DOCUMENT

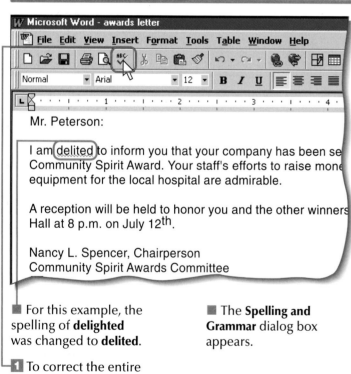

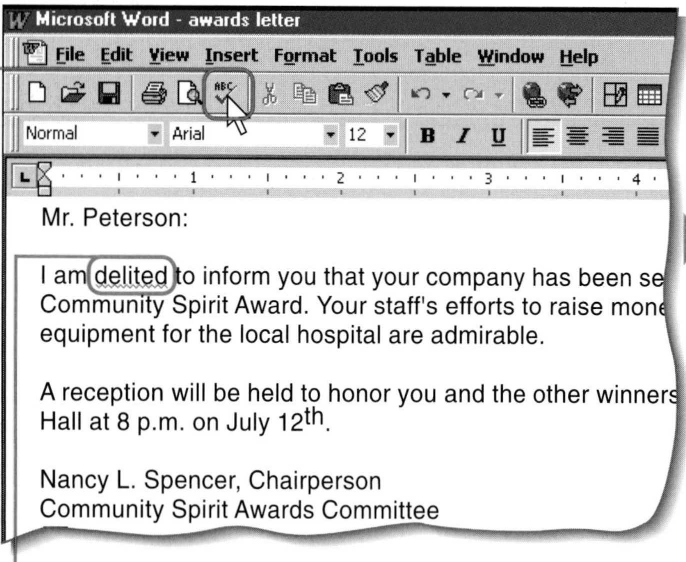

Microsoft Word - awards letter
File Edit View Insert Format Tools Table Window Help
Normal
Arial
12
Mr. Peterson:
I am delited to inform you that your company has been se
Community Spirit Award. Your staff's efforts to raise mone
equipment for the local hospital are admirable.
A reception will be held to honor you and the other winners
Hall at 8 p.m. on July 12th.
Nancy L. Spencer, Chairperson
Community Spirit Awards Committee

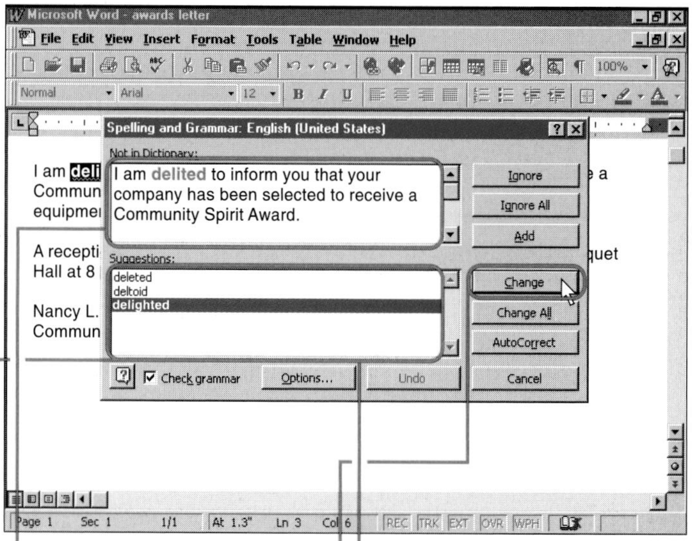

Microsoft Word - awards letter
Spelling and Grammar: English (United States)
Not in Dictionary:
I am delited to inform you that your company has been selected to receive a Community Spirit Award.
Suggestions:
deleted
deltoid
delighted
Ignore
Ignore All
Add
Change
Change All
AutoCorrect
Check grammar
Options...
Undo
Cancel

■ For this example, the spelling of **delighted** was changed to **delited**.

1 To correct the entire document, move the mouse over ABC and then press the left mouse button.

■ The **Spelling and Grammar** dialog box appears.

■ This area displays the first misspelled word or grammar mistake.

■ This area displays suggestions for correcting the text.

CORRECT AN ERROR

2 To select one of the suggestions, move the mouse over the suggestion and then press the left mouse button.

3 Move the mouse over **Change** and then press the left mouse button.

Can Word automatically correct my typing mistakes?

Word automatically corrects common spelling errors as you type.

Note: For more information on using the AutoCorrect feature, refer to page 62.

adn	and
alot	a lot
comittee	committee
don;t	don't
nwe	new
occurence	occurrence
recieve	receive
seperate	separate
teh	the

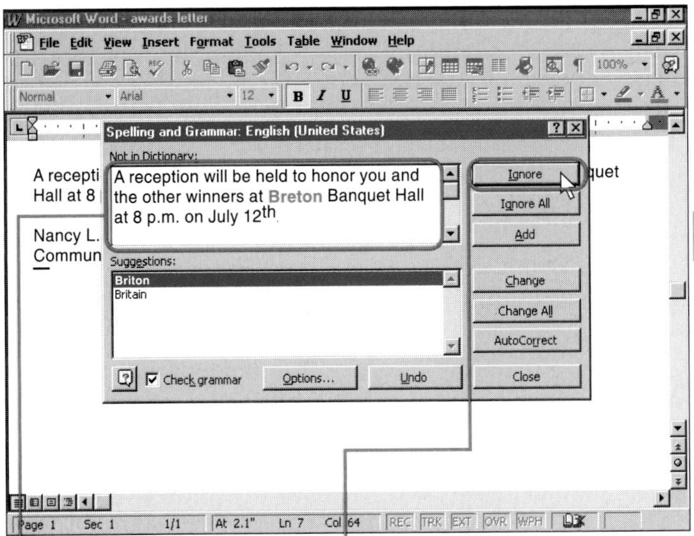

■ This area displays the next misspelled word or grammar mistake.

IGNORE AN ERROR

4 To skip the error and continue checking the document, move the mouse over **Ignore** and then press the left mouse button.

*Note: To skip the error and all occurrences of the error, move the mouse over **Ignore All** and then press the left mouse button.*

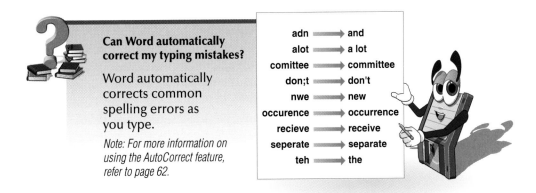

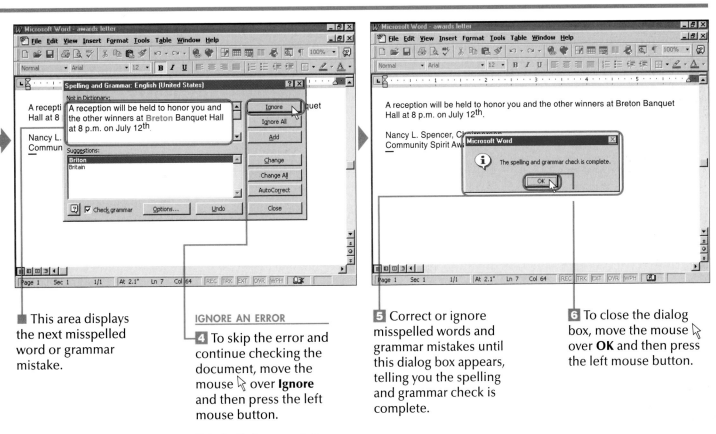

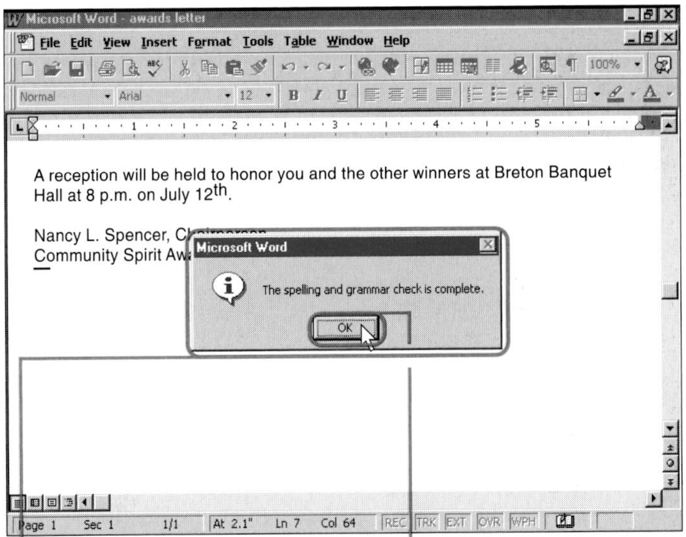

5 Correct or ignore misspelled words and grammar mistakes until this dialog box appears, telling you the spelling and grammar check is complete.

6 To close the dialog box, move the mouse over **OK** and then press the left mouse button.

USING THE THESAURUS

You can use the Thesaurus to replace a word in your document with one that is more suitable.
Word
big
Suggestions
large
immense
huge
gigantic

USING THE THESAURUS

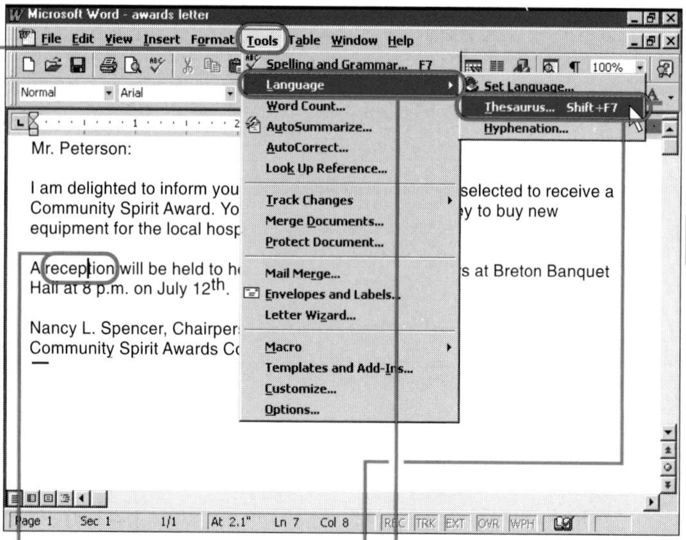

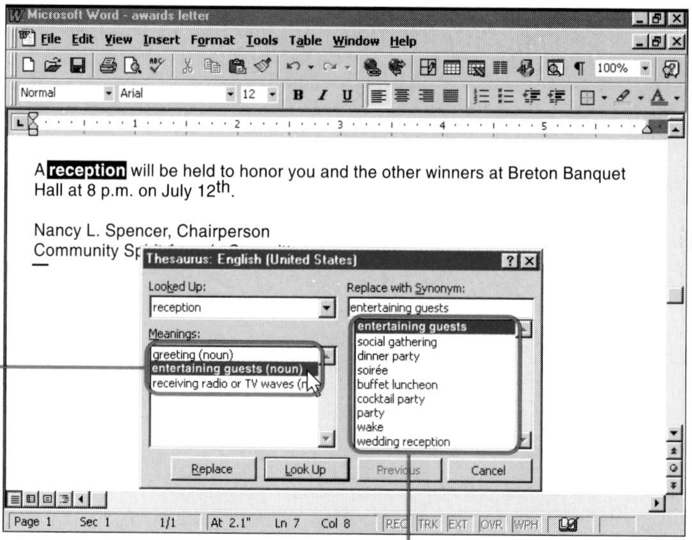

1 Move the mouse I anywhere over the word you want to replace and then press the left mouse button.

2 Move the mouse over **Tools** and then press the left mouse button.

3 Move the mouse over **Language**.

4 Move the mouse over **Thesaurus** and then press the left mouse button.

■ The **Thesaurus** dialog box appears.

5 Move the mouse over the correct meaning of the word and then press the left mouse button.

■ This area displays words that share the meaning you selected.

How can the Thesaurus feature help me?

Using the Thesaurus included with Word is faster and more convenient than searching through a printed thesaurus.

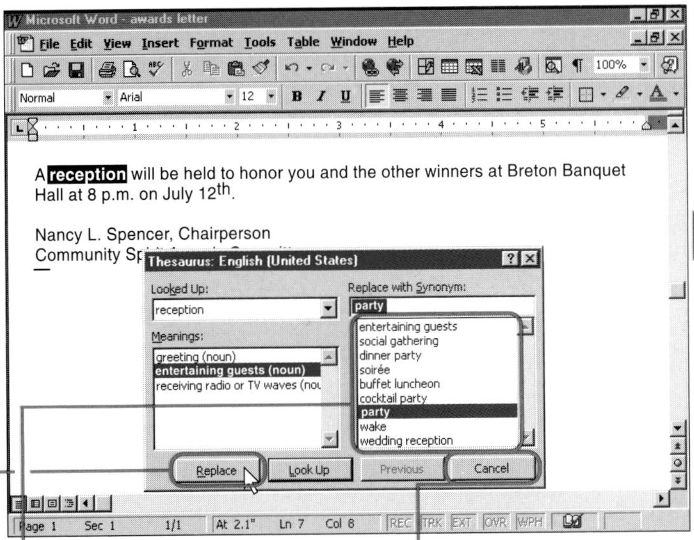

6 To select the word you want to use, move the mouse over the word and then press the left mouse button.

7 To replace the word in the document, move the mouse over **Replace** and then press the left mouse button.

■ If the Thesaurus does not offer a suitable replacement for the word, move the mouse over **Cancel** and then press the left mouse button to close the dialog box.

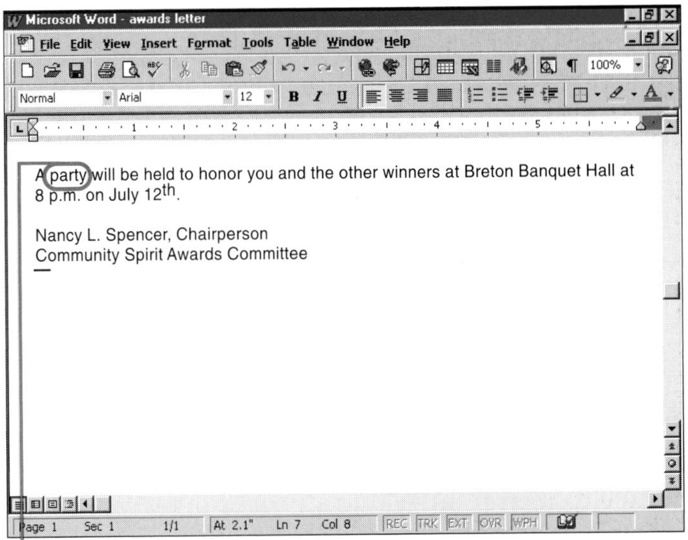

■ Your selection replaces the word in the document.

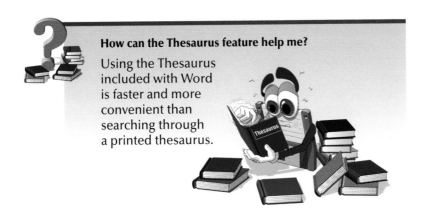

USING AUTOCORRECT

Word automatically corrects hundreds of common typing, spelling and grammar errors as you type. You can create an AutoCorrect entry to add your own words and phrases to the list.
(c) → ©
(tm) → TM
accordingto → according to
ahve → have
can;t → can't
i → I
may of been → may have been
recieve → receive
seperate → separate
teh → the

CREATE AN AUTOCORRECT ENTRY

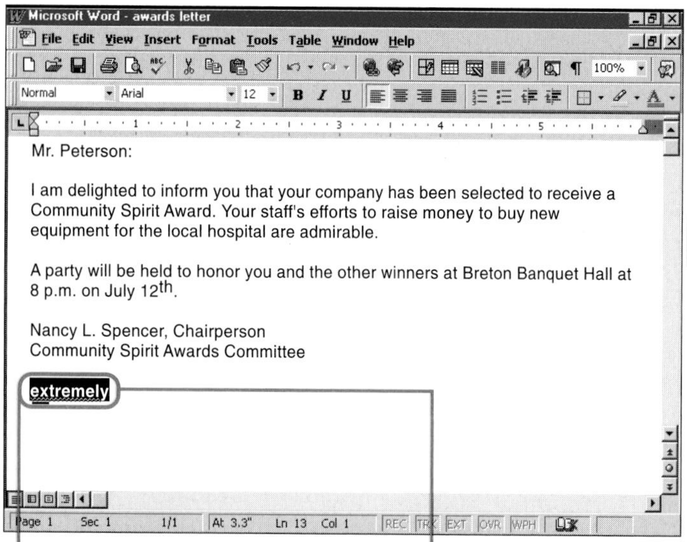

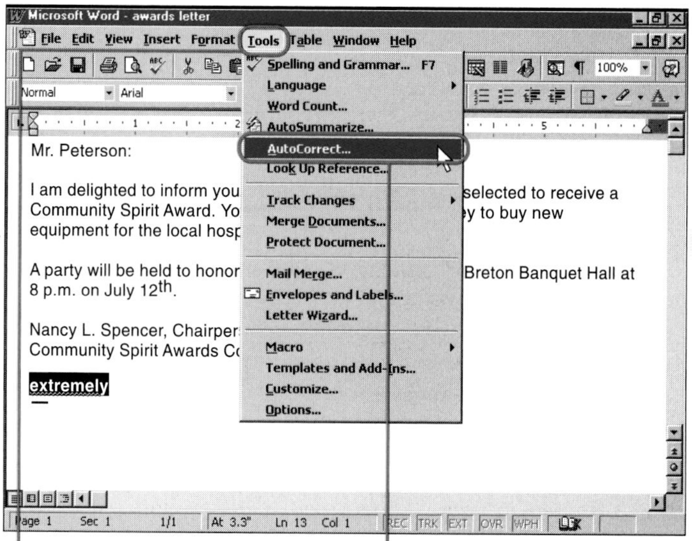

1 Type the text you want Word to automatically place in your documents.

2 Select the text. To select text, refer to page 12.

3 Move the mouse over **Tools** and then press the left mouse button.

4 Move the mouse over **AutoCorrect** and then press the left mouse button.

■ The **AutoCorrect** dialog box appears.

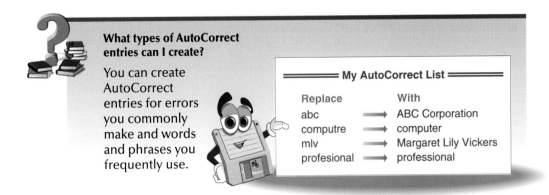

What types of AutoCorrect entries can I create?

You can create AutoCorrect entries for errors you commonly make and words and phrases you frequently use.

My AutoCorrect List

Replace		With
abc	→	ABC Corporation
computre	→	computer
mlv	→	Margaret Lily Vickers
profesional	→	professional

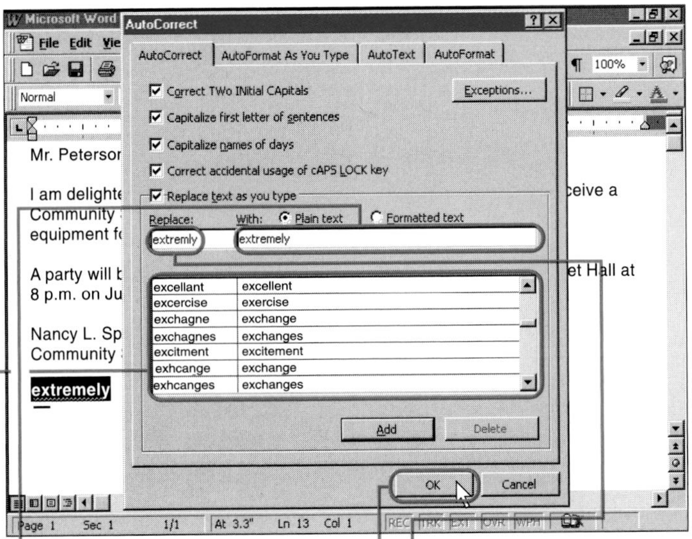

■ This area displays the text you selected in step 2.

■ This area displays a list of all the AutoCorrect entries that come with Word.

5 Type the text you want Word to replace automatically with the text you selected in step 2. The text should not contain spaces and should not be a real word.

6 Move the mouse over **OK** and then press the left mouse button.

INSERT AN AUTOCORRECT ENTRY

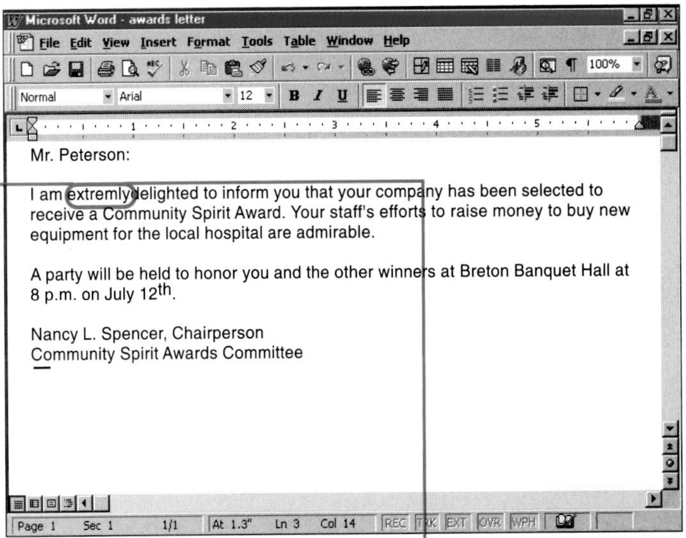

After you create an AutoCorrect entry, Word will automatically insert the entry each time you type the corresponding text.

1 Move the mouse I to where you want the AutoCorrect entry to appear in your document and then press the left mouse button.

2 Type the text Word will automatically replace.

3 Press the **Spacebar** on your keyboard and the AutoCorrect entry replaces the text you typed.

USING AUTOTEXT

CREATE AN AUTOTEXT ENTRY

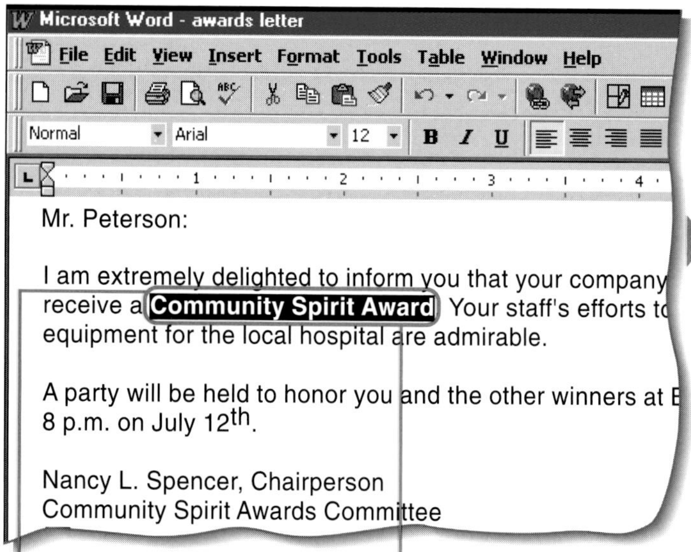

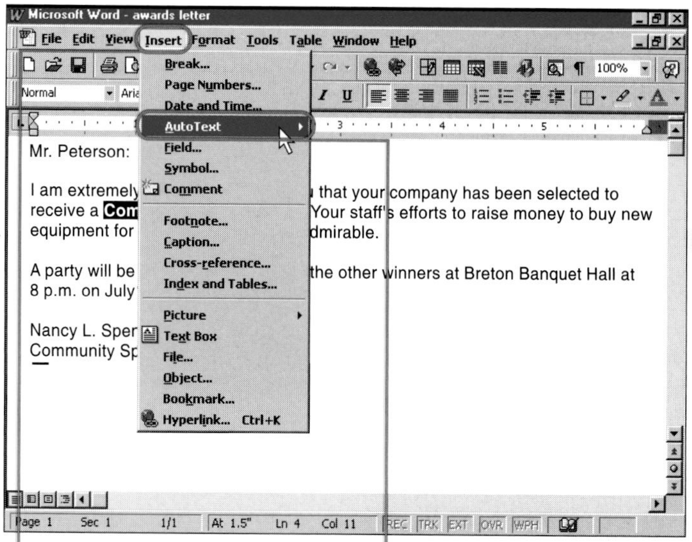

1 Type the text you want to be able to quickly insert.

2 Select the text. To select text, refer to page 12.

3 Move the mouse over **Insert** and then press the left mouse button.

4 Move the mouse over **AutoText**.

What types of AutoText entries can I create?

You can create AutoText entries for text you plan to use often, such as a mailing address, product name, legal disclaimer or closing remark.

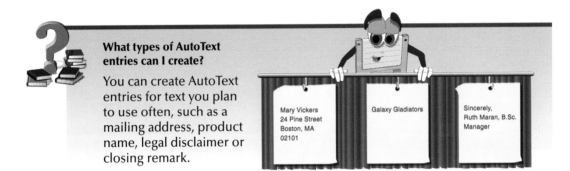

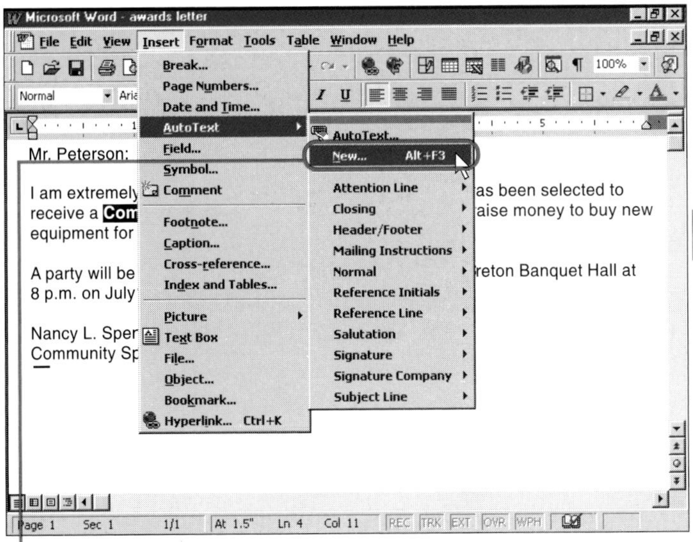

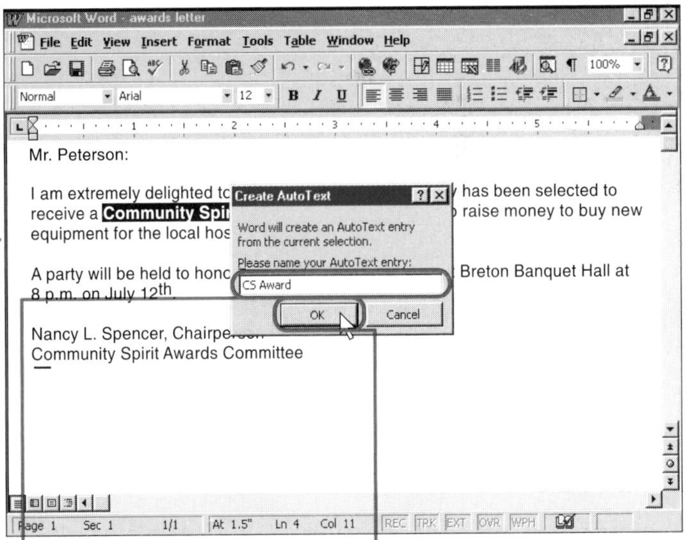

5 Move the mouse over **New** and then press the left mouse button.

■ The **Create AutoText** dialog box appears.

6 This area displays a name for the AutoText entry. To use a different name, type the name.

7 Move the mouse over **OK** and then press the left mouse button.

■ To insert the AutoText entry into a document, refer to page 66.

USING AUTOTEXT

After you create an AutoText entry, you can quickly insert the text into a document.
Dear Susan:
Trafalgar High School celebrates its 50th anniversary this year. We will be celebrating on September 11th with an Open House, followed by a buffet dinner.
Please bring your school photos and memorabilia for our display table.
Becky Flynn
Social Committee

INSERT AN AUTOTEXT ENTRY

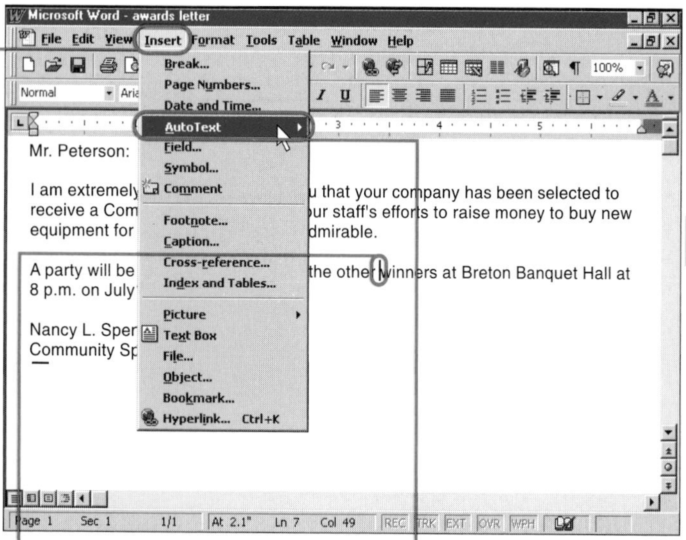

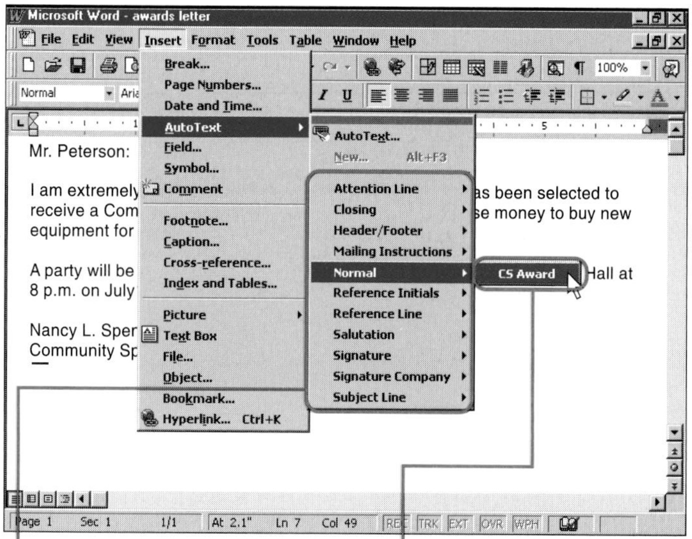

1 Move the mouse I to where you want the AutoText entry to appear in your document and then press the left mouse button.

2 Move the mouse over **Insert** and then press the left mouse button.

3 Move the mouse over **AutoText**.

4 Move the mouse over the category that stores the text you want to use.

5 Move the mouse over the AutoText entry you want to insert and then press the left mouse button.

Does Word come with any AutoText entries?

Word comes with AutoText entries that can help you quickly create a letter.

Some examples include:
Best wishes,
Thank you,
To Whom It May Concern:

Subject:
Reference:
In reply to:
Attention:

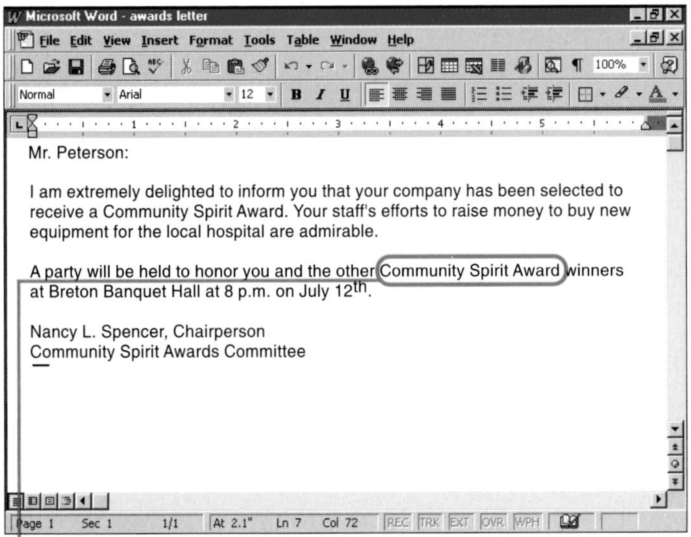
Microsoft Word - awards letter
File Edit View Insert Format Tools Table Window Help
Mr. Peterson:
I am extremely delighted to inform you that your company has been selected to receive a Community Spirit Award. Your staff's efforts to raise money to buy new equipment for the local hospital are admirable.
A party will be held to honor you and the other Community Spirit Award winners at Breton Banquet Hall at 8 p.m. on July 12th.
Nancy L. Spencer, Chairperson
Community Spirit Awards Committee
Page 1 Sec 1 1/1 At 2.1" Ln 7 Col 72

■ The text appears in your document.

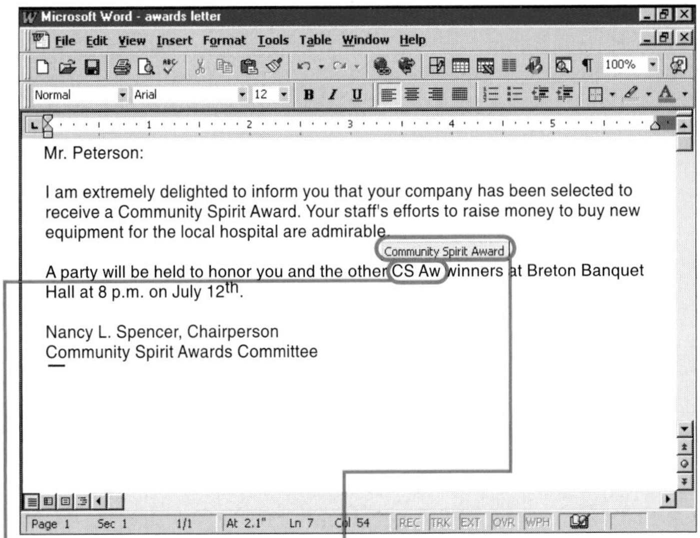
Microsoft Word - awards letter
File Edit View Insert Format Tools Table Window Help
Mr. Peterson:
I am extremely delighted to inform you that your company has been selected to receive a Community Spirit Award. Your staff's efforts to raise money to buy new equipment for the local hospital are admirable.
Community Spirit Award
A party will be held to honor you and the other CS Aw winners at Breton Banquet Hall at 8 p.m. on July 12th.
Nancy L. Spencer, Chairperson
Community Spirit Awards Committee
Page 1 Sec 1 1/1 At 2.1" Ln 7 Col 54

SHORTCUT

1 Type the first few characters of the name of the AutoText entry.

■ A box appears displaying the AutoText entry for the text you typed.

2 To insert the entry, press Enter on your keyboard.

Note: To ignore the AutoText entry, continue typing.

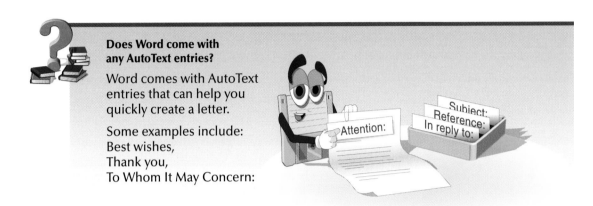

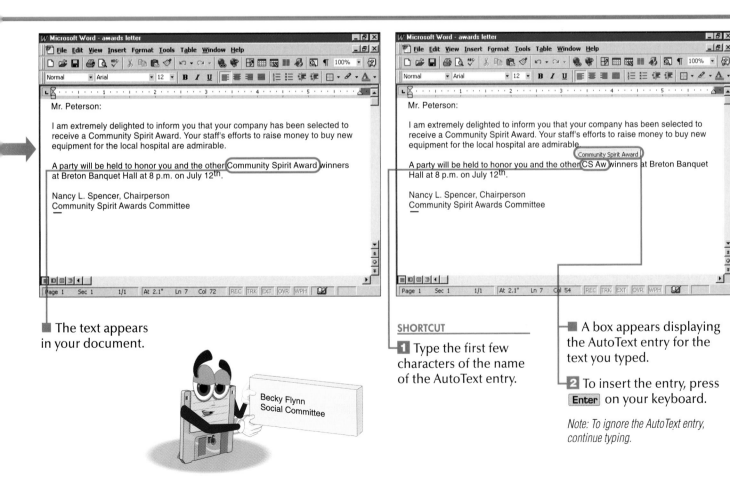

Becky Flynn
Social Committee

COUNT WORDS IN A DOCUMENT

Dear Susan:
Trafalgar High School celebrates its 50th anniversary this year. We will be celebrating on September 11th with an Open House, followed by a buffet dinner.
Please bring your school photos and memorabilia for our display table.
Word Count
38
You can quickly determine the number of words in a document.

At the same time, you can determine the number of pages, characters, paragraphs and lines in the document.

COUNT WORDS IN A DOCUMENT

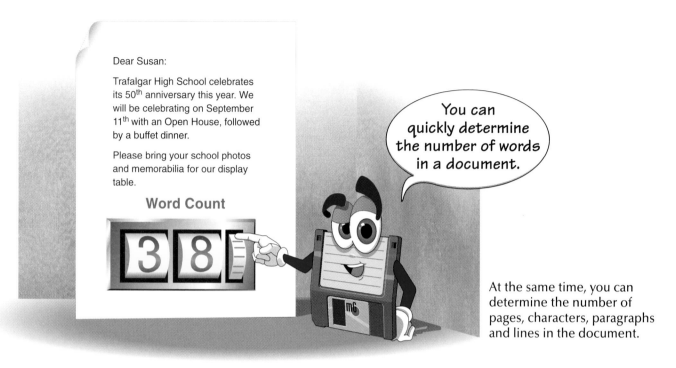

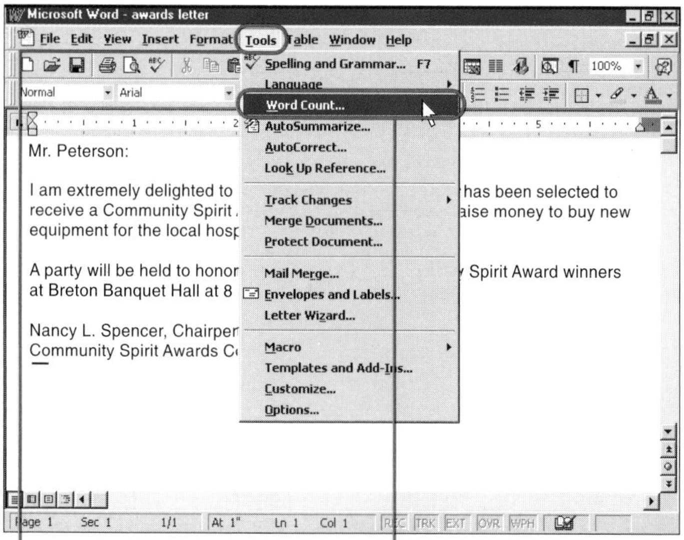

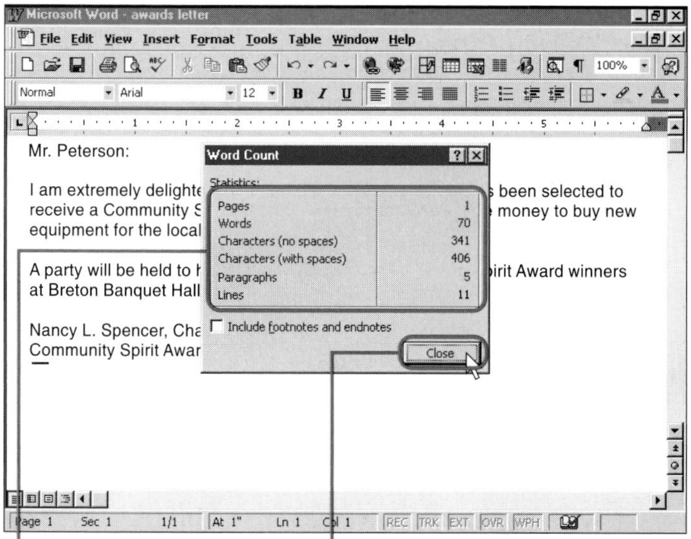

1 Move the mouse over **Tools** and then press the left mouse button.

2 Move the mouse over **Word Count** and then press the left mouse button.

■ The **Word Count** dialog box appears.

■ This area displays information about the document.

3 To close the **Word Count** dialog box, move the mouse over **Close** and then press the left mouse button.

DISPLAY NONPRINTING CHARACTERS

While you view and edit a document, you can display characters that will not appear on a printed page.

Displaying nonprinting characters helps you check for errors, such as extra spaces between words.

DISPLAY NONPRINTING CHARACTERS

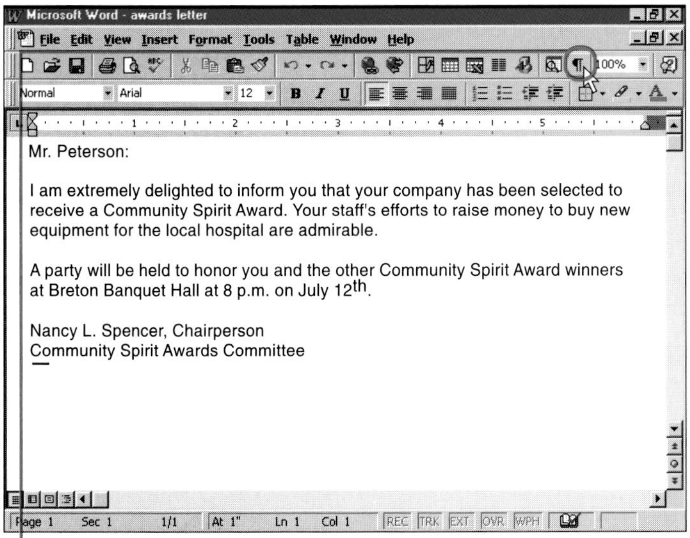

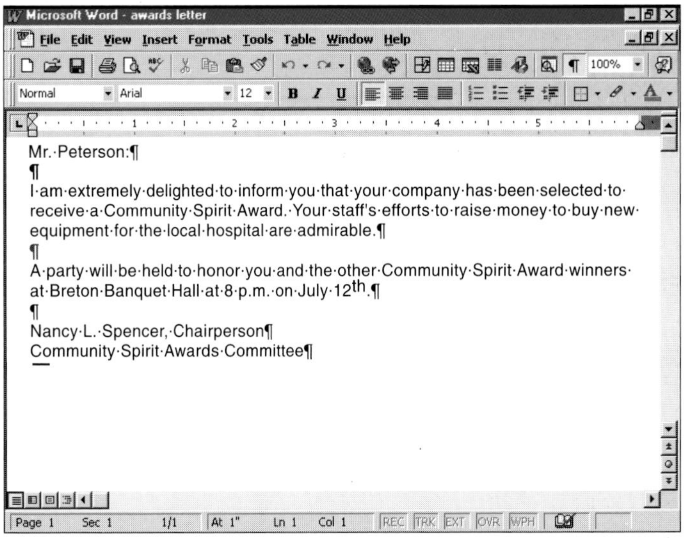

1 To display nonprinting characters in your document, move the mouse over ¶ and then press the left mouse button.

■ Nonprinting characters appear in your document.

Examples include:

¶ Paragraph

· Space

→ Tab

■ To hide the characters, repeat step 1.

TEX

CHAPTER 5

FORMAT TEXT

How can I emphasize information in my documents? This chapter will teach you many different ways to emphasize information so you can create interesting and attractive documents.

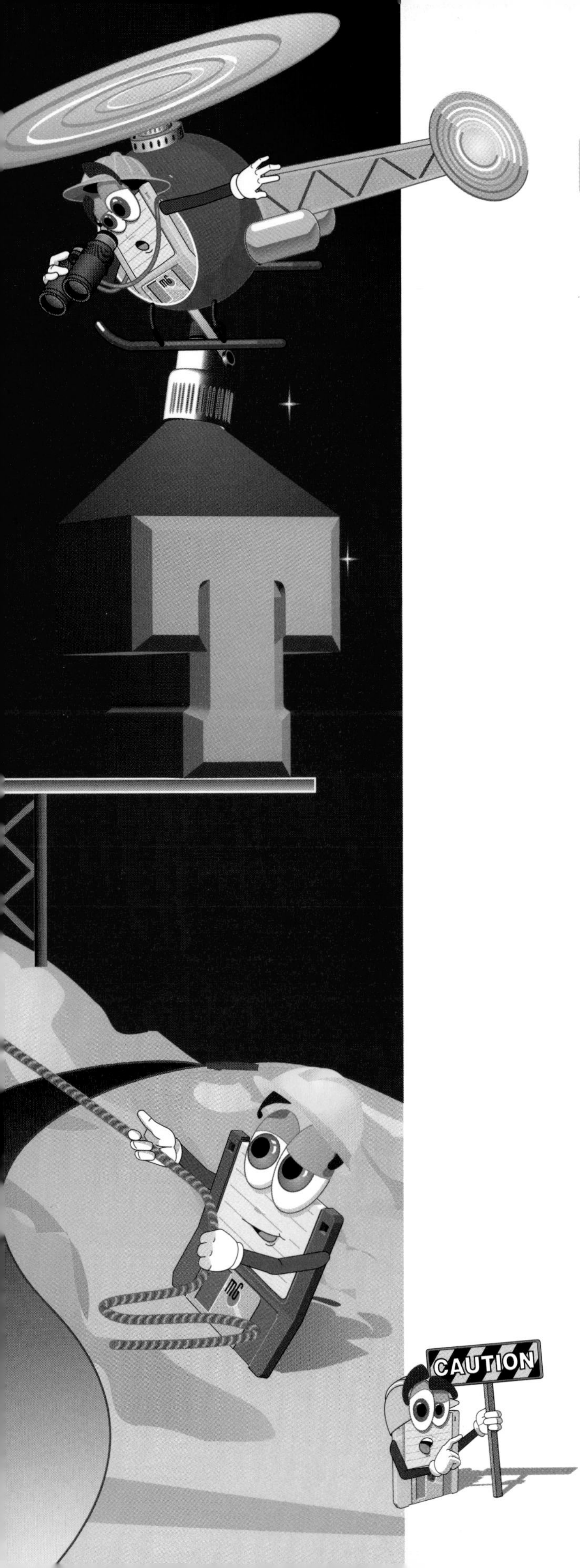

BOLD, ITALIC AND UNDERLINE

You can use the Bold, Italic and Underline features to emphasize information in your document.
Bold
Italic
Underline

BOLD, ITALIC AND UNDERLINE

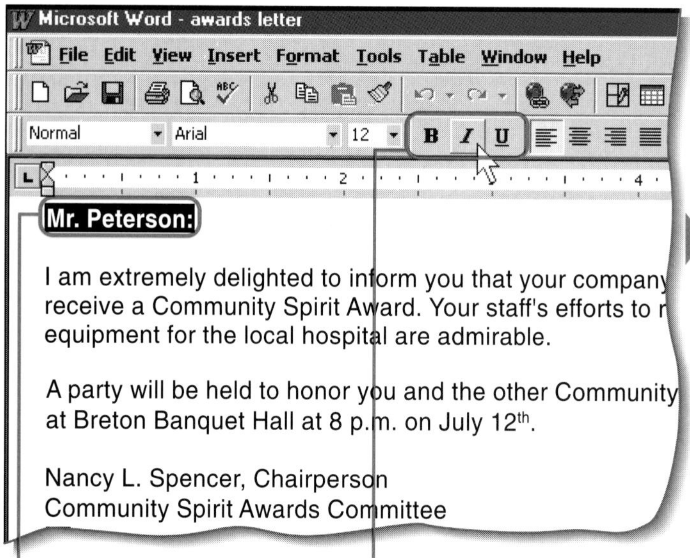

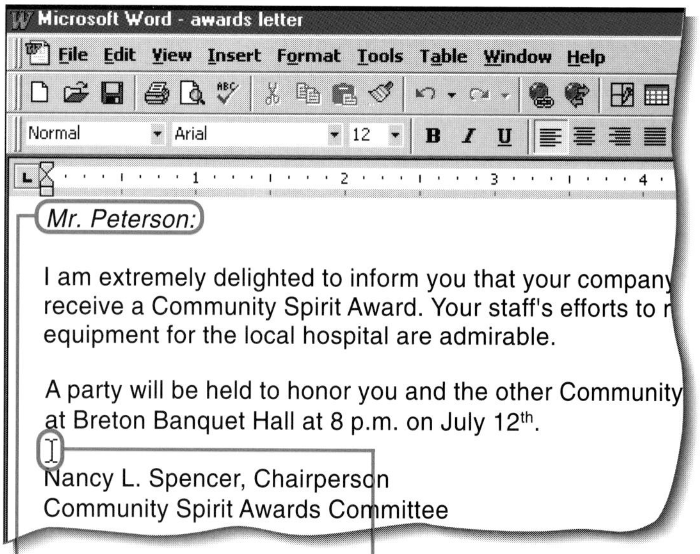

1 Select the text you want to change. To select text, refer to page 12.

2 Move the mouse over one of the following options and then press the left mouse button.

- **B** Bold
- *I* Italic
- U Underline

■ The text you selected appears in the new style.

■ To deselect text, move the mouse outside the selected area and then press the left mouse button.

■ To remove a bold, italic or underline style, repeat steps 1 and 2.

CHANGE ALIGNMENT OF TEXT

You can enhance the appearance of your document by aligning text in different ways.
David C. Thompson
President
Dynamic Advertising Inc.
1223 Lincoln Ave.
New York, NY
10023
Dear Mr. Thompson,
I would like to take this opportunity to congratulate you and your company for winning First Prize in the 1996 Logo Design Contest. It gives me the greatest pleasure to inform you that the Judging Committee's decision was unanimous. Your entry was clearly the best among the hundreds of outstanding entries we received this year.
Enclosed please find a copy of the Judging Committee's remarks. This report states that "the logo designed by Dynamic Advertising Inc. serves to enhance the company's image through the creative use of colors and modern design principles."
Sincerely,
Karen Davis
Align Right
Center
Align Left
Justify

CHANGE ALIGNMENT OF TEXT

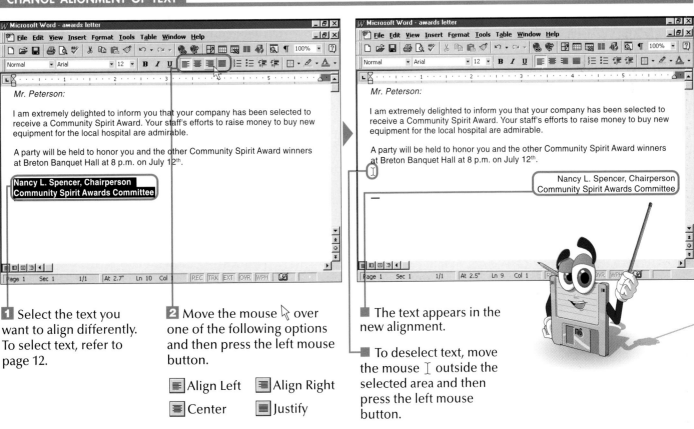

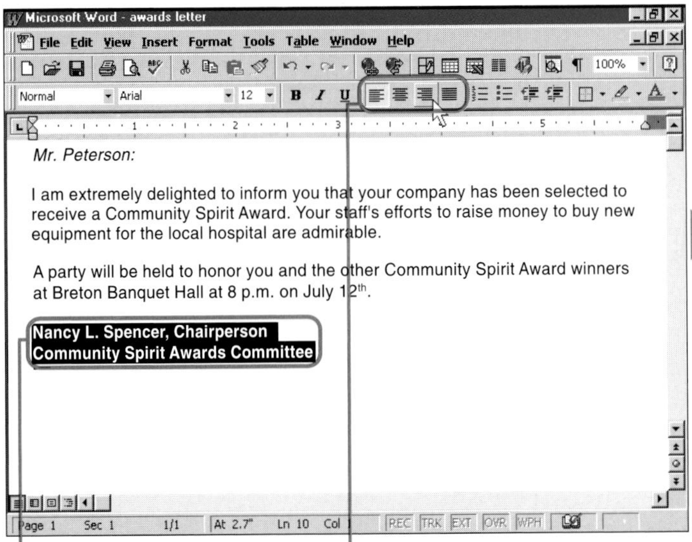
Microsoft Word - awards letter
File Edit View Insert Format Tools Table Window Help
Mr. Peterson:
I am extremely delighted to inform you that your company has been selected to receive a Community Spirit Award. Your staff's efforts to raise money to buy new equipment for the local hospital are admirable.
A party will be held to honor you and the other Community Spirit Award winners at Breton Banquet Hall at 8 p.m. on July 12th.
Nancy L. Spencer, Chairperson
Community Spirit Awards Committee

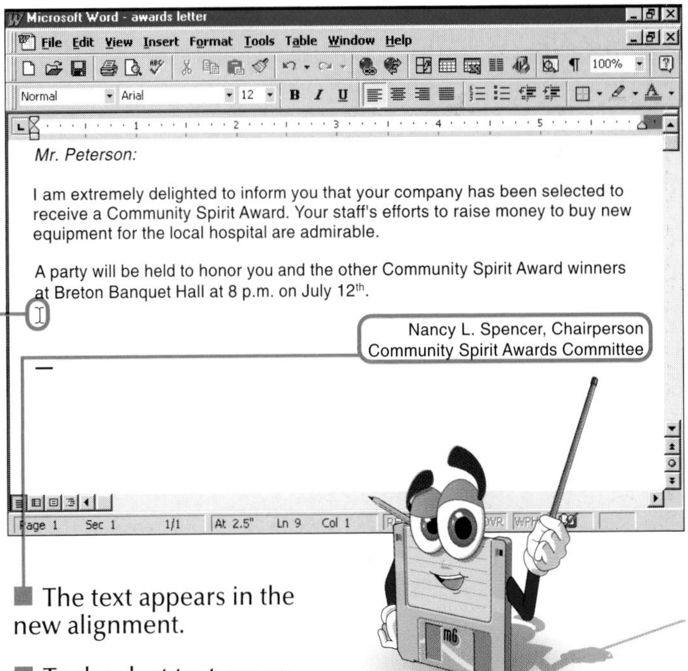
Microsoft Word - awards letter
File Edit View Insert Format Tools Table Window Help
Mr. Peterson:
I am extremely delighted to inform you that your company has been selected to receive a Community Spirit Award. Your staff's efforts to raise money to buy new equipment for the local hospital are admirable.
A party will be held to honor you and the other Community Spirit Award winners at Breton Banquet Hall at 8 p.m. on July 12th.
Nancy L. Spencer, Chairperson
Community Spirit Awards Committee

1 Select the text you want to align differently. To select text, refer to page 12.

2 Move the mouse over one of the following options and then press the left mouse button.

- Align Left
- Align Right
- Center
- Justify

■ The text appears in the new alignment.

■ To deselect text, move the mouse outside the selected area and then press the left mouse button.

CHANGE FONT OF TEXT

You can enhance the appearance of your document by changing the design of the text.
Arial
Times
Courier

CHANGE FONT OF TEXT

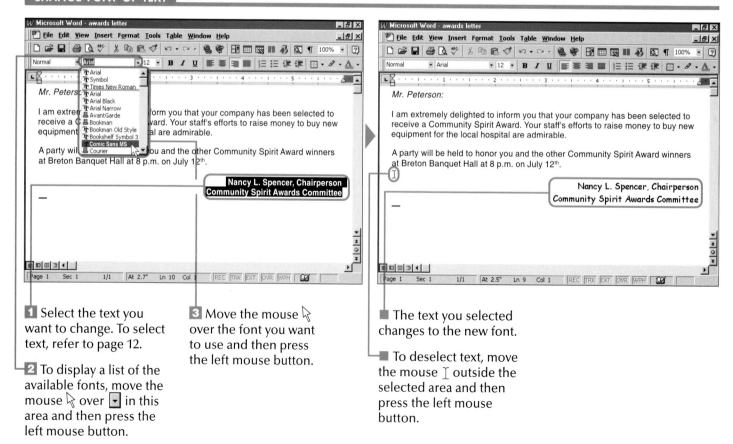

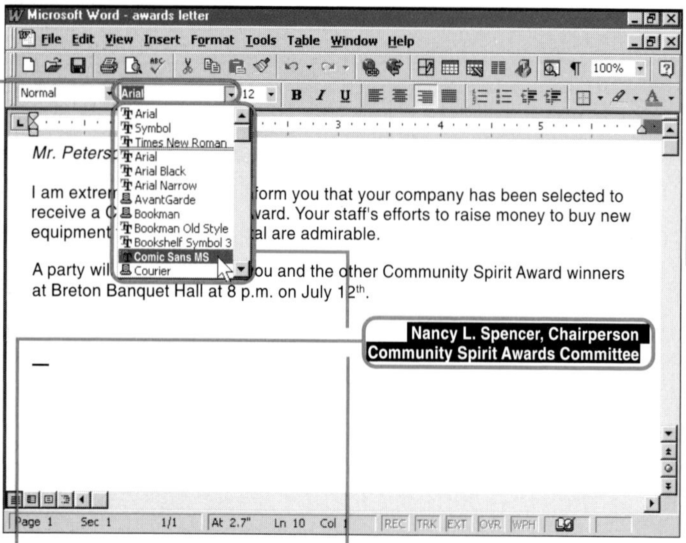

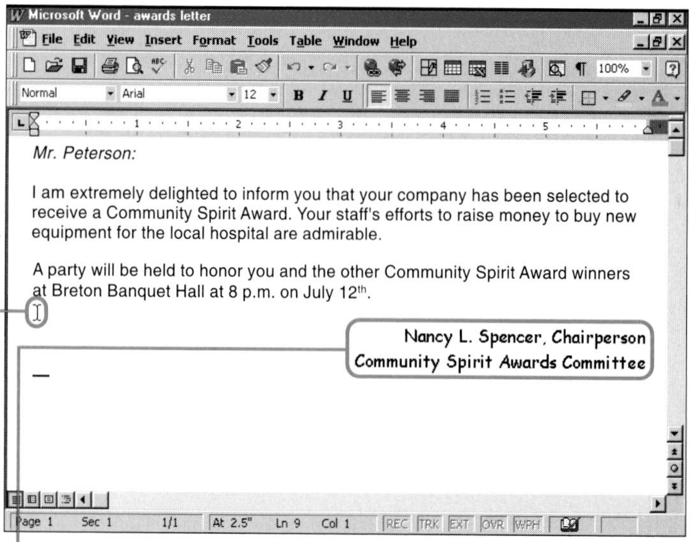

1 Select the text you want to change. To select text, refer to page 12.

2 To display a list of the available fonts, move the mouse over ▾ in this area and then press the left mouse button.

3 Move the mouse over the font you want to use and then press the left mouse button.

■ The text you selected changes to the new font.

■ To deselect text, move the mouse outside the selected area and then press the left mouse button.

CHANGE SIZE OF TEXT

You can increase or decrease the size of text in your document.
8 point
12 point
14 point
18 point
24 point
Word measures the size of text in points. There are approximately 72 points in one inch.

Smaller text lets you fit more information on a page, but larger text is easier to read.

CHANGE SIZE OF TEXT

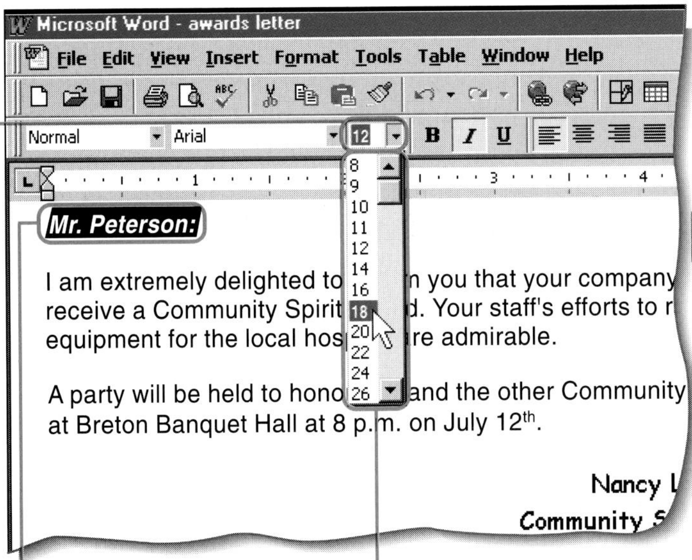

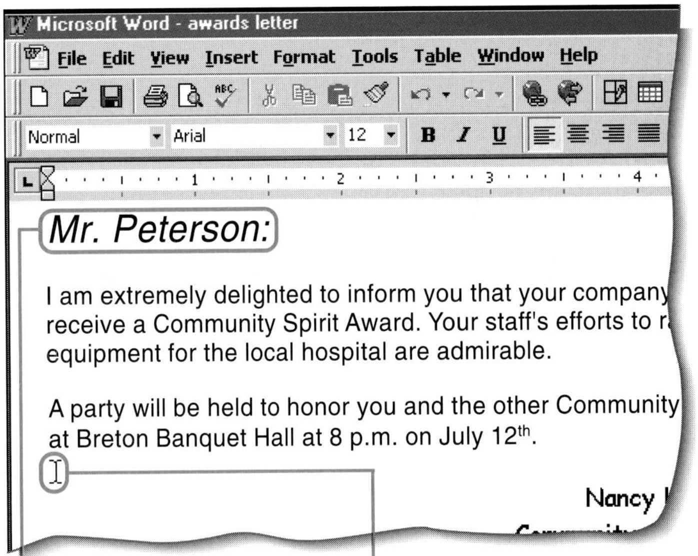

1 Select the text you want to change. To select text, refer to page 12.

2 To display a list of the available sizes, move the mouse over ▾ in this area and then press the left mouse button.

3 Move the mouse over the size you want to use and then press the left mouse button.

■ The text you selected changes to the new size.

■ To deselect text, move the mouse I outside the selected area and then press the left mouse button.

CHANGE TEXT COLOR

You can change the color of text to draw attention to headings or important information in your document.

CHANGE TEXT COLOR

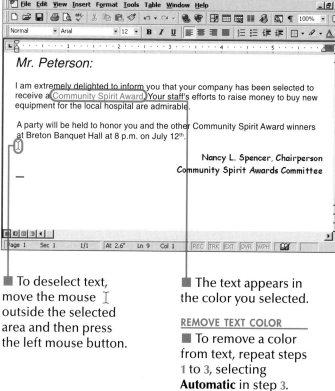

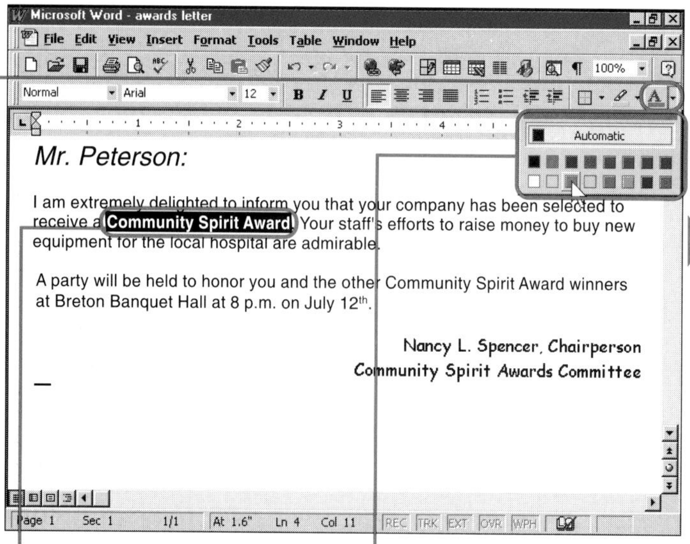

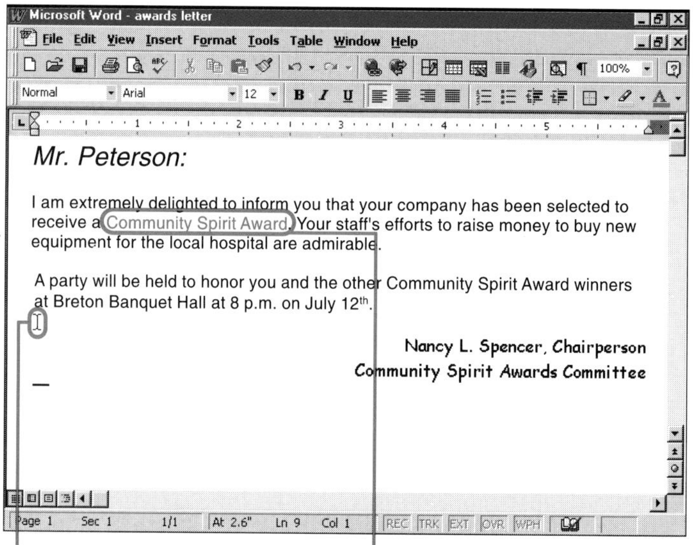

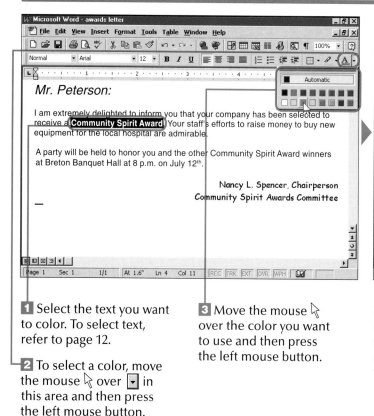

1 Select the text you want to color. To select text, refer to page 12.

2 To select a color, move the mouse over ▾ in this area and then press the left mouse button.

3 Move the mouse over the color you want to use and then press the left mouse button.

■ To deselect text, move the mouse I outside the selected area and then press the left mouse button.

■ The text appears in the color you selected.

REMOVE TEXT COLOR

■ To remove a color from text, repeat steps 1 to 3, selecting **Automatic** in step 3.

HIGHLIGHT TEXT

You can highlight important text in your document. Highlighting text is useful for marking text you want to verify later.
DEAR MRS. GLEDHILL:
There is a 1 h anniversary High School ion on August 8, 9 and 10 lock High School. We all ee you there. Contact Hughes for more information.
usan Hughes

HIGHLIGHT TEXT

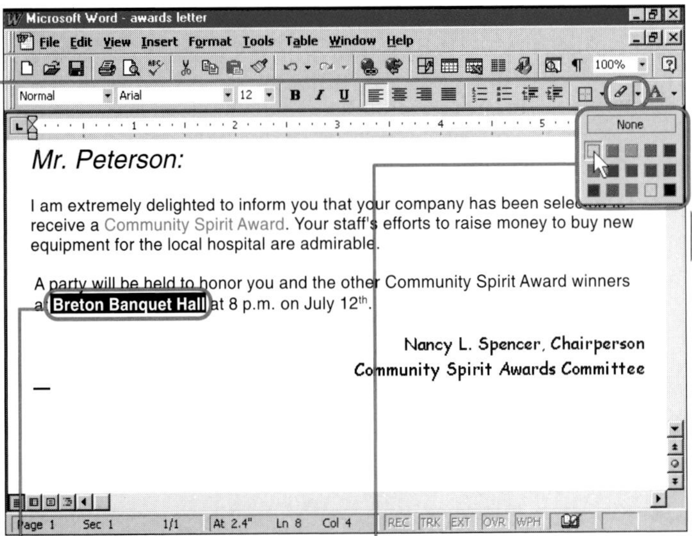

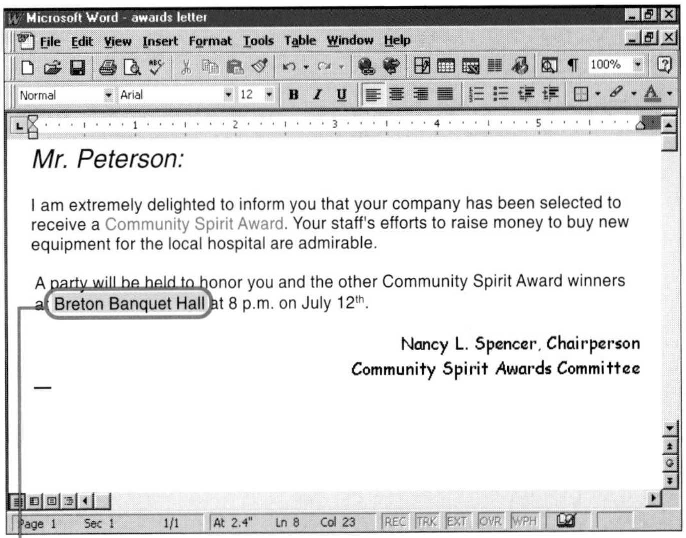

1 Select the text you want to highlight. To select text, refer to page 12.

2 To select a color, move the mouse over ▾ in this area and then press the left mouse button.

3 Move the mouse over the color you want to use and then press the left mouse button.

■ The text appears highlighted in the color you selected.

REMOVE HIGHLIGHT

■ To remove a highlight, repeat steps 1 to 3, selecting **None** in step 3.

CHANGE APPEARANCE OF TEXT

CHANGE APPEARANCE OF TEXT

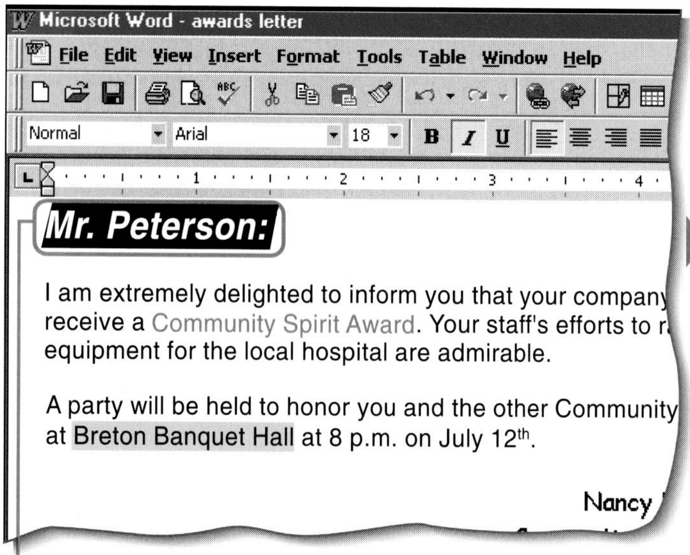

1 Select the text you want to change. To select text, refer to page 12.

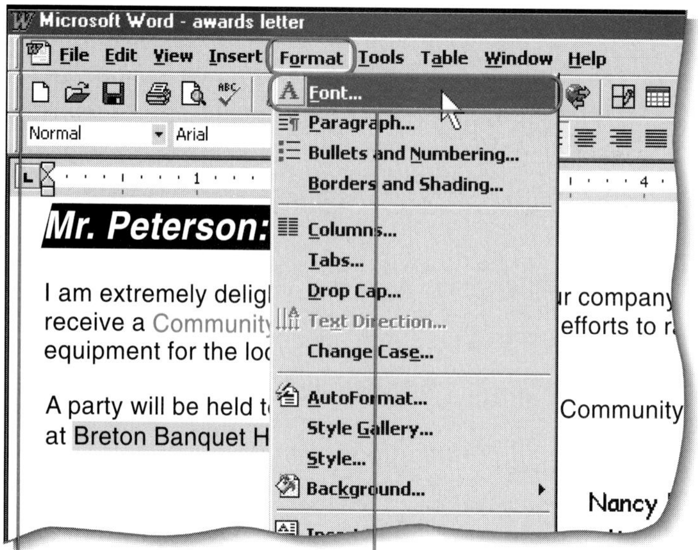

2 Move the mouse over **Format** and then press the left mouse button.

3 Move the mouse over **Font** and then press the left mouse button.

What determines which fonts are available on my computer?

The fonts available on your computer may be different from the fonts on other computers. The available fonts depend on your printer and the setup of your computer.

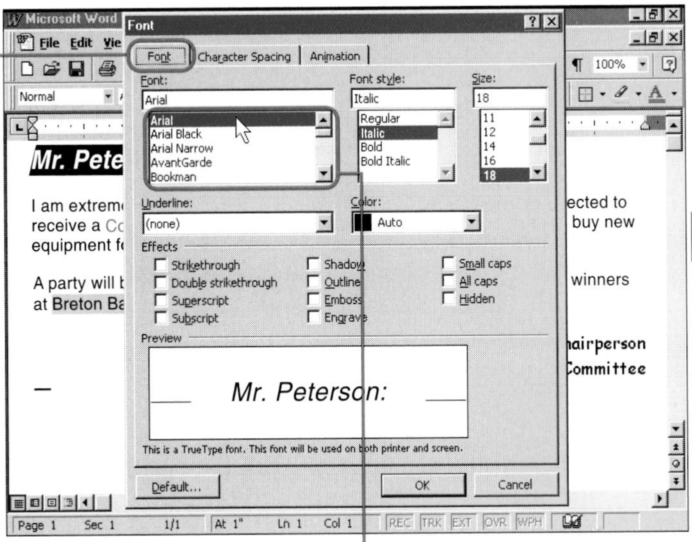

■ The **Font** dialog box appears.

4 Move the mouse over the **Font** tab and then press the left mouse button.

5 To select a design for the text, move the mouse over the font you want to use and then press the left mouse button.

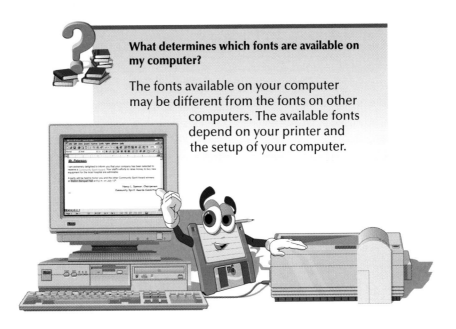

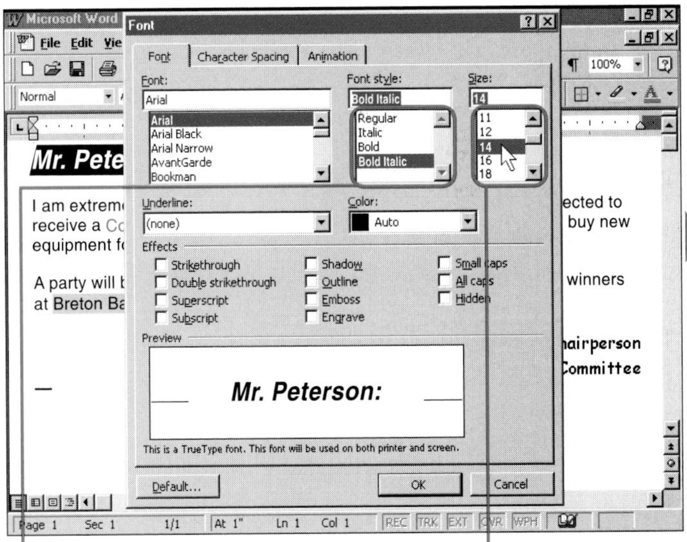

6 To select a style for the text, move the mouse over the style you want to use and then press the left mouse button.

7 To select a size for the text, move the mouse over the size you want to use and then press the left mouse button.

CONTINUED

CHANGE APPEARANCE OF TEXT

CHANGE APPEARANCE OF TEXT (CONTINUED)

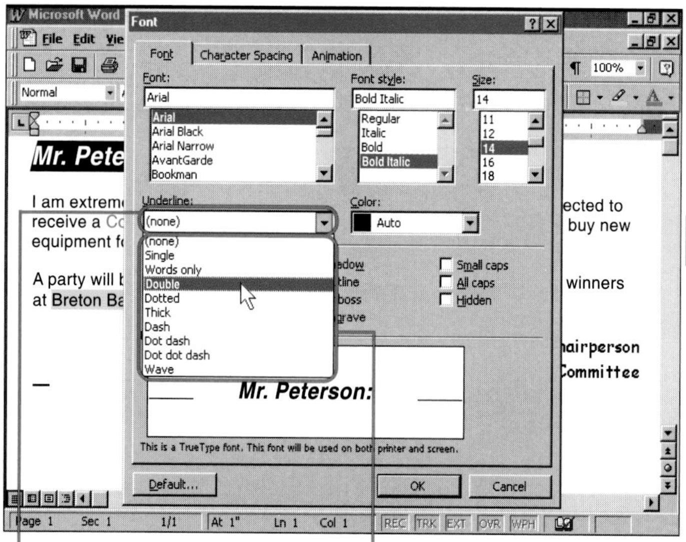

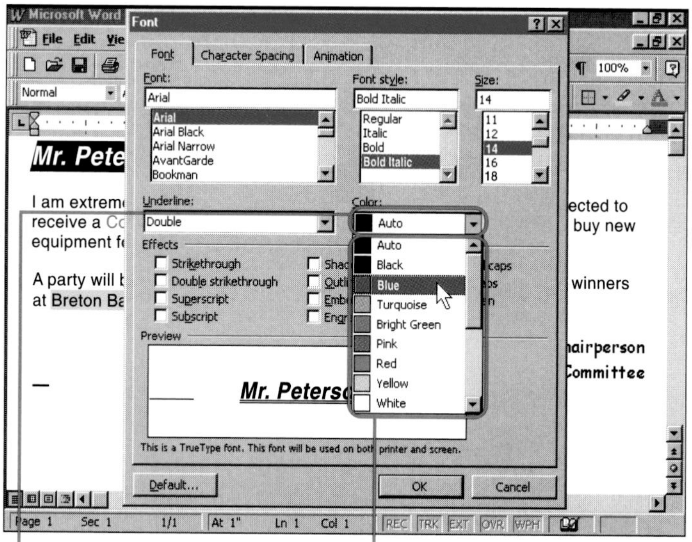

8 To select an underline style, move the mouse over this area and then press the left mouse button.

9 Move the mouse over the underline style you want to use and then press the left mouse button.

10 To select a color for the text, move the mouse over this area and then press the left mouse button.

11 Move the mouse over the color you want to use and then press the left mouse button.

What special effects can I add to my document?

Word offers many special effects.

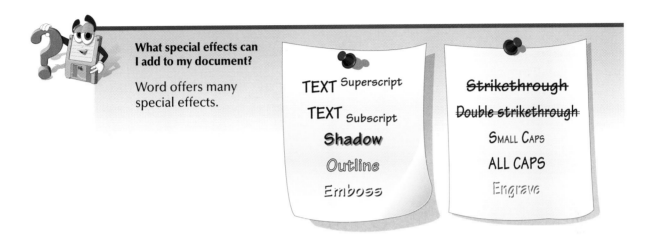

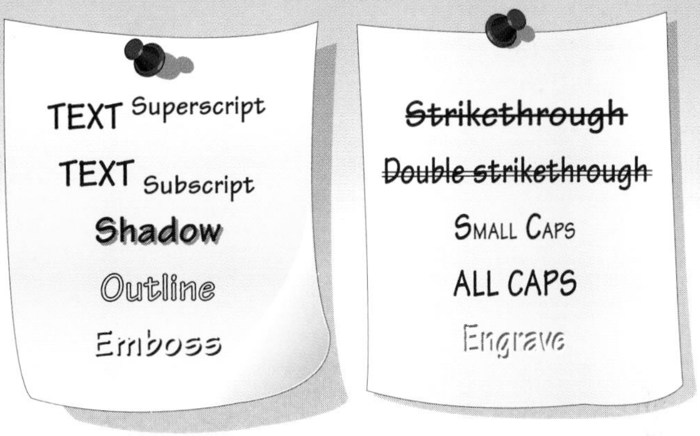

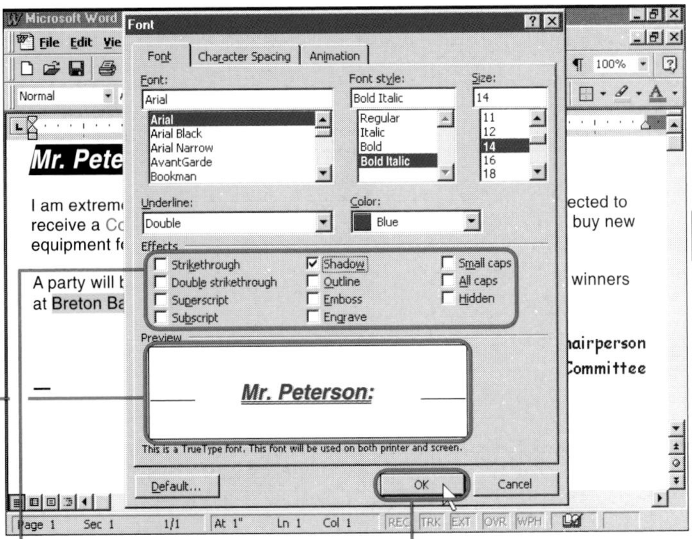

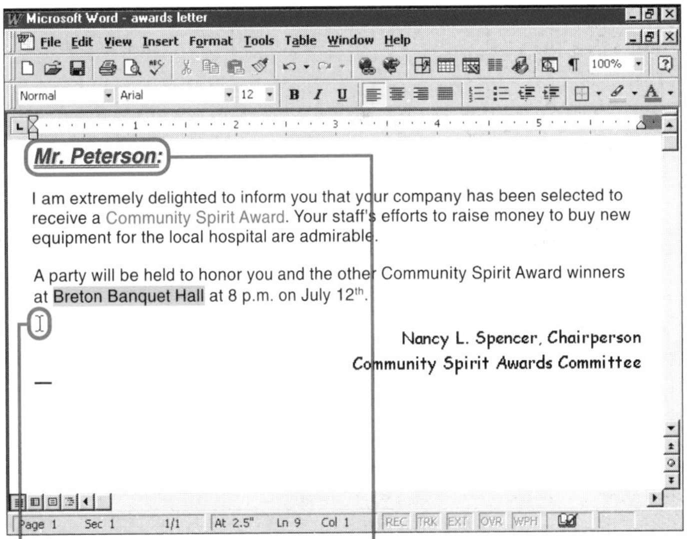

12 To select a special effect, move the mouse over the effect you want to use and then press the left mouse button (☐ changes to ☑).

■ This area displays a preview of all the options you selected.

13 To apply the changes, move the mouse over **OK** and then press the left mouse button.

■ To deselect text, move the mouse outside the selected area and then press the left mouse button.

■ The text you selected displays the changes.

INSERT SYMBOLS

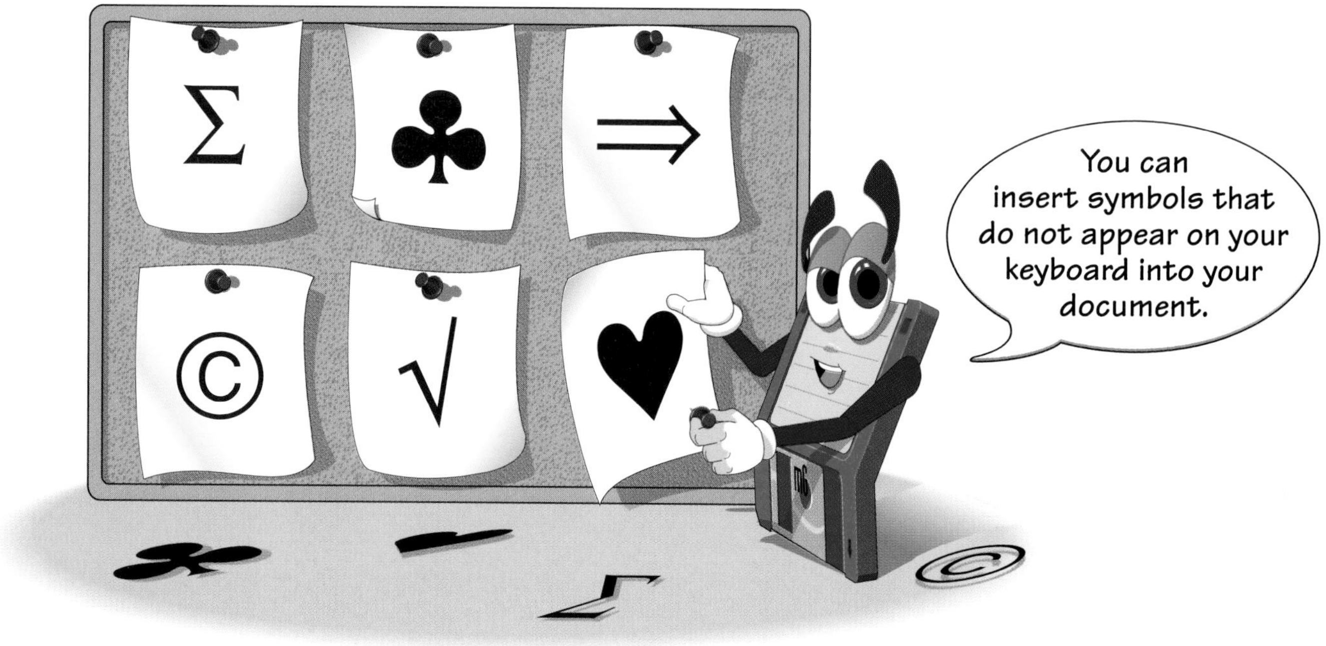

You can insert symbols that do not appear on your keyboard into your document.

INSERT SYMBOLS

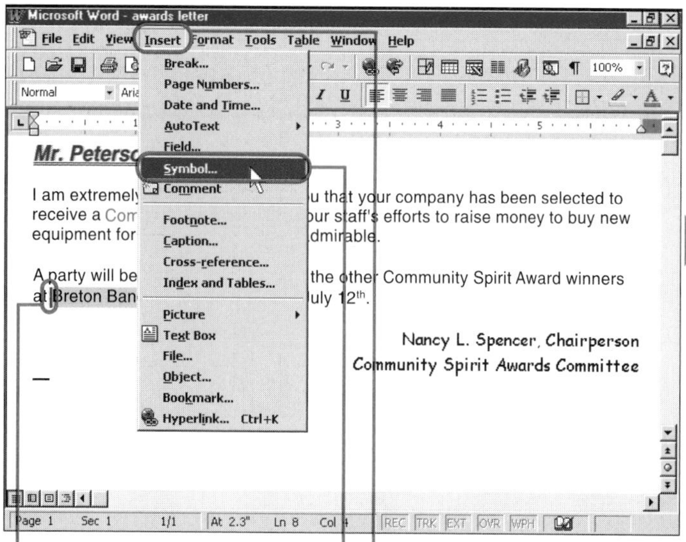

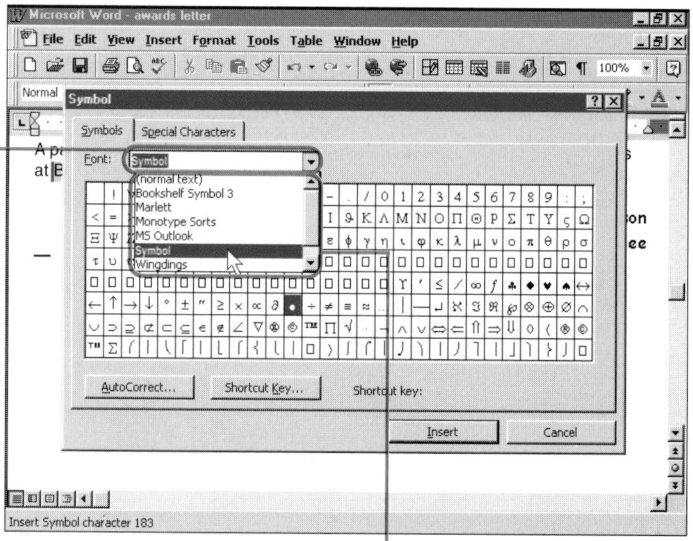

1 Move the mouse I to where you want a symbol to appear in the document and then press the left mouse button.

2 Move the mouse over **Insert** and then press the left mouse button.

3 Move the mouse over **Symbol** and then press the left mouse button.

■ The **Symbol** dialog box appears, displaying the current set of symbols.

4 To display another set of symbols, move the mouse over ▾ in this area and then press the left mouse button.

5 Move the mouse over the set of symbols you want to view and then press the left mouse button.

How can I quickly enter symbols into my document?

If you type one of the following sets of characters, Word will instantly replace the characters with a symbol. This lets you quickly enter symbols that are not available on your keyboard.

(c)	©
(r)	®
(tm)	™
:(	☹
:)	☺
:|	😐
<--	←
-->	→
<==	🡐
==>	🡒
<=>	⇔

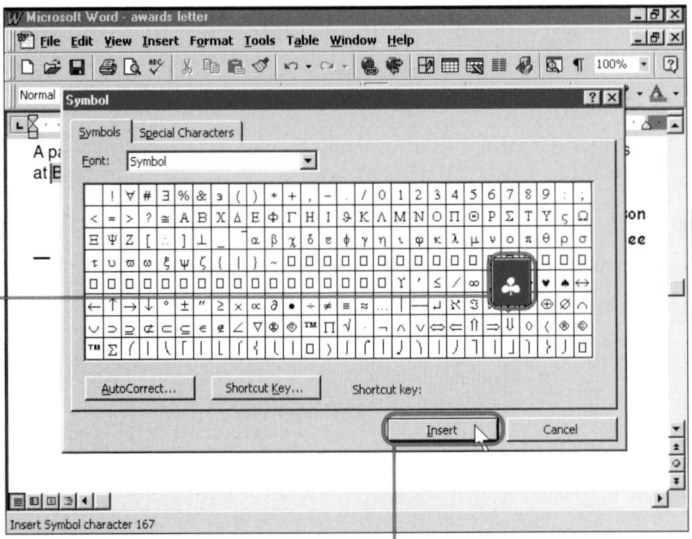

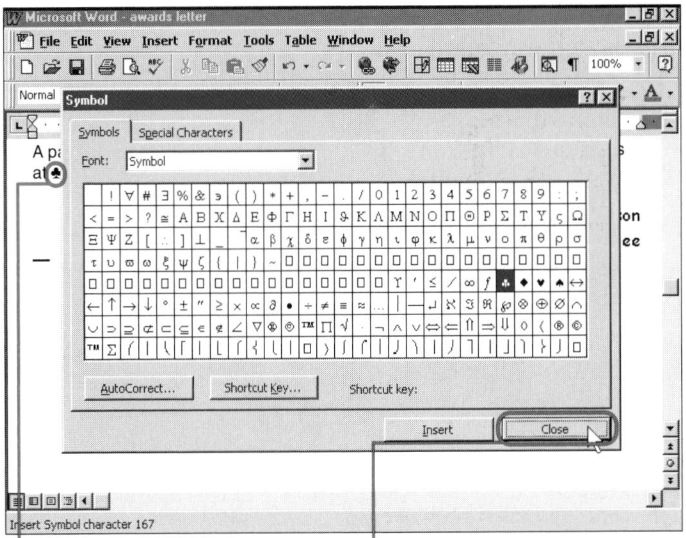

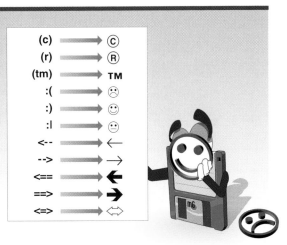

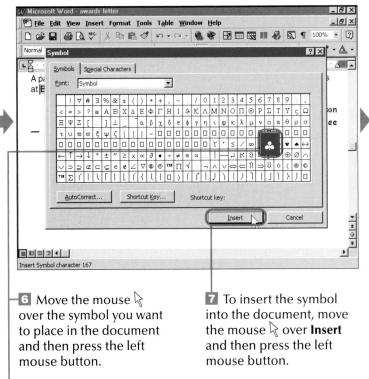

6 Move the mouse over the symbol you want to place in the document and then press the left mouse button.

■ An enlarged version of the symbol appears.

7 To insert the symbol into the document, move the mouse over **Insert** and then press the left mouse button.

■ The symbol appears in the document.

8 To close the **Symbol** dialog box, move the mouse over **Close** and then press the left mouse button.

ADD BULLETS OR NUMBERS

You can separate items in a list by beginning each item with a bullet or number.
WHAP
1
2
3
4
5
6

ADD BULLETS OR NUMBERS

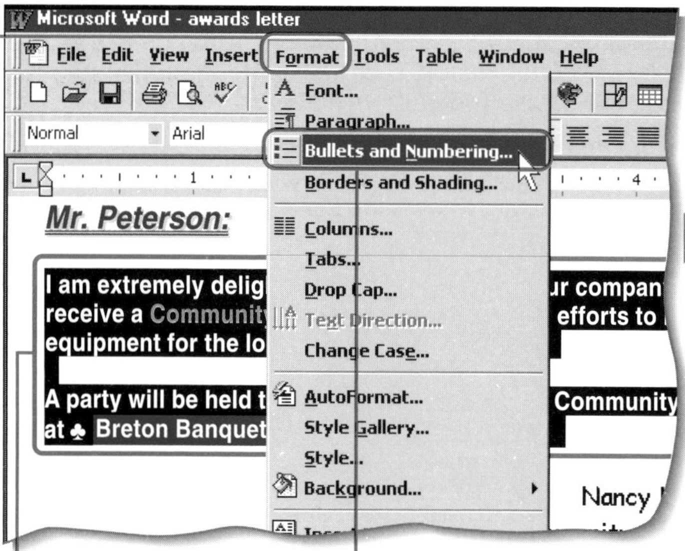

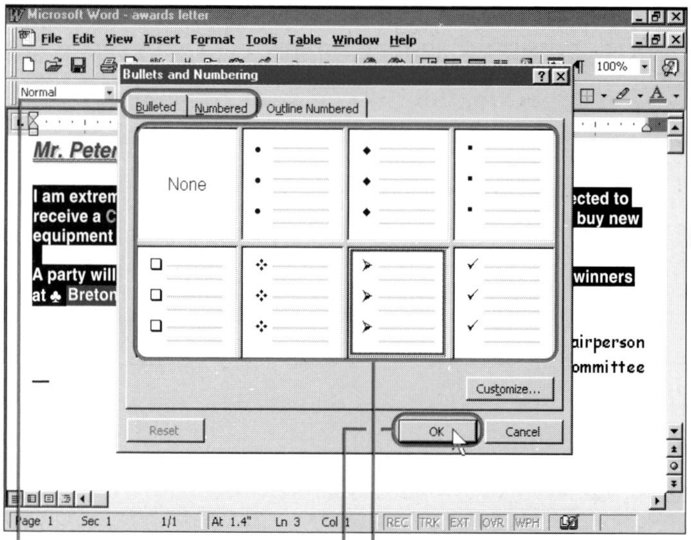

1 Select the text you want to display bullets or numbers. To select text, refer to page 12.

2 Move the mouse over **Format** and then press the left mouse button.

3 Move the mouse over **Bullets and Numbering** and then press the left mouse button.

■ The **Bullets and Numbering** dialog box appears.

4 Move the mouse over the tab for the type of list you want to create and then press the left mouse button.

5 Move the mouse over the style you want to use and then press the left mouse button.

6 Move the mouse over **OK** and then press the left mouse button.

Should I use bullets or numbers in my list?

Bullets are useful for items in no particular order, such as a shopping list.

Shopping List:
• eggs
• butter
• milk
• lettuce
• tomatoes
Recipe:
1. Preheat oven to 300°F
2. Grate 1 cup of cheese
3. Dice 1/4 cup of onions
4. Slice 1/2 a red pepper into strips
5. Add cheese, onions and red pepper to meat sauce
6. Bake for 20 minutes

Numbers are useful for items in a specific order, such as a recipe.

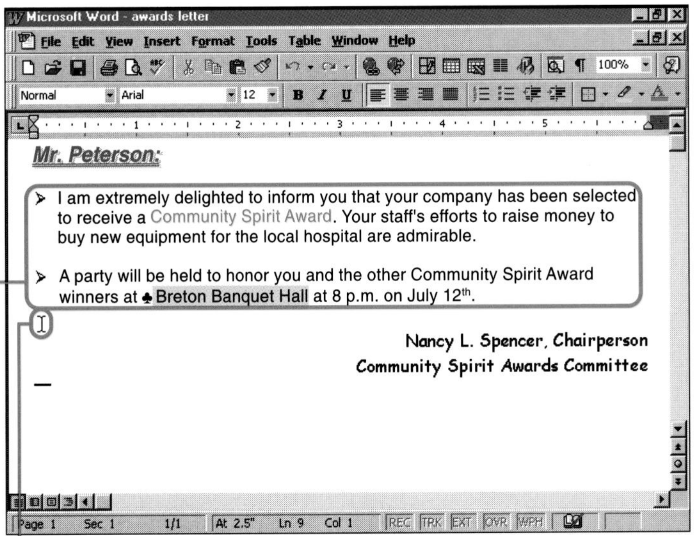
Microsoft Word - awards letter
File Edit View Insert Format Tools Table Window Help
Mr. Peterson:
I am extremely delighted to inform you that your company has been selected to receive a Community Spirit Award. Your staff's efforts to raise money to buy new equipment for the local hospital are admirable.
A party will be held to honor you and the other Community Spirit Award winners at Breton Banquet Hall at 8 p.m. on July 12th.
Nancy L. Spencer, Chairperson
Community Spirit Awards Committee

■ To deselect text, move the mouse I outside the selected area and then press the left mouse button.

■ The bullets or numbers appear in your document.

REMOVE BULLETS OR NUMBERS

■ To remove bullets or numbers from the document, perform steps 1 to 6, selecting **None** in step 5.

ADD BULLETS OR NUMBERS AS YOU TYPE

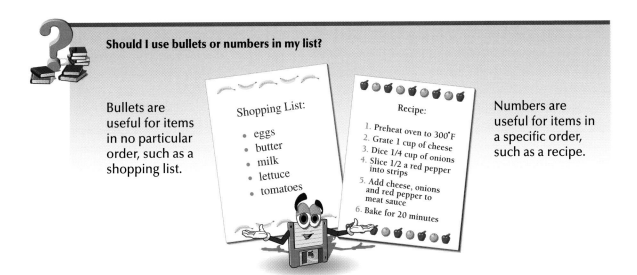

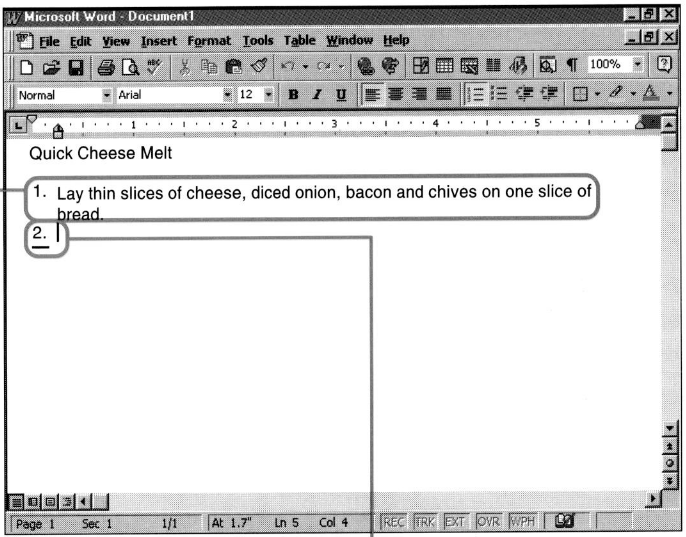
Microsoft Word - Document1
File Edit View Insert Format Tools Table Window Help
Quick Cheese Melt
1. Lay thin slices of cheese, diced onion, bacon and chives on one slice of bread.
2.

1 Move the mouse I to where you want the first number or bullet to appear and then press the left mouse button.

2 Type **1.** or * followed by a space. Then type the first item in the list.

3 Press Enter on your keyboard and Word automatically starts the next item with a number or bullet.

■ To end the numbered or bulleted list, press Enter on your keyboard twice.

ADD A BORDER

Pasta Perfection
• Order our specialty pasta online for fast delivery.
• Browse through our recipe files.
Our Most Popular Types of Pasta:
• Cannelloni
• Lasagna
• Linguine
• Manicotti
• Ravioli
• Spaghetti
Perfect pasta every time!
You can add a border to emphasize an area of text in your document.

ADD A BORDER

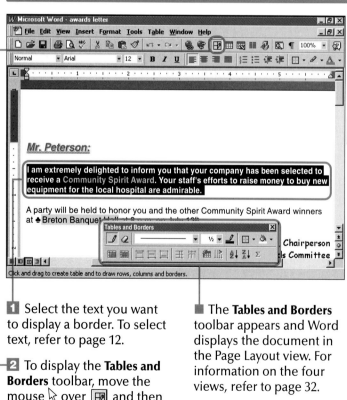

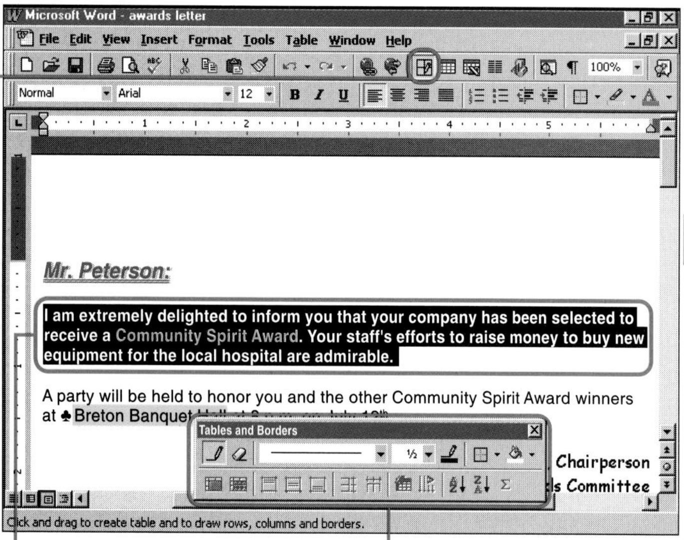
Microsoft Word - awards letter
Mr. Peterson:
I am extremely delighted to inform you that your company has been selected to receive a Community Spirit Award. Your staff's efforts to raise money to buy new equipment for the local hospital are admirable.
A party will be held to honor you and the other Community Spirit Award winners
Tables and Borders
Click and drag to create table and to draw rows, columns and borders.

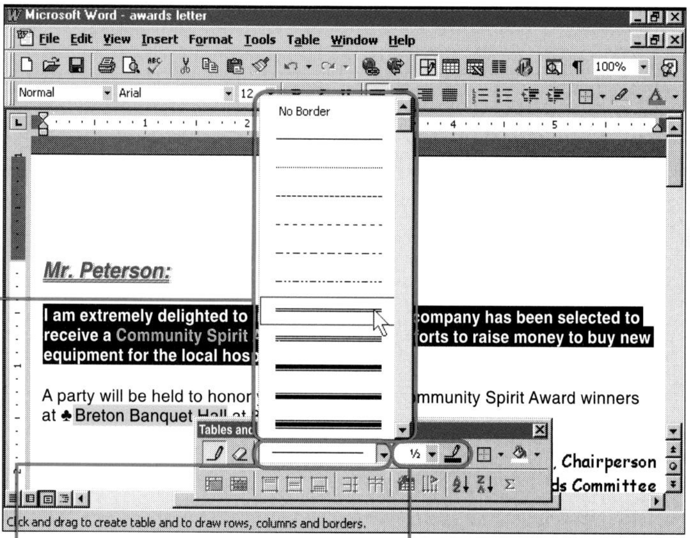
Microsoft Word - awards letter
No Border
Mr. Peterson:
Click and drag to create table and to draw rows, columns and borders.

1 Select the text you want to display a border. To select text, refer to page 12.

2 To display the **Tables and Borders** toolbar, move the mouse over and then press the left mouse button.

■ The **Tables and Borders** toolbar appears and Word displays the document in the Page Layout view. For information on the four views, refer to page 32.

3 To select a line style for the border, move the mouse over this area and then press the left mouse button.

4 Move the mouse over the line style you want to use and then press the left mouse button.

■ Word will use the line thickness and color displayed in these areas for the border.

How can I quickly add a line across my document?

If you type one of the sets of characters in this chart and then press **Enter** on your keyboard, Word will instantly add a line across your document.

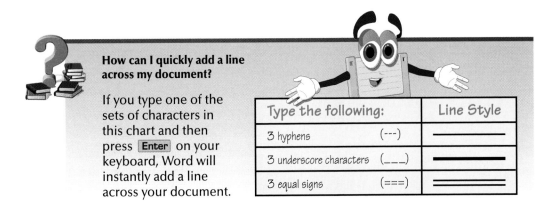

Type the following:	Line Style
3 hyphens (---)	
3 underscore characters (___)	
3 equal signs (===)	

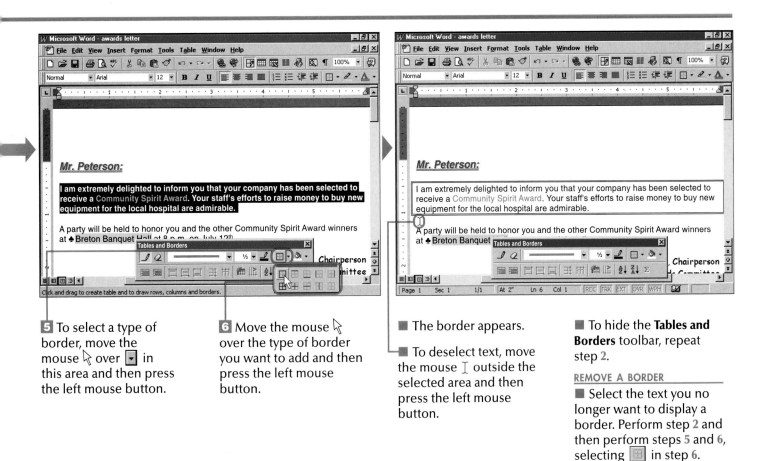

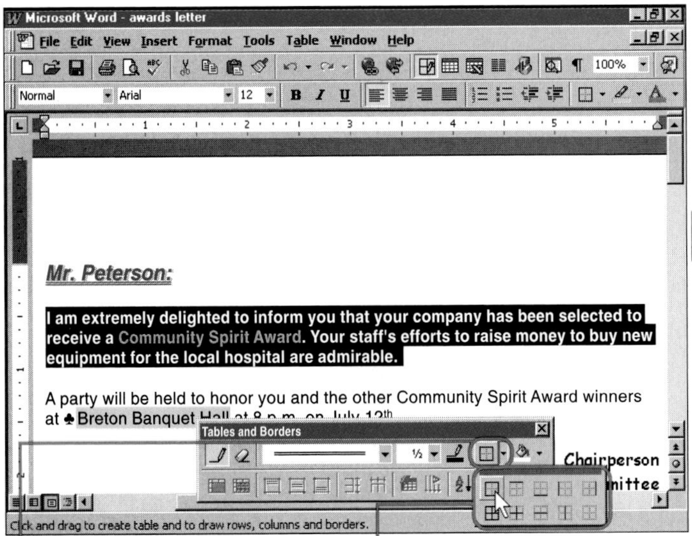
Microsoft Word - awards letter
File Edit View Insert Format Tools Table Window Help
Mr. Peterson:
I am extremely delighted to inform you that your company has been selected to receive a Community Spirit Award. Your staff's efforts to raise money to buy new equipment for the local hospital are admirable.
A party will be held to honor you and the other Community Spirit Award winners
at ♣ Breton Banquet
Tables and Borders
Chairperson
Click and drag to create table and to draw rows, columns and borders.

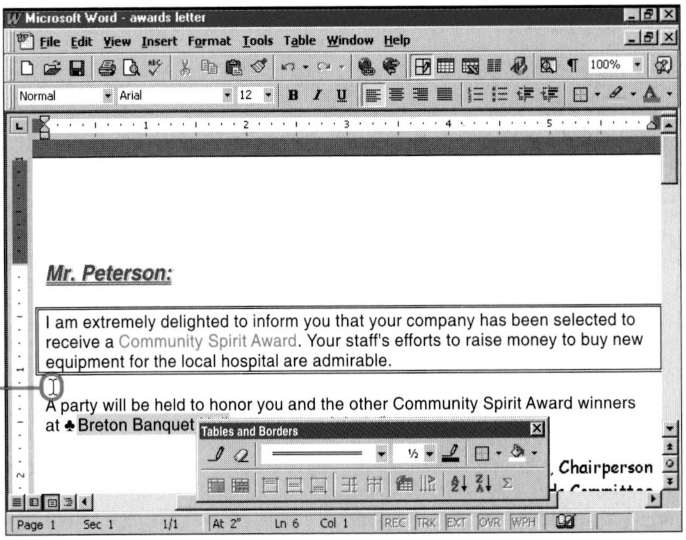
Microsoft Word - awards letter
File Edit View Insert Format Tools Table Window Help
Mr. Peterson:
I am extremely delighted to inform you that your company has been selected to receive a Community Spirit Award. Your staff's efforts to raise money to buy new equipment for the local hospital are admirable.
A party will be held to honor you and the other Community Spirit Award winners
at ♣ Breton Banquet
Tables and Borders
Chairperson
Page 1 Sec 1 1/1 At 2" Ln 6 Col 1

5 To select a type of border, move the mouse over ▾ in this area and then press the left mouse button.

6 Move the mouse over the type of border you want to add and then press the left mouse button.

■ The border appears.

■ To deselect text, move the mouse outside the selected area and then press the left mouse button.

■ To hide the **Tables and Borders** toolbar, repeat step 2.

REMOVE A BORDER

■ Select the text you no longer want to display a border. Perform step 2 and then perform steps 5 and 6, selecting ⊞ in step 6.

ADD SHADING

You can emphasize an area of text in your document by adding shading.
Trafalgar High School celebrates its 50th anniversary this year. We will be celebrating on September 11th with an open house, followed by a buffet dinner.
Trafalgar High School celebrates its 50th anniversary this year. We will be celebrating on September 11th with an open house, followed by a buffet dinner.
Trafalgar High School celebrates its 50th anniversary this year. We will be celebrating on September 11th with an open house, followed by a buffet dinner.
Trafalgar High School celebrates its 50th anniversary this year. We will be celebrating on September 11th with an open house, followed by a buffet dinner.

ADD SHADING

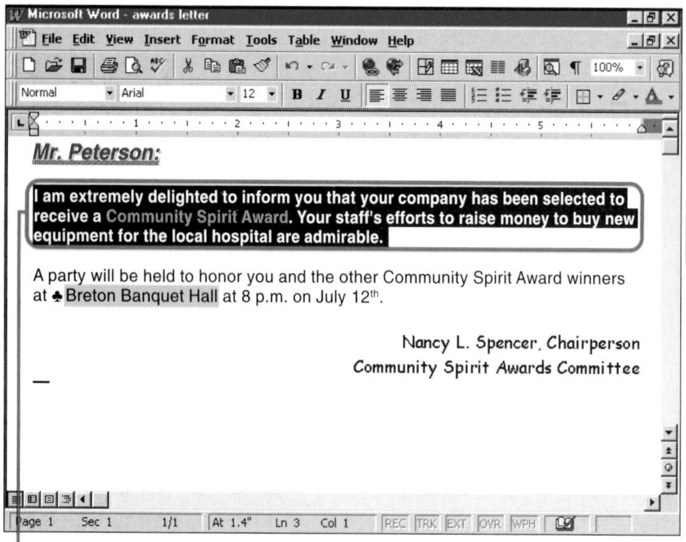
Microsoft Word - awards letter
File Edit View Insert Format Tools Table Window Help
Mr. Peterson:
I am extremely delighted to inform you that your company has been selected to receive a Community Spirit Award. Your staff's efforts to raise money to buy new equipment for the local hospital are admirable.
A party will be held to honor you and the other Community Spirit Award winners at Breton Banquet Hall at 8 p.m. on July 12th.
Nancy L. Spencer, Chairperson
Community Spirit Awards Committee

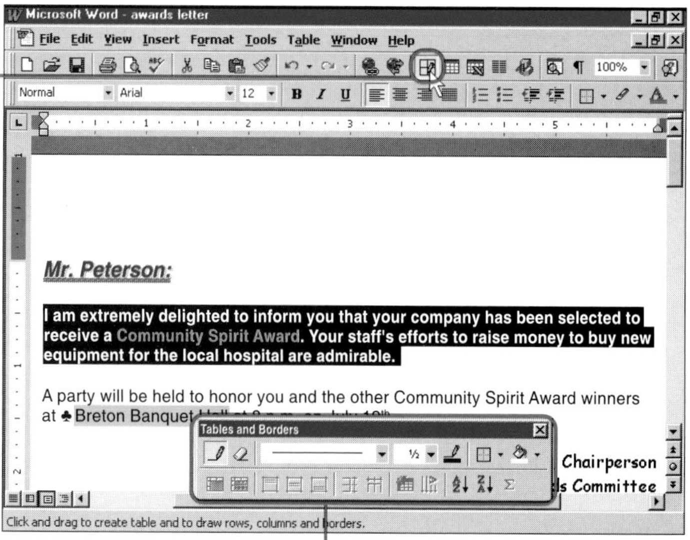
Microsoft Word - awards letter
File Edit View Insert Format Tools Table Window Help
Mr. Peterson:
I am extremely delighted to inform you that your company has been selected to receive a Community Spirit Award. Your staff's efforts to raise money to buy new equipment for the local hospital are admirable.
A party will be held to honor you and the other Community Spirit Award winners
Tables and Borders
Click and drag to create table and to draw rows, columns and borders.

1 Select the text you want to display shading. To select text, refer to page 12.

2 To display the **Tables and Borders** toolbar, move the mouse over and then press the left mouse button.

■ The **Tables and Borders** toolbar appears and Word displays the document in the Page Layout view. For information on the four views, refer to page 32.

How can I quickly add shading to my document?

■ This button (🖌) displays the color of shading you most recently used in your document.

1 To quickly add this shading color, select the text you want to display the shading.

2 Move the mouse over 🖌 and then press the left mouse button.

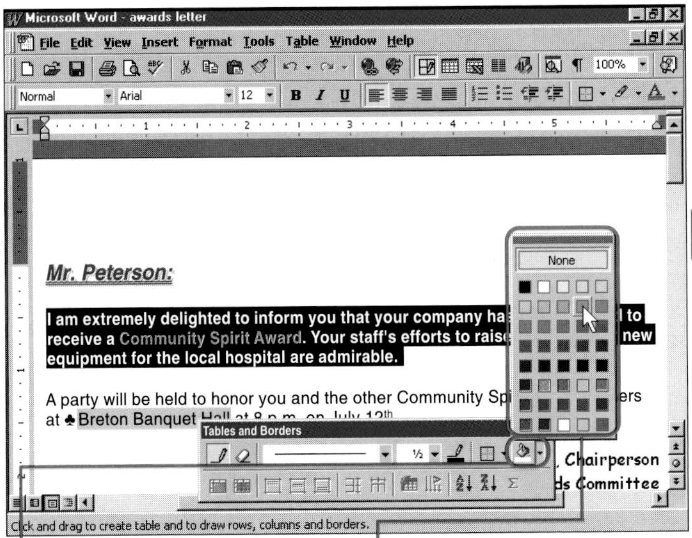

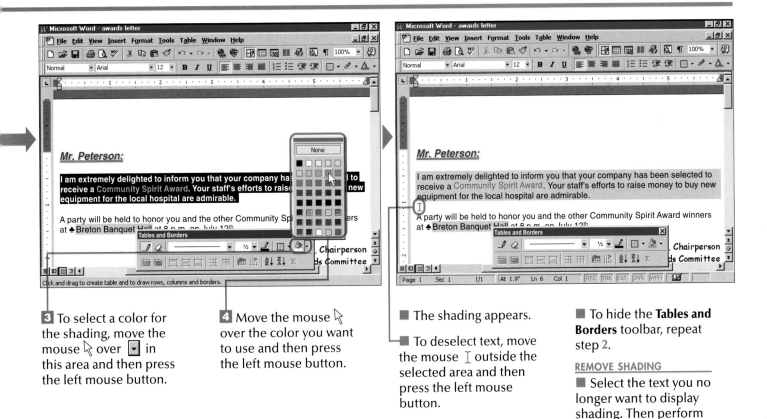

3 To select a color for the shading, move the mouse over ▾ in this area and then press the left mouse button.

4 Move the mouse over the color you want to use and then press the left mouse button.

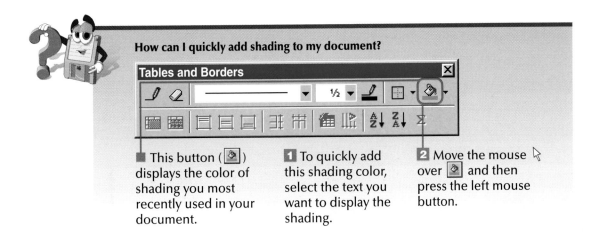

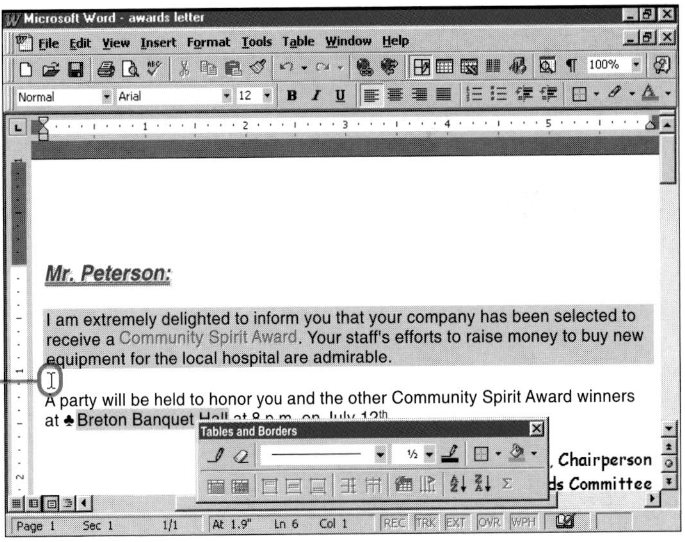

■ The shading appears.

■ To deselect text, move the mouse I outside the selected area and then press the left mouse button.

■ To hide the **Tables and Borders** toolbar, repeat step 2.

REMOVE SHADING

■ Select the text you no longer want to display shading. Then perform steps 2 to 4, selecting **None** in step 4.

CHANGE LINE SPACING

You can change the amount of space between the lines of text in your document to make your document easier to review and edit.
Single
There is a 10th anniversary High School Reunion on August 8, 9 and 10 at Woodblock High School. We all hope to see you there. Contact Susan Hughes for more information.
1.5 Lines
There is a 10th anniversary High School Reunion on August 8, 9 and 10 at Woodblock High School. We all hope to see you there. Contact Susan Hughes for more information.
Double
There is a 10th anniversary High School Reunion on August 8, 9 and 10 at Woodblock High School. We all hope to see you there. Contact Susan Hughes for more information.

CHANGE LINE SPACING

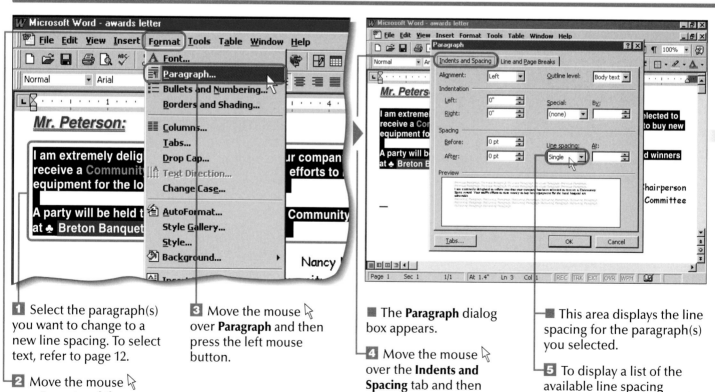

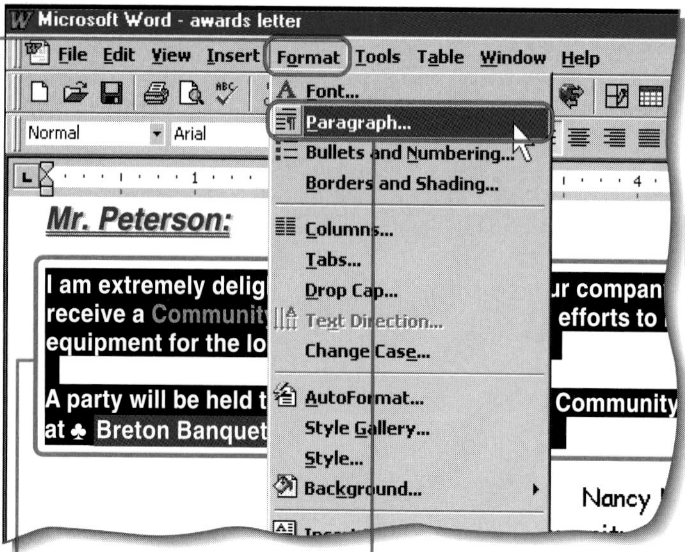

Microsoft Word - awards letter
File Edit View Insert Format Tools Table Window Help
Font...
Paragraph...
Bullets and Numbering...
Borders and Shading...
Columns...
Tabs...
Drop Cap...
Text Direction...
Change Case...
AutoFormat...
Style Gallery...
Style...
Background...
Mr. Peterson:

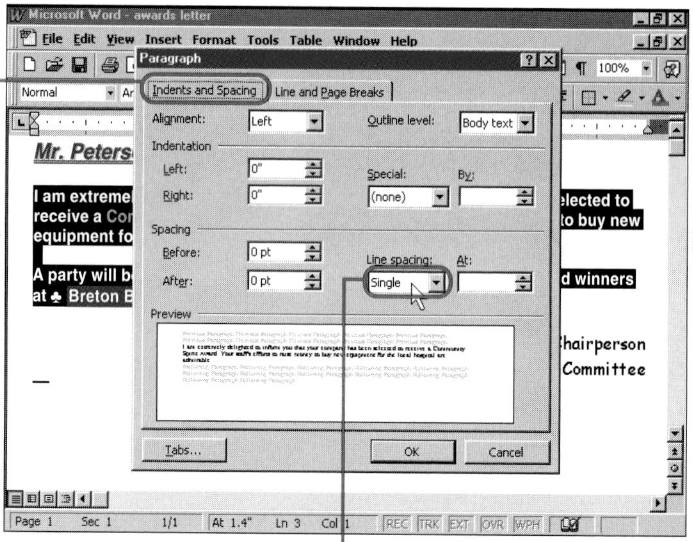

Paragraph
Indents and Spacing
Line and Page Breaks
Alignment: Left
Outline level: Body text
Line spacing: Single
OK
Cancel

1 Select the paragraph(s) you want to change to a new line spacing. To select text, refer to page 12.

2 Move the mouse over **Format** and then press the left mouse button.

3 Move the mouse over **Paragraph** and then press the left mouse button.

■ The **Paragraph** dialog box appears.

4 Move the mouse over the **Indents and Spacing** tab and then press the left mouse button.

■ This area displays the line spacing for the paragraph(s) you selected.

5 To display a list of the available line spacing options, move the mouse over this area and then press the left mouse button.

Does Word ever automatically adjust the line spacing?

Word automatically increases the spacing of lines that contain large characters.

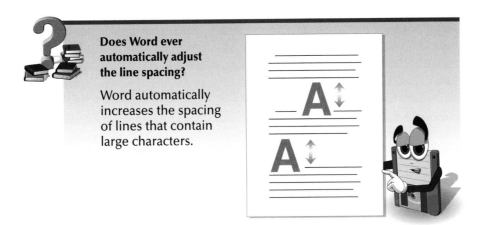

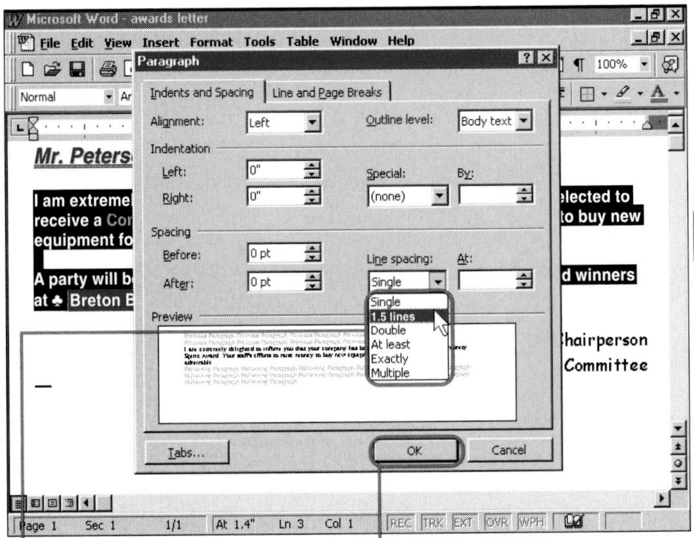

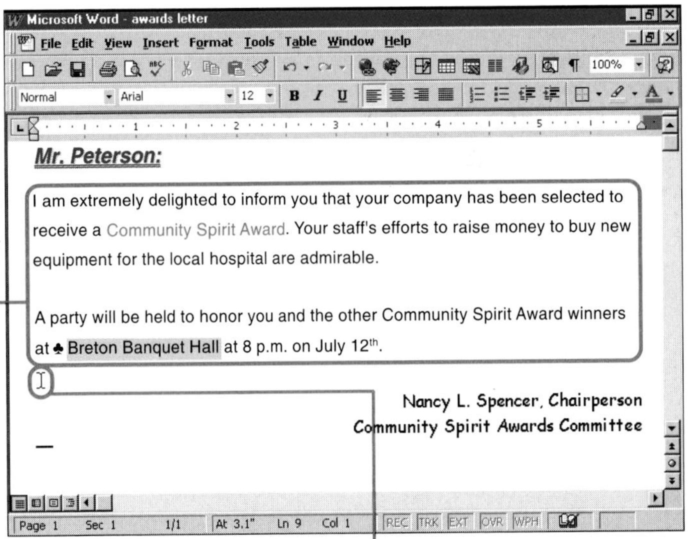

6 Move the mouse over the line spacing option you want to use and then press the left mouse button.

7 Move the mouse over **OK** and then press the left mouse button.

■ Word changes the line spacing of the paragraph(s) you selected.

■ To deselect text, move the mouse outside the selected area and then press the left mouse button.

INDENT PARAGRAPHS

You can use the Indent feature to set off paragraphs in your document.
The spacious grounds of Foster City Zoo were established in 1960 on 350 acres of forest and farmland located five miles west of Foster City, NY.
Indent first line
Indent all but first line
Indent all lines
Indent right edge of all lines

INDENT PARAGRAPHS

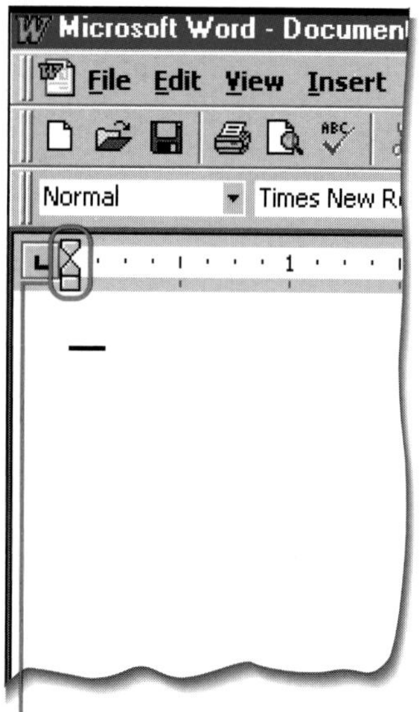

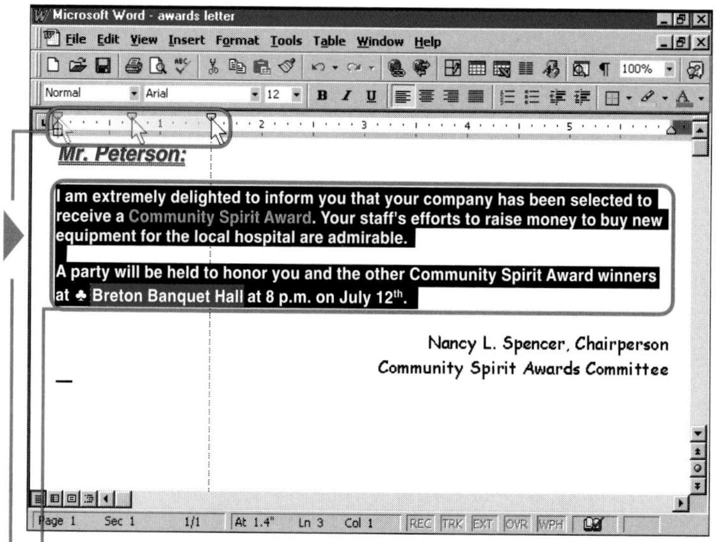

■ These symbols let you indent the left edge of a paragraph.

▽ Indent first line

△ Indent all but first line

□ Indent all lines

■ This symbol (△) lets you indent the right edge of all lines.

Note: If the ruler is not displayed on the screen, refer to page 35 to display the ruler.

1 Select the paragraph(s) you want to indent. To select text, refer to page 12.

2 Move the mouse over the indent symbol and then press and hold down the left mouse button as you move the symbol to a new position.

■ A line shows the new indent position.

What is a hanging indent?

A hanging indent moves all but the first line of a paragraph to the right. Hanging indents are useful when you are creating a résumé, glossary or bibliography.

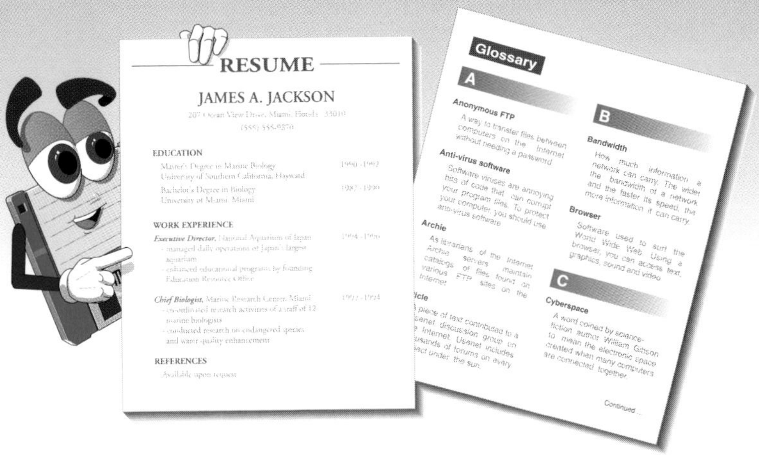
RESUME
JAMES A. JACKSON
EDUCATION
WORK EXPERIENCE
REFERENCES
Glossary
A
Anonymous FTP
Anti-virus software
Archie
B
Bandwidth
Browser
C
Cyberspace

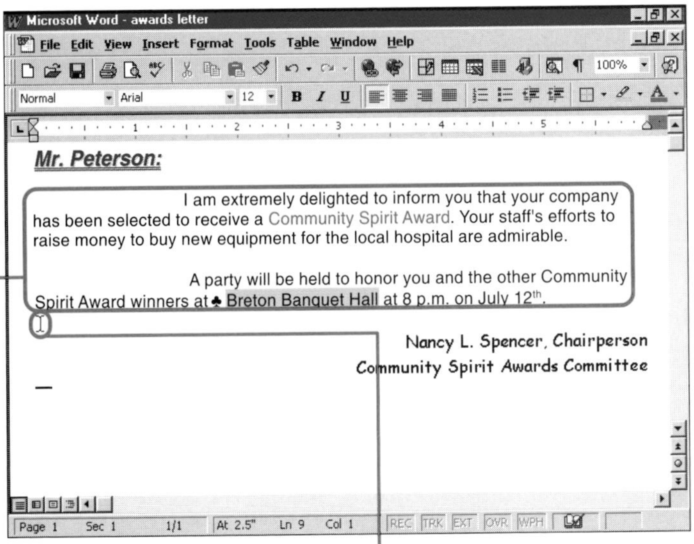
Microsoft Word - awards letter
File Edit View Insert Format Tools Table Window Help
Normal
Arial
12
Mr. Peterson:
I am extremely delighted to inform you that your company has been selected to receive a Community Spirit Award. Your staff's efforts to raise money to buy new equipment for the local hospital are admirable.
A party will be held to honor you and the other Community Spirit Award winners at ♣ Breton Banquet Hall at 8 p.m. on July 12th.
Nancy L. Spencer, Chairperson
Community Spirit Awards Committee
Page 1 Sec 1 1/1 At 2.5" Ln 9 Col 1

3 Release the left mouse button and Word indents the paragraph(s) you selected.

■ To deselect text, move the mouse I outside the selected area and then press the left mouse button.

QUICKLY INDENT ALL LINES IN A PARAGRAPH

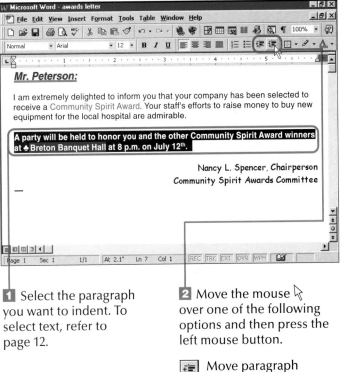

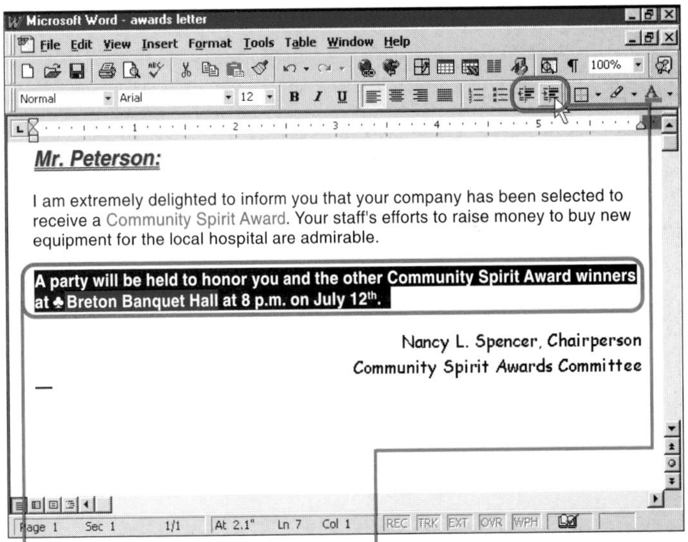
Microsoft Word - awards letter
File Edit View Insert Format Tools Table Window Help
Normal
Arial
12
Mr. Peterson:
I am extremely delighted to inform you that your company has been selected to receive a Community Spirit Award. Your staff's efforts to raise money to buy new equipment for the local hospital are admirable.
A party will be held to honor you and the other Community Spirit Award winners at ♣ Breton Banquet Hall at 8 p.m. on July 12th.
Nancy L. Spencer, Chairperson
Community Spirit Awards Committee
Page 1 Sec 1 1/1 At 2.1" Ln 7 Col 1

1 Select the paragraph you want to indent. To select text, refer to page 12.

2 Move the mouse over one of the following options and then press the left mouse button.

 Move paragraph to the left

 Move paragraph to the right

CHANGE TAB SETTINGS

You can use tabs to line up columns of information in your document. Word offers four types of tabs.
Left Tab
Right Tab
Center Tab
1156 93
42 67
835 02
77 86
Decimal Tab

Word automatically places a tab every 0.5 inches across each page.

ADD A TAB

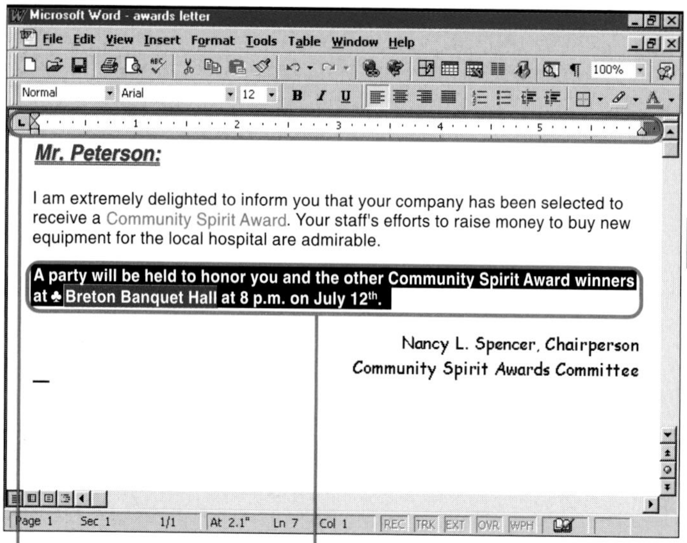
Microsoft Word - awards letter
Mr. Peterson:
I am extremely delighted to inform you that your company has been selected to receive a Community Spirit Award. Your staff's efforts to raise money to buy new equipment for the local hospital are admirable.
A party will be held to honor you and the other Community Spirit Award winners at Breton Banquet Hall at 8 p.m. on July 12th.
Nancy L. Spencer, Chairperson
Community Spirit Awards Committee

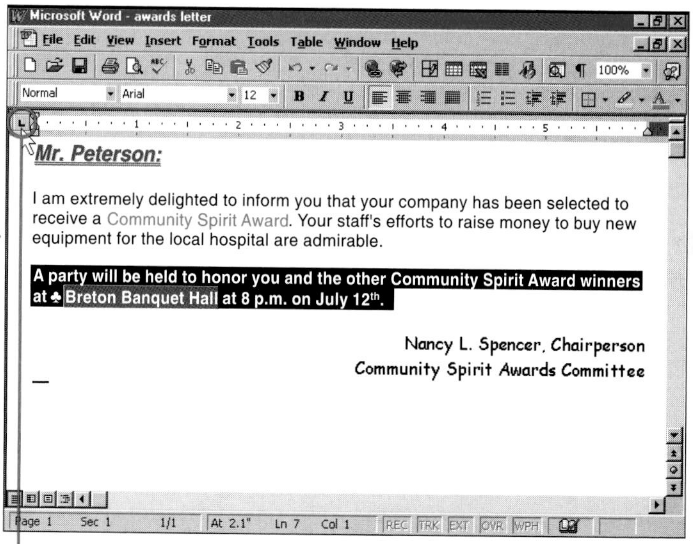
Microsoft Word - awards letter
Mr. Peterson:
I am extremely delighted to inform you that your company has been selected to receive a Community Spirit Award. Your staff's efforts to raise money to buy new equipment for the local hospital are admirable.
A party will be held to honor you and the other Community Spirit Award winners at Breton Banquet Hall at 8 p.m. on July 12th.
Nancy L. Spencer, Chairperson
Community Spirit Awards Committee

■ If the ruler is not displayed on the screen, refer to page 35 to display the ruler.

1 To add a tab, select the text you want to contain the new tab. To select text, refer to page 12.

■ To add a tab to text you are about to type, move the mouse I to where you want to type the text and then press the left mouse button.

2 Move the mouse over this area and then press the left mouse button until the type of tab you want to add appears.

- ∟ Left Tab
- ⊥ Center Tab
- ┘ Right Tab
- ⊥ Decimal Tab

What happens if I use spaces instead of tabs to line up columns of text?

Your document may not print correctly if you use spaces instead of tabs to line up columns of text.

Spaces were used to line up these columns.
Tabs were used to line up these columns.

USING TABS

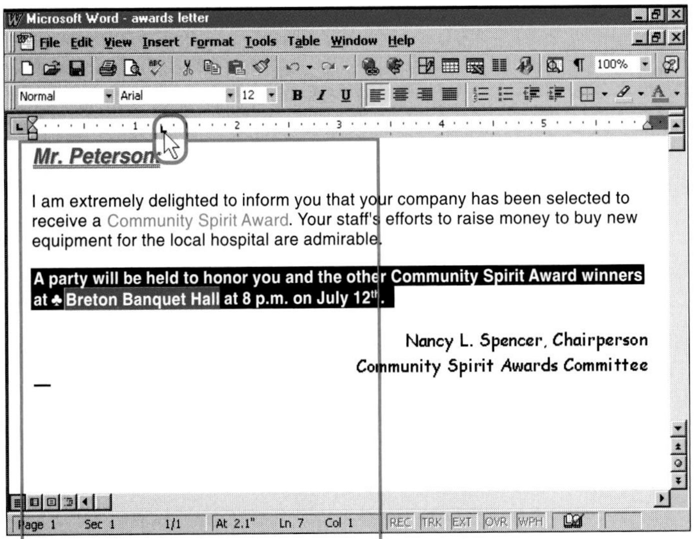

3 Move the mouse over the bottom half of the ruler to where you want to add the tab and then press the left mouse button.

■ The new tab appears on the ruler.

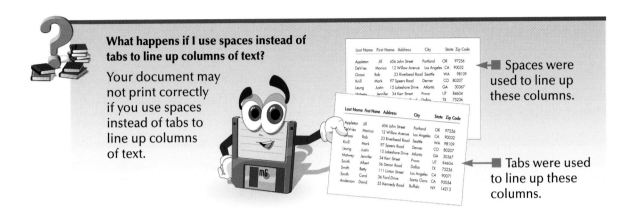

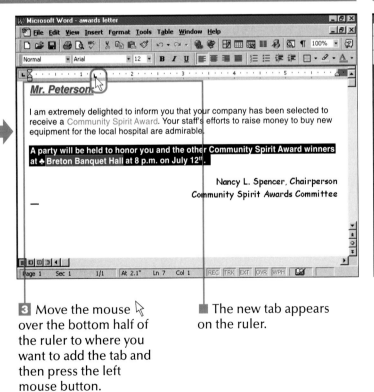

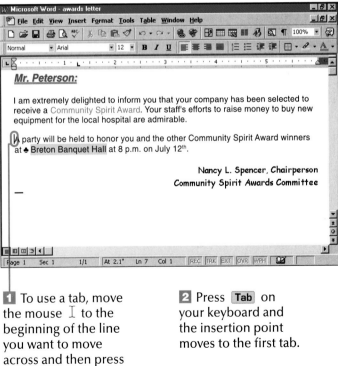

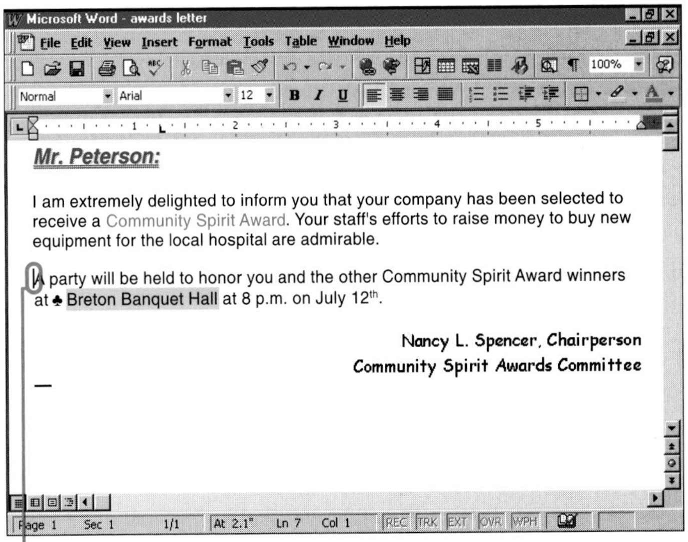

1 To use a tab, move the mouse to the beginning of the line you want to move across and then press the left mouse button.

2 Press **Tab** on your keyboard and the insertion point moves to the first tab.

CHANGE TAB SETTINGS

You can easily move a tab to a different position on the ruler.

MOVE A TAB

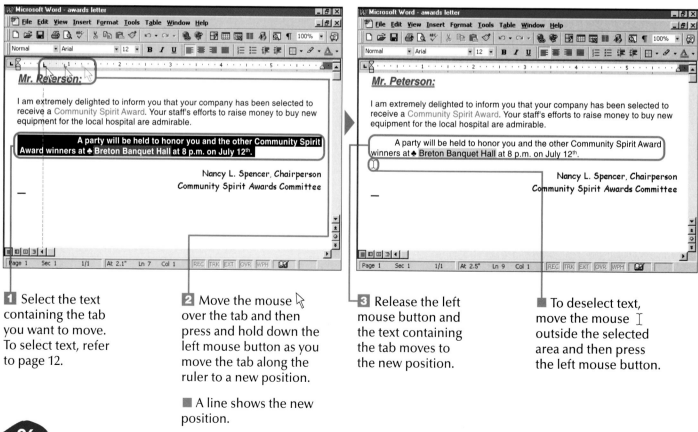

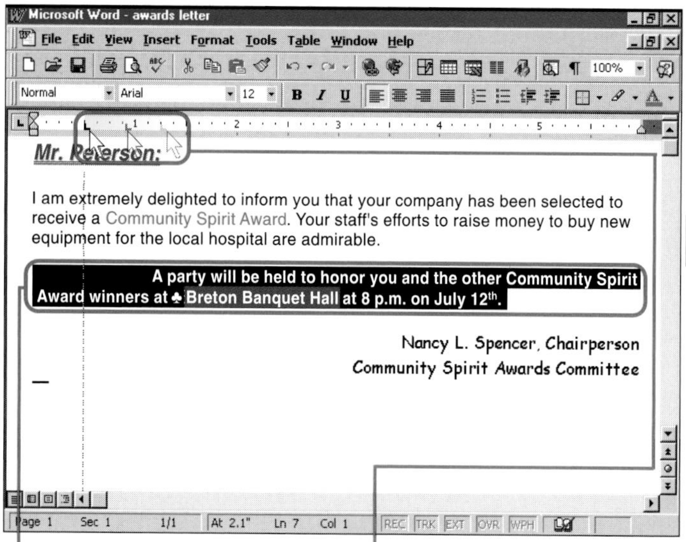

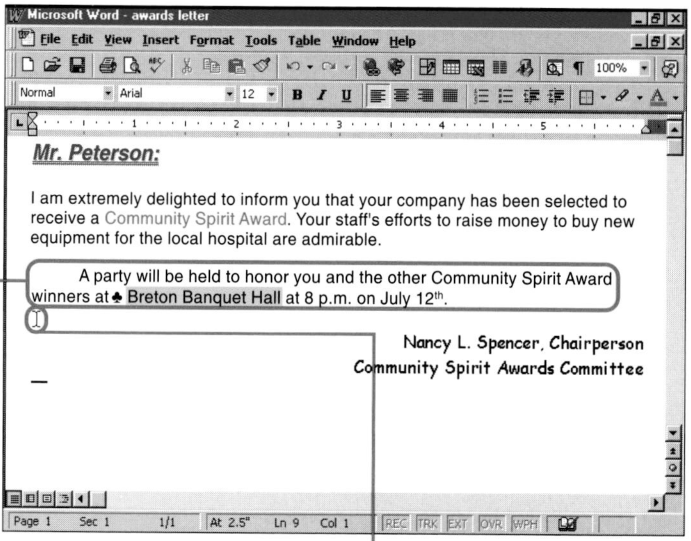

1 Select the text containing the tab you want to move. To select text, refer to page 12.

2 Move the mouse over the tab and then press and hold down the left mouse button as you move the tab along the ruler to a new position.

■ A line shows the new position.

3 Release the left mouse button and the text containing the tab moves to the new position.

■ To deselect text, move the mouse outside the selected area and then press the left mouse button.

When you no longer need a tab, you can remove it from the ruler.

REMOVE A TAB

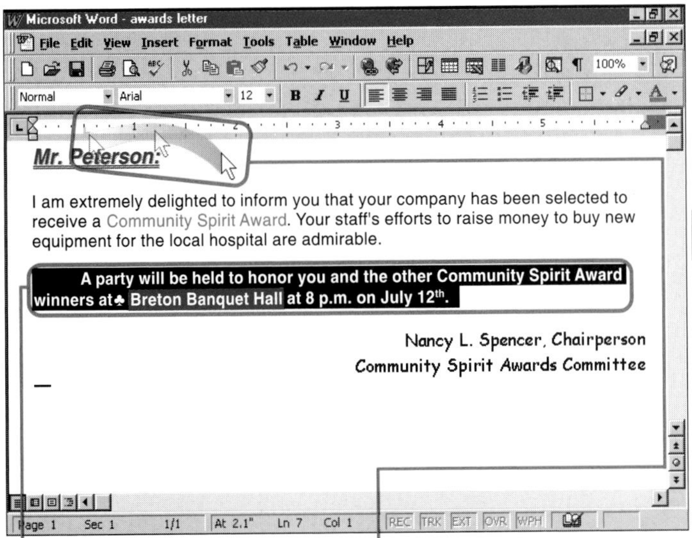

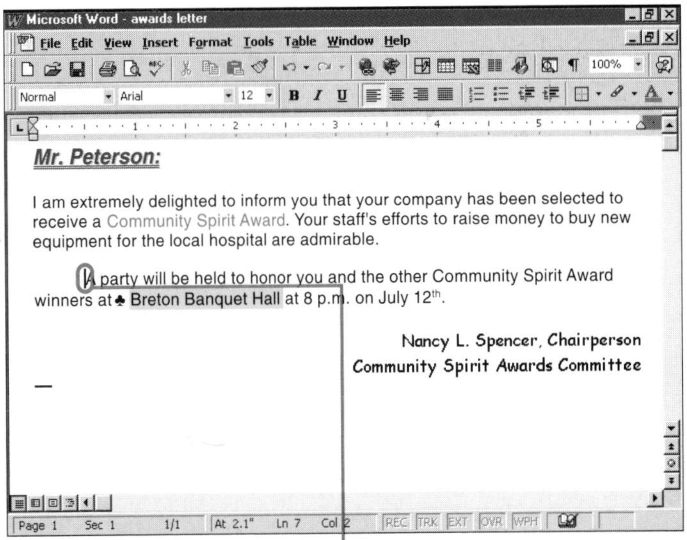

1 Select the text containing the tab you want to remove. To select text, refer to page 12.

2 Move the mouse over the tab and then press and hold down the left mouse button as you move the tab downward off the ruler.

3 Release the left mouse button and the tab disappears from the ruler.

■ To move text back to the left margin, move the mouse I to the left of the first character in the paragraph and then press the left mouse button. Then press ←Backspace on your keyboard.

CHANGE TAB SETTINGS

ADD A TAB WITH LEADER CHARACTERS

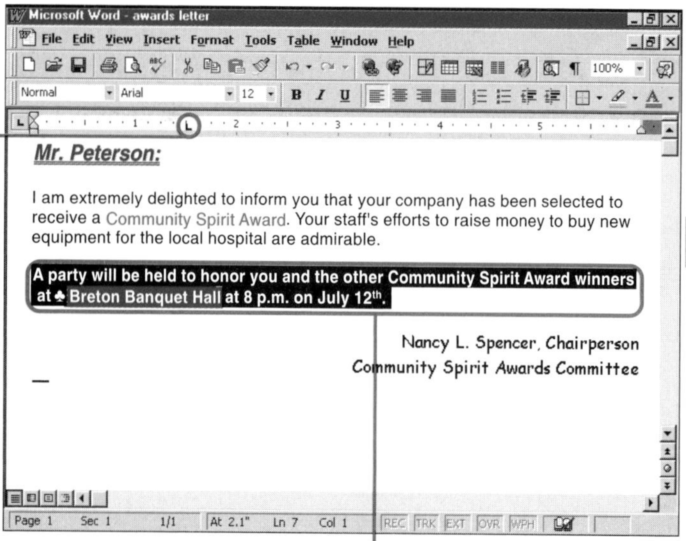

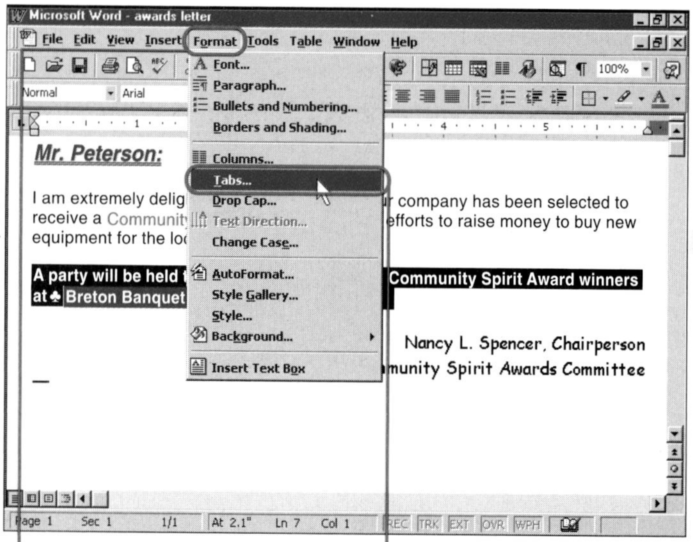

1 Add a tab to the text you want to display leader characters. To add a tab, refer to page 94.

Note: You can also add a tab to text you are about to type.

2 Select the text containing the tab. To select text, refer to page 12.

3 Move the mouse over **Format** and then press the left mouse button.

4 Move the mouse over **Tabs** and then press the left mouse button.

■ The **Tabs** dialog box appears.

Why would I use leader characters?

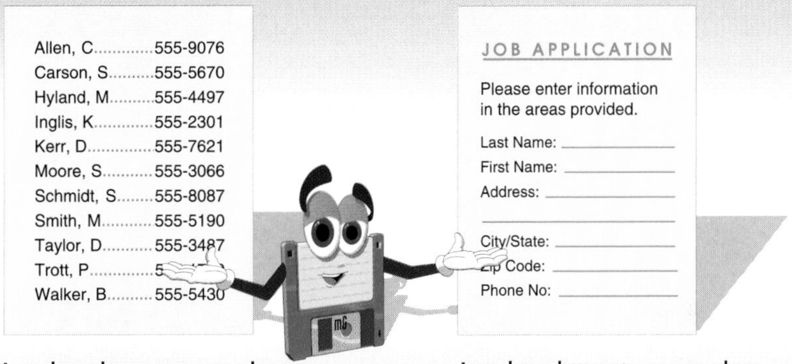

Allen, C............555-9076
Carson, S..........555-5670
Hyland, M..........555-4497
Inglis, K............555-2301
Kerr, D..............555-7621
Moore, S...........555-3066
Schmidt, S........555-8087
Smith, M...........555-5190
Taylor, D...........555-3487
Trott, P
Walker, B..........555-5430
JOB APPLICATION
Please enter information in the areas provided.
Last Name:
First Name:
Address:
City/State:
Code:
Phone No:

Leader characters make information such as a table of contents or a list of telephone numbers easier to read.

Leader characters are also used in forms to create areas where people can enter information.

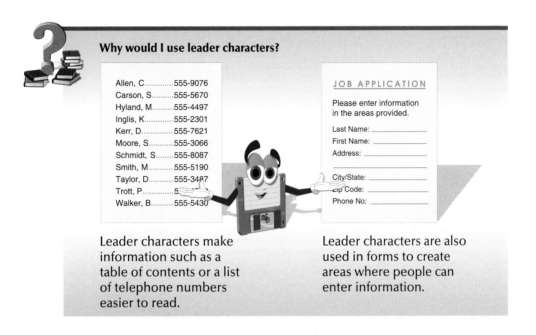

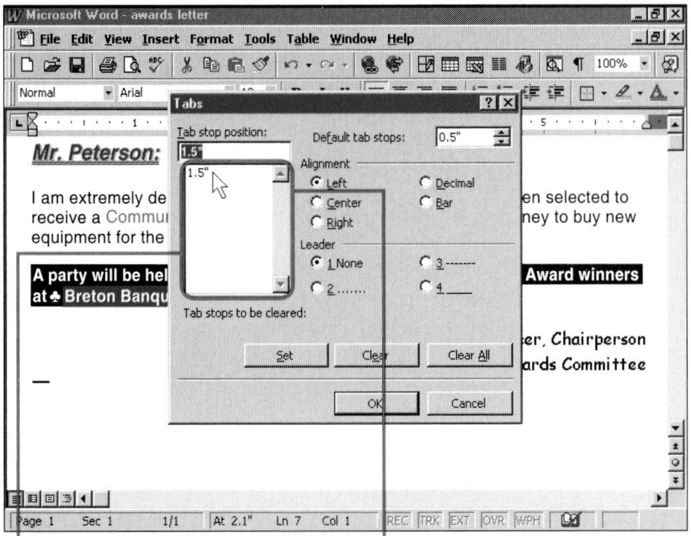

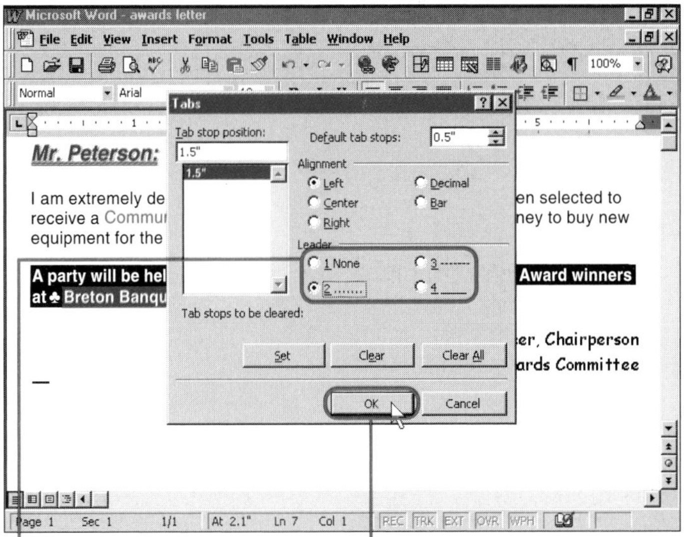

■ This area displays the positions of all the tabs for the text you selected.

5 Move the mouse over the tab you want to display leader characters and then press the left mouse button.

6 Move the mouse over the type of leader character you want to display and then press the left mouse button (○ changes to ◉).

7 Move the mouse over **OK** and then press the left mouse button.

■ You use a tab with leader characters as you would use any tab. To use a tab, refer to page 95.

COPY FORMATTING

You can easily make one area of text look exactly like another.
Great Composers
Bach
Mozart
Beethoven
Holst

COPY FORMATTING

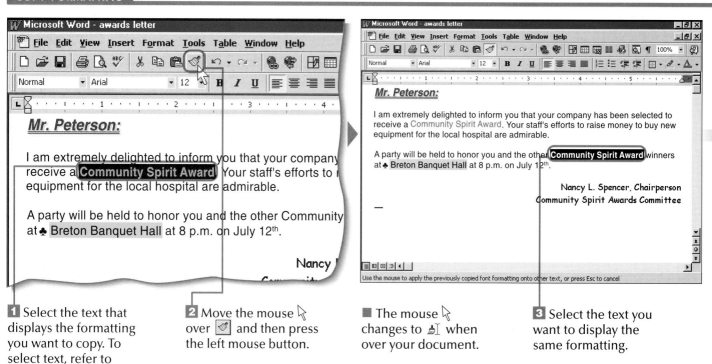

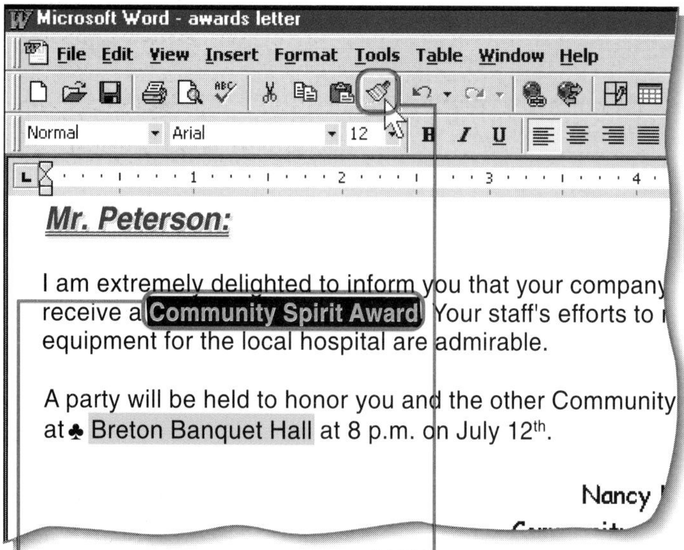
Microsoft Word - awards letter
File Edit View Insert Format Tools Table Window Help
Normal
Arial
12
Mr. Peterson:
I am extremely delighted to inform you that your company
receive a Community Spirit Award. Your staff's efforts to
equipment for the local hospital are admirable.
A party will be held to honor you and the other Community
at Breton Banquet Hall at 8 p.m. on July 12th.
Nancy

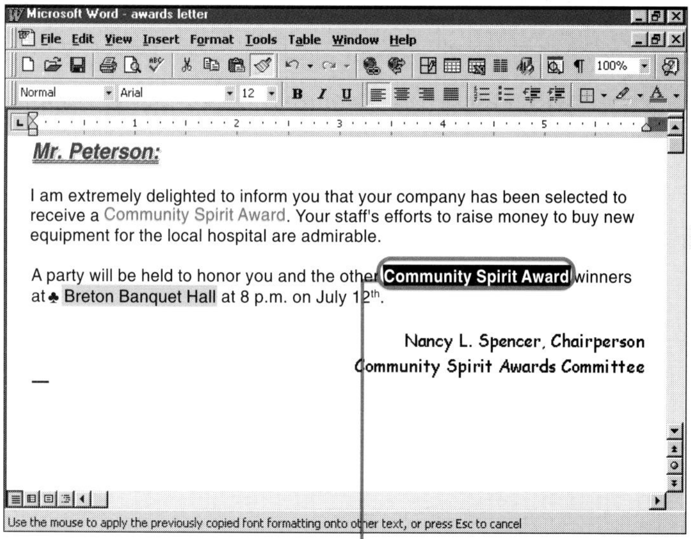
Microsoft Word - awards letter
File Edit View Insert Format Tools Table Window Help
Normal
Arial
12
100%
Mr. Peterson:
I am extremely delighted to inform you that your company has been selected to receive a Community Spirit Award. Your staff's efforts to raise money to buy new equipment for the local hospital are admirable.
A party will be held to honor you and the other Community Spirit Award winners at Breton Banquet Hall at 8 p.m. on July 12th.
Nancy L. Spencer, Chairperson
Community Spirit Awards Committee
Use the mouse to apply the previously copied font formatting onto other text, or press Esc to cancel

1 Select the text that displays the formatting you want to copy. To select text, refer to page 12.

2 Move the mouse over the Format Painter button and then press the left mouse button.

■ The mouse changes to a paintbrush I-beam when over your document.

3 Select the text you want to display the same formatting.

Why would I want to copy the formatting of text?

You may want to copy the formatting of text to make all the headings or important words in your document look the same. This will give your document a consistent appearance.

Strings
Drums
Horns
Piano
Vocals

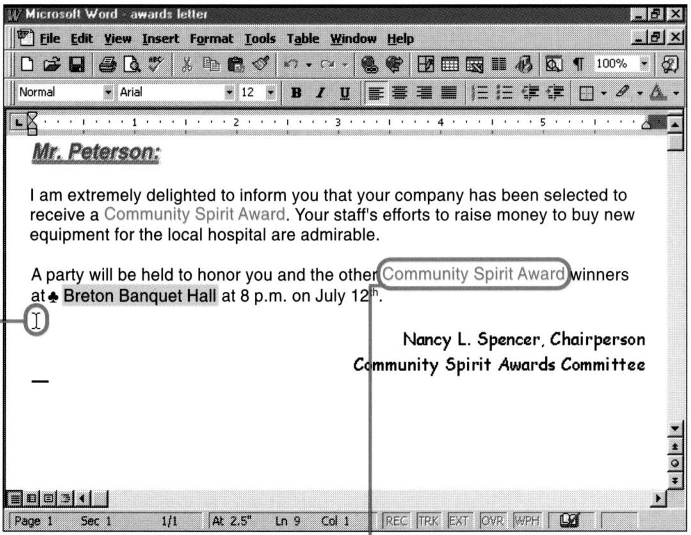
Microsoft Word - awards letter
File Edit View Insert Format Tools Table Window Help
Mr. Peterson:
I am extremely delighted to inform you that your company has been selected to receive a Community Spirit Award. Your staff's efforts to raise money to buy new equipment for the local hospital are admirable.
A party will be held to honor you and the other Community Spirit Award winners at Breton Banquet Hall at 8 p.m. on July 12th.
Nancy L. Spencer, Chairperson
Community Spirit Awards Committee

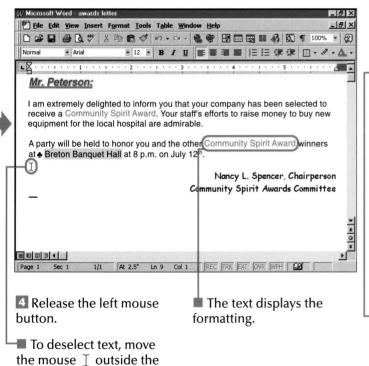

4 Release the left mouse button.

■ To deselect text, move the mouse I outside the selected area and then press the left mouse button.

■ The text displays the formatting.

You can copy formatting to several locations in your document.

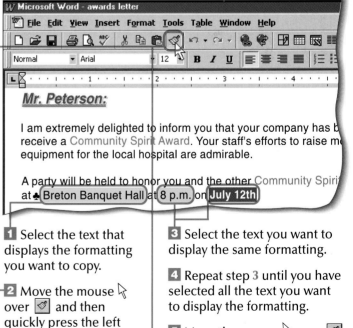

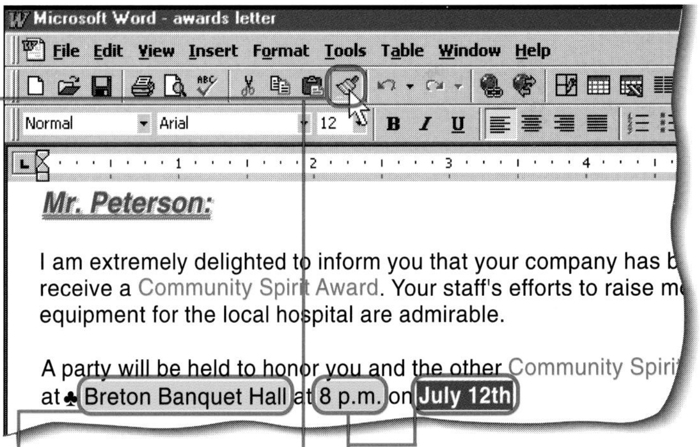
Microsoft Word - awards letter
File Edit View Insert Format Tools Table Window Help
Mr. Peterson:
A party will be held to honor you and the other Community Spiri
at Breton Banquet Hall at 8 p.m. on July 12th

1 Select the text that displays the formatting you want to copy.

2 Move the mouse over and then quickly press the left mouse button twice.

3 Select the text you want to display the same formatting.

4 Repeat step 3 until you have selected all the text you want to display the formatting.

5 Move the mouse over and then press the left mouse button.

USING STYLES

CREATE A STYLE

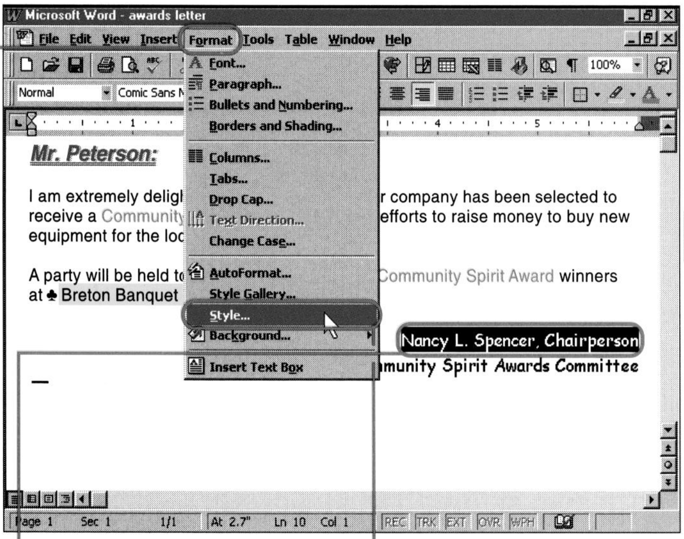

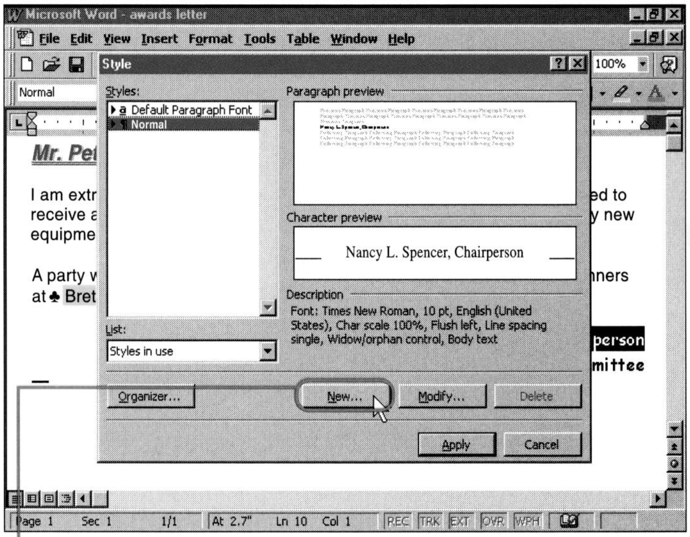

1 Select the text that displays the formatting you want to store. To select text, refer to page 12.

2 Move the mouse over **Format** and then press the left mouse button.

3 Move the mouse over **Style** and then press the left mouse button.

■ The **Style** dialog box appears.

4 Move the mouse over **New** and then press the left mouse button.

■ The **New Style** dialog box appears.

What is the difference between paragraph and character styles?

Character style

A character style includes formatting that changes the appearance of individual characters, such as **bold**, underline and text color.

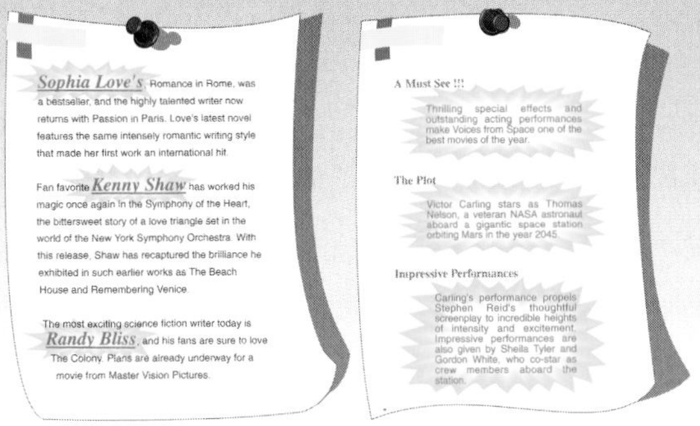

Paragraph style

A paragraph style includes formatting that changes the appearance of individual characters and entire paragraphs, such as text alignment, tab settings and line spacing.

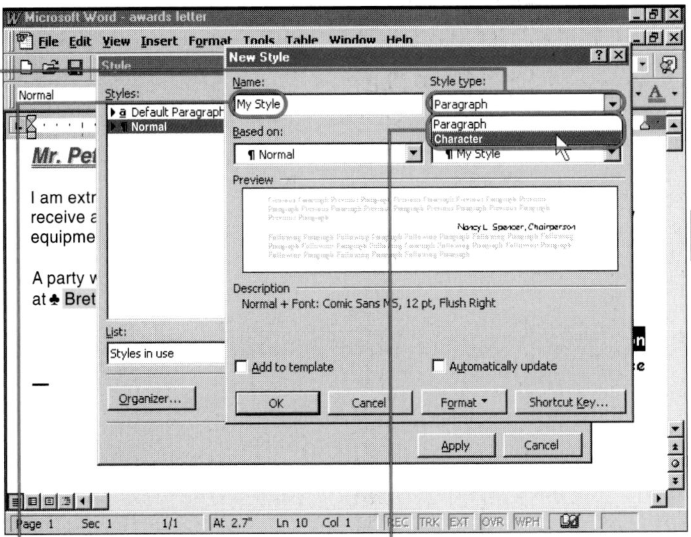

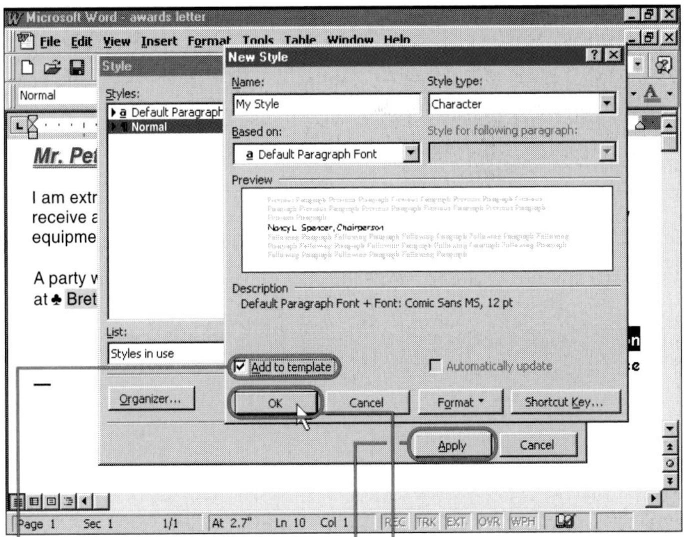

5 Type a name for the new style (example: **My Style**).

6 To select a type of style, move the mouse over this area and then press the left mouse button.

7 Move the mouse over the type of style you want to create and then press the left mouse button.

Note: For information on the types of styles, refer to the top of this page.

8 If you want the style to be available for all new documents you create, move the mouse over **Add to template** and then press the left mouse button (☐ changes to ☑).

9 Move the mouse over **OK** and then press the left mouse button.

10 In the **Style** dialog box, move the mouse over **Apply** and then press the left mouse button.

USING STYLES

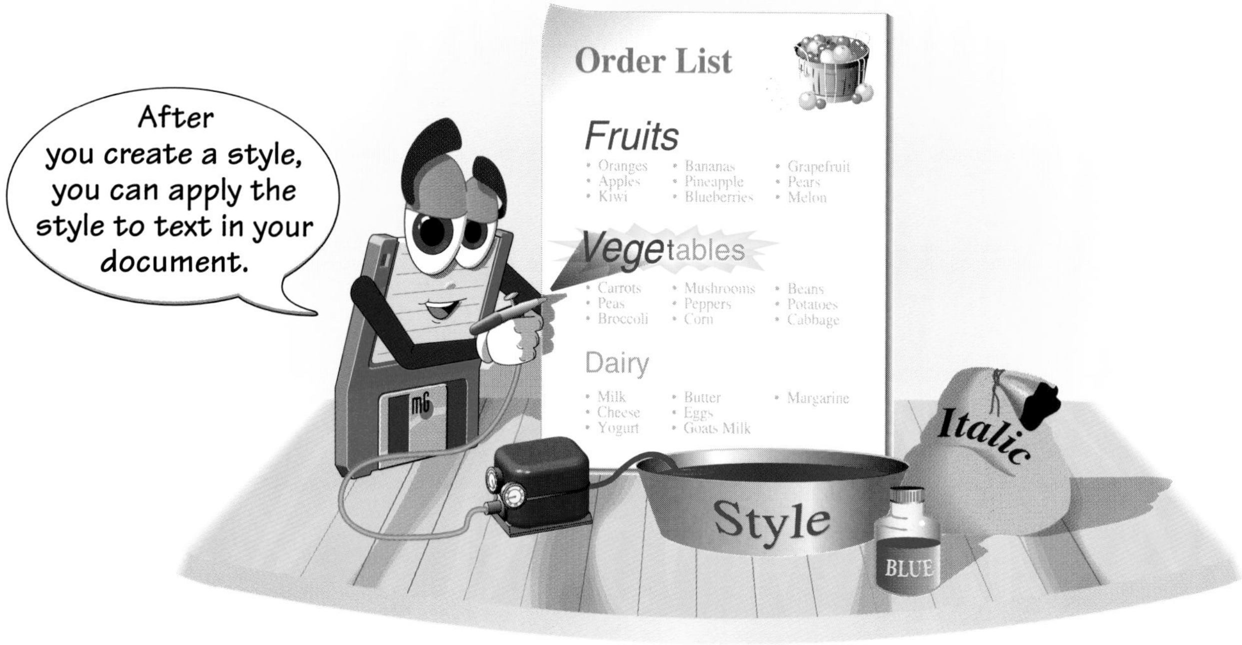

APPLY A STYLE

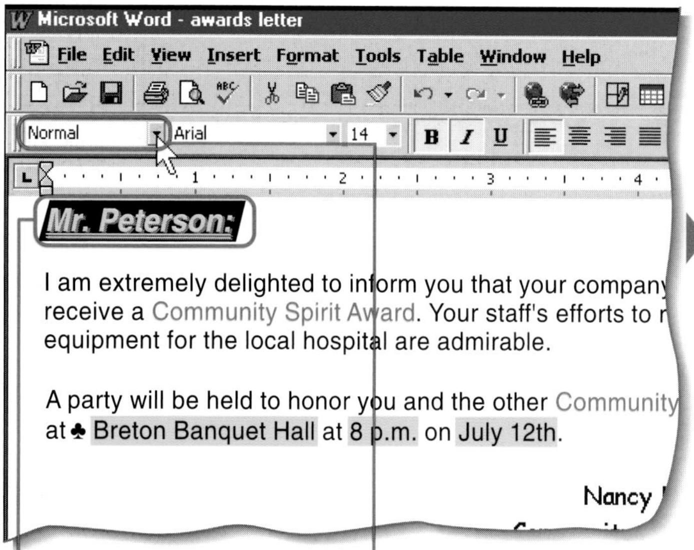

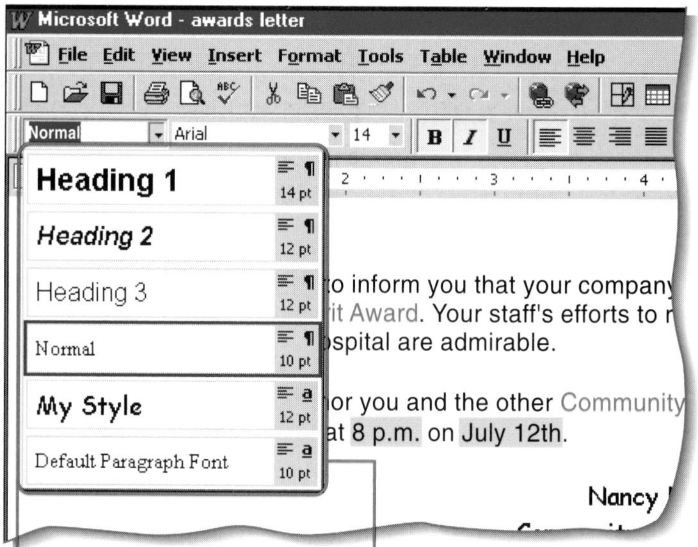

1 Select the text you want to apply a style to. To select text, refer to page 12.

2 Move the mouse over ▾ in this area and then press the left mouse button.

■ A list of styles appears. Word comes with several built-in styles.

■ A symbol to the right of each style indicates the type of style.

a Character style

¶ Paragraph style

Note: For information on the types of styles, refer to the top of page 103.

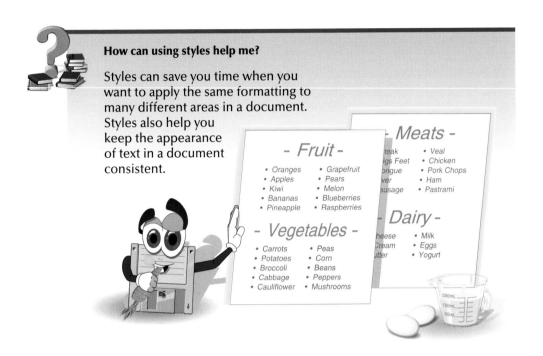

How can using styles help me?

Styles can save you time when you want to apply the same formatting to many different areas in a document. Styles also help you keep the appearance of text in a document consistent.

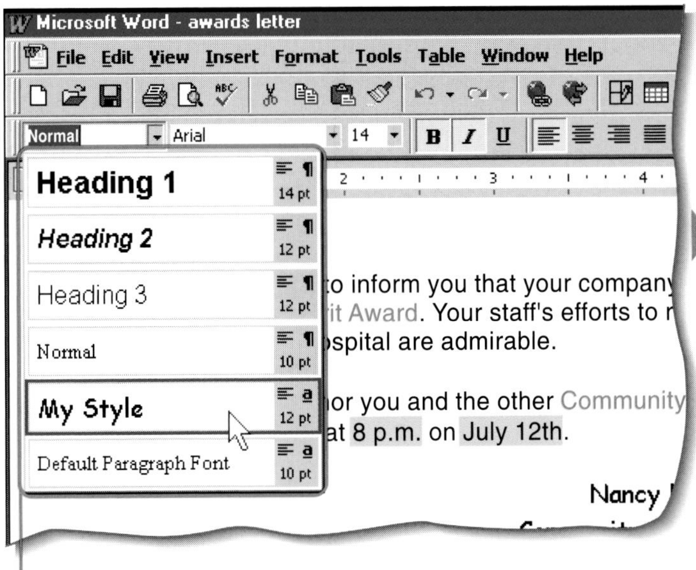

3 Move the mouse over the style you want to use and then press the left mouse button.

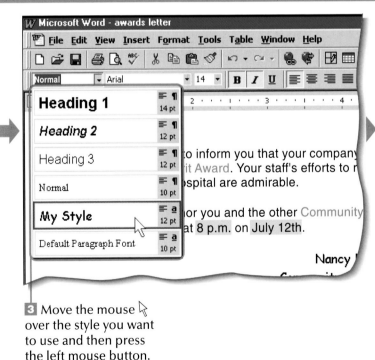

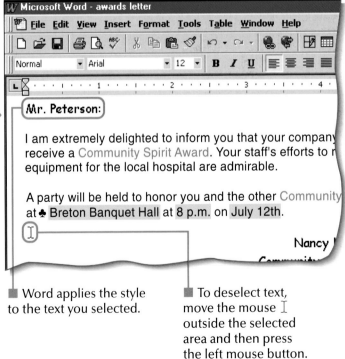

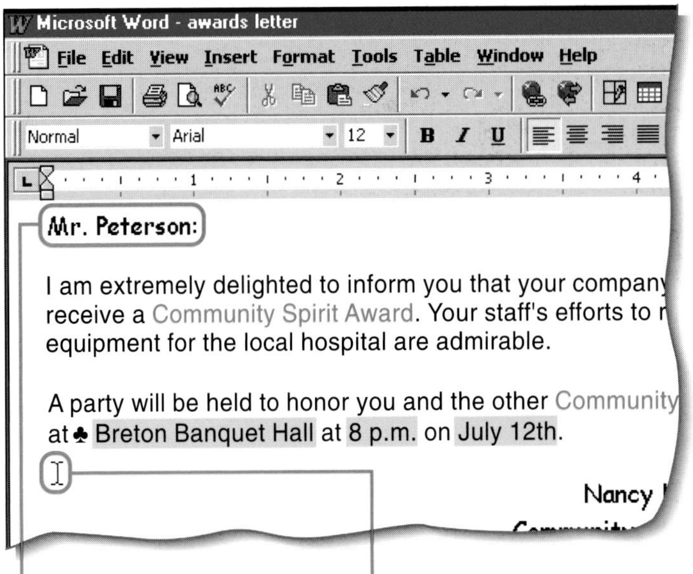

■ Word applies the style to the text you selected.

■ To deselect text, move the mouse outside the selected area and then press the left mouse button.

USING STYLES

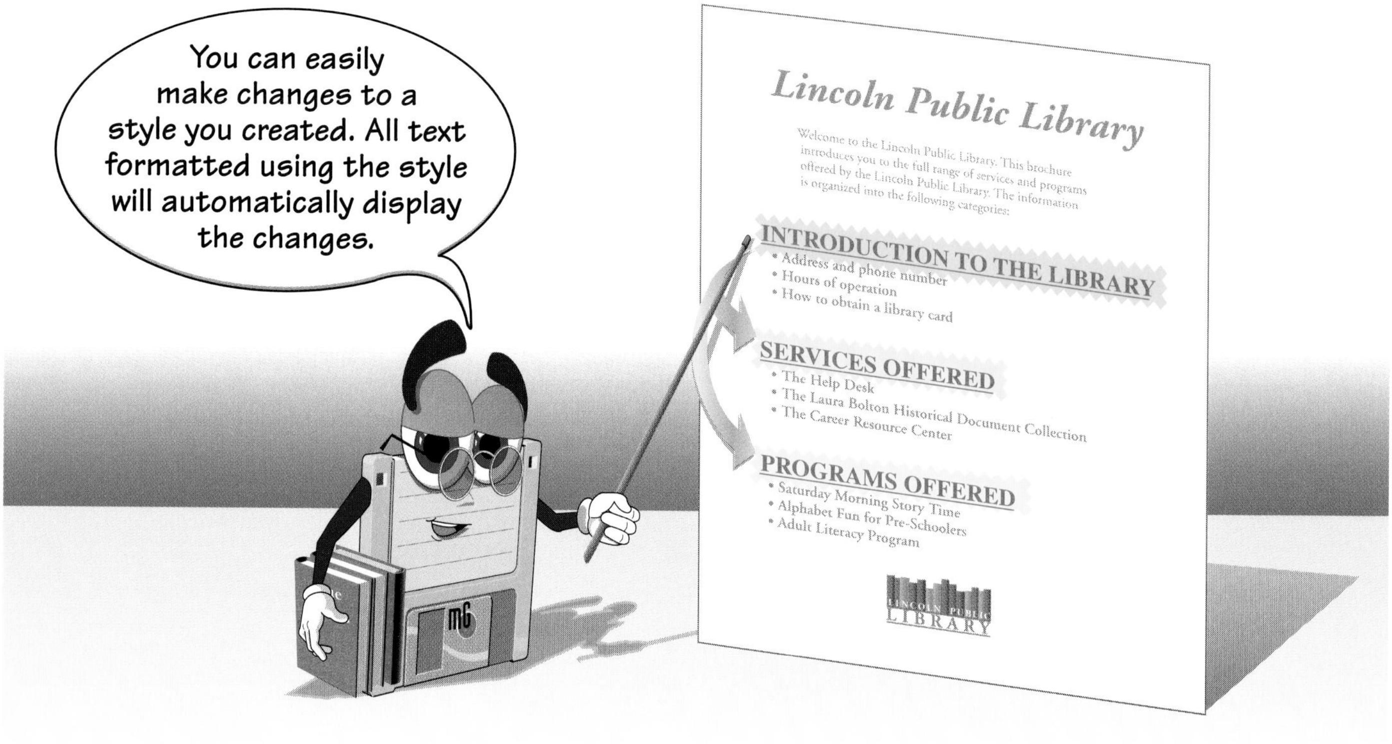

You can easily make changes to a style you created. All text formatted using the style will automatically display the changes.
Lincoln Public Library
Welcome to the Lincoln Public Library. This brochure introduces you to the full range of services and programs offered by the Lincoln Public Library. The information is organized into the following categories:
INTRODUCTION TO THE LIBRARY
• Address and phone number
• Hours of operation
• How to obtain a library card
SERVICES OFFERED
• The Help Desk
• The Laura Bolton Historical Document Collection
• The Career Resource Center
PROGRAMS OFFERED
• Saturday Morning Story Time
• Alphabet Fun for Pre-Schoolers
• Adult Literacy Program

CHANGE A STYLE

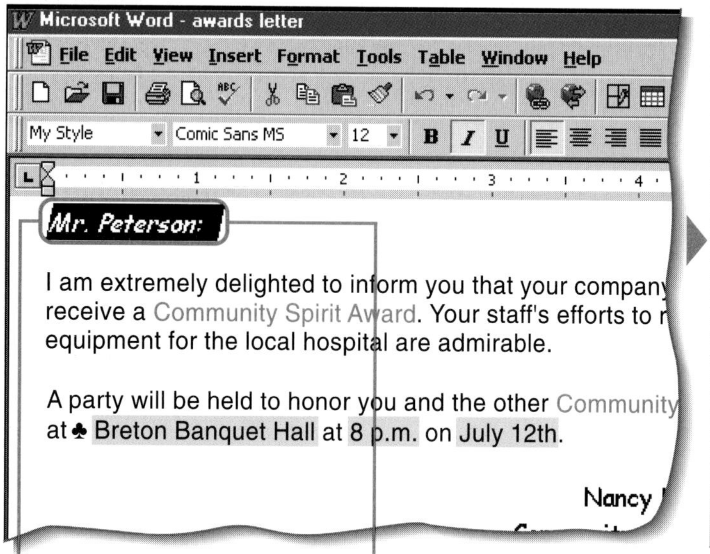

Microsoft Word - awards letter
File Edit View Insert Format Tools Table Window Help
My Style
Comic Sans MS
12
Mr. Peterson:
I am extremely delighted to inform you that your company
receive a Community Spirit Award. Your staff's efforts to r
equipment for the local hospital are admirable.
A party will be held to honor you and the other Community
at Breton Banquet Hall at 8 p.m. on July 12th.
Nancy

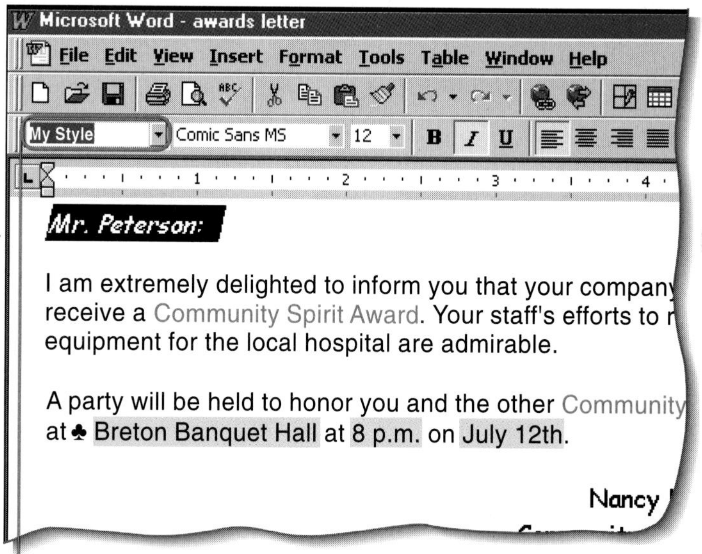

Microsoft Word - awards letter
File Edit View Insert Format Tools Table Window Help
My Style
Comic Sans MS
12
Mr. Peterson:
I am extremely delighted to inform you that your company
receive a Community Spirit Award. Your staff's efforts to r
equipment for the local hospital are admirable.
A party will be held to honor you and the other Community
at Breton Banquet Hall at 8 p.m. on July 12th.
Nancy

1 Select an area of text that is formatted with the style you want to change. To select text, refer to page 12.

2 Change the appearance of the text you selected.

Note: To change the appearance of text, refer to pages 78 to 81.

3 Move the mouse I over this area and then press the left mouse button.

4 Press **Enter** on your keyboard.

When would I want to change a style?

You may want to change an existing style to quickly change the appearance of a document. You can try several formats until the document appears the way you want.

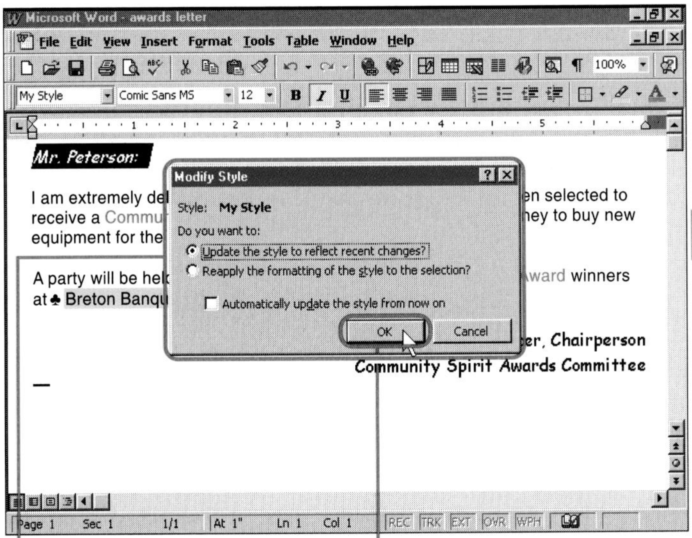
Microsoft Word - awards letter
File Edit View Insert Format Tools Table Window Help
My Style
Comic Sans MS
12
Mr. Peterson:
Modify Style
Style: My Style
Do you want to:
Update the style to reflect recent changes?
Reapply the formatting of the style to the selection?
Automatically update the style from now on
OK
Cancel
Community Spirit Awards Committee
Page 1 Sec 1 1/1 At 1" Ln 1 Col 1

■ The **Modify Style** dialog box appears.

5 To change the style, move the mouse over **OK** and then press the left mouse button.

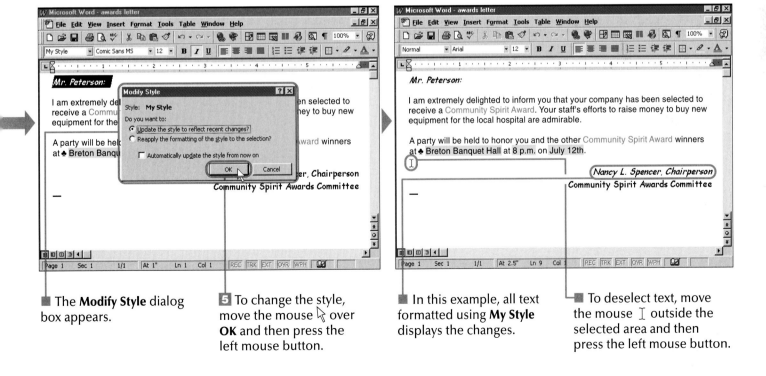

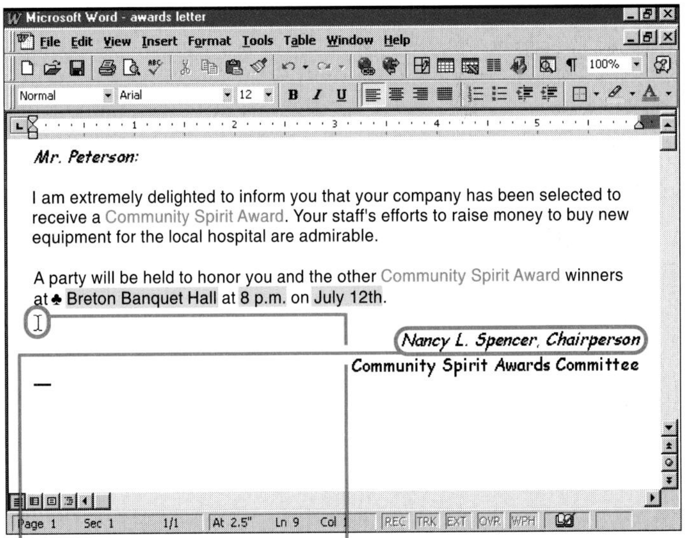
Microsoft Word - awards letter
File Edit View Insert Format Tools Table Window Help
Normal
Arial
12
Mr. Peterson:
I am extremely delighted to inform you that your company has been selected to receive a Community Spirit Award. Your staff's efforts to raise money to buy new equipment for the local hospital are admirable.
A party will be held to honor you and the other Community Spirit Award winners at ♣ Breton Banquet Hall at 8 p.m. on July 12th.
Nancy L. Spencer, Chairperson
Community Spirit Awards Committee
Page 1 Sec 1 1/1 At 2.5" Ln 9

■ In this example, all text formatted using **My Style** displays the changes.

■ To deselect text, move the mouse outside the selected area and then press the left mouse button.

When was the last time you heard someone boast about the trophy large mouth bass they reeled in on their last fishing outing? Have you always wanted to go fishing but didn't know where to start? Whether you assume this popular sport is as easy as finding a pond and plopping yourself down with a line, or whether you are intimidated by the large array of rods, reels, baits, lures and fish, these few basic guidelines will help you get started.

The choices in the world of fishing are enormous. Do you want to fish for fun, for trophy or for supper? Are you looking for a particular type of fish or for the most convenient location? Are you handy with a boat or more comfortable sticking to shore?

No matter what your preferences are, try to choose a quiet location in the cool still of the early morning or evening. Make sure you are aware of the weather forecast before you set out so you can dress appropriately. Remember that temperatures are often cooler by the water, with different wind factors.[1] Don't be discouraged by light rain since some of the best fishing can be done in the rain! And don't forget to pack plenty to eat for an enjoyable outing.

Some good guides to fishing spots in your area can be obtained from local tourism information.[2]

[1] Bob Jones, Coastal Weather Conditions. (Maine: Devries, 1995) 104.

[2] Kathy MacDonald, Fishing in North America. (Montana: Matway, 1996)

3

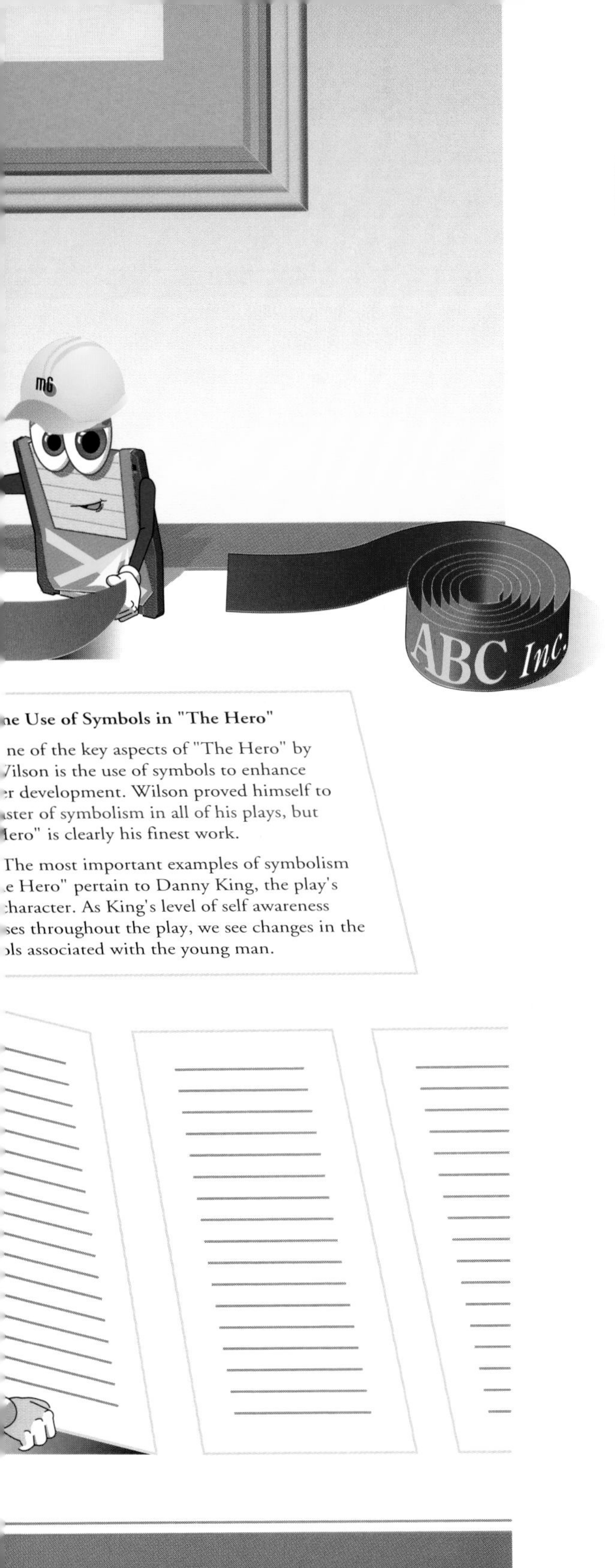
ABC Inc.
ne Use of Symbols in "The Hero"
ne of the key aspects of "The Hero" by
/ilson is the use of symbols to enhance
er development. Wilson proved himself to
ster of symbolism in all of his plays, but
lero" is clearly his finest work.
The most important examples of symbolism
e Hero" pertain to Danny King, the play's
character. As King's level of self awareness
ses throughout the play, we see changes in the
ols associated with the young man.

CHAPTER 6

FORMAT PAGES

Unsure of how to format your pages to include such things as footnotes or columns? Confused by changing your margins or paper size? Do not be intimidated—Word allows you to use many sophisticated formatting options with ease.

ADD PAGE NUMBERS

ADD PAGE NUMBERS

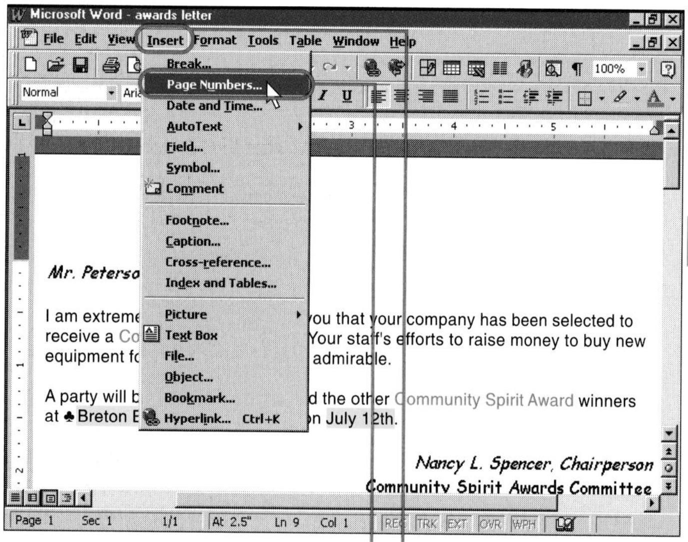

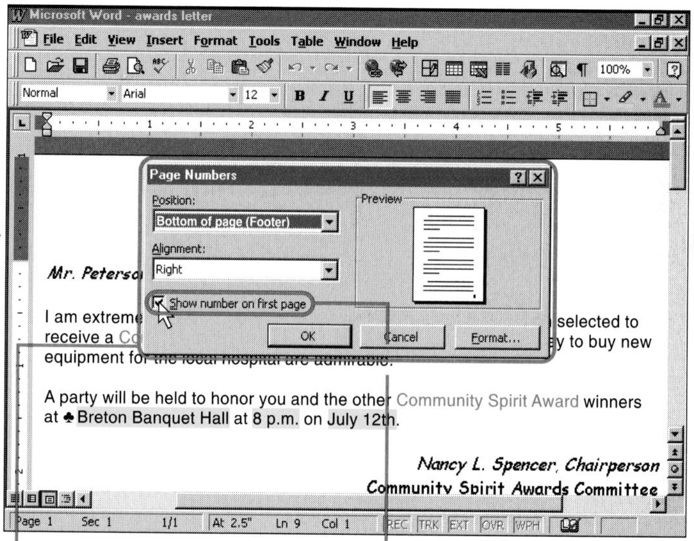

1 Display the document in the Page Layout view. To change the view, refer to page 32.

Note: Word does not display page numbers in the Normal view.

2 Move the mouse over **Insert** and then press the left mouse button.

3 Move the mouse over **Page Numbers** and then press the left mouse button.

■ The **Page Numbers** dialog box appears.

4 To hide the page number on the first page of the document, move the mouse over this option and then press the left mouse button (☑ changes to ☐).

Note: This option is useful if the first page of the document is a title page.

Will Word adjust the page numbers if I change my document?

If you add, remove or rearrange text in your document, Word will automatically adjust the page numbers for you.

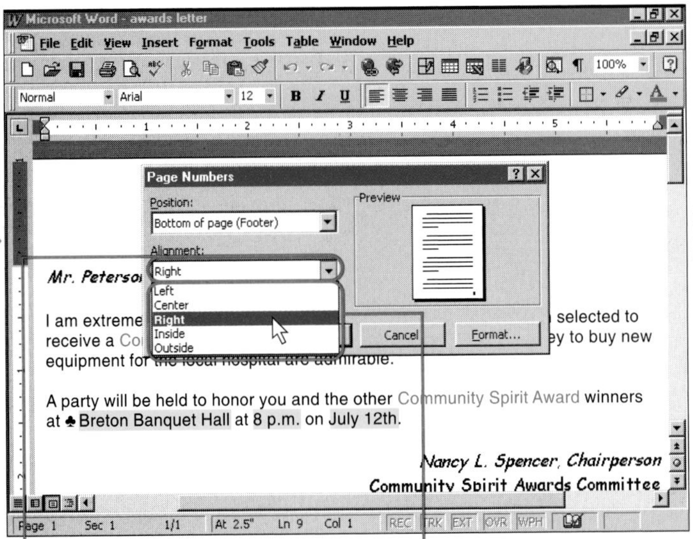

5 To select an alignment for the page numbers, move the mouse over this area and then press the left mouse button.

6 Move the mouse over the alignment you want to use and then press the left mouse button.

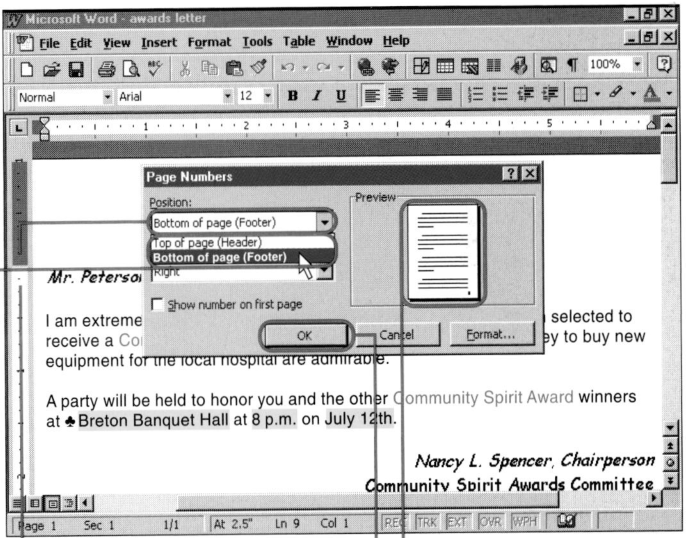

7 To select a position for the page numbers, move the mouse over this area and then press the left mouse button.

8 Move the mouse over the position where you want the page numbers to appear and then press the left mouse button.

■ This area displays a sample of the page numbering.

9 Move the mouse over **OK** and then press the left mouse button.

ADD FOOTNOTES

Word ensures that the footnote text always appears on the same page as the footnote number.

ADD FOOTNOTES

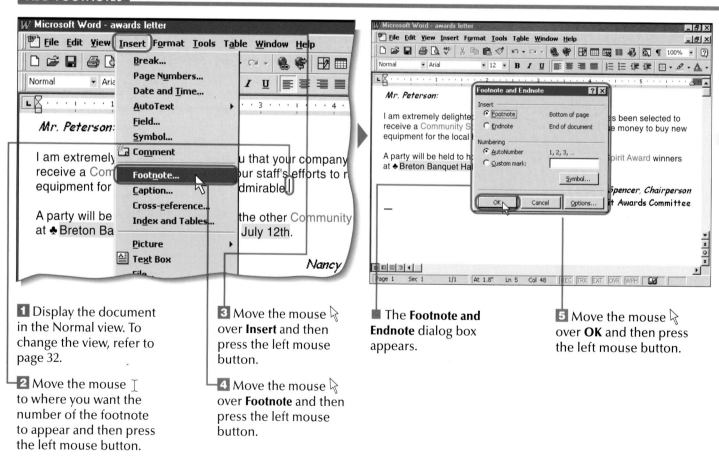

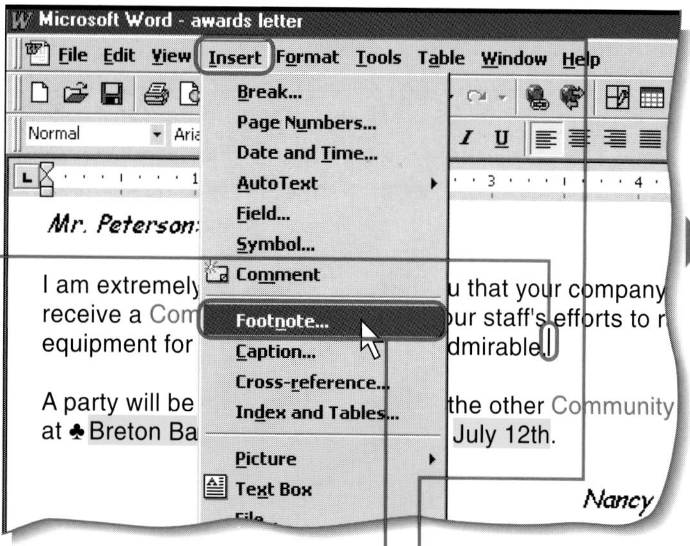

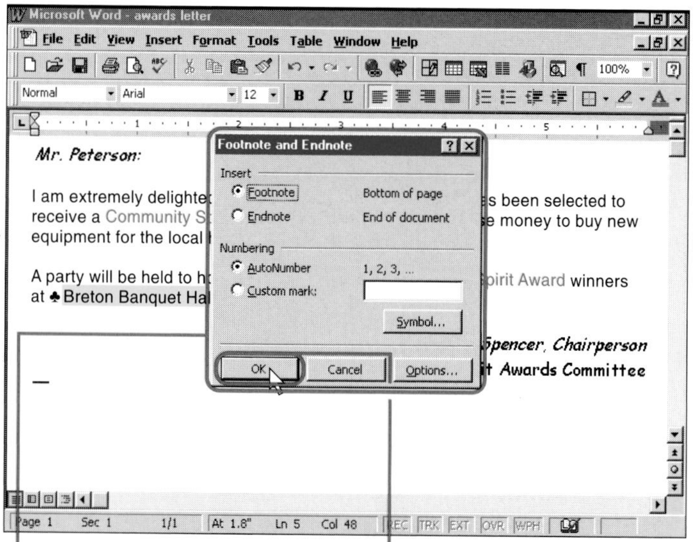

1 Display the document in the Normal view. To change the view, refer to page 32.

2 Move the mouse I to where you want the number of the footnote to appear and then press the left mouse button.

3 Move the mouse over **Insert** and then press the left mouse button.

4 Move the mouse over **Footnote** and then press the left mouse button.

■ The **Footnote and Endnote** dialog box appears.

5 Move the mouse over **OK** and then press the left mouse button.

Will Word adjust the footnote numbers if I add or remove footnotes?

If you add or remove footnotes in your document, Word will automatically renumber the footnotes for you.

1
2
3

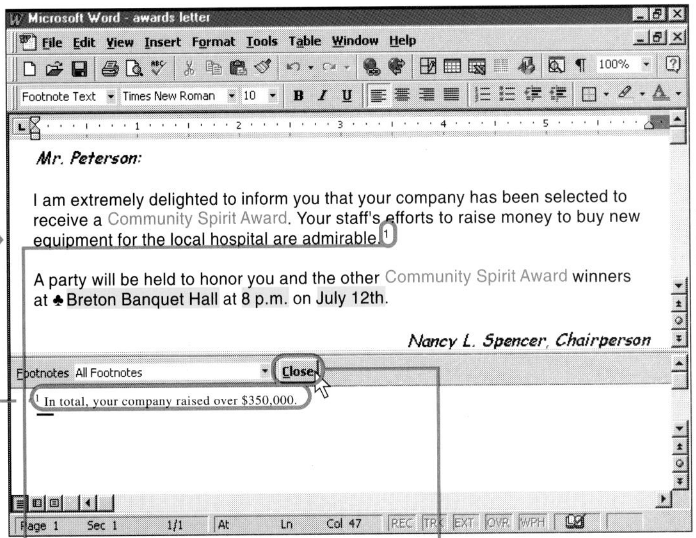
Microsoft Word - awards letter
File Edit View Insert Format Tools Table Window Help
Footnote Text
Times New Roman
10
Mr. Peterson:
I am extremely delighted to inform you that your company has been selected to receive a Community Spirit Award. Your staff's efforts to raise money to buy new equipment for the local hospital are admirable.1
A party will be held to honor you and the other Community Spirit Award winners at ♣Breton Banquet Hall at 8 p.m. on July 12th.
Nancy L. Spencer, Chairperson
Footnotes All Footnotes
Close
1 In total, your company raised over $350,000.
Page 1 Sec 1 1/1 At Ln Col 47 REC TRK EXT OVR WPH

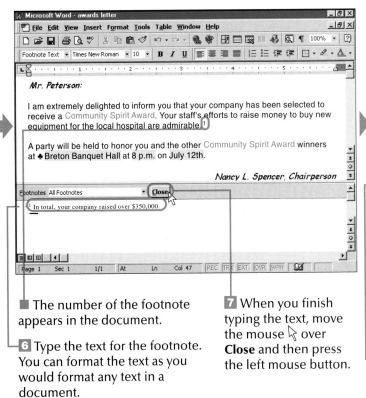

■ The number of the footnote appears in the document.

6 Type the text for the footnote. You can format the text as you would format any text in a document.

Note: To format text, refer to pages 72 to 107.

7 When you finish typing the text, move the mouse over **Close** and then press the left mouse button.

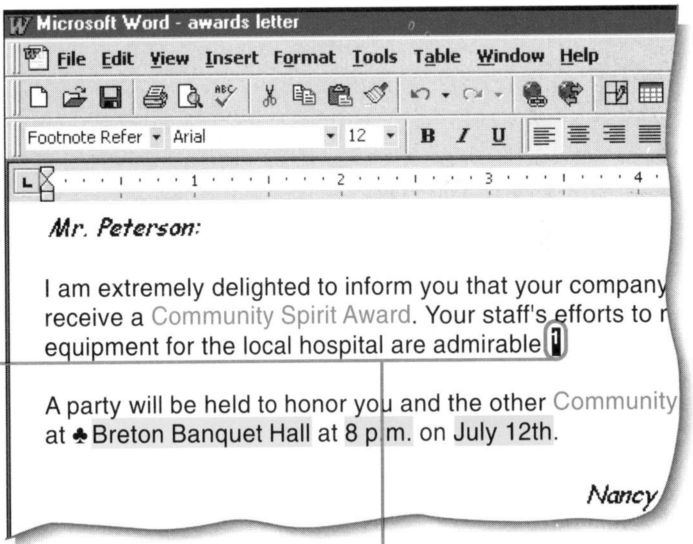
Microsoft Word - awards letter
File Edit View Insert Format Tools Table Window Help
Footnote Refer
Arial
12
Mr. Peterson:
I am extremely delighted to inform you that your company
receive a Community Spirit Award. Your staff's efforts to r
equipment for the local hospital are admirable.1
A party will be held to honor you and the other Community
at ♣Breton Banquet Hall at 8 p.m. on July 12th.
Nancy

■ The footnote text disappears from the screen.

■ To redisplay the footnote text so you can edit the footnote, move the mouse I over the number of the footnote and then quickly press the left mouse button twice.

DELETE A FOOTNOTE

1 Select the number of the footnote in the document. To select text, refer to page 12.

2 Press **Delete** on your keyboard.

ADD A HEADER AND FOOTER

■ A header appears at the top of each page.

■ A footer appears at the bottom of each page.

ADD A HEADER AND FOOTER

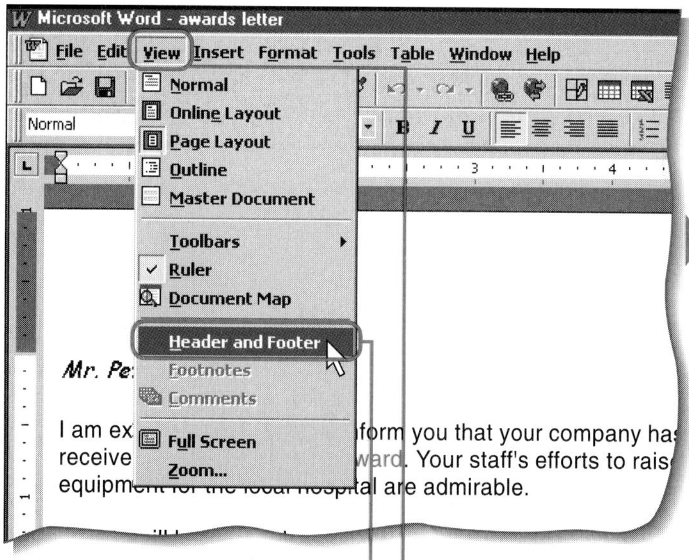

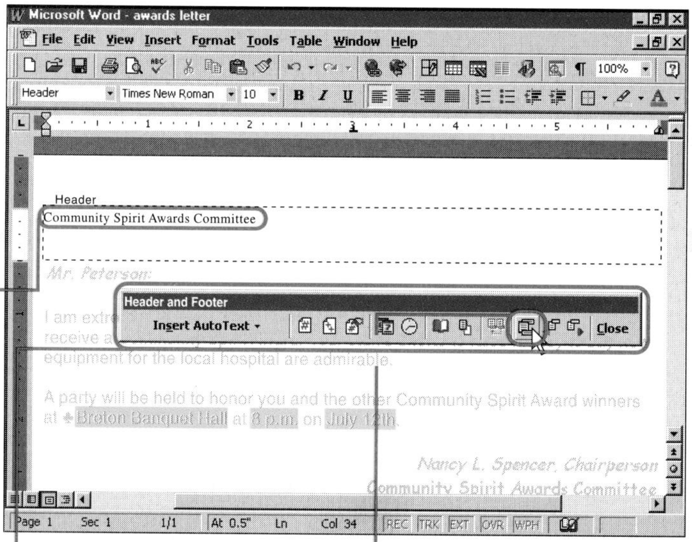

1 Display the document in the Page Layout view. To change the view, refer to page 32.

Note: Word does not display headers and footers in the Normal view.

2 Move the mouse over **View** and then press the left mouse button.

3 Move the mouse over **Header and Footer** and then press the left mouse button.

■ Word displays the **Header and Footer** toolbar and dims the text in the document.

4 To create a header, type the header text. You can format the text as you would format any text in a document.

5 To create a footer, move the mouse over the footer button and then press the left mouse button.

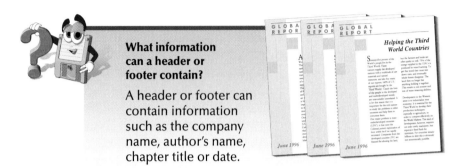

What information can a header or footer contain?

A header or footer can contain information such as the company name, author's name, chapter title or date.

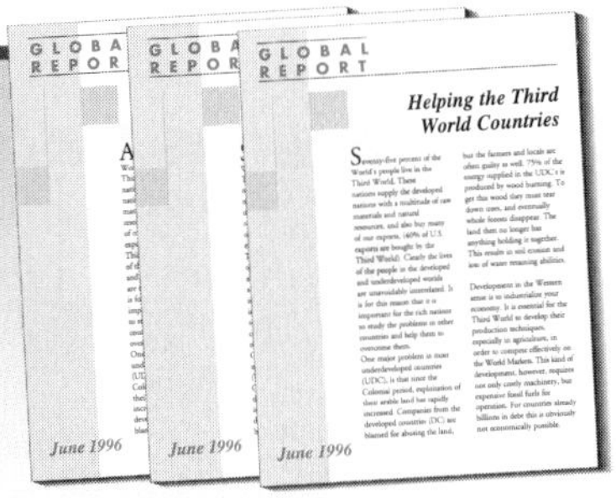

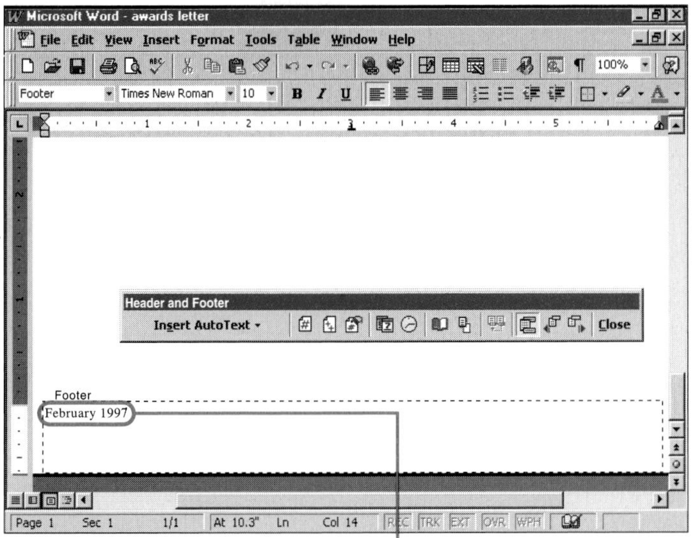

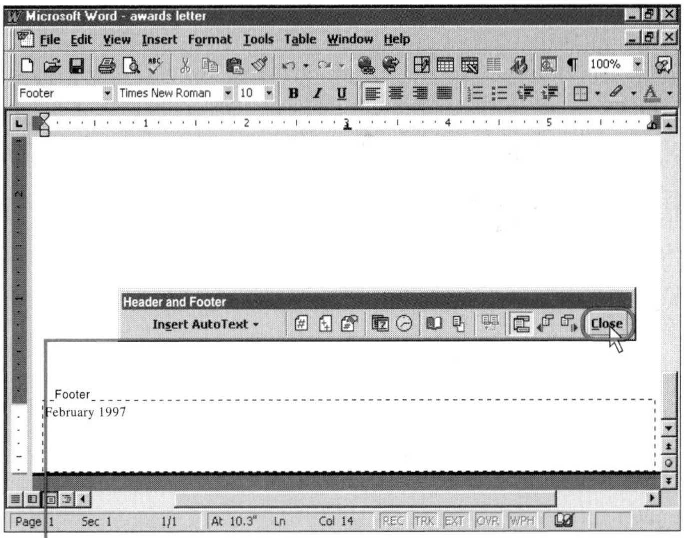

■ The **Footer** area appears.

Note: To return to the header area at any time, repeat step 5.

6 Type the footer text. You can format the text as you would format any text in a document.

Note: To format text, refer to pages 72 to 107.

7 When you have finished creating the header and footer, move the mouse over **Close** and then press the left mouse button.

EDIT A HEADER OR FOOTER

1 To edit a header or footer, repeat steps 1 to 7.

INSERT A PAGE BREAK

If you want to start a new page at a specific place in your document, you can insert a page break. A page break shows where one page ends and another begins.

INSERT A PAGE BREAK

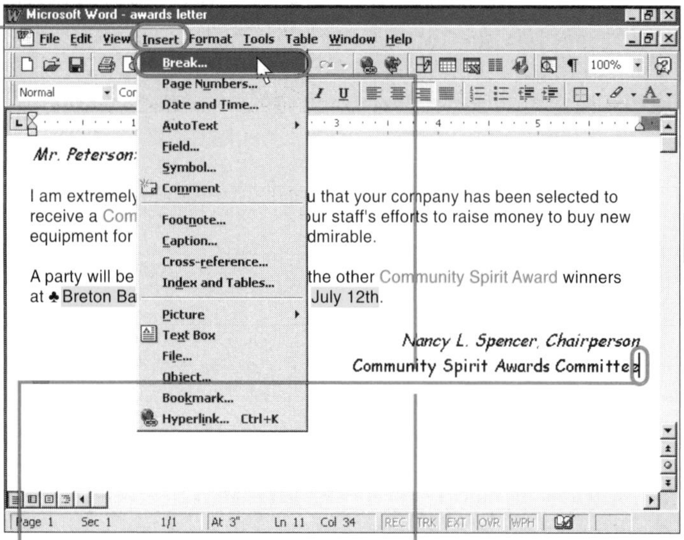

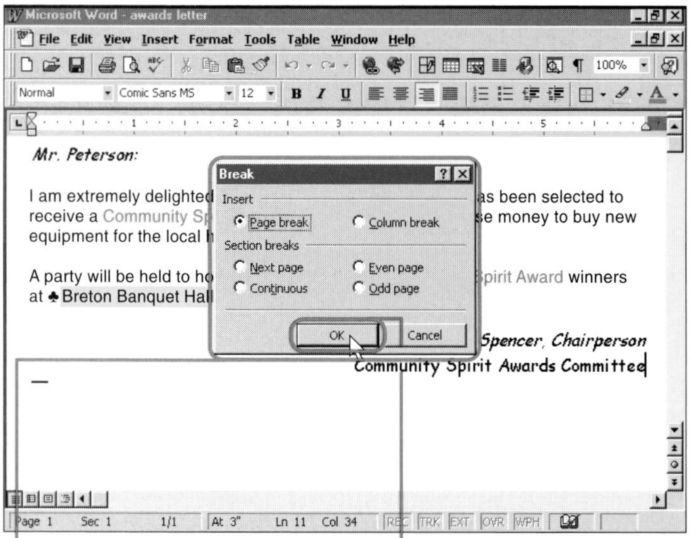

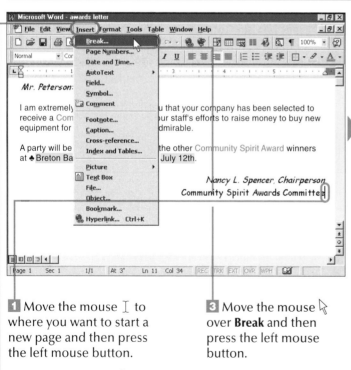

1 Move the mouse I to where you want to start a new page and then press the left mouse button.

2 Move the mouse over **Insert** and then press the left mouse button.

3 Move the mouse over **Break** and then press the left mouse button.

■ The **Break** dialog box appears.

4 Move the mouse over **OK** and then press the left mouse button.

Will Word ever insert page breaks automatically?

When you fill a page with text, Word automatically starts a new page by inserting a page break for you.

The Use of Symbols in "The Hero"
One of the key aspects of "The Hero" by James Wilson is the use of symbols to enhance character development. Wilson proved himself to be a master of symbolism in all of his plays, but "The Hero" is clearly his finest work.
The most important examples of symbolism in "The Hero" pertain to Danny King, the play's main character. As King's level of self awareness increases throughout the play, we see changes in the symbols associated with the young man.
In the play's opening scene, King is a first-year college student filled with optimism about the future. We see this optimism reflected in witty dialogue between King and his friends. We also see this optimism reflected in the symbols associated with him.

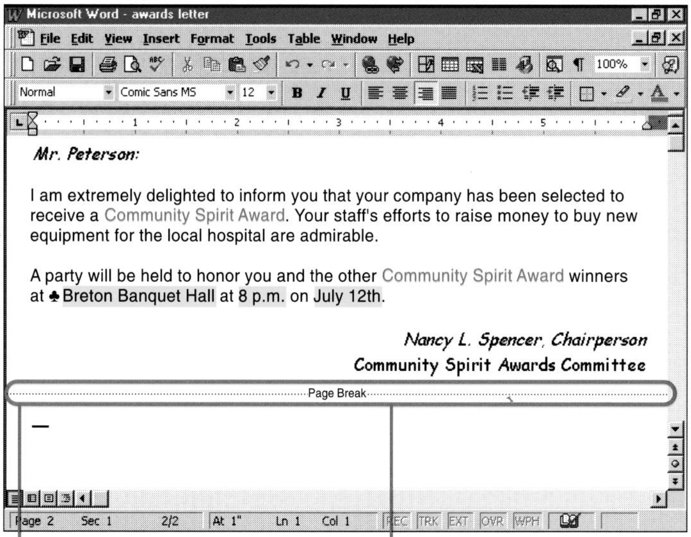
Microsoft Word - awards letter
Mr. Peterson:
I am extremely delighted to inform you that your company has been selected to receive a Community Spirit Award. Your staff's efforts to raise money to buy new equipment for the local hospital are admirable.
A party will be held to honor you and the other Community Spirit Award winners at Breton Banquet Hall at 8 p.m. on July 12th.
Nancy L. Spencer, Chairperson
Community Spirit Awards Committee
Page Break

■ If the document is displayed in the Normal view, a line with the words **Page Break** appears across the screen.

■ The **Page Break** line shows where one page ends and another begins. The line will not appear when you print the document.

REMOVE A PAGE BREAK

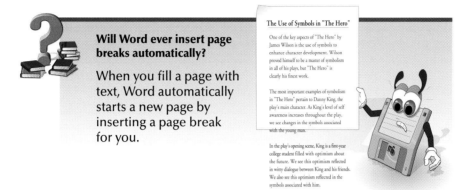

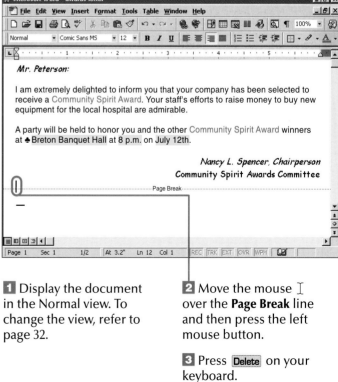

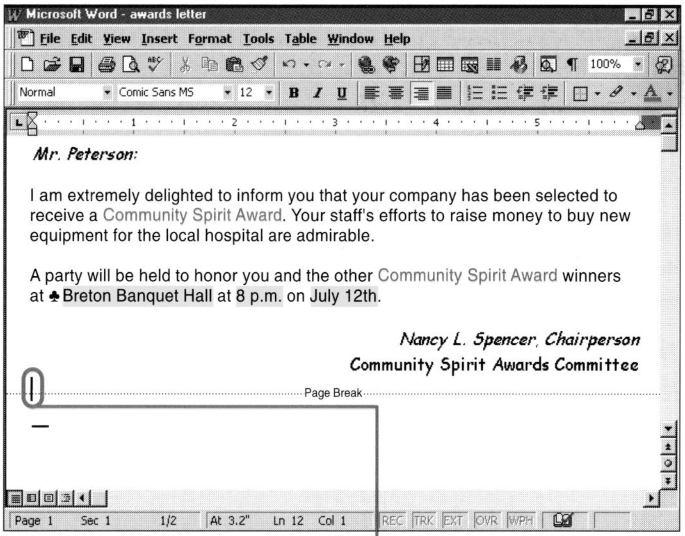
Microsoft Word - awards letter
Mr. Peterson:
I am extremely delighted to inform you that your company has been selected to receive a Community Spirit Award. Your staff's efforts to raise money to buy new equipment for the local hospital are admirable.
A party will be held to honor you and the other Community Spirit Award winners at Breton Banquet Hall at 8 p.m. on July 12th.
Nancy L. Spencer, Chairperson
Community Spirit Awards Committee
Page Break

1 Display the document in the Normal view. To change the view, refer to page 32.

2 Move the mouse I over the **Page Break** line and then press the left mouse button.

3 Press Delete on your keyboard.

INSERT A SECTION BREAK

You need to divide a document into sections to change margins, create columns or vertically center text for only part of your document.

INSERT A SECTION BREAK

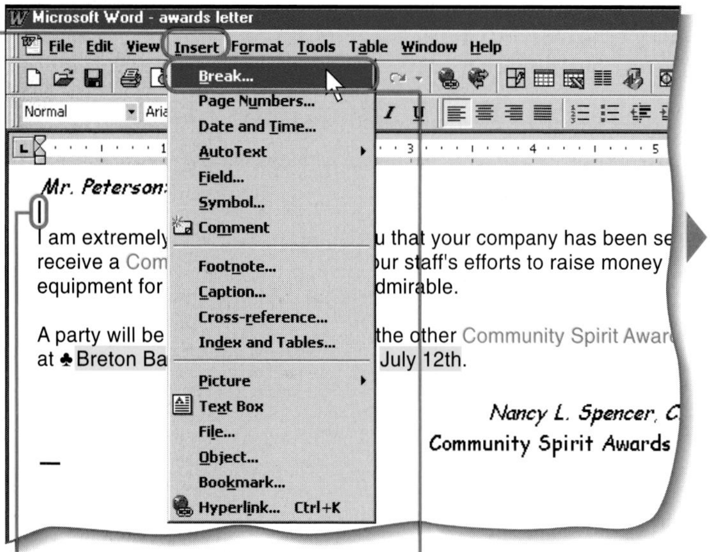

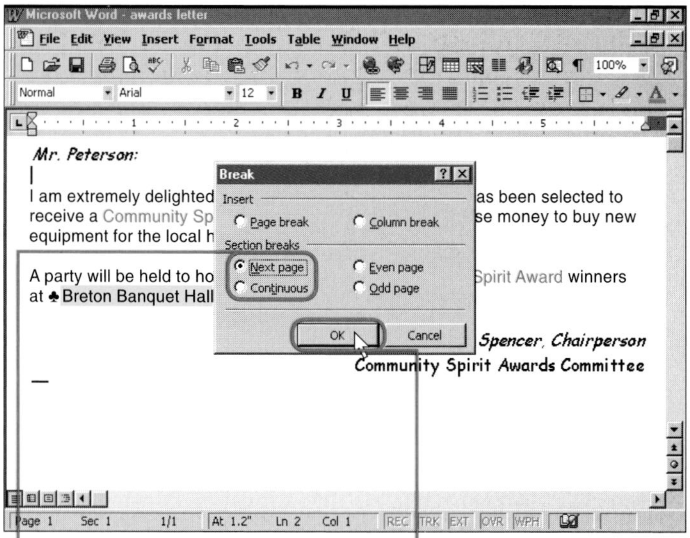

1 Move the mouse I to where you want to start a new section and then press the left mouse button.

2 Move the mouse over **Insert** and then press the left mouse button.

3 Move the mouse over **Break** and then press the left mouse button.

■ The **Break** dialog box appears.

4 Move the mouse over one of the following options and then press the left mouse button (○ changes to ◉).

Next page - Creates a new section on a new page.

Continuous - Creates a new section on the current page.

5 Move the mouse over **OK** and then press the left mouse button.

If I remove a section break will the appearance of my document change?

When you remove a section break, the text above the break assumes the appearance of the following section.

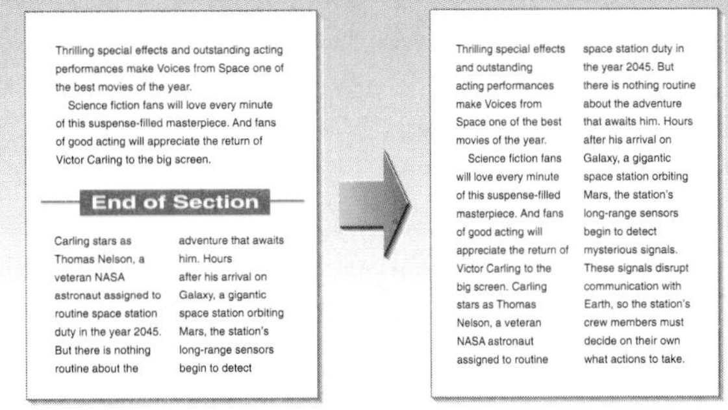
Thrilling special effects and outstanding acting performances make Voices from Space one of the best movies of the year.
Science fiction fans will love every minute of this suspense-filled masterpiece. And fans of good acting will appreciate the return of Victor Carling to the big screen.
End of Section
Carling stars as Thomas Nelson, a veteran NASA astronaut assigned to routine space station duty in the year 2045. But there is nothing routine about the adventure that awaits him. Hours after his arrival on Galaxy, a gigantic space station orbiting Mars, the station's long-range sensors begin to detect
Thrilling special effects and outstanding acting performances make Voices from Space one of the best movies of the year.
Science fiction fans will love every minute of this suspense-filled masterpiece. And fans of good acting will appreciate the return of Victor Carling to the big screen. Carling stars as Thomas Nelson, a veteran NASA astronaut assigned to routine space station duty in the year 2045. But there is nothing routine about the adventure that awaits him. Hours after his arrival on Galaxy, a gigantic space station orbiting Mars, the station's long-range sensors begin to detect mysterious signals. These signals disrupt communication with Earth, so the station's crew members must decide on their own what actions to take.

REMOVE A SECTION BREAK

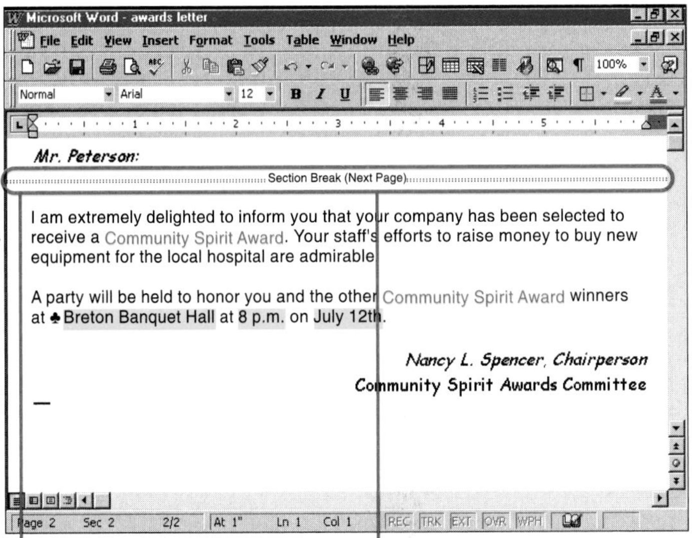
Microsoft Word - awards letter
File Edit View Insert Format Tools Table Window Help
Normal Arial 12
Mr. Peterson:
Section Break (Next Page)
I am extremely delighted to inform you that your company has been selected to receive a Community Spirit Award. Your staff's efforts to raise money to buy new equipment for the local hospital are admirable.
A party will be held to honor you and the other Community Spirit Award winners at Breton Banquet Hall at 8 p.m. on July 12th.
Nancy L. Spencer, Chairperson
Community Spirit Awards Committee
Page 2 Sec 2 2/2 At 1" Ln 1 Col 1

If the document is displayed in the Normal view, a double line with the words **Section Break** appears across the screen.

The **Section Break** line shows where one section ends and another begins. The line will not appear when you print the document.

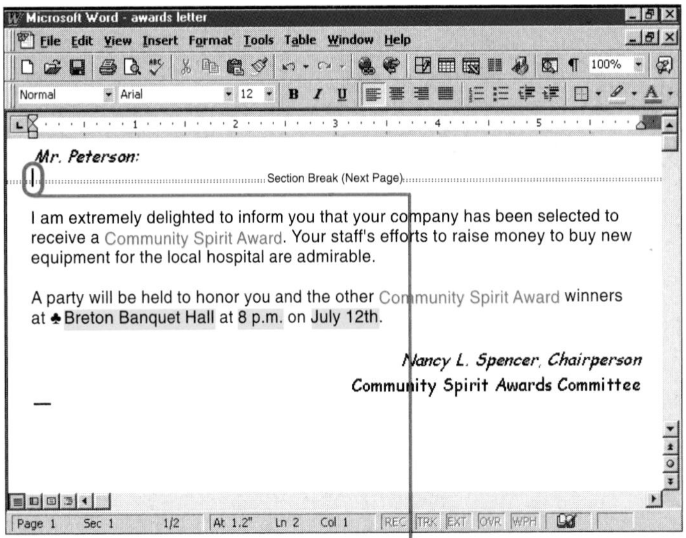
Microsoft Word - awards letter
File Edit View Insert Format Tools Table Window Help
Normal Arial 12
Mr. Peterson:
Section Break (Next Page)
I am extremely delighted to inform you that your company has been selected to receive a Community Spirit Award. Your staff's efforts to raise money to buy new equipment for the local hospital are admirable.
A party will be held to honor you and the other Community Spirit Award winners at Breton Banquet Hall at 8 p.m. on July 12th.
Nancy L. Spencer, Chairperson
Community Spirit Awards Committee
Page 1 Sec 1 1/2 At 1.2" Ln 2 Col 1

1 Display the document in the Normal view. To change the view, refer to page 32.

2 Move the mouse I over the **Section Break** line and then press the left mouse button.

3 Press Delete on your keyboard.

CENTER TEXT ON A PAGE

CENTER TEXT ON A PAGE

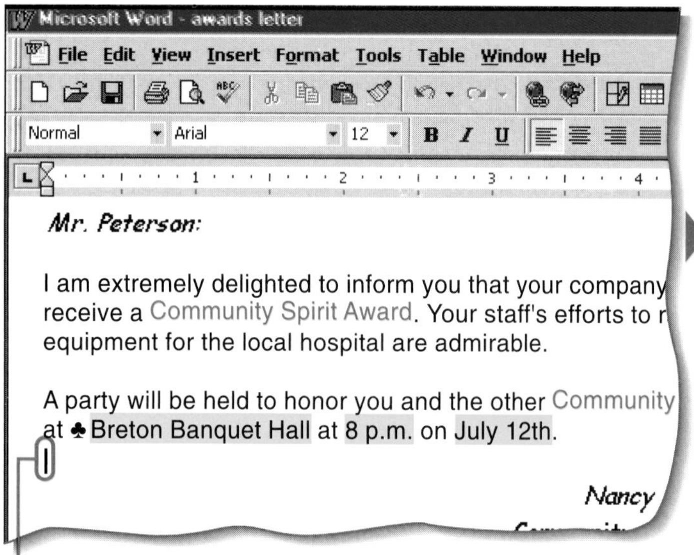

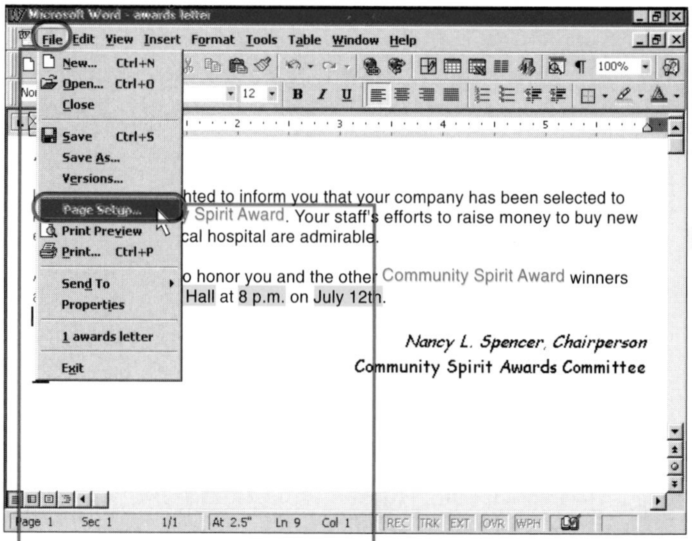

1 Move the mouse I anywhere over the document or section you want to vertically center and then press the left mouse button.

Note: To vertically center only some of the text in a document, you must divide the document into sections. To divide a document into sections, refer to page 118.

2 Move the mouse over **File** and then press the left mouse button.

3 Move the mouse over **Page Setup** and then press the left mouse button.

■ The **Page Setup** dialog box appears.

How can I see what text centered on a page will look like when printed?

You can use the Print Preview feature to display a page on your screen. This lets you see how the page will look when printed.

Note: For information on using Print Preview, refer to page 132.

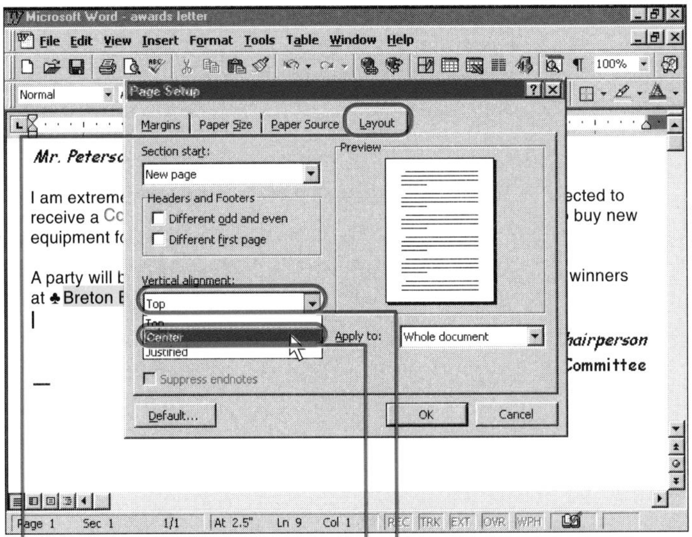

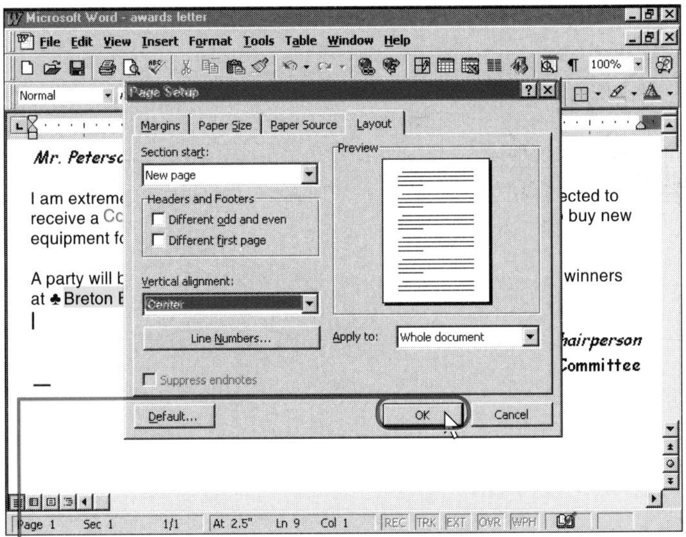

4 Move the mouse over the **Layout** tab and then press the left mouse button.

5 Move the mouse over this area and then press the left mouse button.

6 Move the mouse over **Center** and then press the left mouse button.

7 Move the mouse over **OK** and then press the left mouse button.

REMOVE CENTERING

■ Perform steps 1 to 7, selecting **Top** in step 6.

CHANGE MARGINS

A margin is the amount of space between text and the edge of your paper. You can easily change the margins to suit your document.

Changing margins lets you accommodate letterhead and other specialty paper.

CHANGE MARGINS

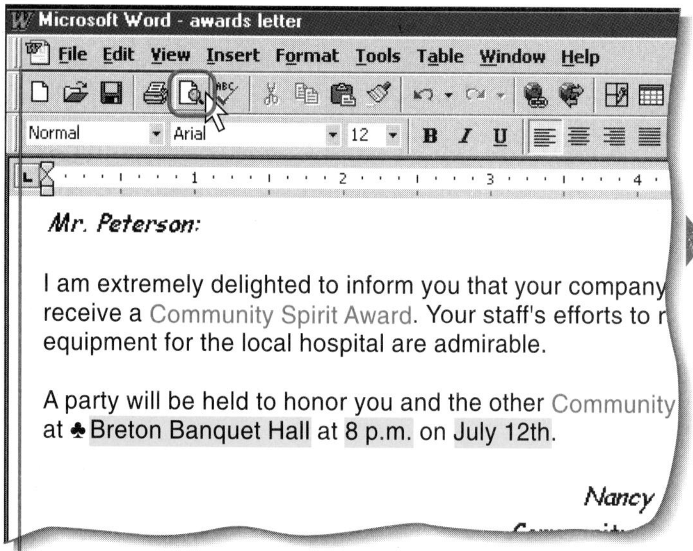

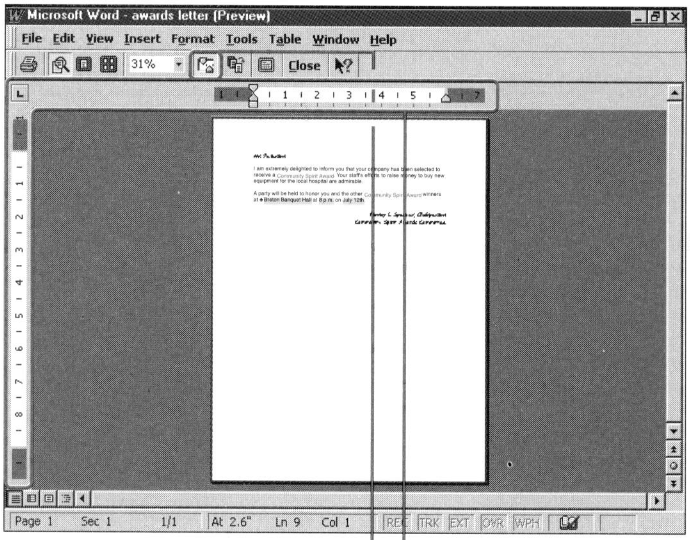

1 To change the margins for the entire document, move the mouse over and then press the left mouse button.

Note: To change the margins for only part of your document, refer to the top of page 123.

■ The document appears in the Print Preview window. For more information on using Print Preview, refer to page 132.

■ This area displays the ruler.

■ If the ruler is not displayed, move the mouse over and then press the left mouse button.

How can I change the margins for only part of my document?

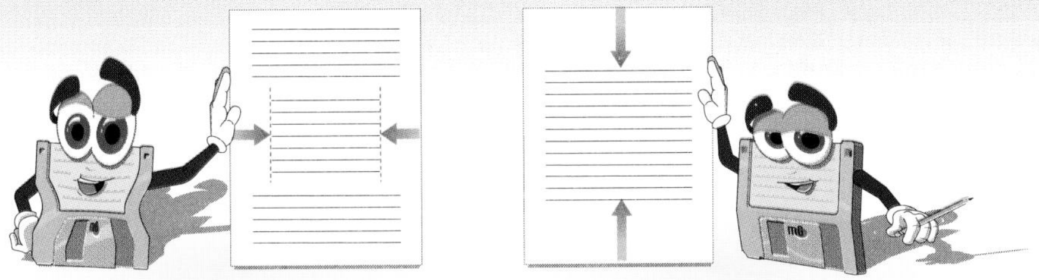

If you want to change the left and right margins for only part of your document, change the indentation of paragraphs. To indent paragraphs, refer to page 92.

If you want to change the top and bottom margins for only part of your document, you must divide the document into sections. To divide a document into sections, refer to page 118.

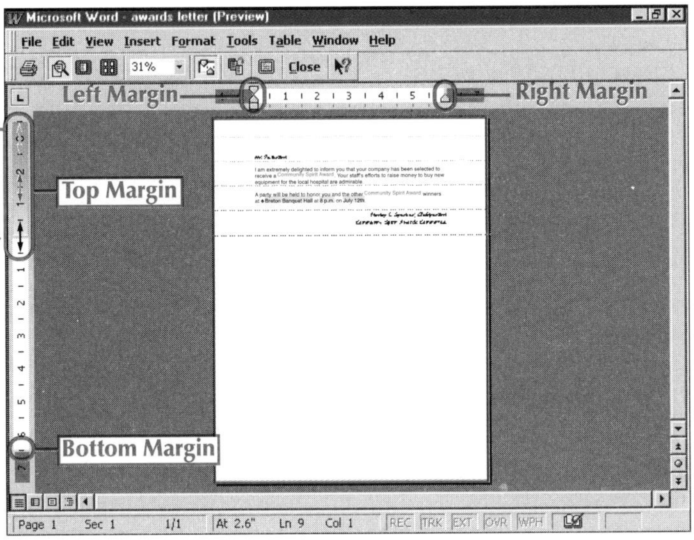

2 Move the mouse over the margin you want to move (changes to ↕ or ↔) and then press and hold down the left mouse button as you move the margin to a new location.

■ A line shows the new location.

Note: To view the exact measurement of a margin, press and hold down **Alt** *on your keyboard as you perform step* ***2****.*

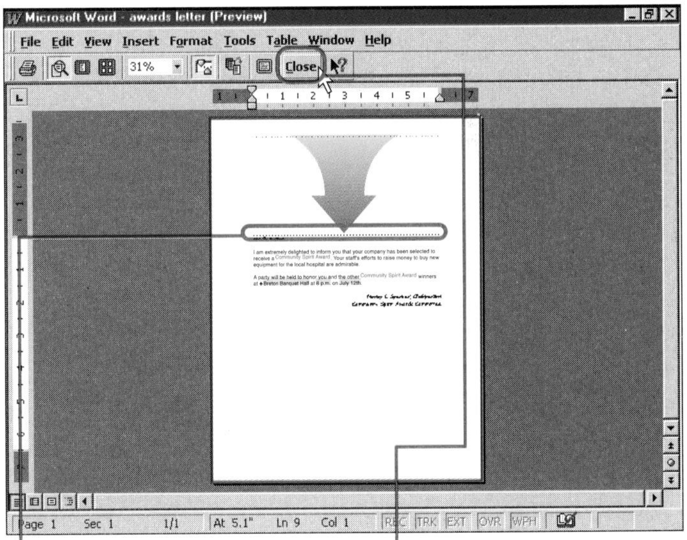

3 Release the left mouse button and the margin moves to the new location.

4 Repeat steps **2** and **3** for each margin you want to move.

5 To close the Print Preview window, move the mouse over **Close** and then press the left mouse button.

CHANGE PAPER SIZE

Word sets each page in your document to print on letter-sized paper. If you want to use a different paper size, you can change this setting.

CHANGE PAPER SIZE

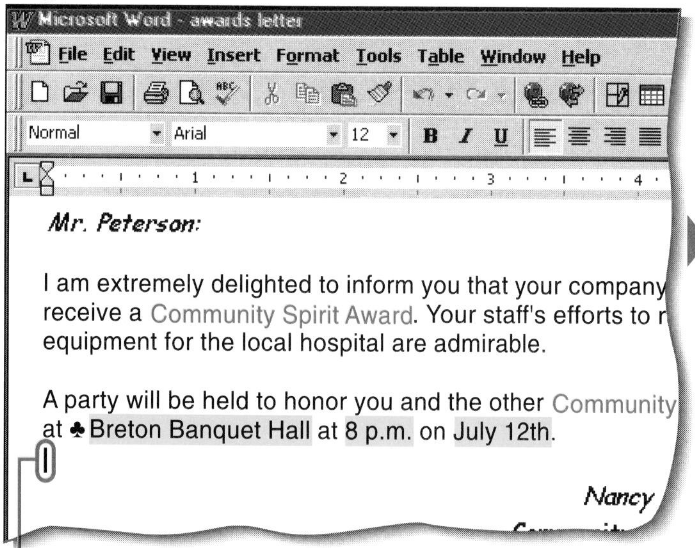

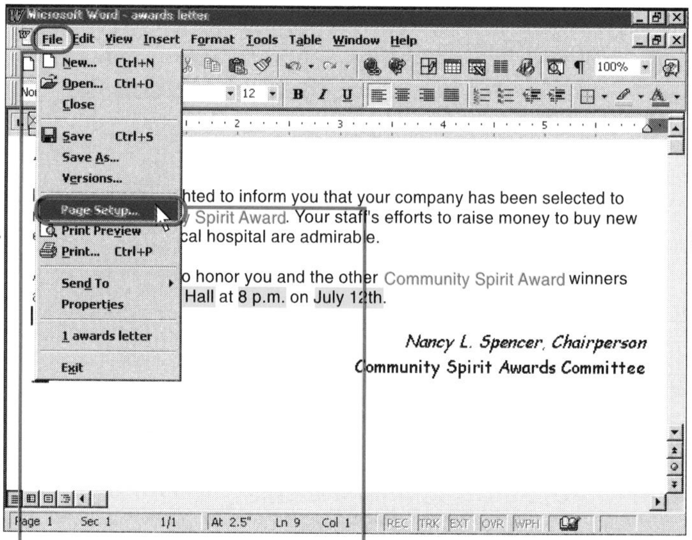

1 Move the mouse I anywhere over the document or section you want to print on a different paper size and then press the left mouse button.

Note: To change the paper size for only part of your document, you must divide the document into sections. To divide a document into sections, refer to page 118.

2 Move the mouse over **File** and then press the left mouse button.

3 Move the mouse over **Page Setup** and then press the left mouse button.

■ The **Page Setup** dialog box appears.

What paper sizes can I use?

The paper sizes listed in the **Page Setup** dialog box depend on the printer you are using.

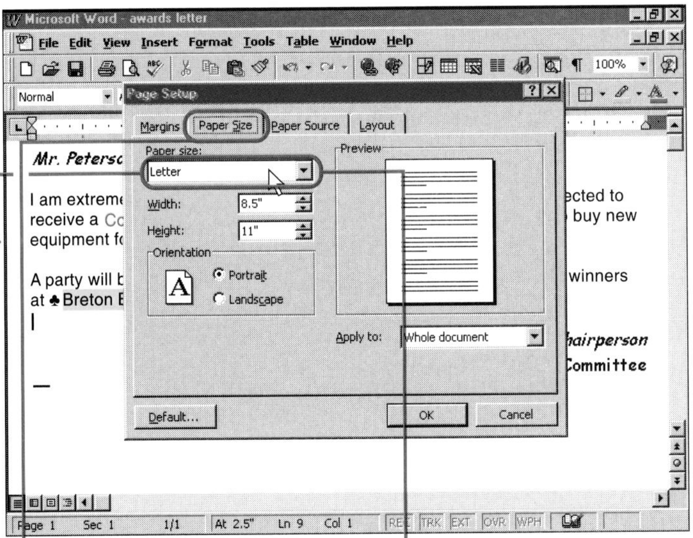

4 Move the mouse over the **Paper Size** tab and then press the left mouse button.

■ This area displays the current paper size.

5 To display a list of the paper sizes supported by your printer, move the mouse over this area and then press the left mouse button.

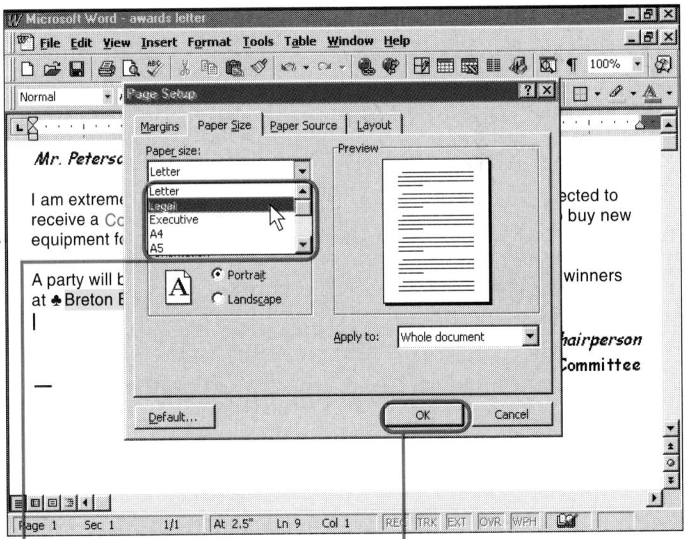

6 Move the mouse over the paper size you want to use and then press the left mouse button.

7 Move the mouse over **OK** and then press the left mouse button.

CHANGE PAGE ORIENTATION

You can change the orientation of pages in your document.
PORTRAIT
One of the key aspects of "The Hero" by James Wilson is the use of symbols to enhance character development. Wilson proved himself to be a master of symbolism in all of his plays, but "The Hero" is clearly his finest work.
The most important examples of symbolism in "The Hero" pertain to Danny King, the play's main character. As King's level of self awareness increases throughout the play, we see changes in the symbols associated with the young man.
LANDSCAPE
One of the key aspects of "The Hero" by James Wilson is the use of symbols to enhance character development. Wilson proved himself to be a master of symbolism in all of his plays, but "The Hero" is clearly his finest work.
The most important examples of symbolism in "The Hero" pertain to Danny King, the play's main character. As King's level of self awareness increases throughout the play, we see changes in the symbols associated with the young man.

CHANGE PAGE ORIENTATION

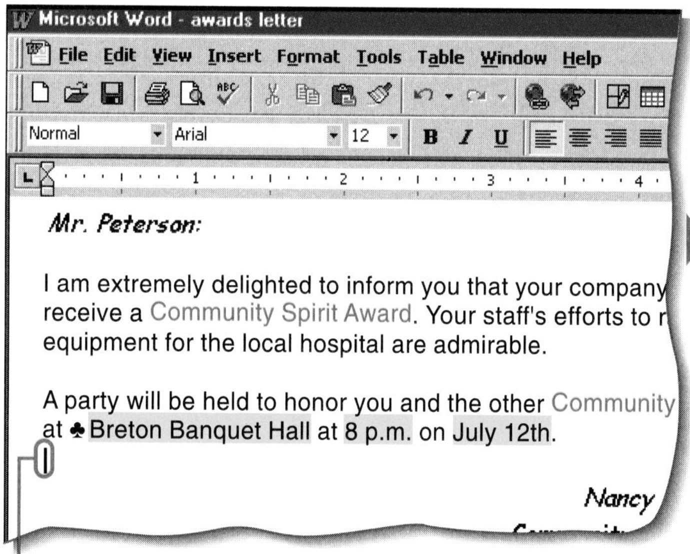
Microsoft Word - awards letter
File Edit View Insert Format Tools Table Window Help
Normal
Arial
12
Mr. Peterson:
I am extremely delighted to inform you that your company
receive a Community Spirit Award. Your staff's efforts to r
equipment for the local hospital are admirable.
A party will be held to honor you and the other Community
at ♣ Breton Banquet Hall at 8 p.m. on July 12th.
Nancy

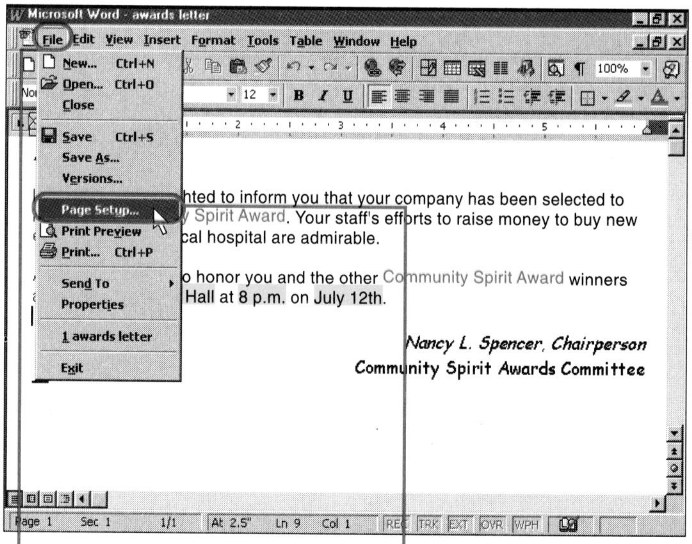
Microsoft Word - awards letter
File Edit View Insert Format Tools Table Window Help
New... Ctrl+N
Open... Ctrl+O
Close
Save Ctrl+S
Save As...
Versions...
Page Setup...
Print Preview
Print... Ctrl+P
Send To
Properties
1 awards letter
Exit
Nancy L. Spencer, Chairperson
Community Spirit Awards Committee
Page 1 Sec 1 1/1 At 2.5" Ln 9 Col 1

1 Move the mouse anywhere over the document or section you want to change to a different page orientation and then press the left mouse button.

Note: To change the page orientation for only part of your document, you must divide the document into sections. To divide a document into sections, refer to page 118.

2 Move the mouse over **File** and then press the left mouse button.

3 Move the mouse over **Page Setup** and then press the left mouse button.

■ The **Page Setup** dialog box appears.

When would I use each page orientation?

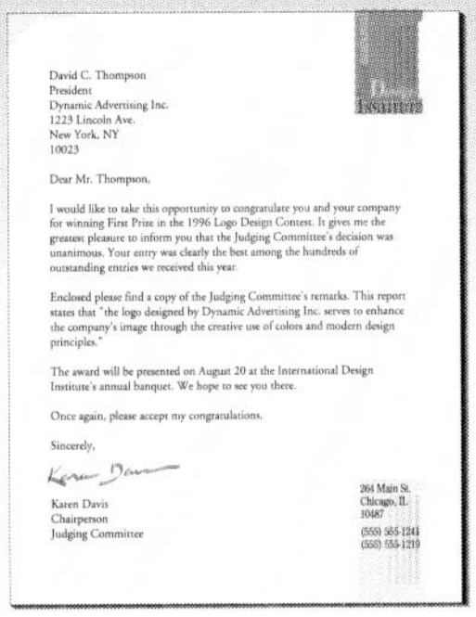

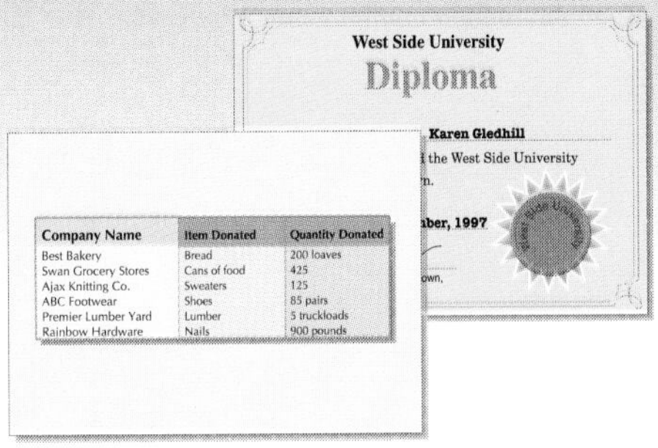

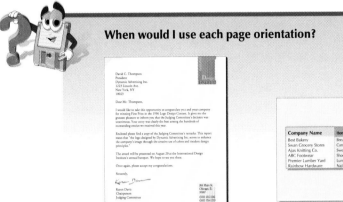

Portrait

This is the standard page orientation. Most documents use the Portrait orientation.

Landscape

Certificates and tables often use the Landscape orientation.

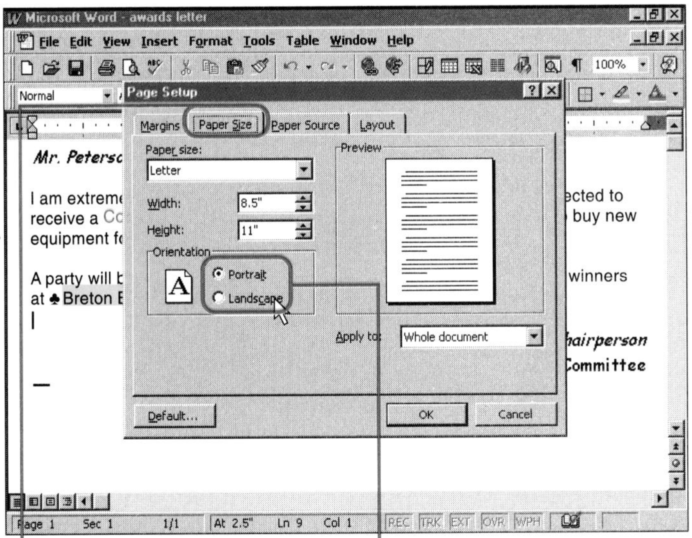

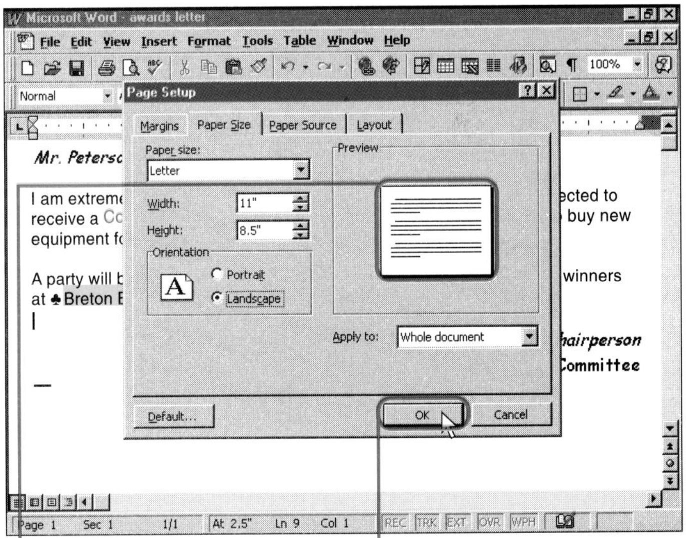

4 Move the mouse over the **Paper Size** tab and then press the left mouse button.

5 Move the mouse over the page orientation you want to use and then press the left mouse button (○ changes to ◉).

■ This area displays a preview of the page orientation you selected.

6 Move the mouse over **OK** and then press the left mouse button.

CREATE NEWSPAPER COLUMNS

You can display your text in columns like those found in a newspaper. This is useful for creating documents such as newsletters and brochures.
Fishing Guide
Fishing Guide

CREATE NEWSPAPER COLUMNS

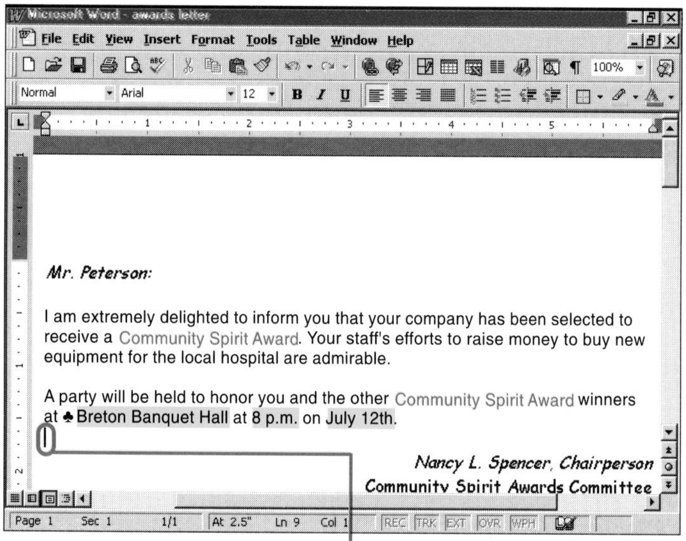

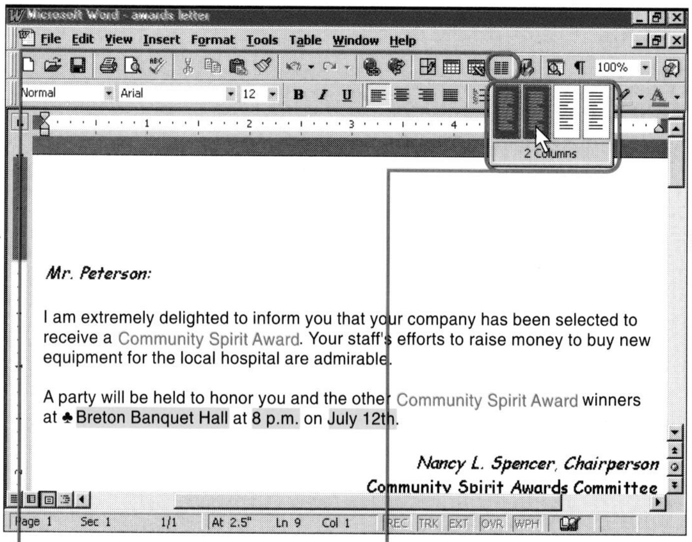

1 Display the document in the Page Layout view. To change the view, refer to page 32.

Note: Word does not display newspaper columns side-by-side in the Normal view.

2 Move the mouse I anywhere over the document or section you want to display newspaper columns and then press the left mouse button.

Note: To create newspaper columns for only part of the document, you must divide the document into sections. To divide a document into sections, refer to page 118.

3 Move the mouse ↖ over ▤ and then press the left mouse button.

4 Move the mouse ↖ over the number of columns you want to create and then press the left mouse button.

Why is there text in only one of my columns?

Word fills one column with text before starting a new column.

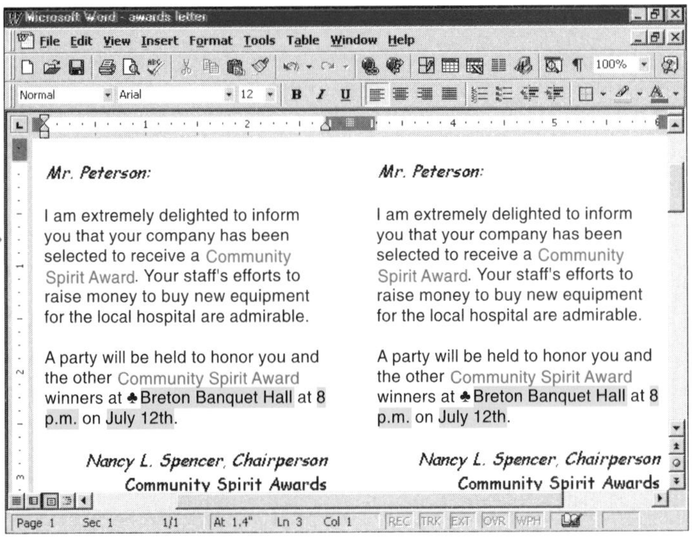
Microsoft Word - awards letter
File Edit View Insert Format Tools Table Window Help
Mr. Peterson:
I am extremely delighted to inform you that your company has been selected to receive a Community Spirit Award. Your staff's efforts to raise money to buy new equipment for the local hospital are admirable.
A party will be held to honor you and the other Community Spirit Award winners at Breton Banquet Hall at 8 p.m. on July 12th.
Nancy L. Spencer, Chairperson
Community Spirit Awards
Page 1 Sec 1 1/1 At 1.4" Ln 3 Col 1

■ The text in the document appears in newspaper columns.

Note: For this example, the existing text was copied to show the newspaper columns. To copy text, refer to page 50.

REMOVE NEWSPAPER COLUMNS

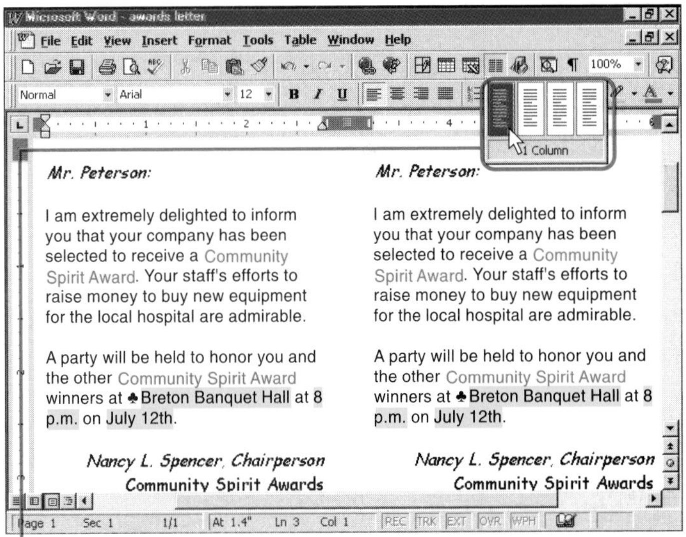
Microsoft Word - awards letter
File Edit View Insert Format Tools Table Window Help
1 Column
Mr. Peterson:
I am extremely delighted to inform you that your company has been selected to receive a Community Spirit Award. Your staff's efforts to raise money to buy new equipment for the local hospital are admirable.
A party will be held to honor you and the other Community Spirit Award winners at Breton Banquet Hall at 8 p.m. on July 12th.
Nancy L. Spencer, Chairperson
Community Spirit Awards
Page 1 Sec 1 1/1 At 1.4" Ln 3 Col 1

■ Repeat steps 2 to 4, selecting **1 Column** in step 4.

Dear Susan,
I'm delighted you'll be coming to Chicago this summer. I've requested
the same vacation time, so we'll be able to spend lots of time together.
Gwen Yates
16 Maple Drive
Baltimore, Maryland
21201
David C. Thompson
President
Dynamic Advertising Inc.
1223 Lincoln Ave.
New York, NY
10023
Dear Mr. Thompson,
Sincerely,
Karen Davis
Chairperson

CHAPTER 7

PRINT YOUR DOCUMENTS

Now that I have created my document, how do I produce a paper copy? Find out how to print your documents, envelopes and labels in this chapter.

PREVIEW A DOCUMENT

You can use the Print Preview feature to see how your document will look when printed.

PREVIEW A DOCUMENT

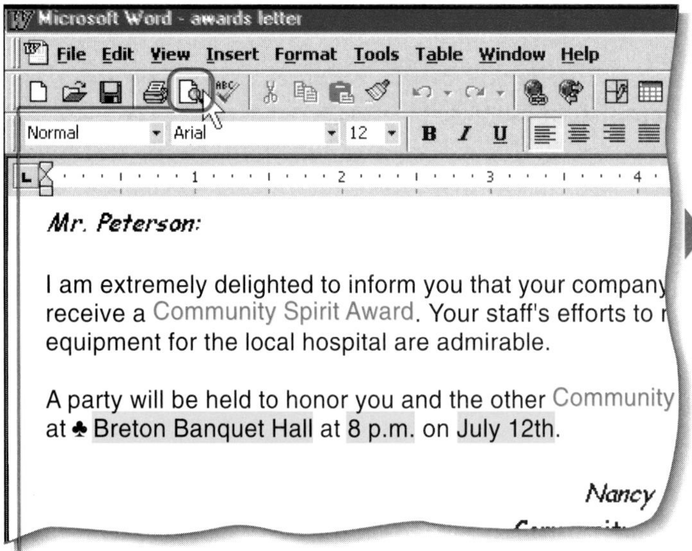

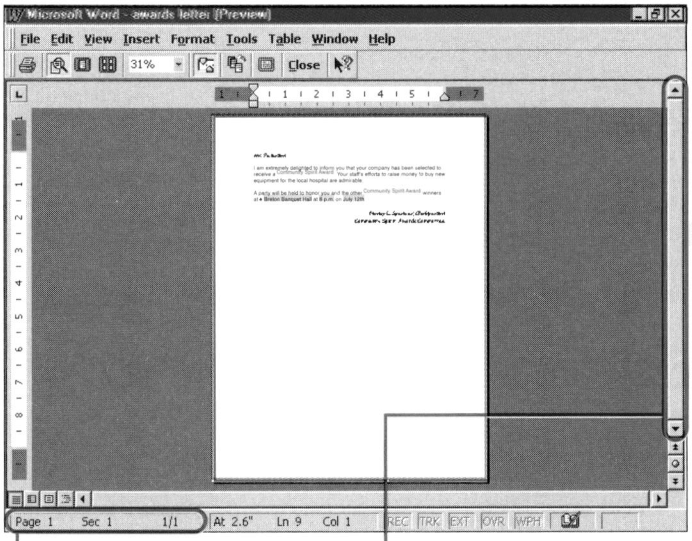

1 Move the mouse over and then press the left mouse button.

■ The Print Preview window appears.

■ This area tells you which page is displayed and the number of pages in the document. In this example, the document contains one page.

■ If your document contains more than one page, use the scroll bar to view the other pages.

When can I edit my document in the Print Preview window?

If the mouse looks like I when over your document, you can edit the document.

If the mouse looks like 🔍+ or 🔍− when over your document, you can magnify or shrink the page displayed on your screen.

*Note: To change the shape of the mouse, perform step **3** below.*

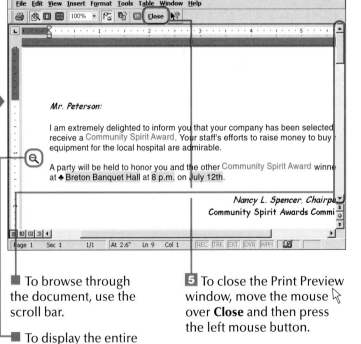

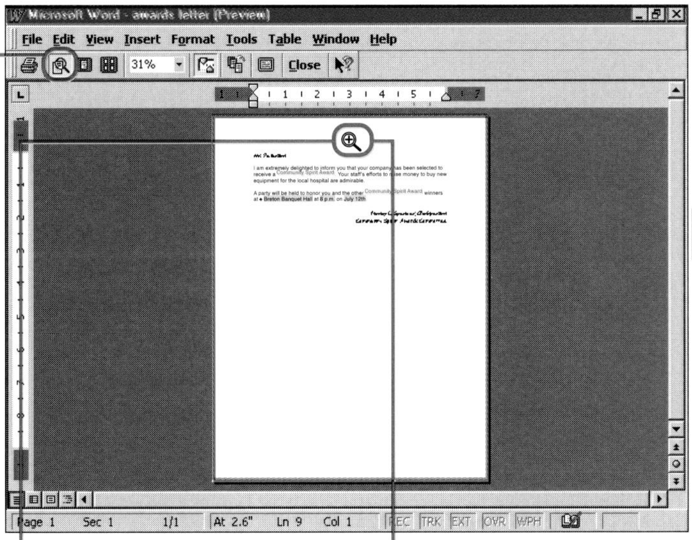

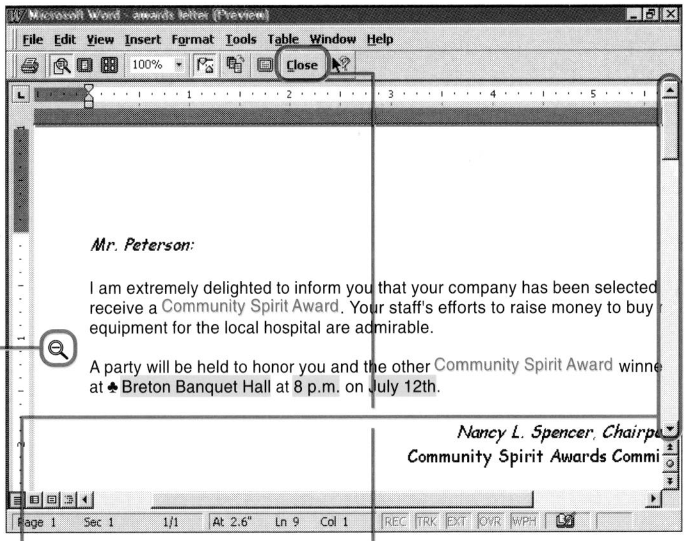

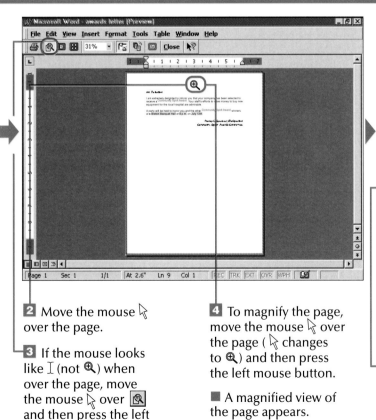

2 Move the mouse ↖ over the page.

3 If the mouse looks like I (not 🔍+) when over the page, move the mouse ↖ over 🔍 and then press the left mouse button.

4 To magnify the page, move the mouse ↖ over the page (↖ changes to 🔍+) and then press the left mouse button.

■ A magnified view of the page appears.

■ To browse through the document, use the scroll bar.

■ To display the entire page again, move the mouse ↖ over the page (↖ changes to 🔍−) and then press the left mouse button.

5 To close the Print Preview window, move the mouse ↖ over **Close** and then press the left mouse button.

PRINT A DOCUMENT

You can produce a paper copy of the document displayed on your screen.

PRINT A DOCUMENT

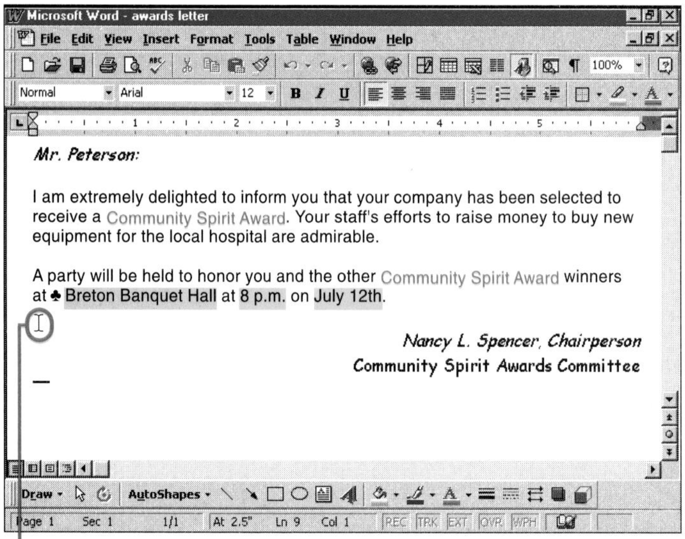

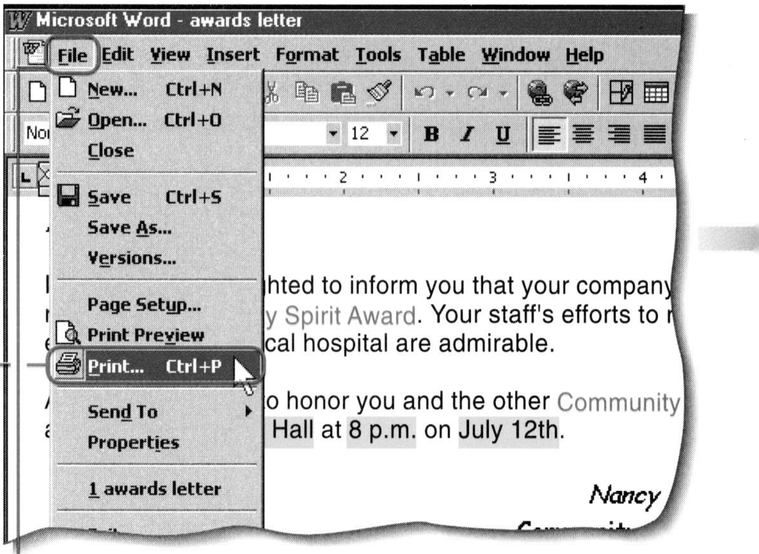

1 Move the mouse I anywhere over the document or page you want to print and then press the left mouse button.

■ To print part of your document, select the text you want to print. To select text, refer to page 12.

2 Move the mouse over **File** and then press the left mouse button.

3 Move the mouse over **Print** and then press the left mouse button.

■ The **Print** dialog box appears.

How do I prepare my printer to print documents?

Before printing, always make sure your printer is turned on and contains paper.

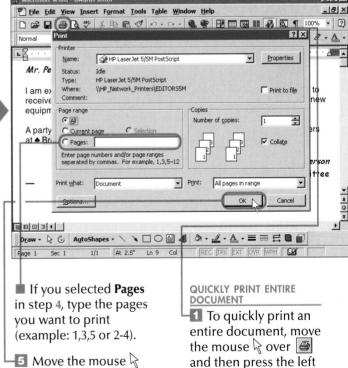

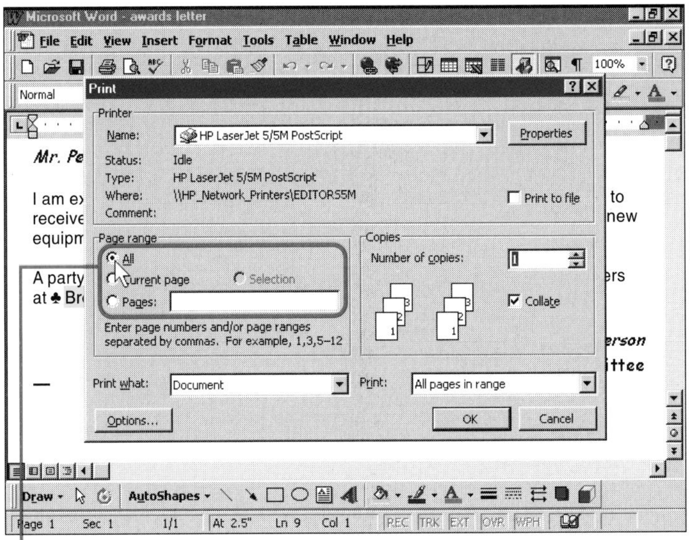

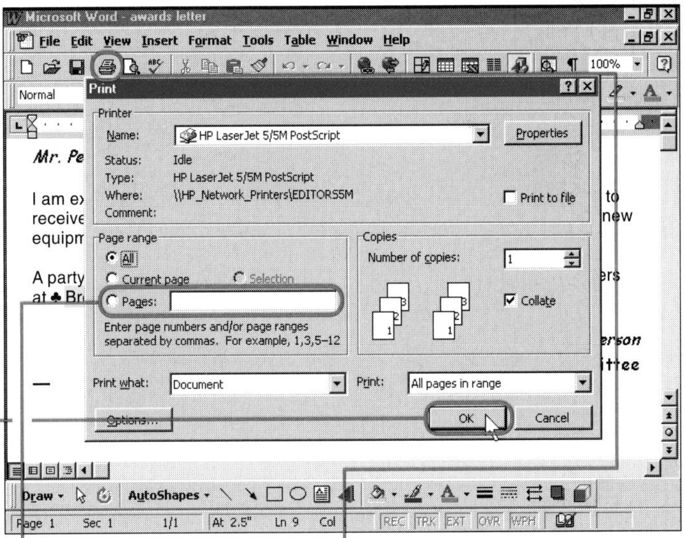

4 Move the mouse over the print option you want to use and then press the left mouse button (○ changes to ◉).

All - Prints every page in the document.

Current page - Prints the page containing the insertion point.

Pages - Prints the pages you specify.

Selection - Prints the text you selected.

■ If you selected **Pages** in step 4, type the pages you want to print (example: 1,3,5 or 2-4).

5 Move the mouse over **OK** and then press the left mouse button.

QUICKLY PRINT ENTIRE DOCUMENT

1 To quickly print an entire document, move the mouse over 🖨 and then press the left mouse button.

PRINT AN ENVELOPE

PRINT AN ENVELOPE

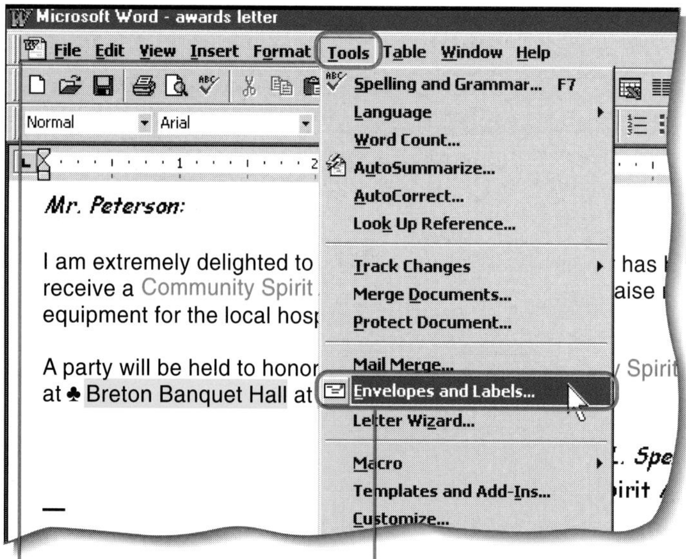

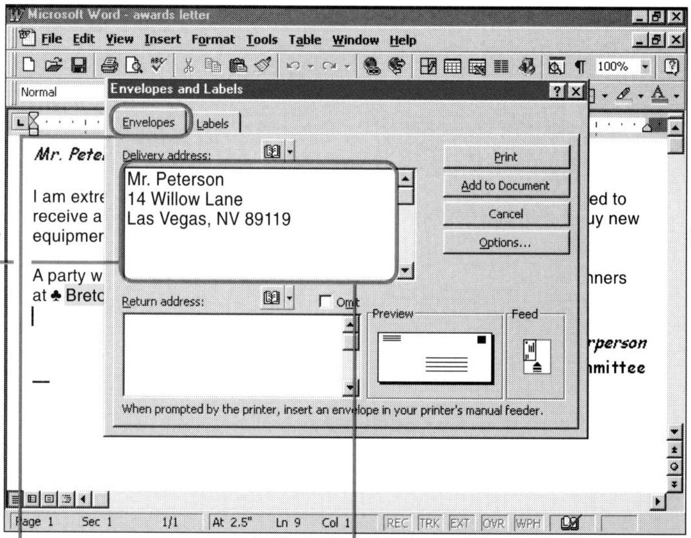

1 Move the mouse over **Tools** and then press the left mouse button.

2 Move the mouse over **Envelopes and Labels** and then press the left mouse button.

■ The **Envelopes and Labels** dialog box appears.

3 Move the mouse over the **Envelopes** tab and then press the left mouse button.

■ This area displays the delivery address. If Word finds an address in your document, Word will enter the address for you.

4 To enter a delivery address, move the mouse I over this area and then press the left mouse button. Then type the delivery address.

Note: To remove any existing text before typing an address, press **Delete** *or* **←Backspace** *on your keyboard.*

Why would I omit the return address on an envelope?

You would omit the return address if your envelope already displays a return address. Company stationery often displays a return address.

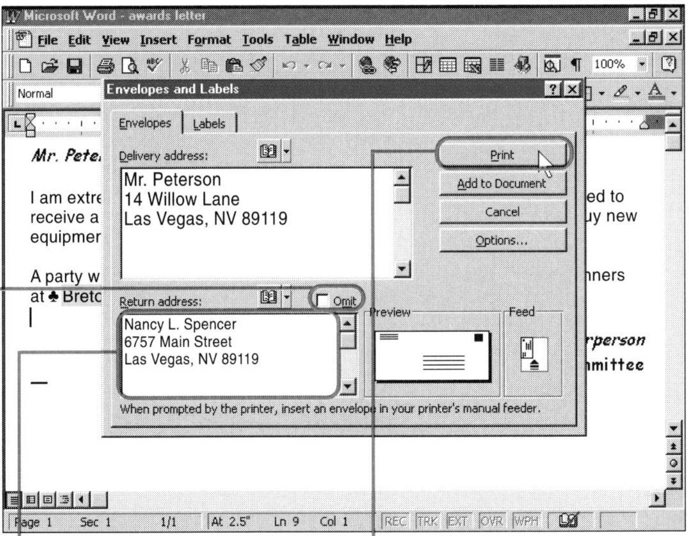

5 To enter a return address, move the mouse over this area and then press the left mouse button. Then type the return address.

■ If you do not want to print a return address, move the mouse over **Omit** and then press the left mouse button (☐ changes to ☑).

6 To print the envelope, move the mouse over **Print** and then press the left mouse button.

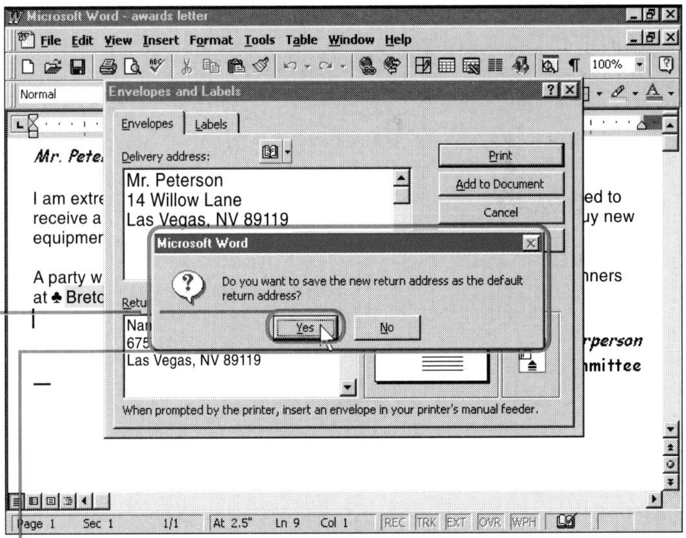

■ This dialog box appears if you entered a return address.

7 To save the return address, move the mouse over **Yes** and then press the left mouse button.

*Note: If you selected **Yes** in step 7, the address will appear as the return address every time you print an envelope. This saves you from constantly having to retype the address.*

PRINT LABELS

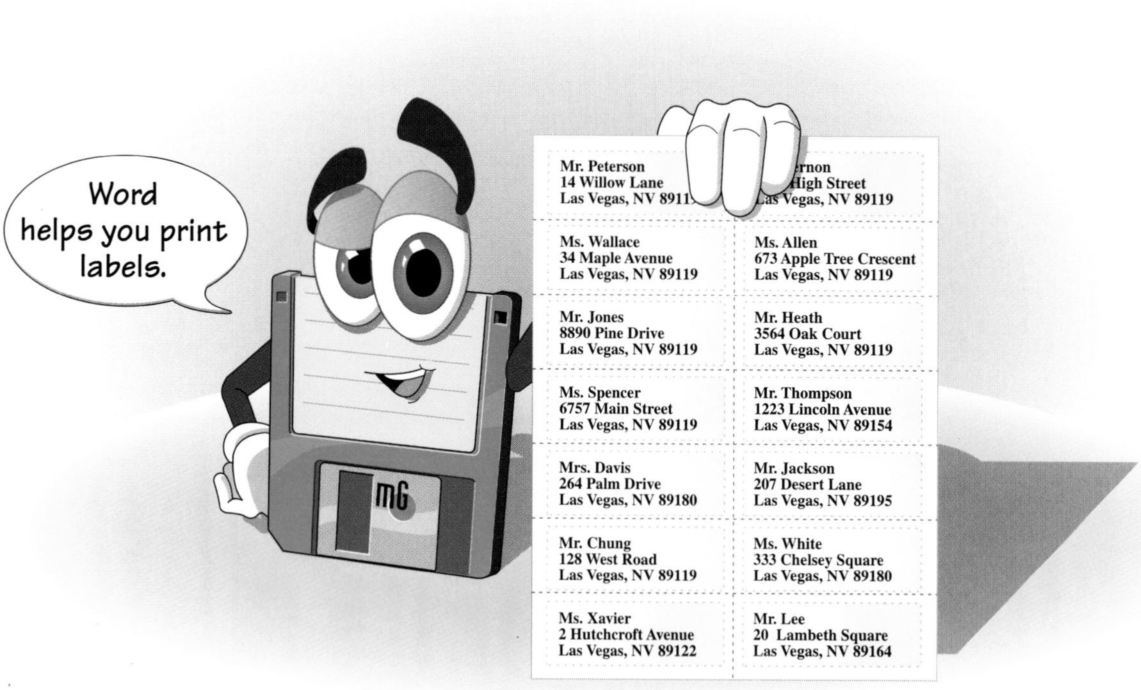

PRINT LABELS

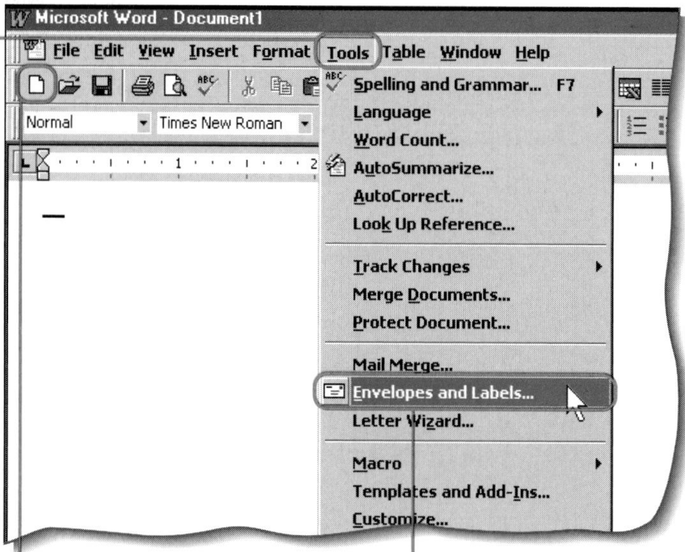

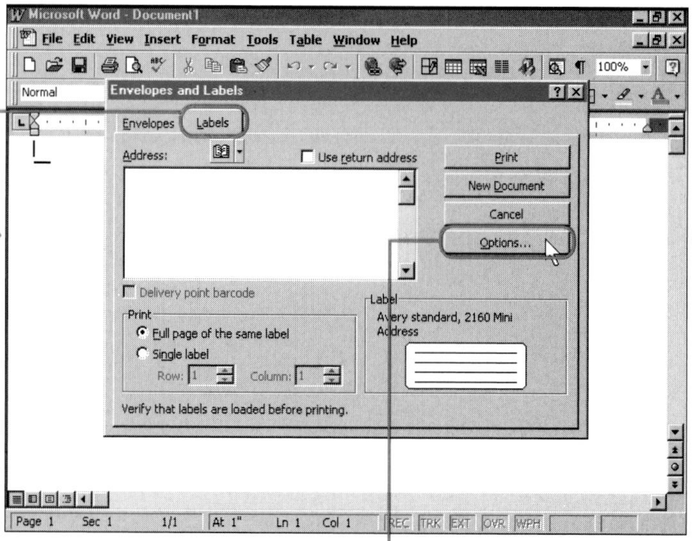

1 To create a new document, move the mouse over ▢ and then press the left mouse button.

2 Move the mouse over **Tools** and then press the left mouse button.

3 Move the mouse over **Envelopes and Labels** and then press the left mouse button.

■ The **Envelopes and Labels** dialog box appears.

4 Move the mouse over the **Labels** tab and then press the left mouse button.

5 To select the type of label you want to use, move the mouse over **Options** and then press the left mouse button.

How can I tell which label product I am using?

You can check your label packaging to determine which label product to select in step 7 below.

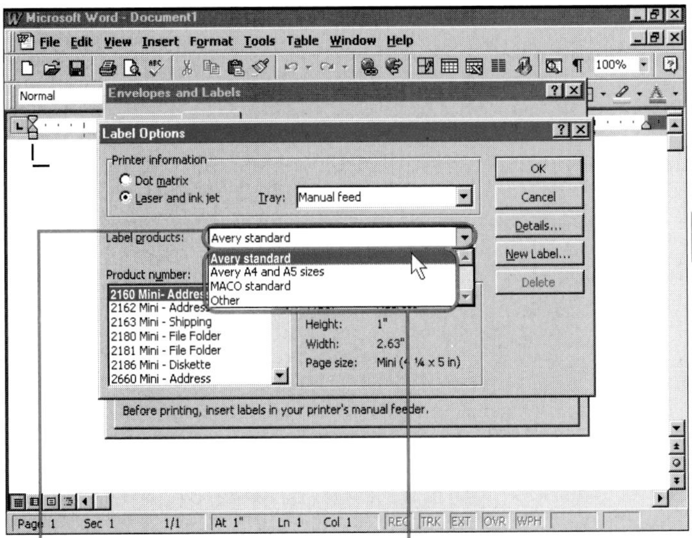

■ The **Label Options** dialog box appears.

6 To display a list of label products, move the mouse over this area and then press the left mouse button.

7 Move the mouse over the label product you want to use and then press the left mouse button.

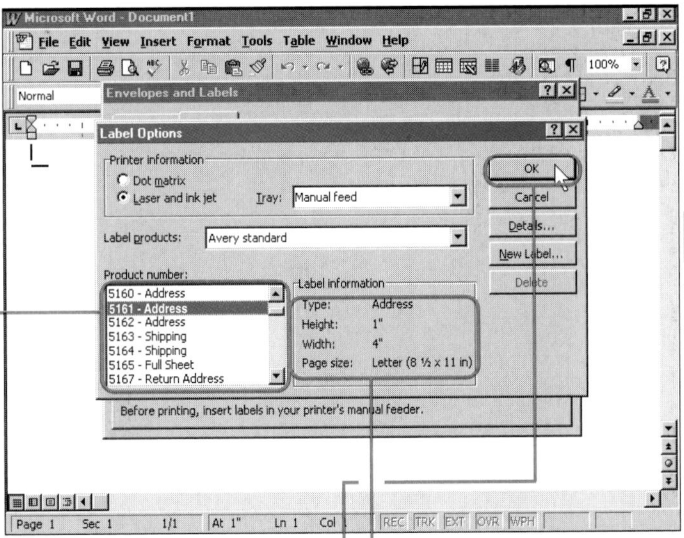

■ This area displays the types of labels for the product you selected.

8 Move the mouse over the type of label you want to use and then press the left mouse button.

■ This area displays information about the type of label you selected.

9 Move the mouse over **OK** and then press the left mouse button.

CONTINUED

PRINT LABELS

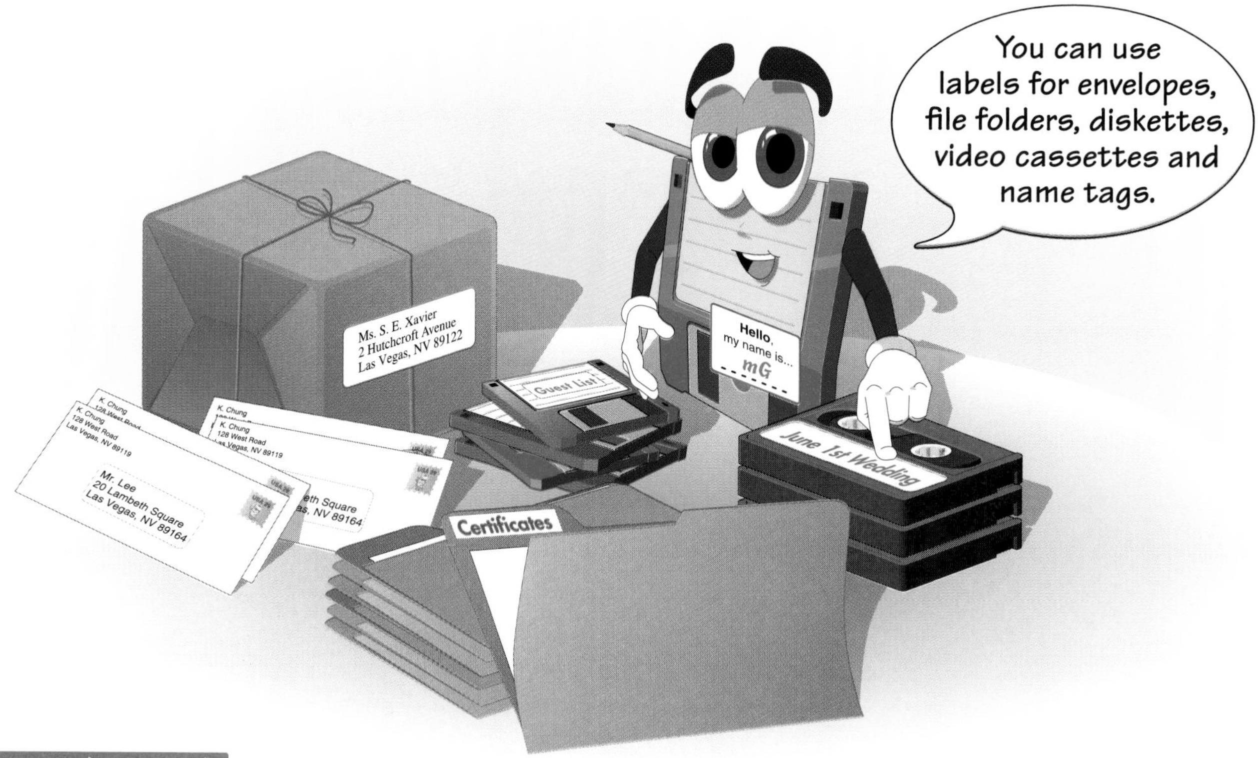

PRINT LABELS (CONTINUED)

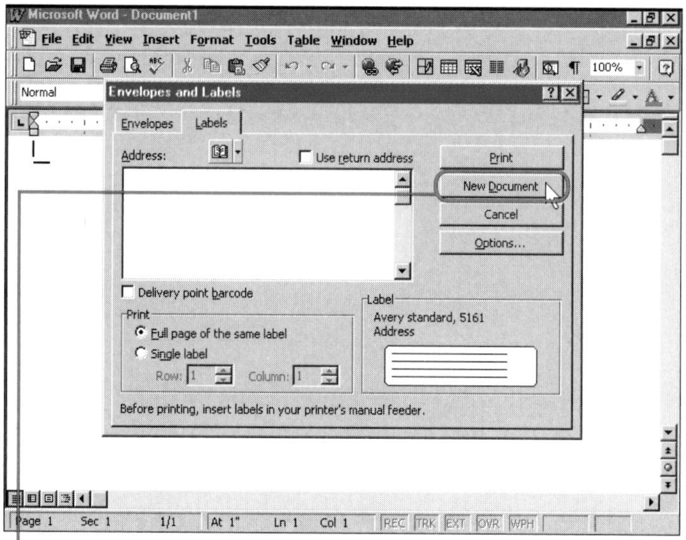

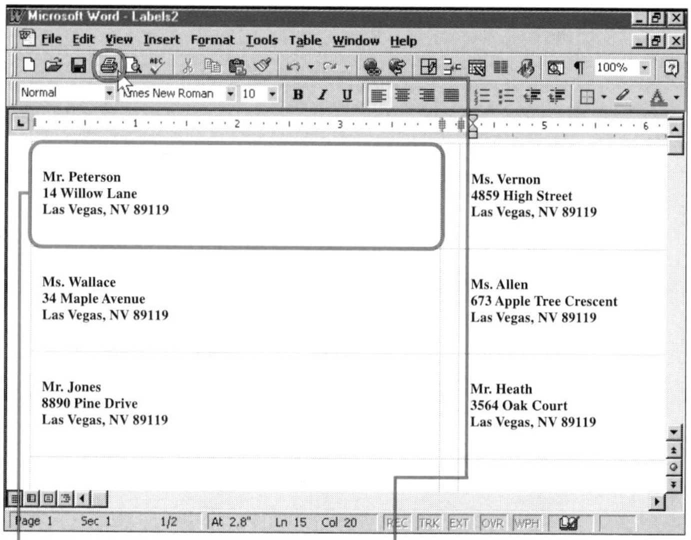

10 To add the labels to a new document, move the mouse over **New Document** and then press the left mouse button.

■ The labels appear.

11 Move the mouse over the label where you want to type text and then press the left mouse button. Then type the text.

Note: You can format the text as you would format any text in a document. To format text, refer to pages 72 to 107.

12 Repeat step 11 for each label.

13 To print the labels, move the mouse over the print button and then press the left mouse button.

Can I quickly create a label for each person on my mailing list?

You can use the Mail Merge feature included with Word to quickly create a label for each person on your mailing list. For more information, refer to page 198.

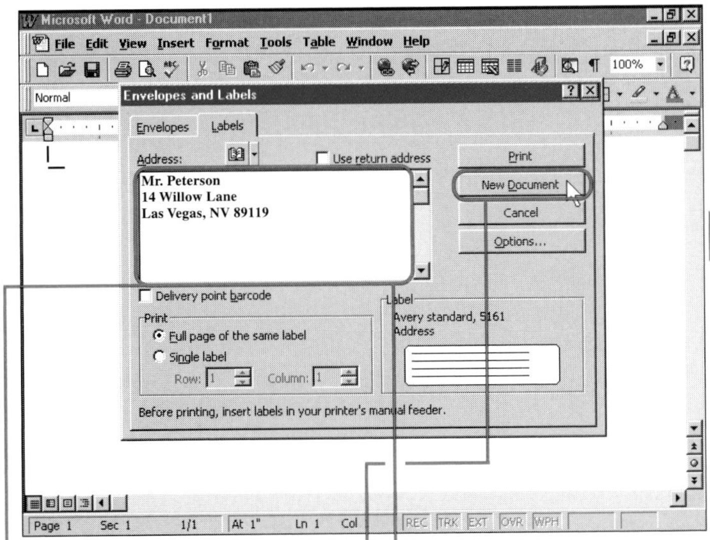

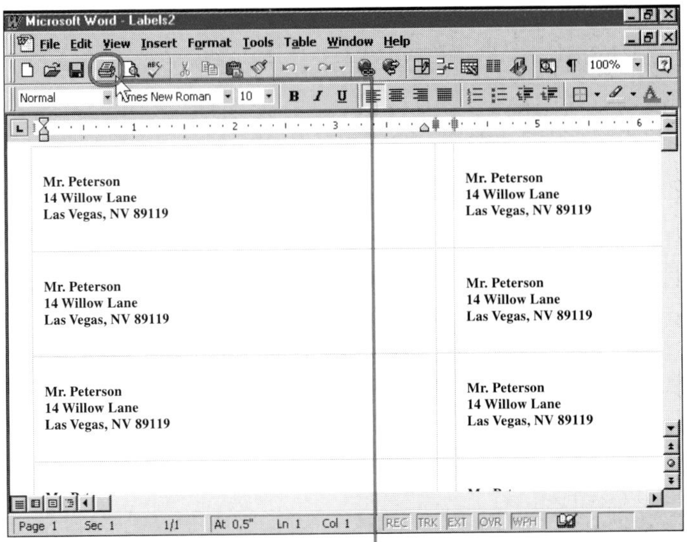

PRINT THE SAME TEXT ON EVERY LABEL

1 Perform steps 1 to 9 starting on page 138.

2 Move the mouse over this area and then press the left mouse button.

3 Type the text you want to appear on every label.

4 Move the mouse over **New Document** and then press the left mouse button.

■ The labels appear. Each label displays the same text.

5 To print the labels, move the mouse over 🖨 and then press the left mouse button.

David C. Thompson
President
Dynamic Advertising Inc.
1223 Lincoln Ave.
10023
Dear Mr. Thompson,
outstanding entries
cept my congratulations.
THE CITY OF SEATTLE • THE CITY OF SEATTLE
For more information
Contact: Susan Nelson
announced today.
Quantity Donated
Company Name
Best Bakery
Swan Grocery Stores
Ajax Knitting Co.
ABC Footwear
Premier Lumber Yard
Rainbow Hardware
425
125
85 pairs
said Moore. "It's a proud moment in our history."
For more information
Contact: Susan Nelson, Deputy Mayor
Phone: (555) 555-4645

CHAPTER 8

WORK WITH MULTIPLE DOCUMENTS

Wondering how to create new documents and work with more than one document? Learn how in this chapter.

CREATE A NEW DOCUMENT

You can create a new document to start writing a letter, report or memo.

CREATE A NEW DOCUMENT

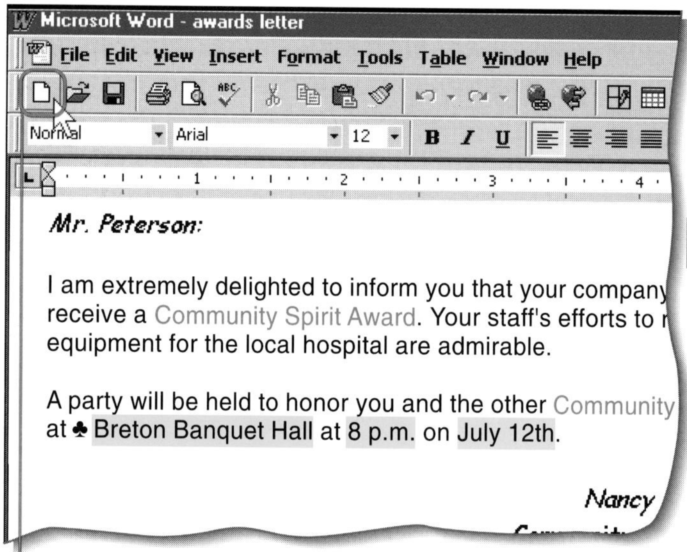

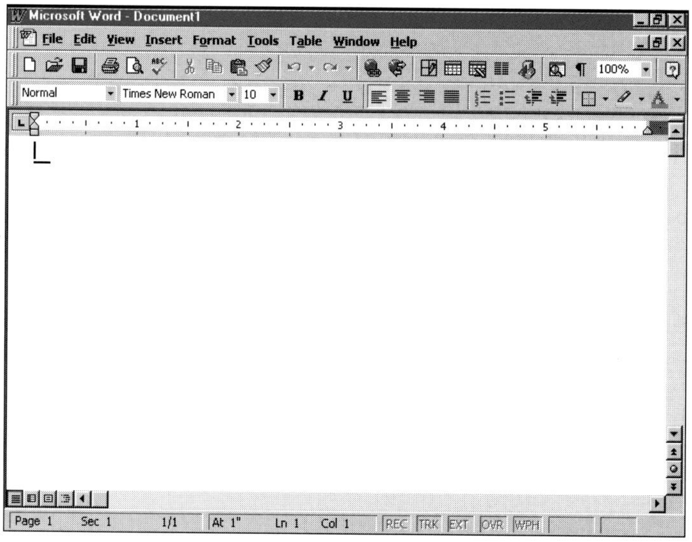

1 Move the mouse ⬚ over □ and then press the left mouse button.

■ A new document appears. The previous document is now hidden behind the new document.

■ Think of each document as a separate piece of paper. When you create a document, you are placing a new piece of paper on the screen.

SWITCH BETWEEN DOCUMENTS

Word lets you have many documents open at once. You can easily switch from one open document to another.

SWITCH BETWEEN DOCUMENTS

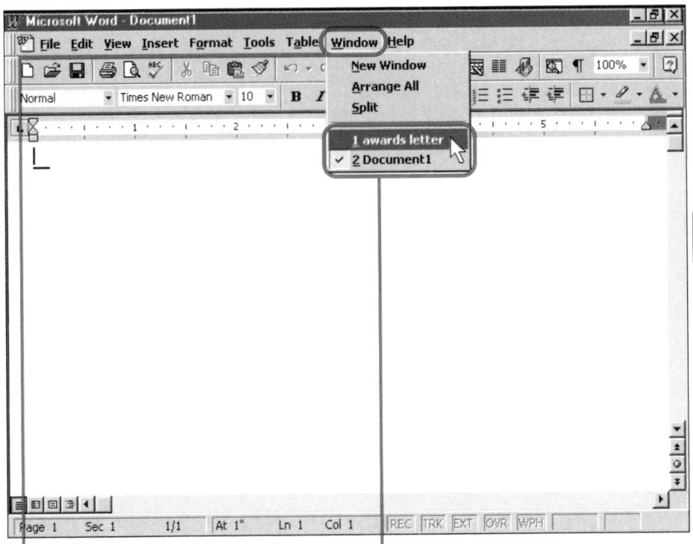

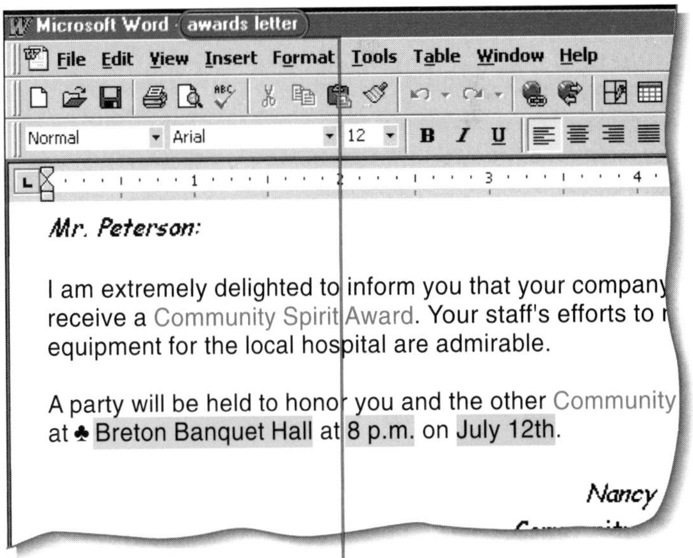

1 To display a list of all open documents, move the mouse over **Window** and then press the left mouse button.

2 Move the mouse over the name of the document you want to display and then press the left mouse button.

■ The document appears.

■ Word displays the name of the document at the top of your screen.

COPY OR MOVE TEXT BETWEEN DOCUMENTS

You can copy or move text from one document to another. This will save you time when you want to use text from another document.
ABC Corp.
Feb 21, 1997
106 Campbell Road
Burbank, CA
91505
Dear Mr. Cooke,
We would like to reschedule our quarterly meeting to April 7th, 1997 at 2:30 p.m.
Can you let me know if this time is OK?
Thanks,
John Dobson
ABC Corp.
Quarterly Report
1997
Includes: Financial Statistics
Company History
Sales Statistics

COPY OR MOVE TEXT BETWEEN DOCUMENTS

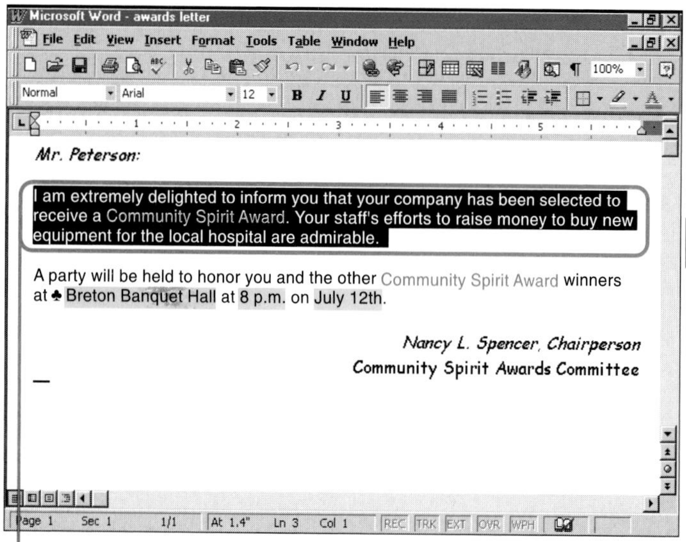

Microsoft Word - awards letter
File Edit View Insert Format Tools Table Window Help
Mr. Peterson:
I am extremely delighted to inform you that your company has been selected to receive a Community Spirit Award. Your staff's efforts to raise money to buy new equipment for the local hospital are admirable.
A party will be held to honor you and the other Community Spirit Award winners at Breton Banquet Hall at 8 p.m. on July 12th.
Nancy L. Spencer, Chairperson
Community Spirit Awards Committee

1 Select the text you want to place in another document. To select text, refer to page 12.

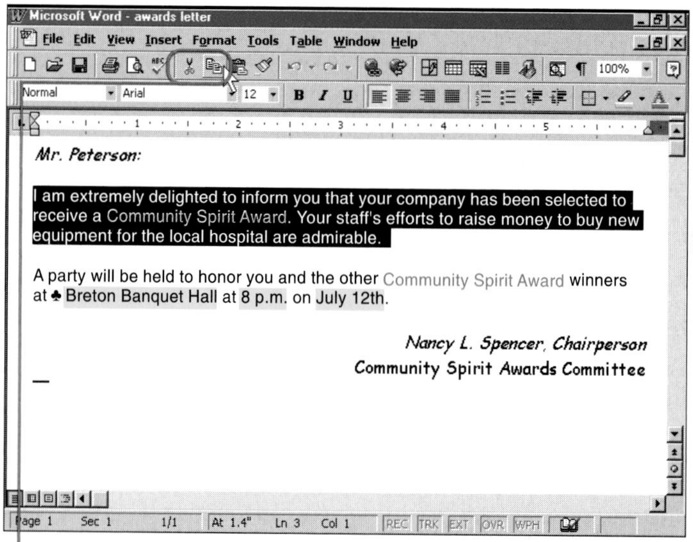

Microsoft Word - awards letter
File Edit View Insert Format Tools Table Window Help
Mr. Peterson:
I am extremely delighted to inform you that your company has been selected to receive a Community Spirit Award. Your staff's efforts to raise money to buy new equipment for the local hospital are admirable.
A party will be held to honor you and the other Community Spirit Award winners at Breton Banquet Hall at 8 p.m. on July 12th.
Nancy L. Spencer, Chairperson
Community Spirit Awards Committee

2 Move the mouse over one of the following options and then press the left mouse button.

- Move the text
- Copy the text

Note: For information on the difference between moving and copying text, refer to the top of page 147.

What is the difference between moving and copying text?

Move Text
When you move text, the original text disappears.

Copy Text
When you copy text, the original text remains in its place.

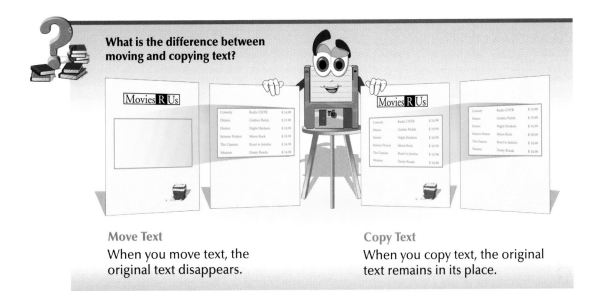

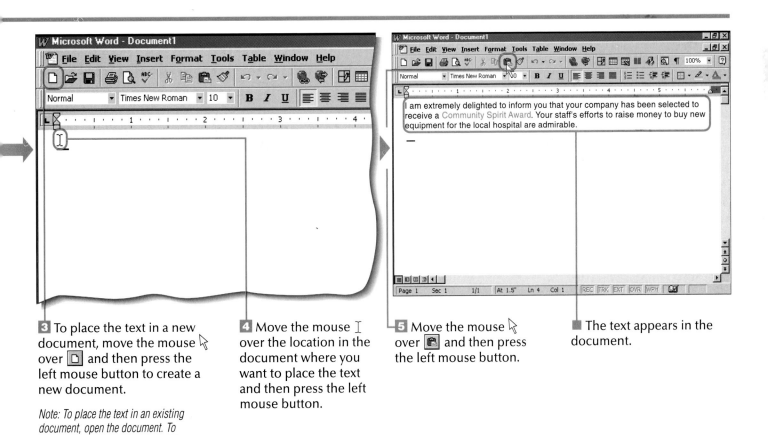

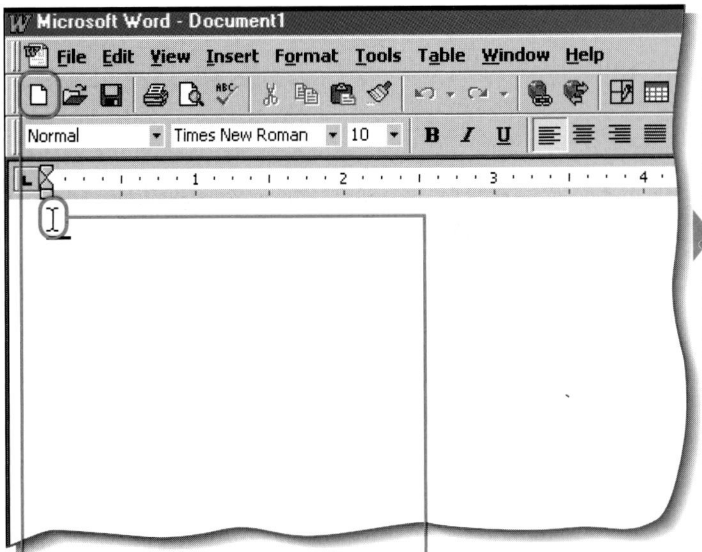

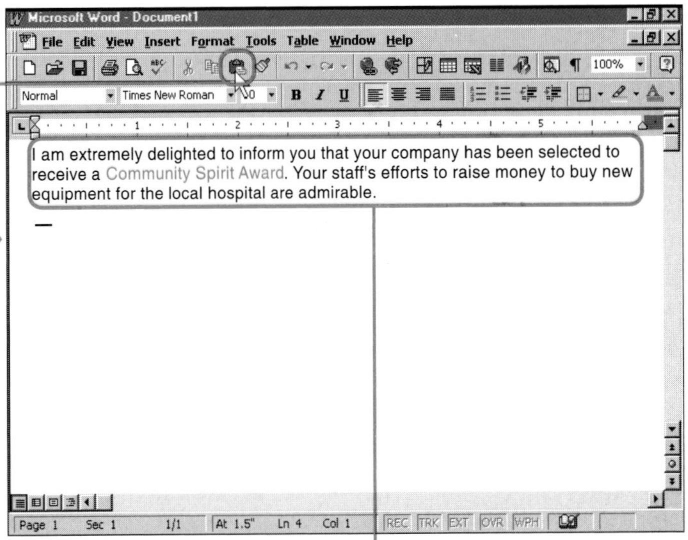

3 To place the text in a new document, move the mouse over and then press the left mouse button to create a new document.

Note: To place the text in an existing document, open the document. To open a document, refer to page 24.

4 Move the mouse over the location in the document where you want to place the text and then press the left mouse button.

5 Move the mouse over and then press the left mouse button.

■ The text appears in the document.

USING TEMPLATES AND WIZARDS

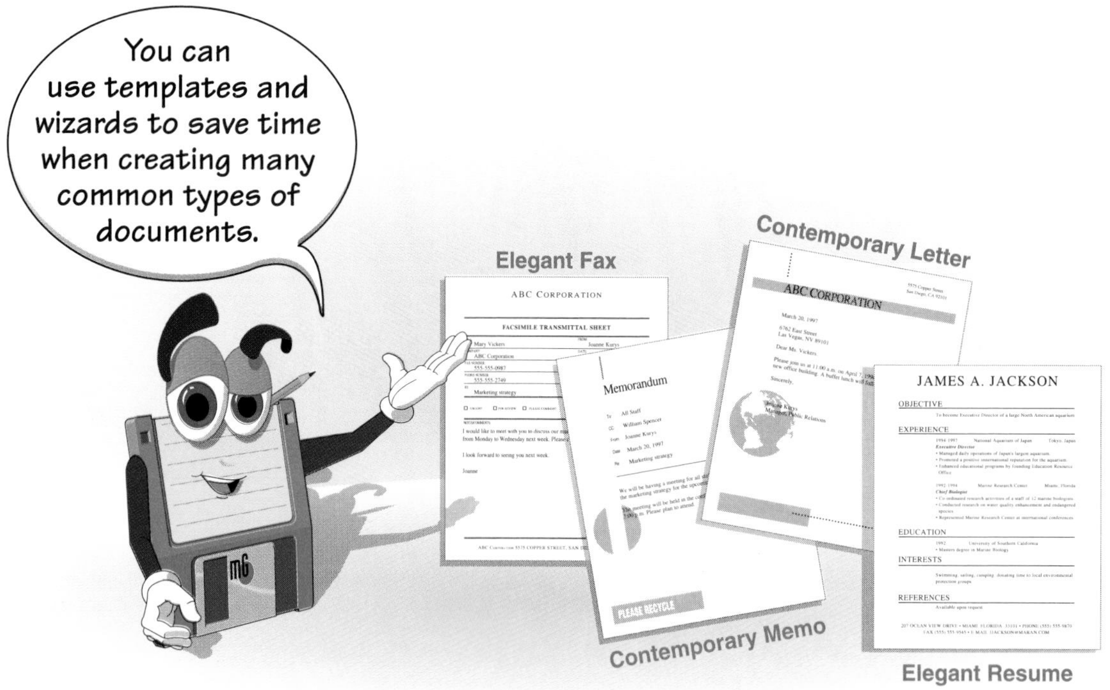

Templates and wizards provide the layout and formatting so you can concentrate on the content of your document.

USING TEMPLATES AND WIZARDS

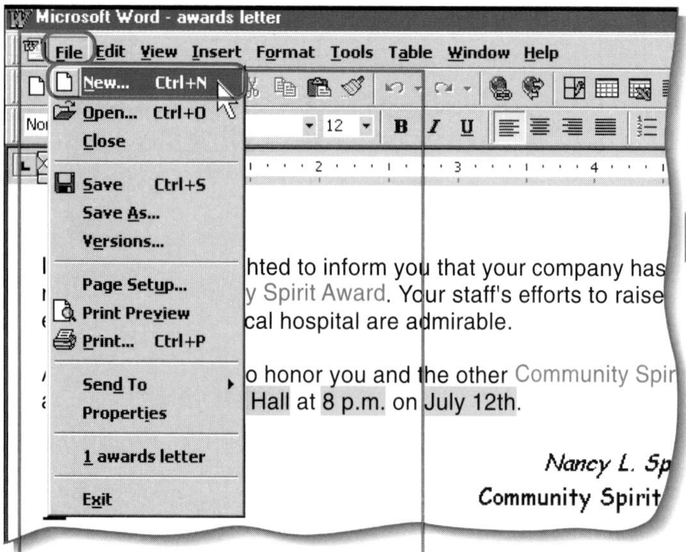

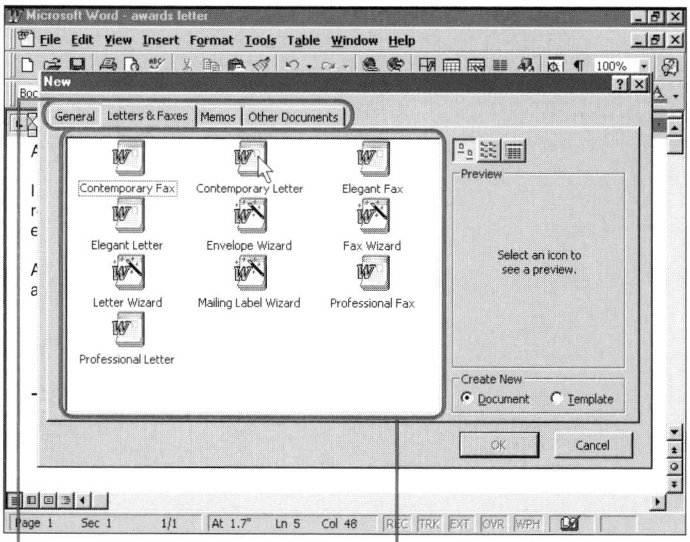

1 Move the mouse over **File** and then press the left mouse button.

2 Move the mouse over **New** and then press the left mouse button.

■ The **New** dialog box appears.

3 Move the mouse over the tab for the type of document you want to create and then press the left mouse button.

4 Move the mouse over the document you want to create and then press the left mouse button.

*Note: If the document has **Wizard** in its name, Word will help you prepare the document step-by-step.*

What is the difference between a template and a wizard?

Template

When you select a template, a document immediately appears with areas for you to fill in your personalized information.

Wizard

When you select a wizard, you will be asked a series of questions. The wizard uses your answers to help complete the document.

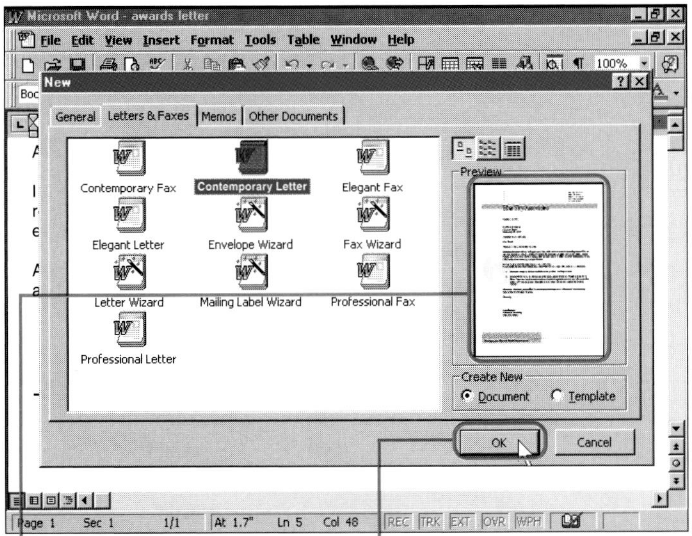

■ This area displays a preview of the document you selected.

5 To create the document, move the mouse over **OK** and then press the left mouse button.

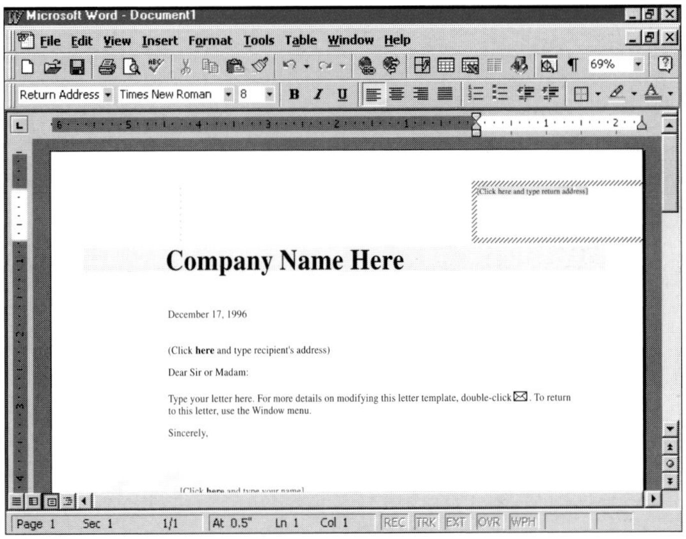

■ The document appears on your screen.

Note: If you selected a wizard in step 4, Word will ask you a series of questions before creating the document.

6 Type information where required to complete the document.

CHAPTER 9

WORK WITH TABLES

Do you want to learn how to display information in a table? This chapter teaches you how to create and work with a table in your document.

CREATE A TABLE

You can create a table to neatly display information in your document.

Word lets you draw a table on the screen as you would draw a table with a pen and paper.

CREATE A TABLE

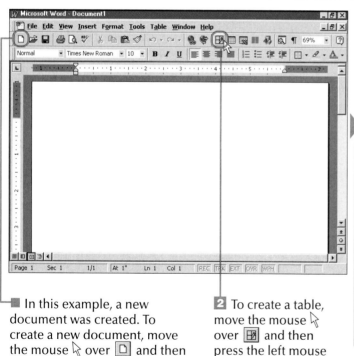

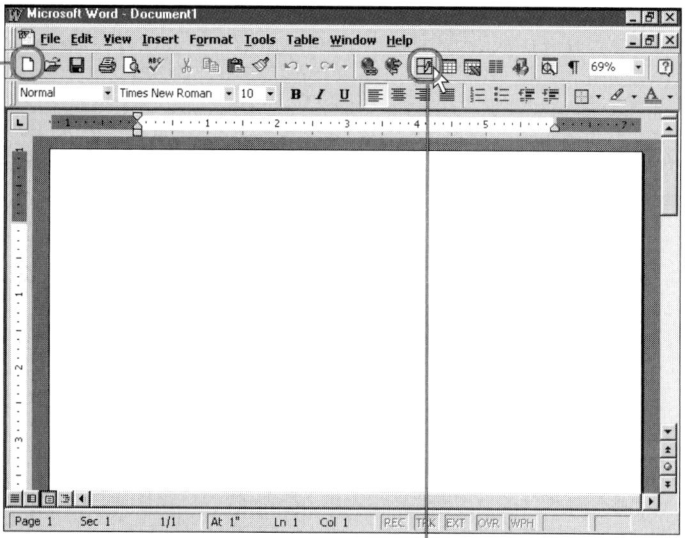

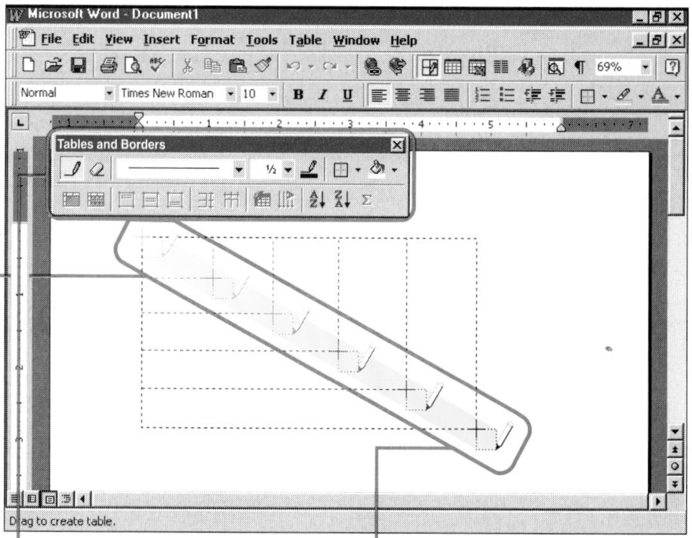

■ In this example, a new document was created. To create a new document, move the mouse over ▢ and then press the left mouse button.

1 Display the document in the Page Layout view. To change the view, refer to page 32.

2 To create a table, move the mouse over ▦ and then press the left mouse button.

■ The **Tables and Borders** toolbar appears.

3 Move the mouse ✎ to where you want the top left corner of the table to appear.

4 Press and hold down the left mouse button as you move the mouse until the outline of the table displays the size you want. Then release the mouse button.

Can I move a toolbar out of the way?

If a toolbar is in the way, you can easily move the toolbar to a new location.

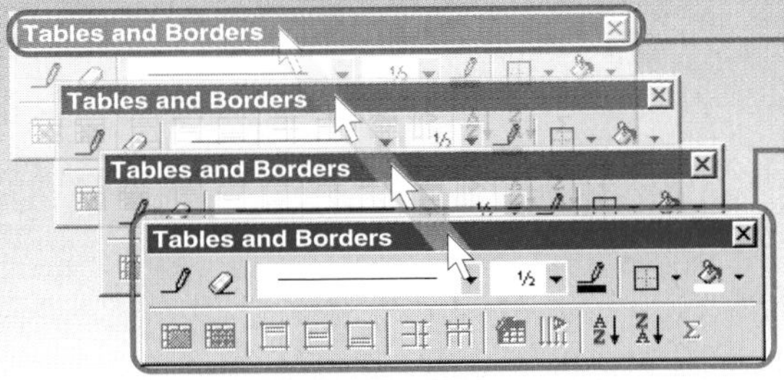

1 Move the mouse over the title bar.

2 Press and hold down the left mouse button as you move the toolbar to a new location. Then release the mouse button.

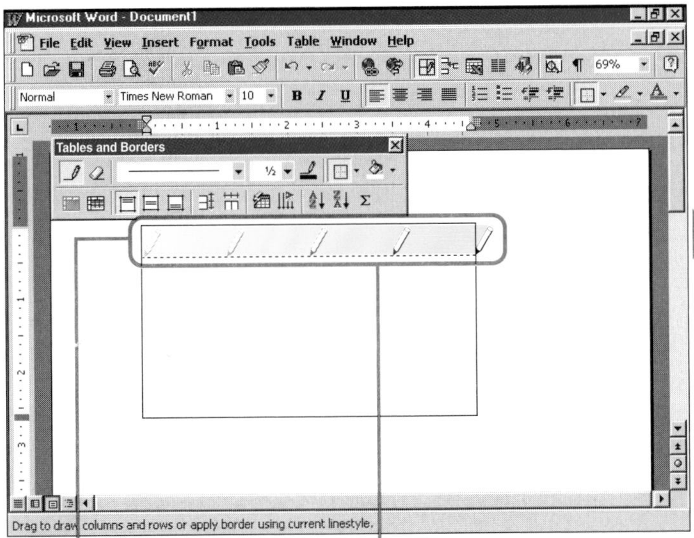

■ The outline of the table appears in the document.

5 To add a line to the table, move the mouse to where you want the line to begin.

6 Press and hold down the left mouse button as you move the mouse to where you want the line to end. Then release the mouse button.

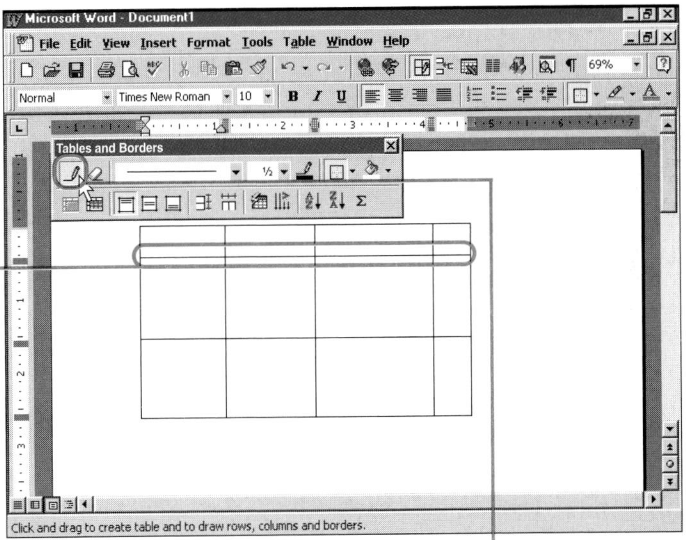

■ The line appears in your table.

7 Repeat steps 5 and 6 until you have added all the lines you want.

8 When you finish adding lines, move the mouse over and then press the left mouse button.

CHANGE ROW HEIGHT OR COLUMN WIDTH

After you have created a table, you can change the height of rows or the width of columns.

CHANGE ROW HEIGHT

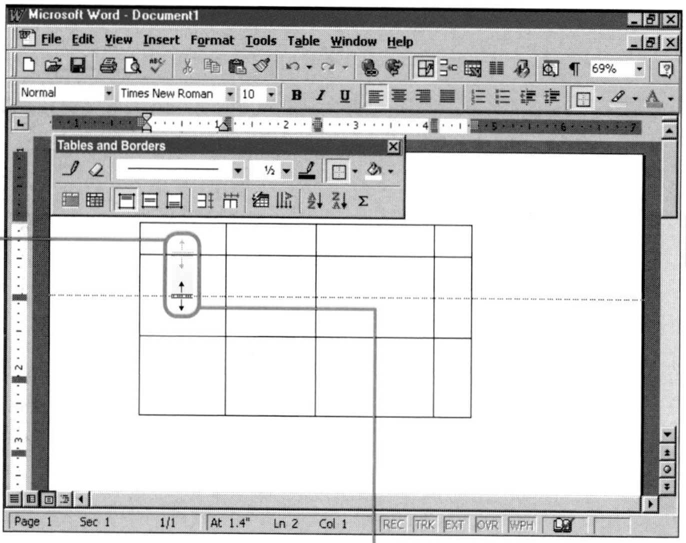

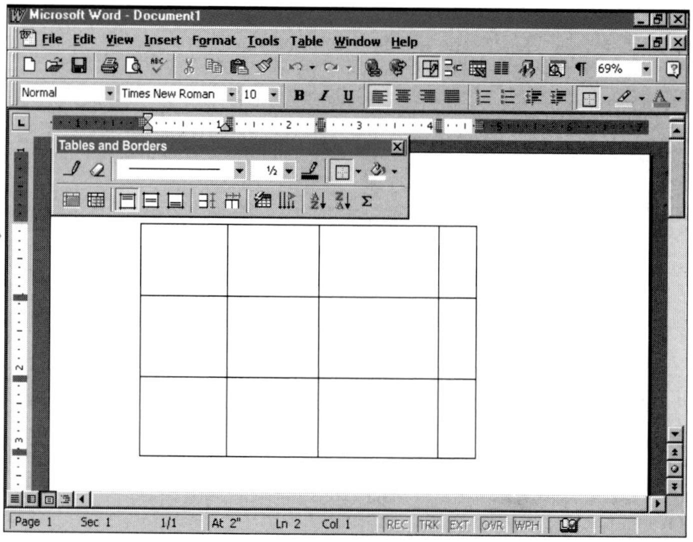

1 Move the mouse I over the bottom edge of the row you want to change (I changes to ÷).

2 Press and hold down the left mouse button as you move the row edge to a new position.

■ A line shows the new position.

3 Release the left mouse button and the row displays the new height.

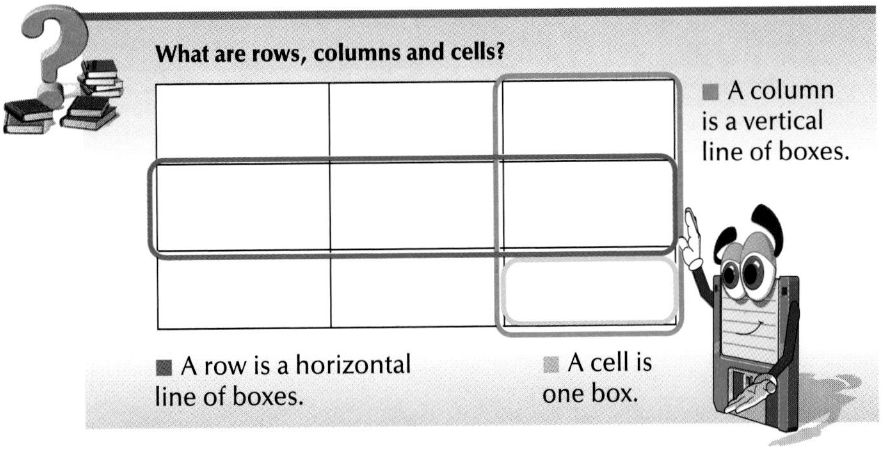
What are rows, columns and cells?
A column is a vertical line of boxes.
A row is a horizontal line of boxes.
A cell is one box.

CHANGE COLUMN WIDTH

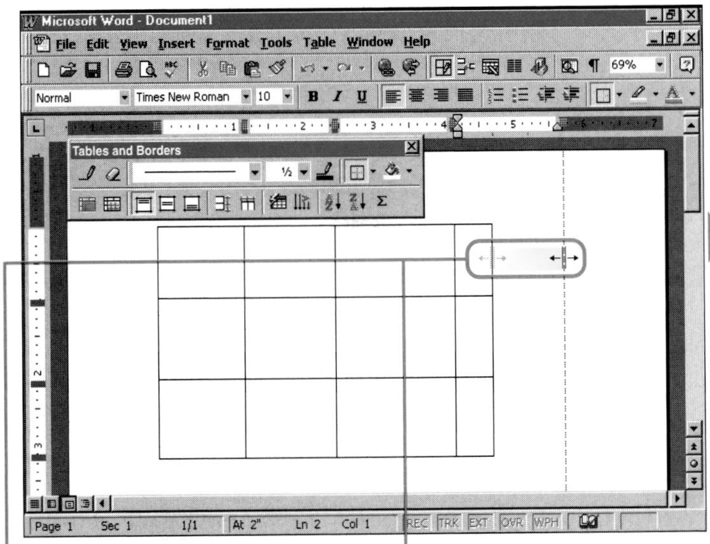

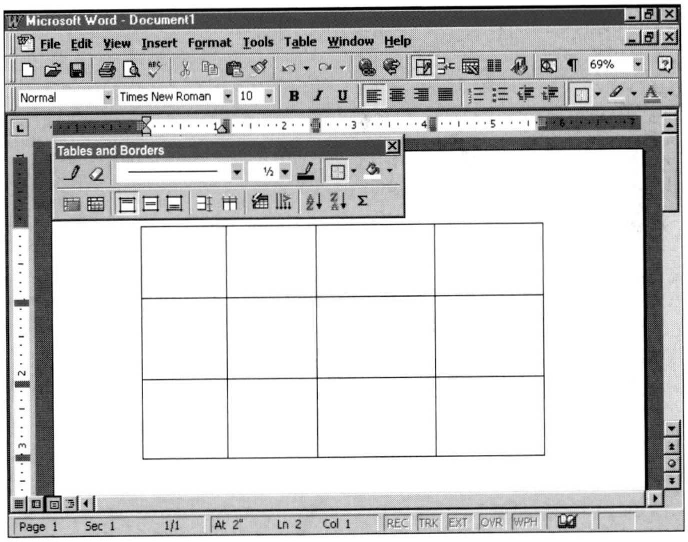

1 Move the mouse I over the right edge of the column you want to change (I changes to ⟛).

2 Press and hold down the left mouse button as you move the column edge to a new position.

■ A line shows the new position.

3 Release the left mouse button and the column displays the new width.

ERASE LINES

ERASE LINES

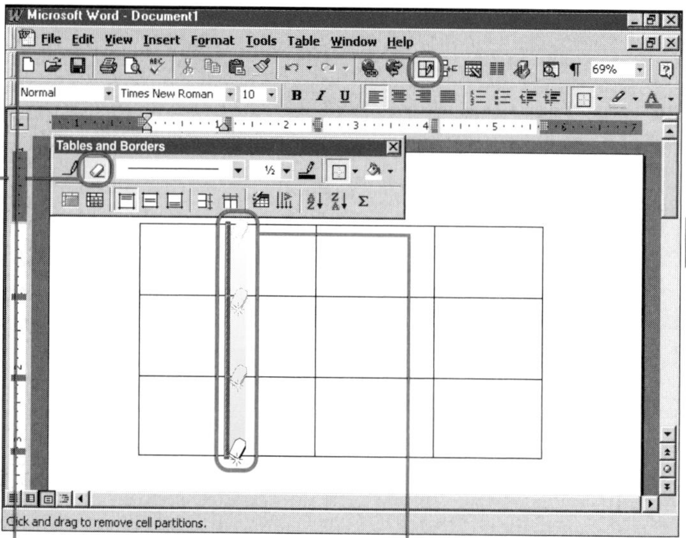

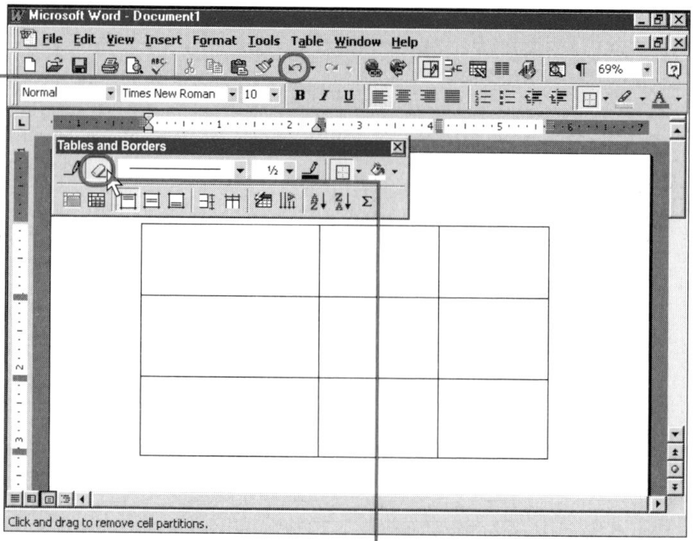

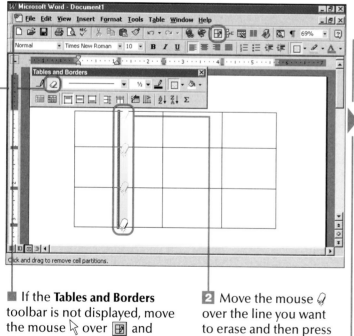

■ If the **Tables and Borders** toolbar is not displayed, move the mouse over ▦ and then press the left mouse button to display the toolbar.

1 Move the mouse over ▦ and then press the left mouse button.

2 Move the mouse over the line you want to erase and then press and hold down the left mouse button as you move the mouse along the line.

3 Release the left mouse button and the line disappears.

■ To immediately return the line to the table, move the mouse over ↶ and then press the left mouse button.

4 Repeat steps 2 and 3 for all the lines you want to erase.

5 When you finish erasing lines, move the mouse over ▦ and then press the left mouse button.

ENTER TEXT

ENTER TEXT

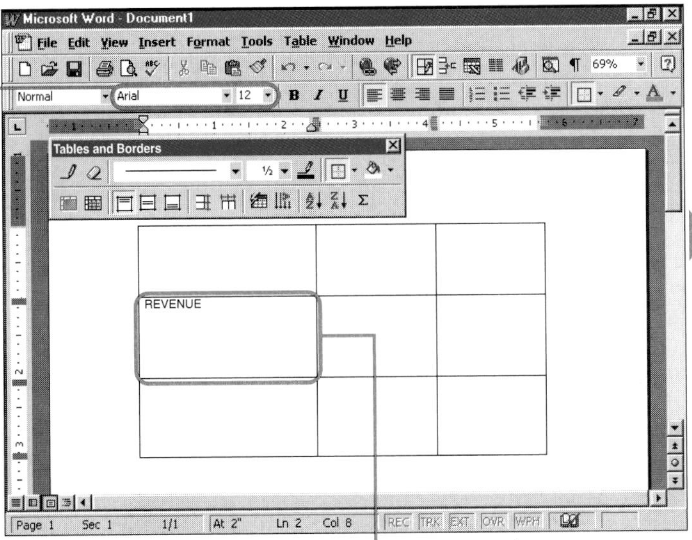

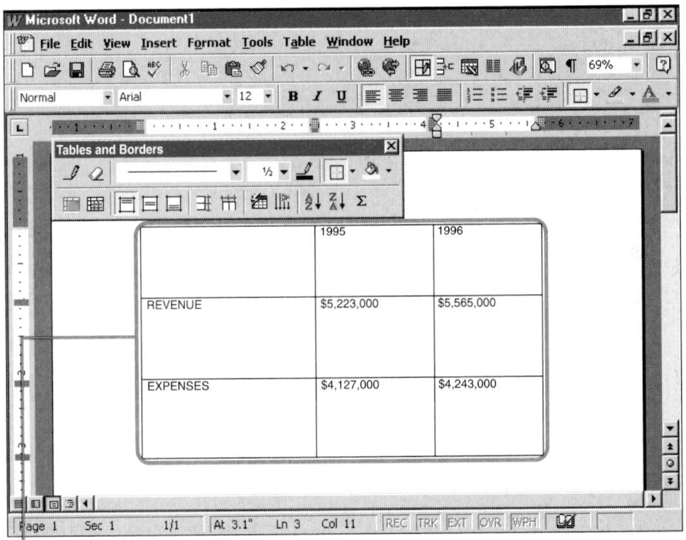

■ For this example, the design and size of text were changed to make the text easier to read. To change the design and size of text, refer to pages 74 and 75.

1 Move the mouse I over the cell where you want to type text and then press the left mouse button. Then type the text.

Note: To quickly move through the cells in a table, press ←, ↑, ↓ or → on your keyboard.

2 Repeat step 1 until you have typed all the text.

■ You can edit and format the text in a table as you would edit and format any text in a document.

ADD A ROW OR COLUMN

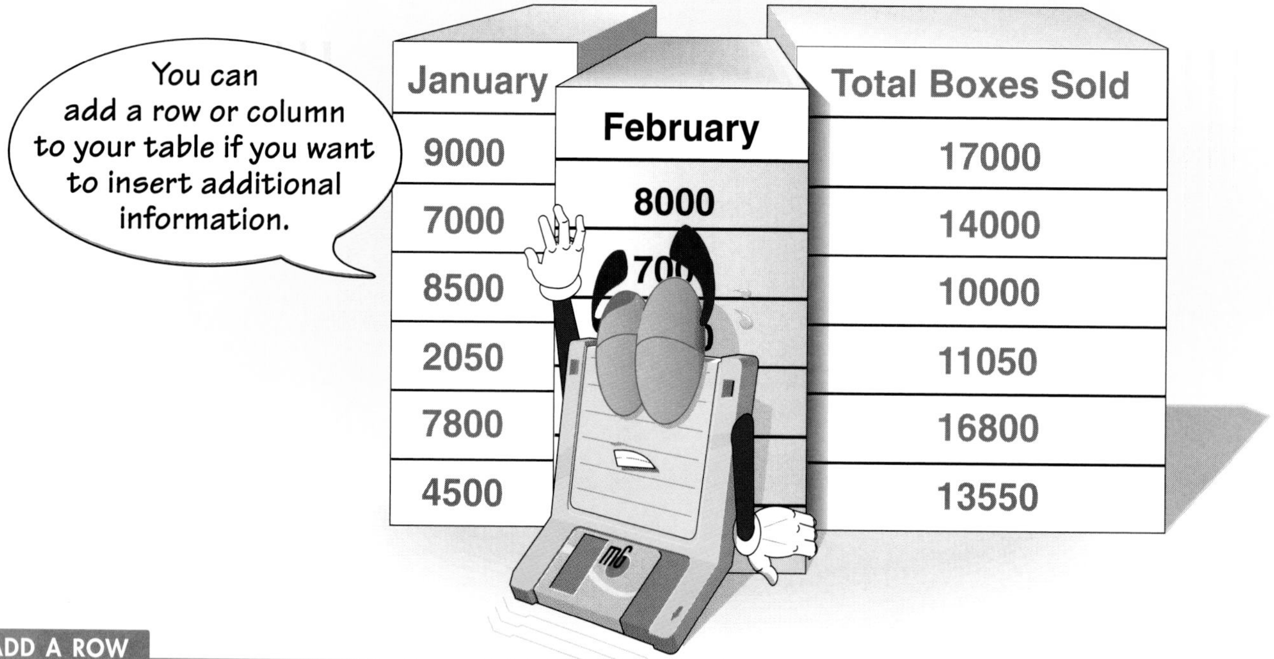

You can add a row or column to your table if you want to insert additional information.
January
9000
7000
8500
2050
7800
4500
February
8000
Total Boxes Sold
17000
14000
10000
11050
16800
13550

ADD A ROW

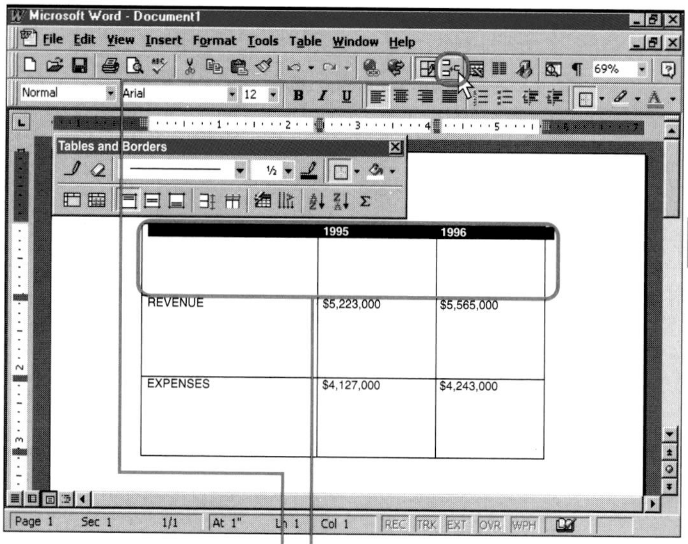

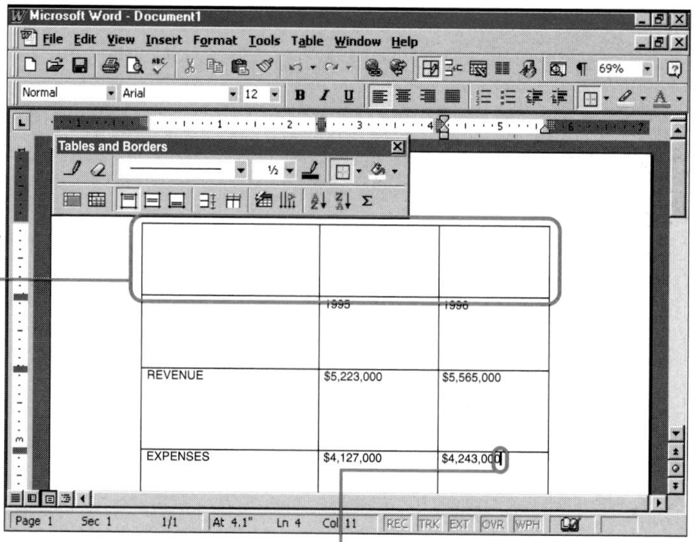

Word will insert a row above the row you select.

1 To select a row, move the mouse I to the left of the row (I changes to ↗) and then press the left mouse button.

2 Move the mouse ↖ over [Insert Rows] and then press the left mouse button.

■ A new row appears.

ADD A ROW TO THE BOTTOM OF A TABLE

1 Move the mouse I over the bottom right cell in the table and then press the left mouse button.

2 Press Tab on your keyboard.

Is there another way to add a row or column to a table?

You can add a row or column by drawing a line for the new row or column.

1 Move the mouse over on the **Tables and Borders** toolbar and then press the left mouse button.

2 To draw the line in your table, perform steps 5 and 6 on page 153.

ADD A COLUMN

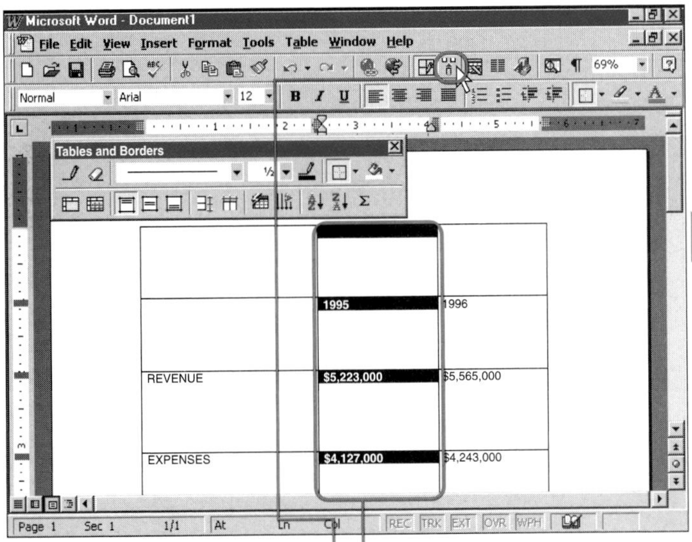

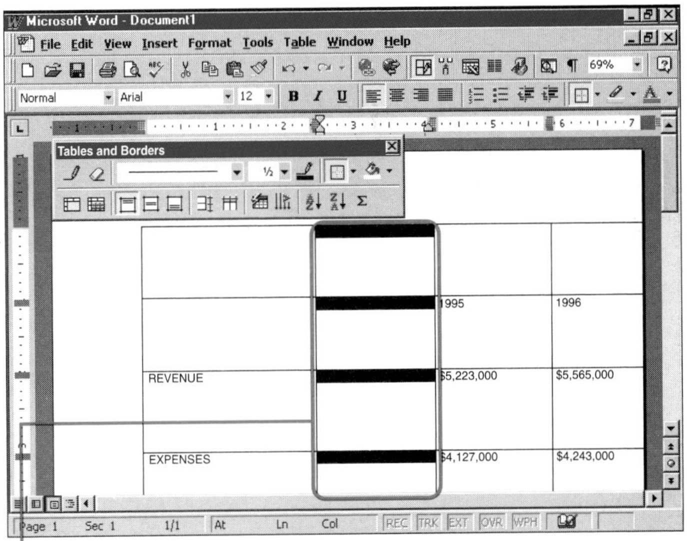

Word will insert a column to the left of the column you select.

1 To select a column, move the mouse I to the top of the column (I changes to ↓) and then press the left mouse button.

2 Move the mouse over and then press the left mouse button.

■ A new column appears.

DELETE A ROW OR COLUMN

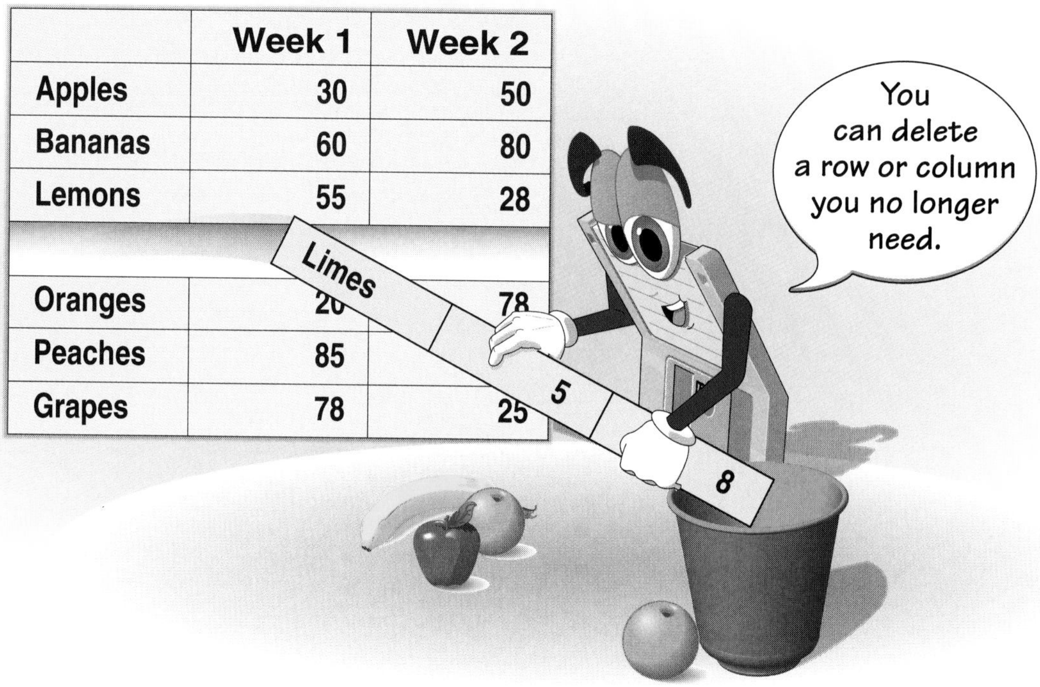

Week 1
Week 2
Apples 30 50
Bananas 60 80
Lemons 55 28
Limes
5
8
Oranges 78
Peaches 85
Grapes 78 25
You can delete a row or column you no longer need.

DELETE A ROW OR COLUMN

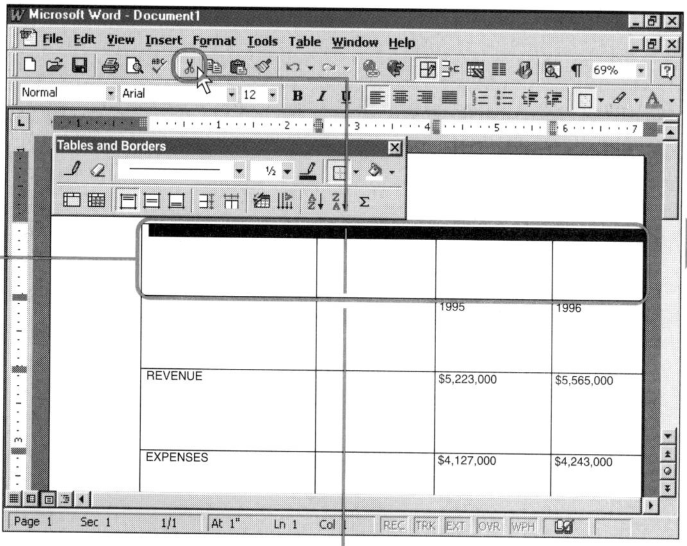

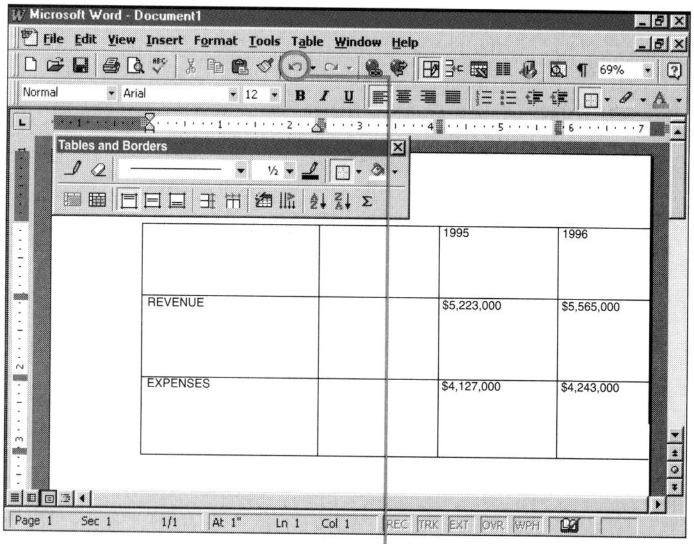

1 To select the row you want to delete, move the mouse I to the left of the row (I changes to ↗) and then press the left mouse button.

■ To select the column you want to delete, move the mouse I to the top of the column (I changes to ↓) and then press the left mouse button.

2 Move the mouse ↖ over ✂ and then press the left mouse button.

■ The row or column disappears.

■ To immediately return the row or column to the table, move the mouse ↖ over ↶ and then press the left mouse button.

DELETE A TABLE

DELETE A TABLE

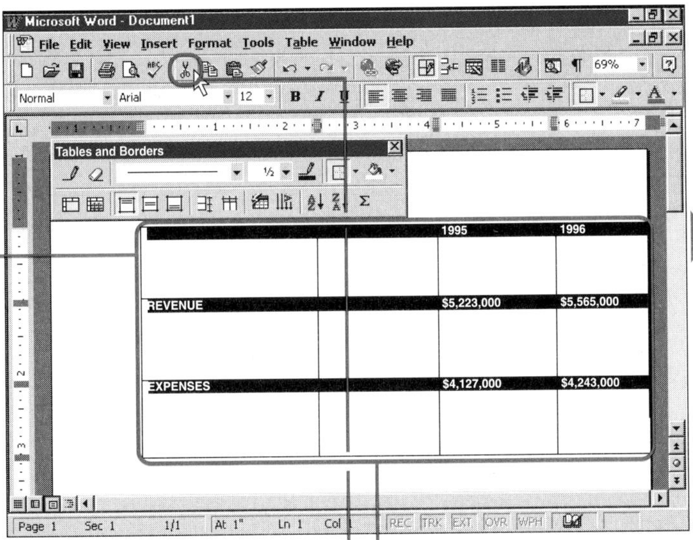

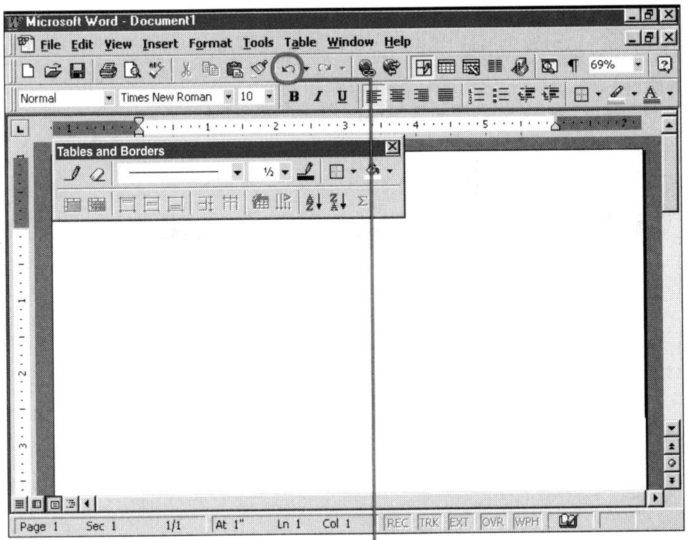

1 To select all the cells in the table, move the mouse to the left of the first row in the table (changes to).

2 Press and hold down the left mouse button as you move the mouse until you highlight all the cells in the table. Then release the mouse button.

3 Move the mouse over and then press the left mouse button.

■ The table disappears.

■ To immediately return the table to the document, move the mouse over and then press the left mouse button.

CHANGE TABLE BORDERS

You can enhance the appearance of a table by changing the borders.

CHANGE TABLE BORDERS

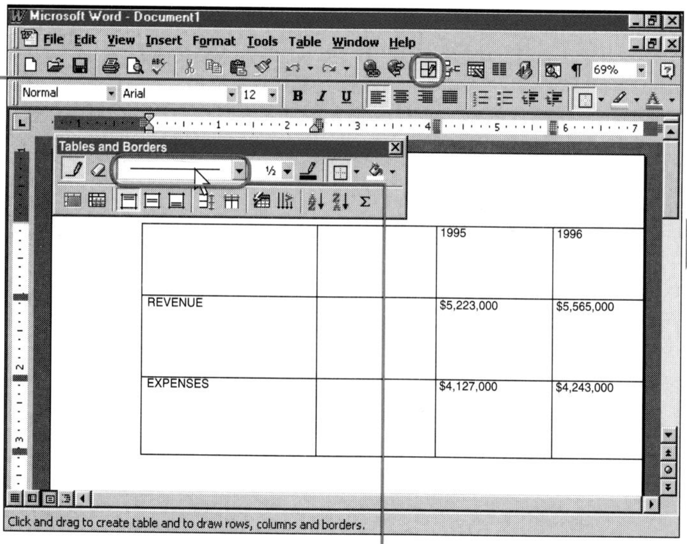

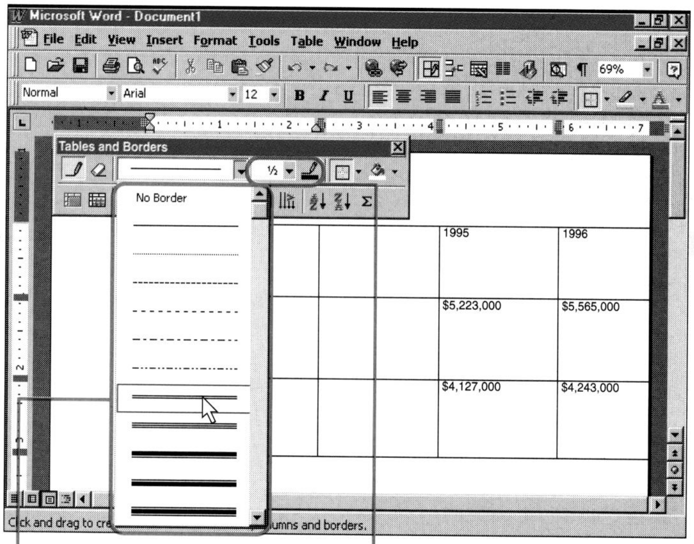

■ If the **Tables and Borders** toolbar is not displayed, move the mouse over the toolbar button and then press the left mouse button to display the toolbar.

1 To view a list of the available line styles, move the mouse over this area and then press the left mouse button.

2 Move the mouse over the line style you want to use and then press the left mouse button.

■ Word will use the line thickness and color displayed in these areas for the border.

How can I quickly enhance the appearance of a table?

Company Name	Item Donated	Quantity Donated
Best Bakery	Bread	200 loaves
Swan Grocery Stores	Cans of food	425
Ajax Knitting Co.	Sweaters	125
ABC Footwear	Shoes	85 pairs
Premier Lumber Yard	Lumber	5 truckloads
Rainbow Hardware	Nails	900 pounds

Company Name	Item Donated	Quantity Donated
Best Bakery	**Bread**	**200 loaves**
Swan Grocery Stores	**Cans of food**	**425**
Ajax Knitting Co.	**Sweaters**	**125**
ABC Footwear	**Shoes**	**85 pairs**
Premier Lumber Yard	**Lumber**	**5 truckloads**
Rainbow Hardware	**Nails**	**900 pounds**

You can have Word automatically add borders and shading to a table by using the Table AutoFormat feature. For information on the Table AutoFormat feature, refer to page 164.

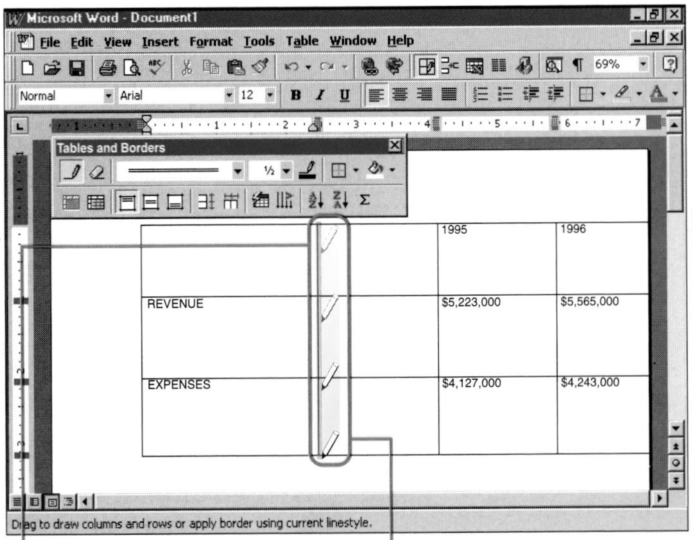

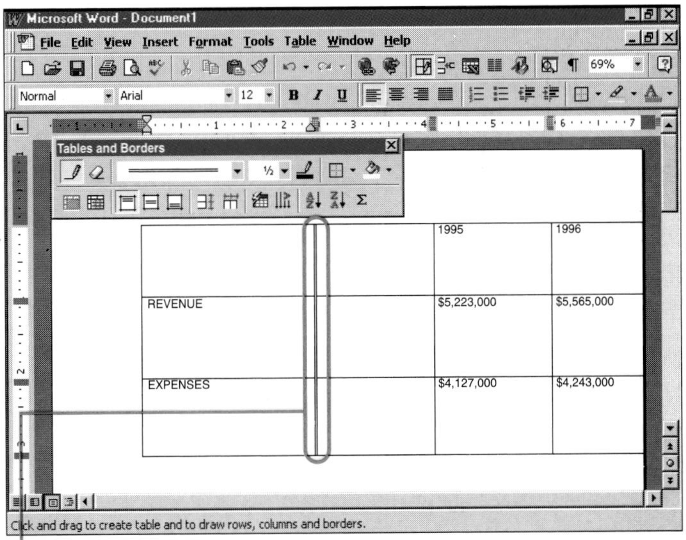

3 Move the mouse ⇖ over the border you want to change (⇖ changes to ✎).

4 Press and hold down the left mouse button as you move the mouse ✎ along the entire length of the border you want to change. Then release the mouse button.

■ The border changes.

5 Repeat steps 3 and 4 for each border you want to change.

6 When you finish changing borders, move the mouse ⇖ over ✎ and then press the left mouse button.

■ Word will use the line style you selected in step 2 to create new tables until you exit the program.

FORMAT A TABLE

Word offers many ready-to-use designs that you can choose from to give your table a new appearance.
Ready-To-Use
Designs

FORMAT A TABLE

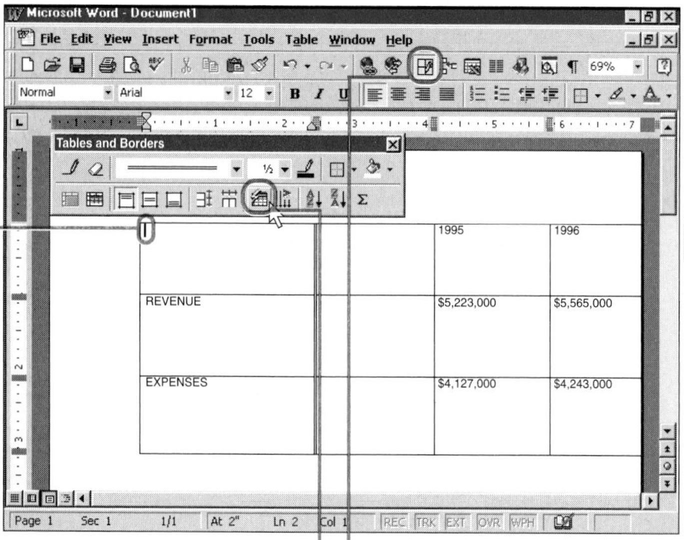

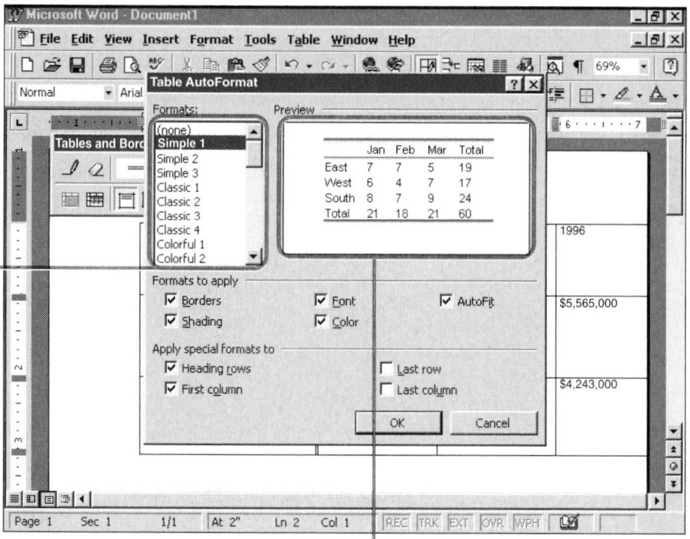

1 Move the mouse I anywhere over the table you want to change and then press the left mouse button.

■ If the **Tables and Borders** toolbar is not displayed, move the mouse over and then press the left mouse button to display the toolbar.

2 Move the mouse over and then press the left mouse button.

■ The **Table AutoFormat** dialog box appears.

■ This area displays a list of the available table designs.

■ This area displays a sample of the highlighted table design.

3 Press ↓ or ↑ on your keyboard until a design you like appears.

What are some of the table designs offered by Word?

	Jan	Feb	Mar	Total
East	7	7	5	19
West	6	4	7	17
South	8	7	9	24
Total	21	18	21	60

Colorful 1

	Jan	Feb	Mar	Total
East	7	7	5	19
West	6	4	7	17
South	8	7	9	24
Total	21	18	21	60

Grid 8

	Jan	Feb	Mar	Total
East	7	7	5	19
West	6	4	7	17
South	8	7	9	24
Total	21	18	21	60

Classic 3

	Jan	Feb	Mar	Total
East	7	7	5	19
West	6	4	7	17
South	8	7	9	24
Total	21	18	21	60

Columns 5

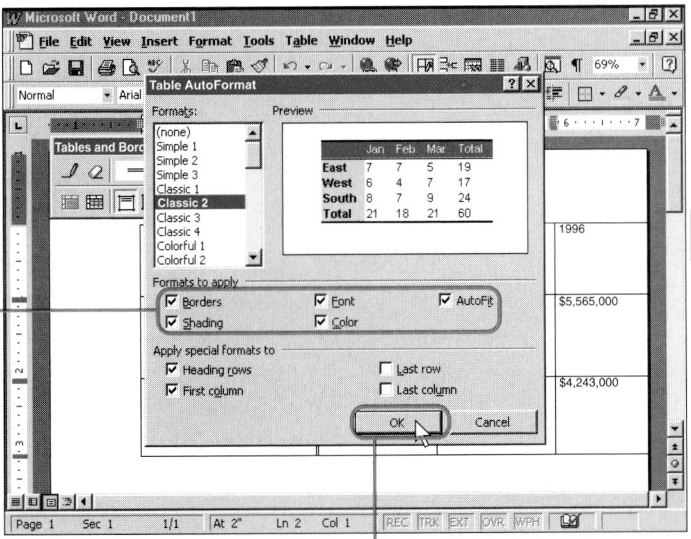

■ A check mark (✔) beside an option tells you that Word will apply the option to the table.

4 To add or remove a check mark (✔) for an option, move the mouse over the check box beside the option and then press the left mouse button.

5 To apply the design to the table, move the mouse over **OK** and then press the left mouse button.

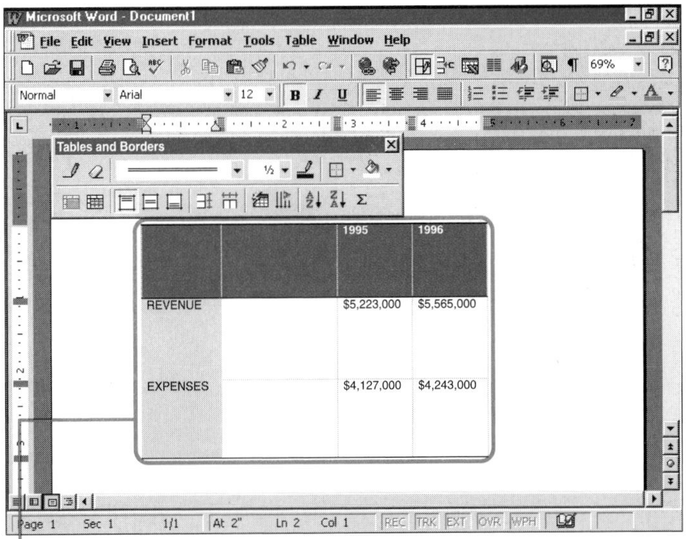

■ The table displays the design you selected.

REMOVE AUTOFORMAT

■ Perform steps 1 to 3, selecting **Grid 1** in step 3. Then press Enter on your keyboard.

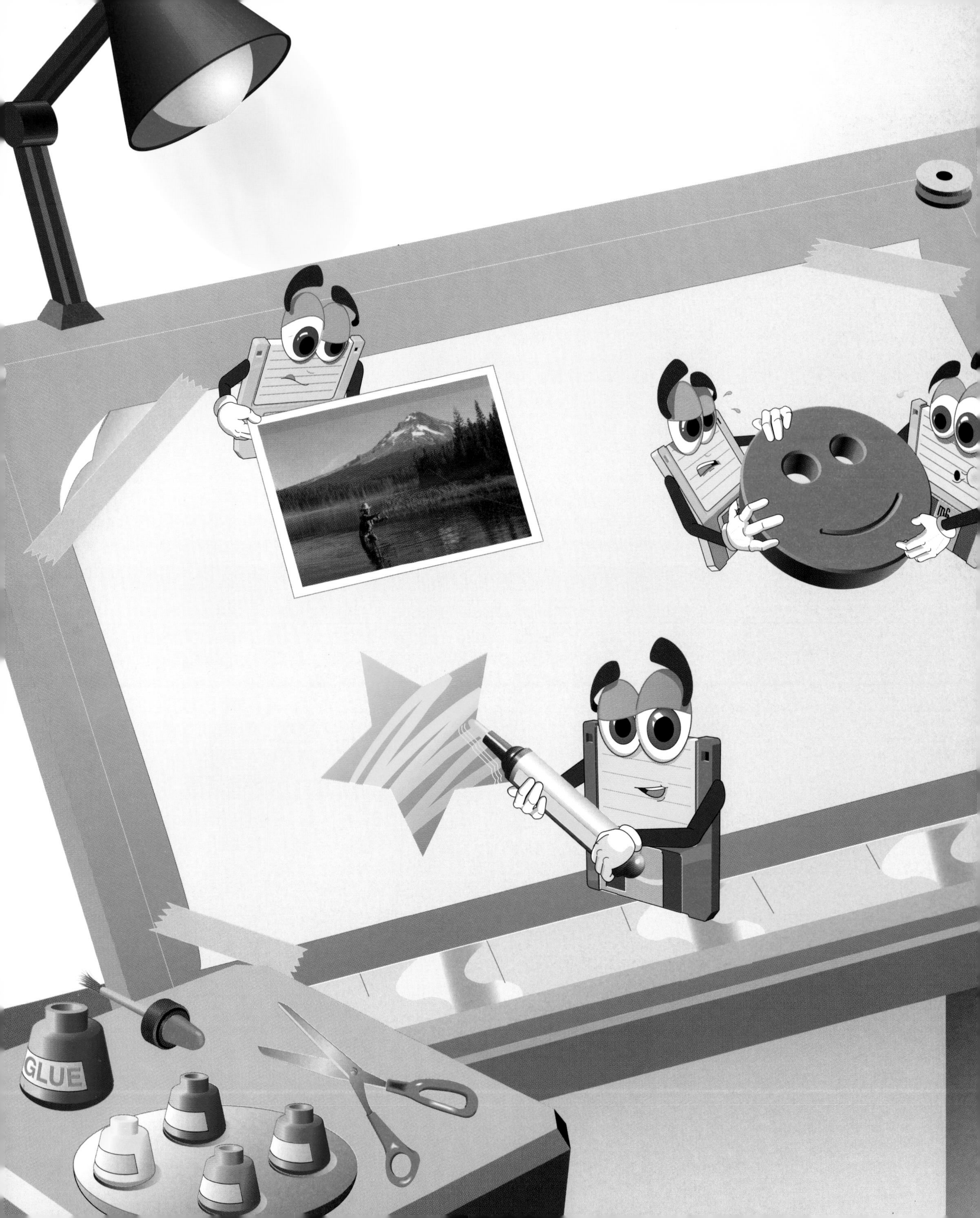
GLUE

CHAPTER 10

WORK WITH GRAPHICS

What can I do to enhance the appearance of my documents? Learn how to add colorful graphics and text effects to your documents.

ADD A SIMPLE SHAPE

Word provides many ready-made shapes, called AutoShapes, that you can easily add to your document.

Word can only display graphics in the Page Layout and Online Layout views. For information on the four views, refer to page 32.

ADD A SIMPLE SHAPE

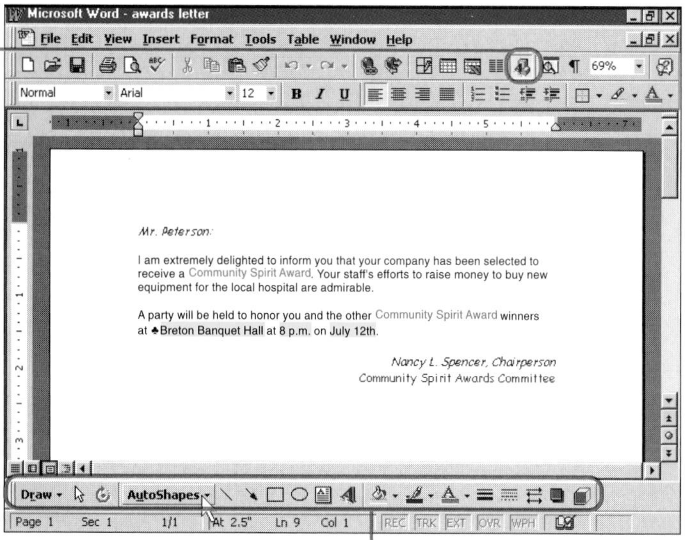

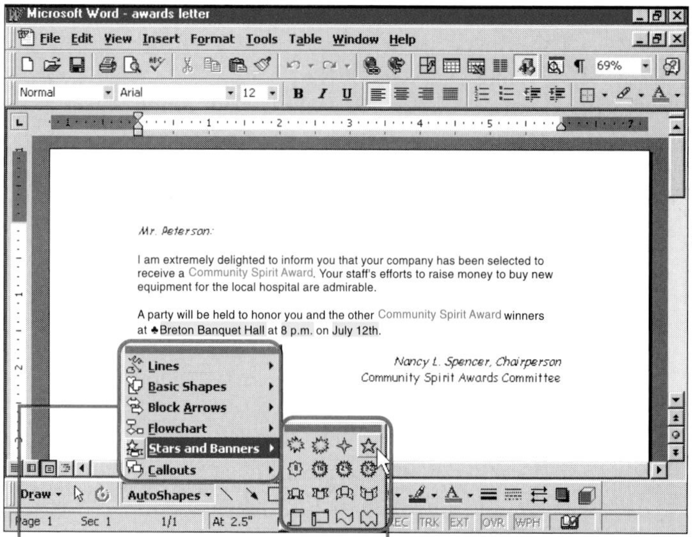

1 To display the **Drawing** toolbar, move the mouse over the Drawing button and then press the left mouse button.

■ The **Drawing** toolbar appears and your document is displayed in the Page Layout view.

2 To add a shape, move the mouse over **AutoShapes** and then press the left mouse button.

3 Move the mouse over the type of shape you want to add.

4 Move the mouse over the shape you want to add and then press the left mouse button.

How do I delete a shape?

To delete a shape, move the mouse ✥ over the shape and then press the left mouse button. Then press Delete on your keyboard.

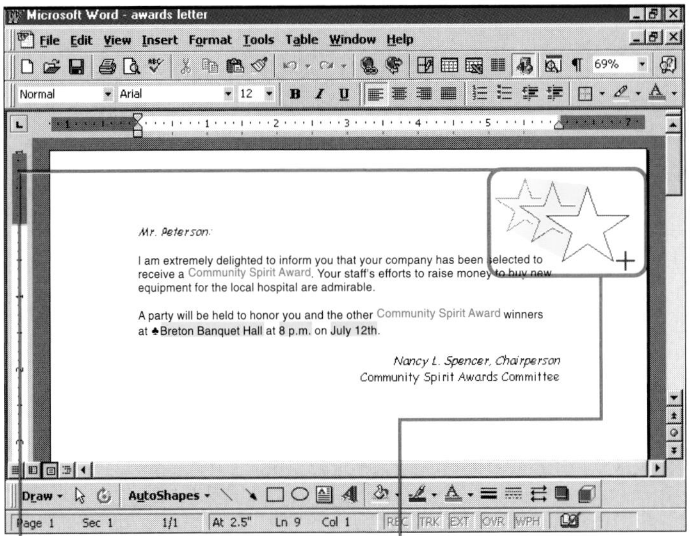
Microsoft Word - awards letter
File Edit View Insert Format Tools Table Window Help
Normal
Arial
12
69%
Mr. Peterson:
I am extremely delighted to inform you that your company has been selected to receive a Community Spirit Award. Your staff's efforts to raise money to buy new equipment for the local hospital are admirable.
A party will be held to honor you and the other Community Spirit Award winners at ♣Breton Banquet Hall at 8 p.m. on July 12th.
Nancy L. Spencer, Chairperson
Community Spirit Awards Committee
Draw
AutoShapes
Page 1 Sec 1 1/1 At 2.5" Ln 9 Col 1 REC TRK EXT OVR WPH

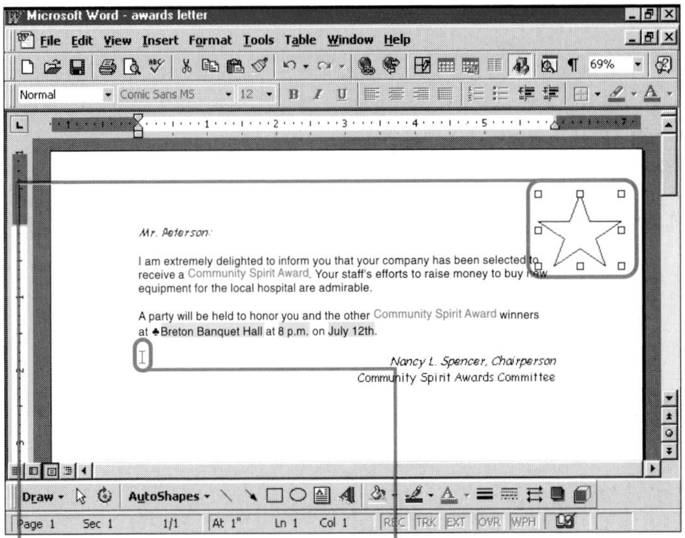
Microsoft Word - awards letter
File Edit View Insert Format Tools Table Window Help
Normal
Comic Sans MS
12
69%
Mr. Peterson:
I am extremely delighted to inform you that your company has been selected to receive a Community Spirit Award. Your staff's efforts to raise money to buy new equipment for the local hospital are admirable.
A party will be held to honor you and the other Community Spirit Award winners at ♣Breton Banquet Hall at 8 p.m. on July 12th.
Nancy L. Spencer, Chairperson
Community Spirit Awards Committee
Draw
AutoShapes
Page 1 Sec 1 1/1 At 1" Ln 1 Col 1 REC TRK EXT OVR WPH

5 Move the mouse ↖ to where you want the top left corner of the shape to appear (↖ changes to +).

6 Press and hold down the left mouse button as you move the mouse + until the shape is the size you want. Then release the mouse button.

■ The shape appears in your document. The handles (□) around the shape let you change the size of the shape. To resize a graphic, refer to page 175.

7 To hide the handles, move the mouse I outside the shape area and then press the left mouse button.

■ To hide the **Drawing** toolbar, repeat step 1.

ADD CLIP ART OR A PICTURE

You can use professionally designed clip art and pictures that come with Word to enhance your document.
Health News
FISHING NEWS

Word can only display graphics in the Page Layout and Online Layout views. For information on the four views, refer to page 32.

ADD CLIP ART OR A PICTURE

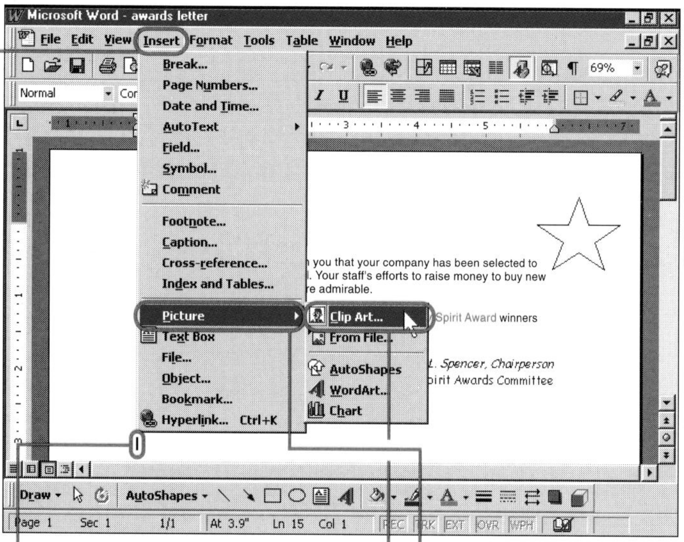
Microsoft Word - awards letter
File Edit View Insert Format Tools Table Window Help
Break...
Page Numbers...
Date and Time...
AutoText
Field...
Symbol...
Comment
Footnote...
Caption...
Cross-reference...
Index and Tables...
Picture
Text Box
File...
Object...
Bookmark...
Hyperlink... Ctrl+K
Clip Art...
From File...
AutoShapes
WordArt...
Chart

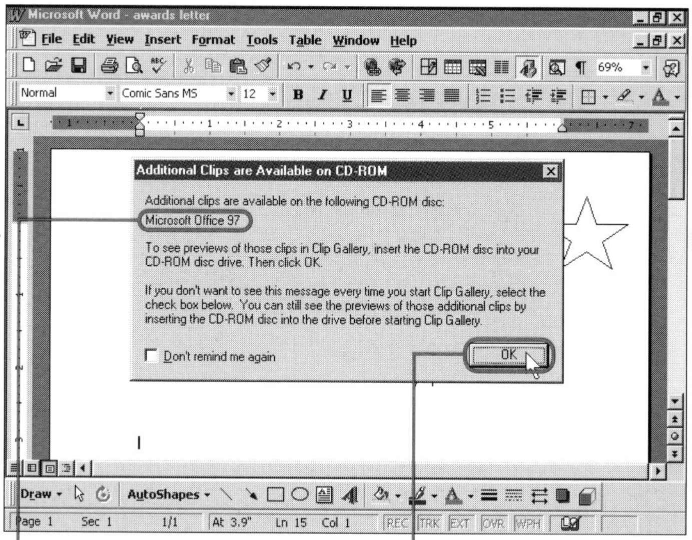
Microsoft Word - awards letter
Additional Clips are Available on CD-ROM
Additional clips are available on the following CD-ROM disc:
Microsoft Office 97
To see previews of those clips in Clip Gallery, insert the CD-ROM disc into your CD-ROM disc drive. Then click OK.
If you don't want to see this message every time you start Clip Gallery, select the check box below. You can still see the previews of those additional clips by inserting the CD-ROM disc into the drive before starting Clip Gallery.
Don't remind me again
OK

1 Move the mouse I to where you want to add a graphic and then press the left mouse button.

2 Move the mouse over **Insert** and then press the left mouse button.

3 Move the mouse over **Picture**.

4 Move the mouse over **Clip Art** and then press the left mouse button.

■ A dialog box appears if additional graphics are available on the CD-ROM disc identified in this area.

5 To view the additional graphics, insert the CD-ROM disc into your CD-ROM disc drive.

6 Move the mouse over **OK** and then press the left mouse button.

■ The **Microsoft Clip Gallery** dialog box appears.

What clip art and pictures does Word offer?

Word offers clip art and pictures of animals, household items, plants, sports and much more.

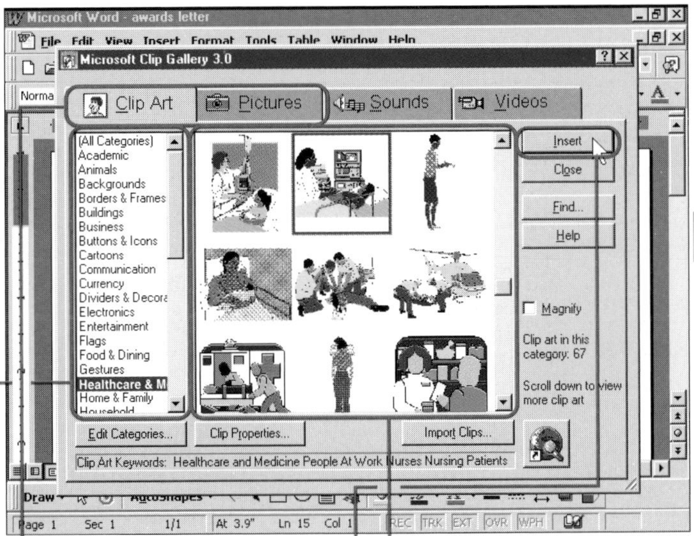

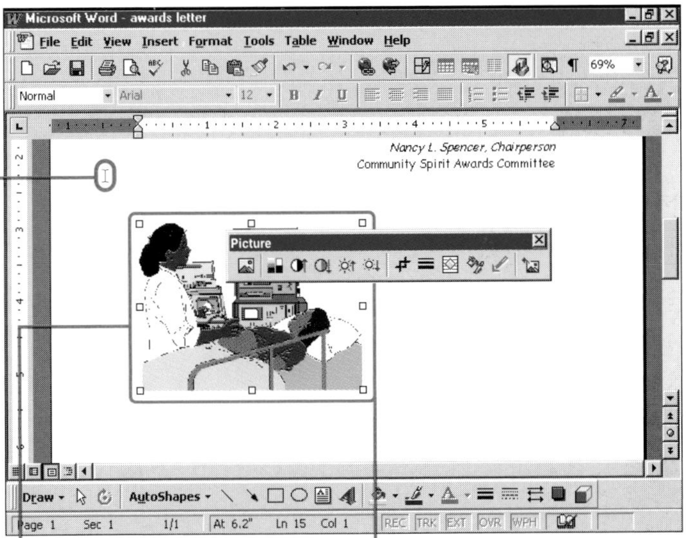

7 Move the mouse over the **Clip Art** or **Pictures** tab and then press the left mouse button.

8 Move the mouse over the category of graphics you want to choose from and then press the left mouse button.

9 Move the mouse over the graphic you want to add and then press the left mouse button.

10 To add the graphic to your document, move the mouse over **Insert** and then press the left mouse button.

■ The graphic appears in your document. The handles (□) around the graphic let you change the size of the graphic. To resize a graphic, refer to page 175.

11 To hide the handles, move the mouse outside the graphic area and then press the left mouse button.

■ To delete a graphic, move the mouse over the graphic and then press the left mouse button. Then press Delete on your keyboard.

ADD A TEXT EFFECT

You can use the WordArt feature to add text effects to your document.

Word can only display graphics in the Page Layout and Online Layout views. For information on the four views, refer to page 32.

ADD A TEXT EFFECT

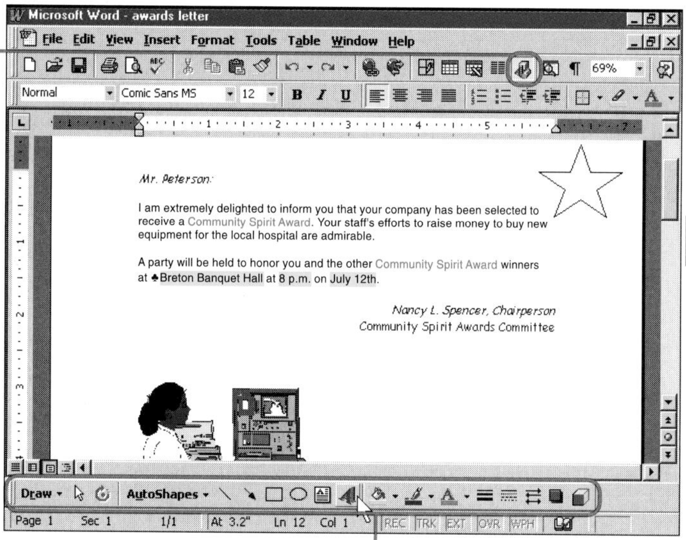

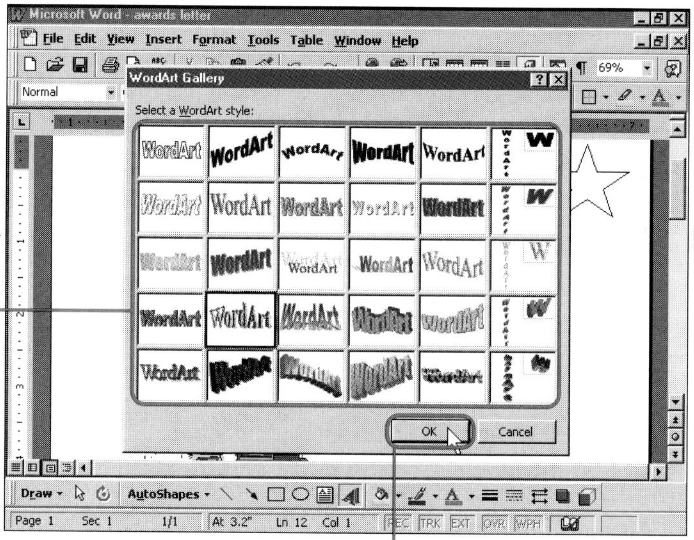

1 To display the **Drawing** toolbar, move the mouse over and then press the left mouse button.

■ The **Drawing** toolbar appears and your document is displayed in the Page Layout view.

2 To add a text effect, move the mouse over and then press the left mouse button.

■ The **WordArt Gallery** dialog box appears.

3 Move the mouse over the type of text effect you want to add to your document and then press the left mouse button.

4 Move the mouse over **OK** and then press the left mouse button.

How do I delete a text effect?

To delete a text effect, move the mouse over the text effect and then press the left mouse button. Then press Delete on your keyboard.

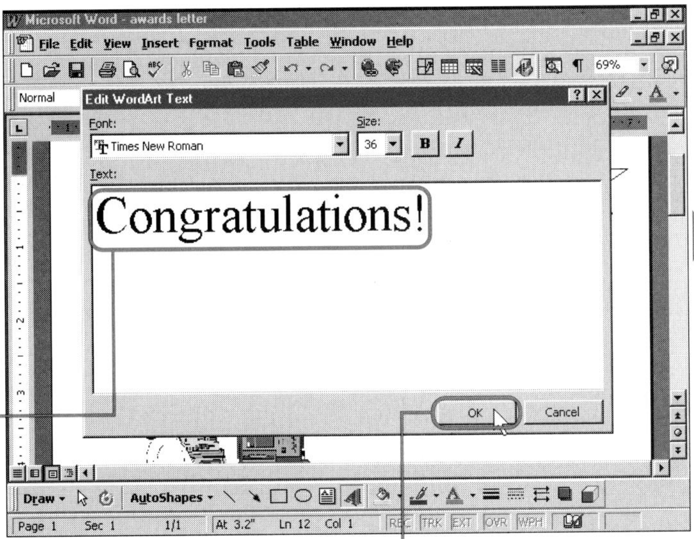

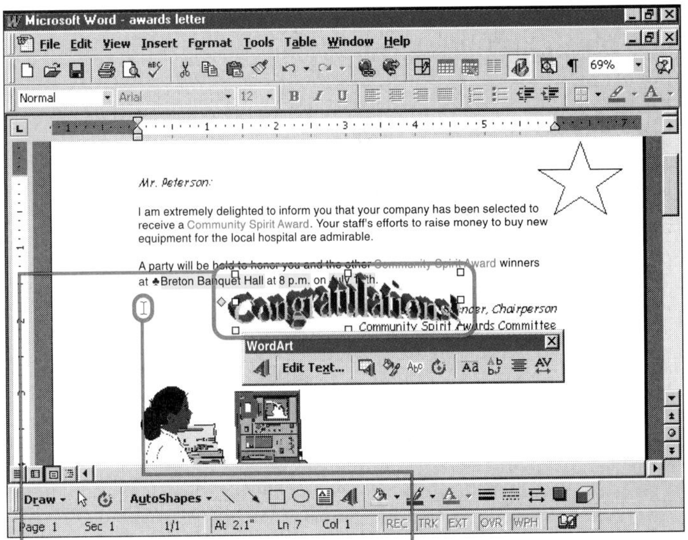

■ The **Edit WordArt Text** dialog box appears.

5 Type the text you want to display the effect you selected in step 3.

6 To add the text effect to your document, move the mouse over **OK** and then press the left mouse button.

■ The text effect appears in your document. The handles (□) around the text effect let you change the size of the text effect. To resize a graphic, refer to page 175.

7 To hide the handles, move the mouse outside the text effect area and then press the left mouse button.

■ To hide the **Drawing** toolbar, repeat step 1.

MOVE OR RESIZE A GRAPHIC

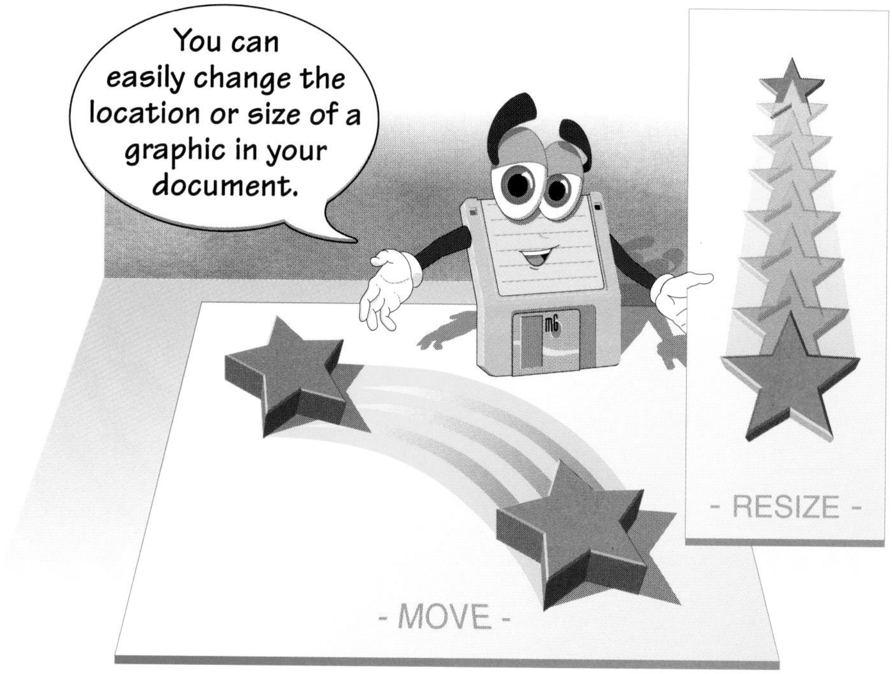

You can easily change the location or size of a graphic in your document.
- RESIZE -
- MOVE -

Word can only display graphics in the Page Layout and Online Layout views. For information on the four views, refer to page 32.

MOVE A GRAPHIC

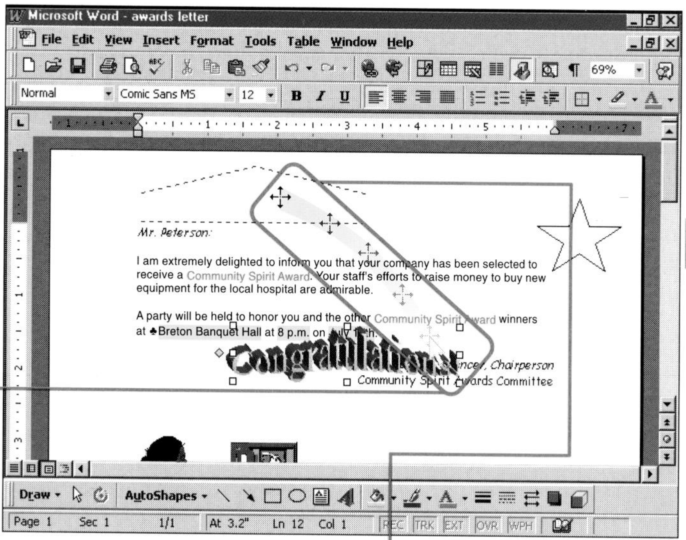

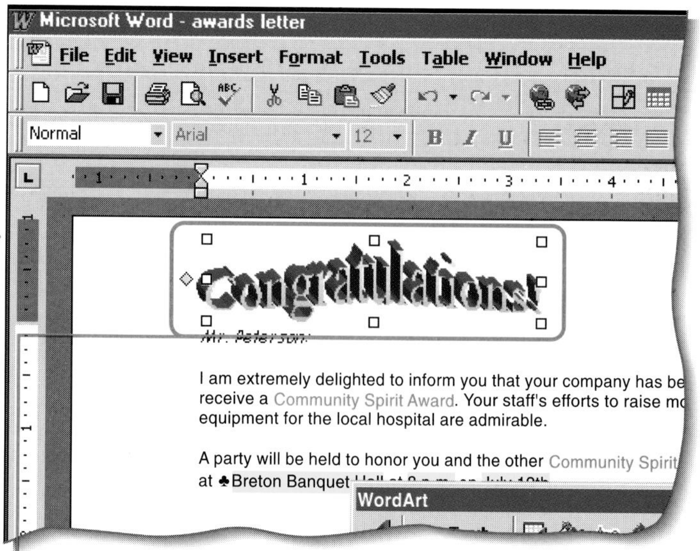

1 Display your document in the Page Layout view. To change the view, refer to page 32.

2 Move the mouse I over the graphic you want to move (I changes to ✥).

3 Press and hold down the left mouse button as you move the graphic to a new location. Then release the mouse button.

■ The graphic appears in the new location.

What are the handles (□) that appear around a selected graphic used for?

The handles around a selected graphic let you change the size of the graphic.

- □ Change the height of a graphic.
- ■ Change the width of a graphic.
- □ Change the height and width of a graphic at the same time.

RESIZE A GRAPHIC

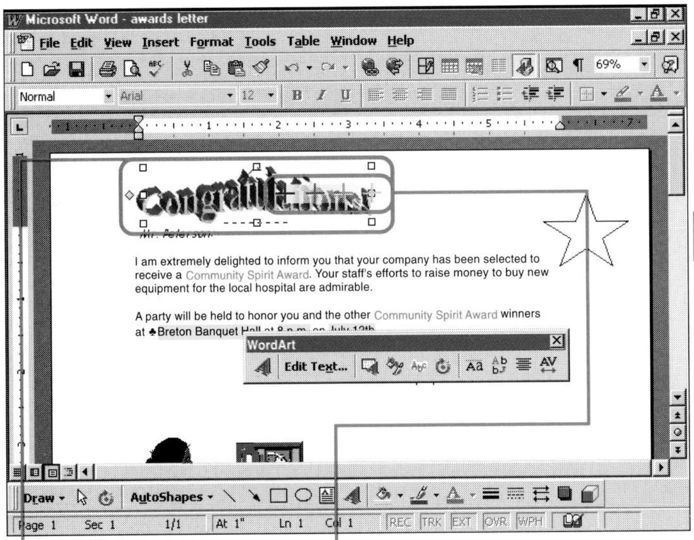
Microsoft Word - awards letter
File Edit View Insert Format Tools Table Window Help
I am extremely delighted to inform you that your company has been selected to receive a Community Spirit Award. Your staff's efforts to raise money to buy new equipment for the local hospital are admirable.
A party will be held to honor you and the other Community Spirit Award winners
WordArt
Edit Text...
Draw
AutoShapes

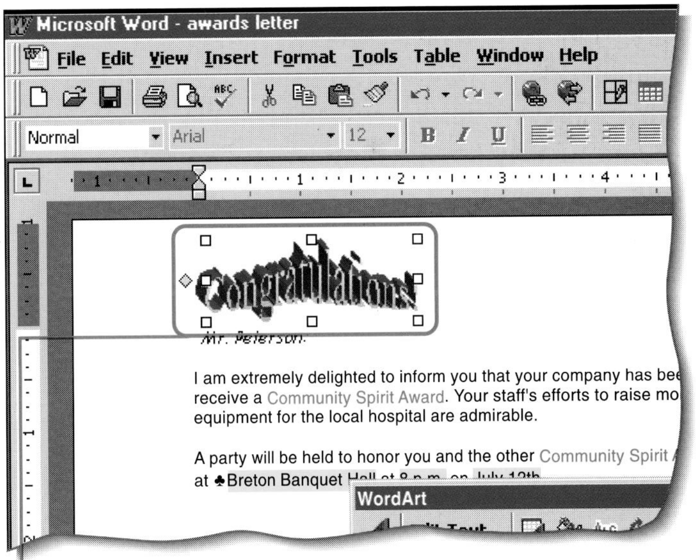
Microsoft Word - awards letter
File Edit View Insert Format Tools Table Window Help
Normal
Arial
I am extremely delighted to inform you that your company has bee
receive a Community Spirit Award. Your staff's efforts to raise mo
equipment for the local hospital are admirable.
A party will be held to honor you and the other Community Spirit
at ♣Breton Banquet
WordArt

1 Move the mouse ✥ over the graphic you want to resize and then press the left mouse button. Handles (□) appear around the graphic.

2 Move the mouse ✥ over one of the handles (✥ changes to ↔ or ↕).

3 Press and hold down the left mouse button as you move the mouse + until the graphic is the size you want. Then release the mouse button.

■ The graphic appears in the new size.

CHANGE COLOR OF GRAPHIC

You can easily change the color of a graphic in your document.
mG

Word can only display graphics in the Page Layout and Online Layout views. For information on the four views, refer to page 32.

CHANGE COLOR OF GRAPHIC

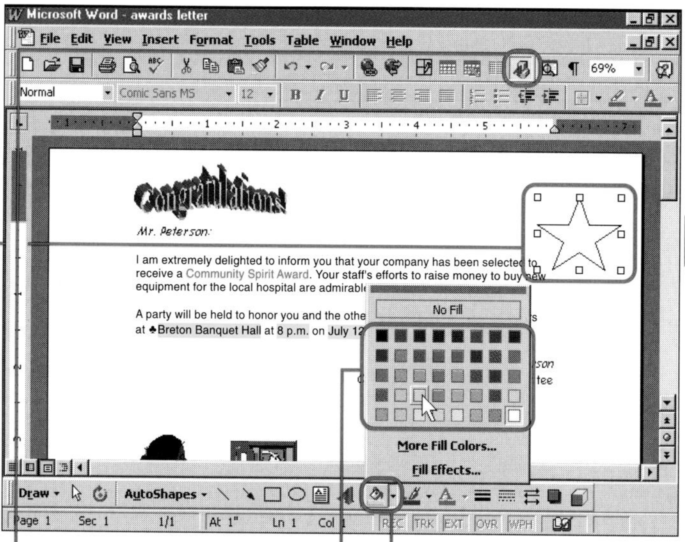

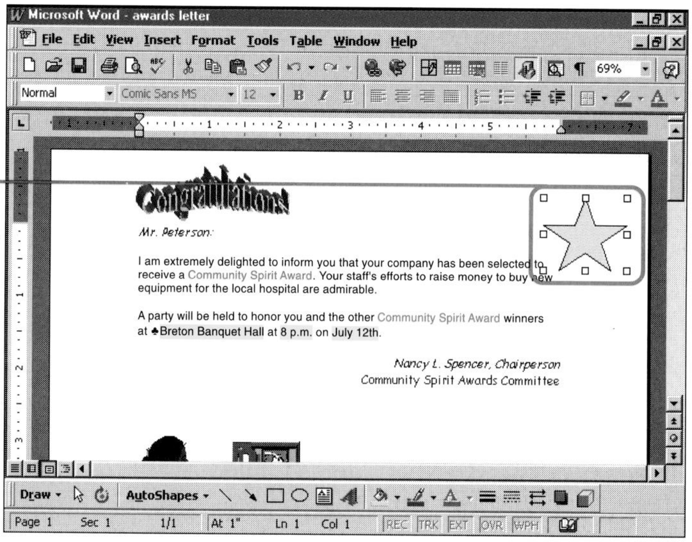

1 To display the **Drawing** toolbar, move the mouse over and then press the left mouse button.

2 Move the mouse over the graphic you want to display a different color and then press the left mouse button.

3 Move the mouse over ▾ in this area and then press the left mouse button.

4 Move the mouse over the color you want to use and then press the left mouse button.

■ The graphic displays the color you selected.

MAKE A GRAPHIC 3-D

Word can only display graphics in the Page Layout and Online Layout views. For information on the four views, refer to page 32.

MAKE A GRAPHIC 3-D

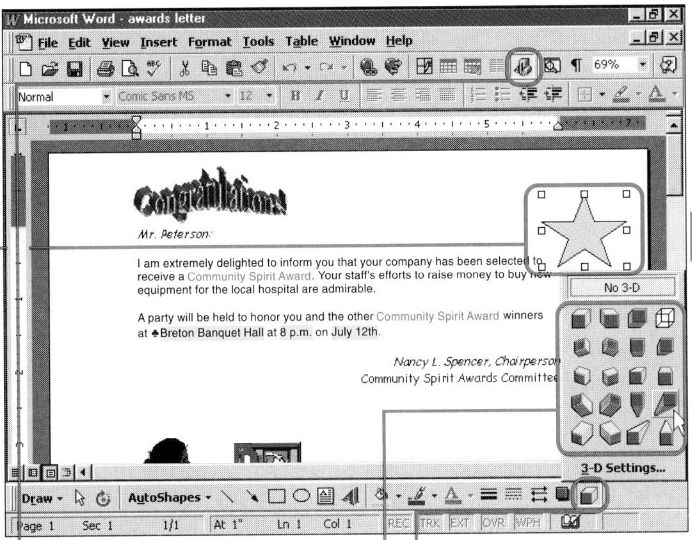

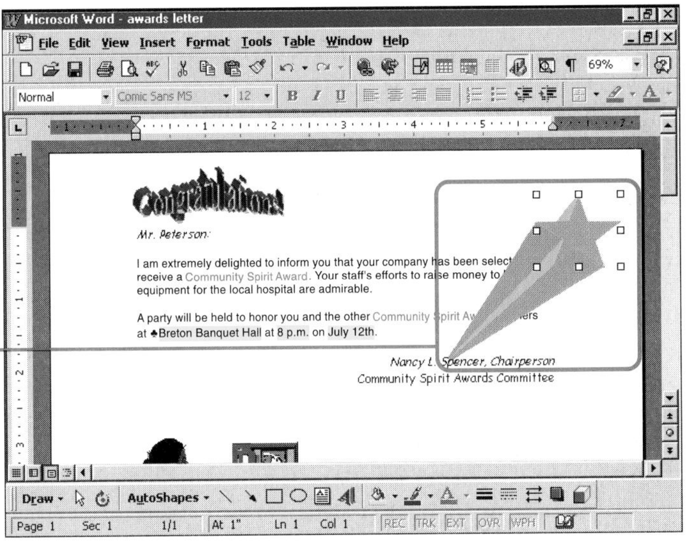

1 To display the **Drawing** toolbar, move the mouse over and then press the left mouse button.

2 Move the mouse over the graphic you want to appear in 3-D and then press the left mouse button.

3 Move the mouse over and then press the left mouse button.

4 Move the mouse over the 3-D effect you want to use and then press the left mouse button.

■ The graphic appears in 3-D.

WRAP TEXT AROUND A GRAPHIC

You can easily wrap text around a graphic in your document.

Word can only display graphics in the Page Layout and Online Layout views. For information on the four views, refer to page 32.

WRAP TEXT AROUND A GRAPHIC

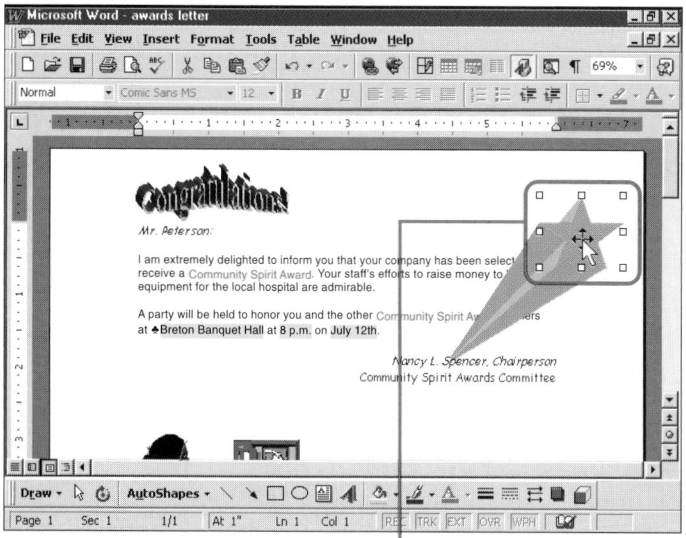

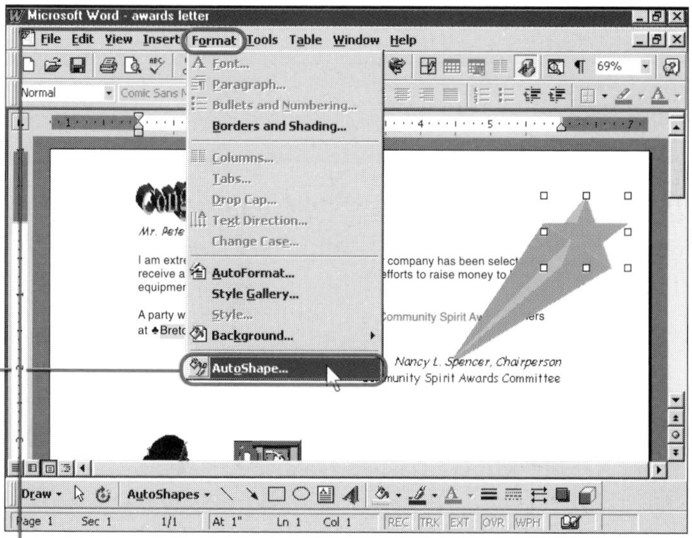

1 Display your document in the Page Layout view. To change the view, refer to page 32.

2 Move the mouse over the graphic you want to wrap text around and then press the left mouse button.

3 Move the mouse over **Format** and then press the left mouse button.

4 Move the mouse over **AutoShape**, **Picture** or **WordArt** and then press the left mouse button.

*Note: The option available in step **4** depends on the type of graphic you selected in step **2**.*

■ The **Format** dialog box appears.

How can I wrap text around a graphic?

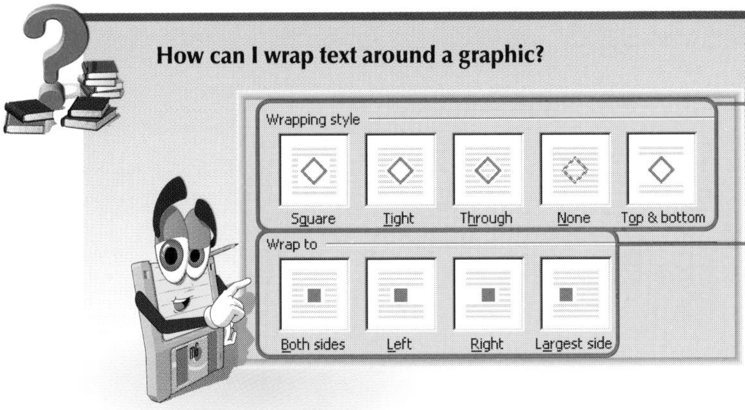

■ You can choose the way you want text to wrap around a graphic.

■ You can choose which side(s) of the graphic you want the text to wrap around.

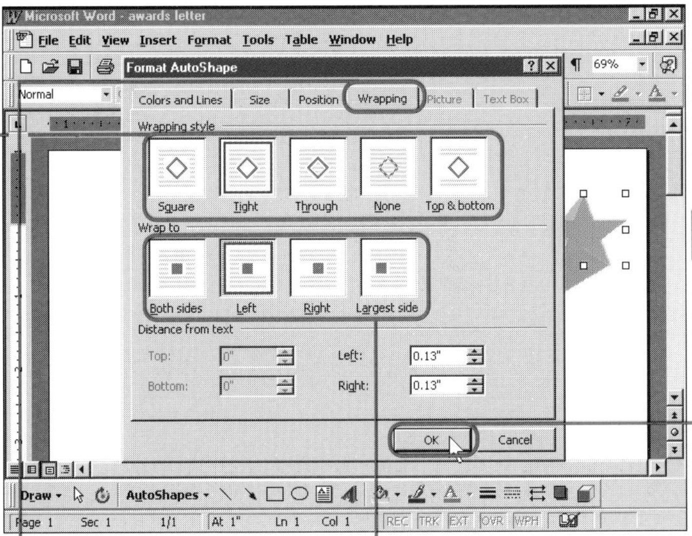

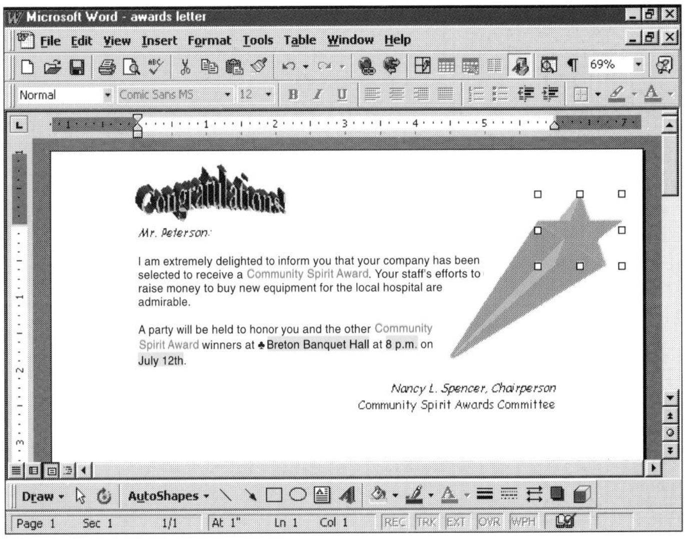

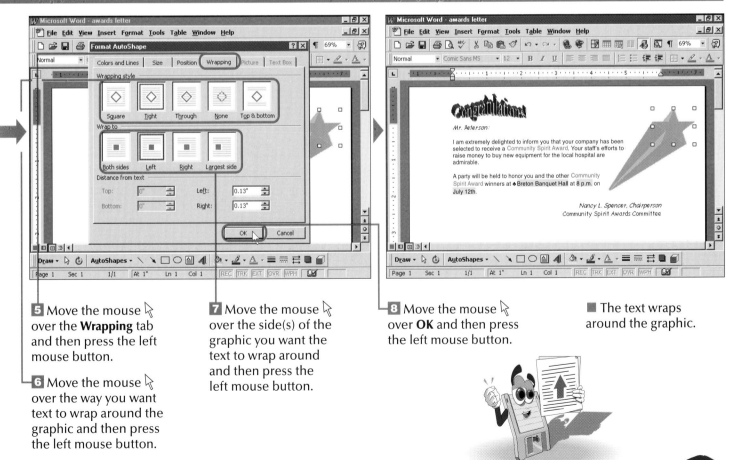

5 Move the mouse over the **Wrapping** tab and then press the left mouse button.

6 Move the mouse over the way you want text to wrap around the graphic and then press the left mouse button.

7 Move the mouse over the side(s) of the graphic you want the text to wrap around and then press the left mouse button.

8 Move the mouse over **OK** and then press the left mouse button.

■ The text wraps around the graphic.

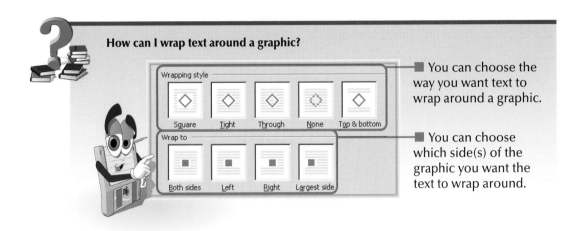

MAIL
MAIL
Mr. John Smith
11 South Street
Los Angeles, CA 90013
32
Mr. Jim Hunter
14 Willow Avenue
Los Angeles, CA 90028
32

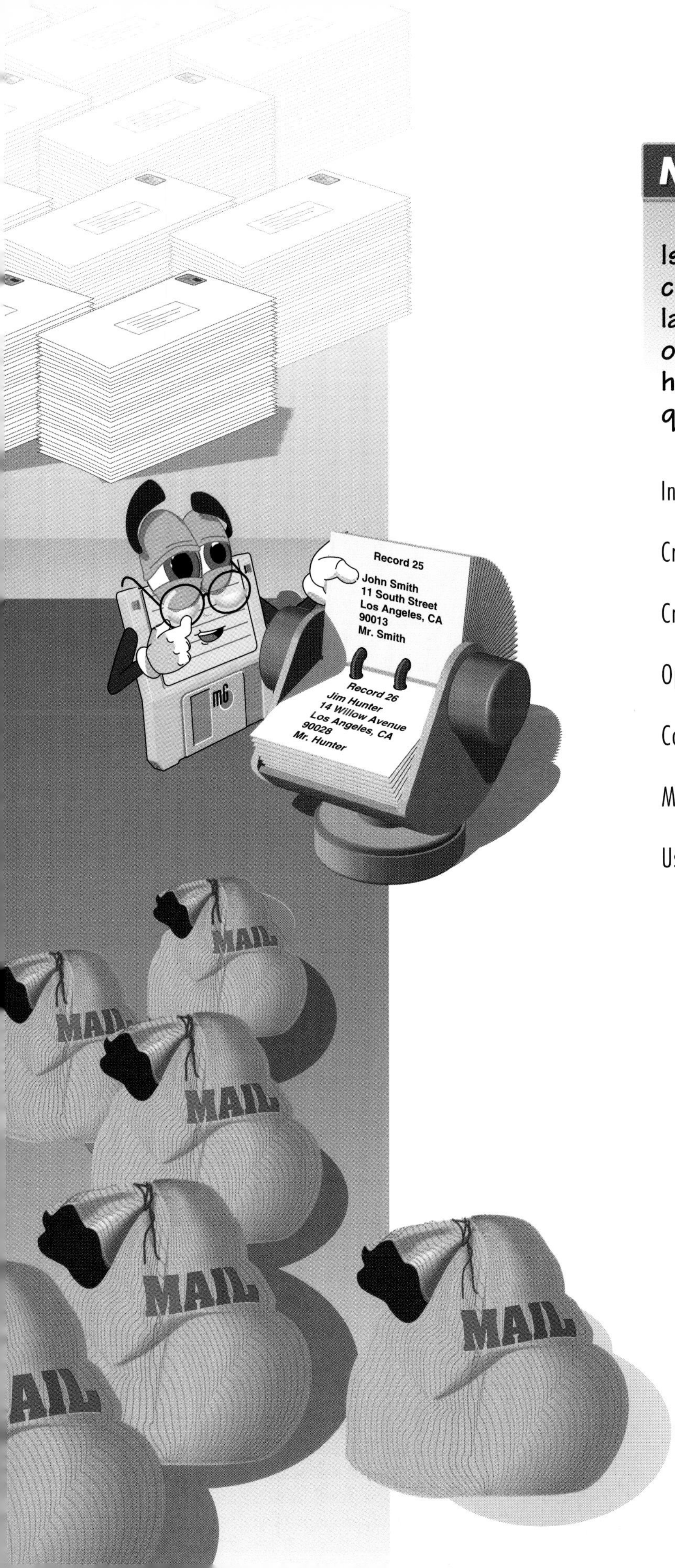

CHAPTER 11

MAIL MERGE

Is there an efficient way to create personalized letters and labels for my customers? Word offers a Mail Merge feature to help you complete these tasks quickly and easily.

INTRODUCTION TO MAIL MERGE

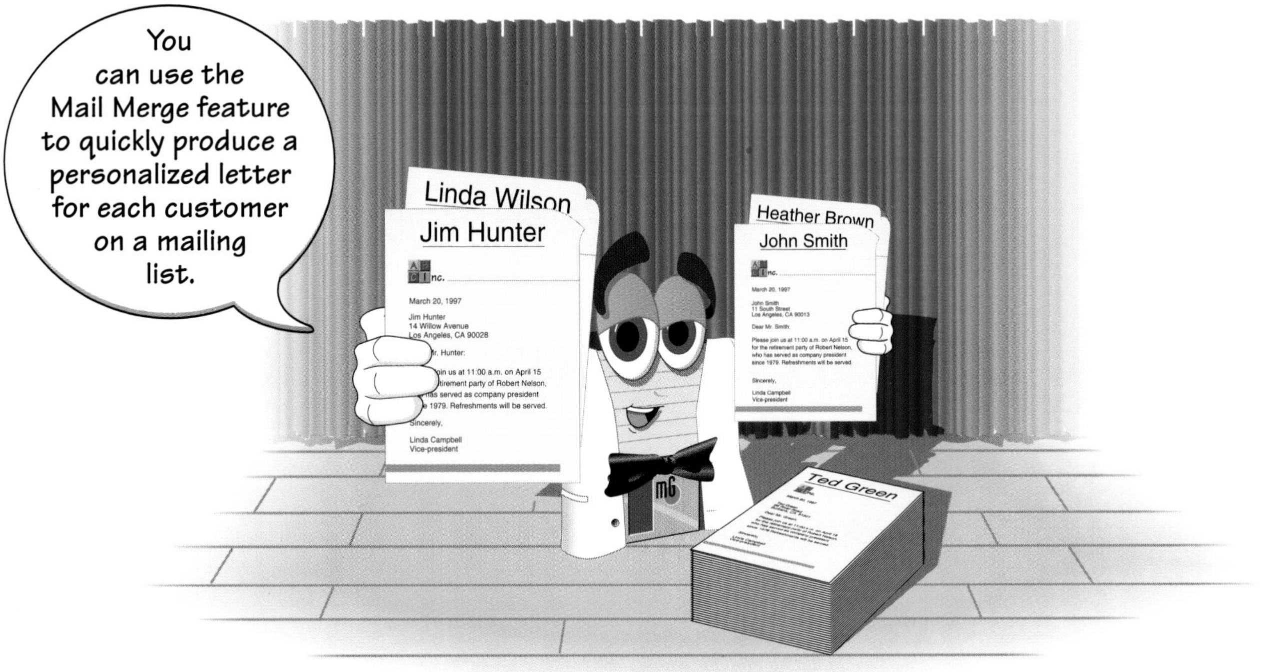
You can use the Mail Merge feature to quickly produce a personalized letter for each customer on a mailing list.
Linda Wilson
Jim Hunter
Heather Brown
John Smith
Ted Green

STEP ONE

Create a Main Document

A main document is a letter you want to send to each customer on your mailing list.

ABC Inc.

March 20, 1997

John Smith
11 South Street
Los Angeles, CA 90013

Dear Mr. Smith:

Please join us at 11:00 a.m. on April 15 for the retirement party of Robert Nelson, who has served as company president since 1979. Refreshments will be served.

Sincerely,

Linda Campbell
Vice-president

STEP TWO

Create a Data Source

A data source contains the information that changes in each letter, such as the name and address of each customer.

You only need to create a data source once. After you create a data source, you can use the data source for every mailing.

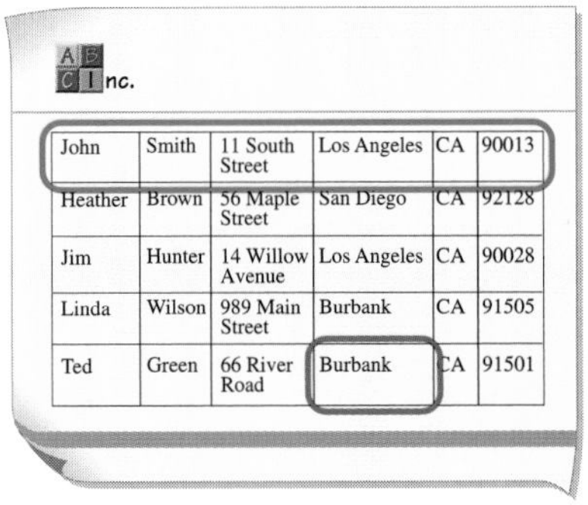

ABC Inc.

John	Smith	11 South Street	Los Angeles	CA	90013
Heather	Brown	56 Maple Street	San Diego	CA	92128
Jim	Hunter	14 Willow Avenue	Los Angeles	CA	90028
Linda	Wilson	989 Main Street	Burbank	CA	91505
Ted	Green	66 River Road	Burbank	CA	91501

All the information for one customer is called a **record.**

Each piece of information about the customer is called a **field.**

What types of documents can I create using the Mail Merge feature?

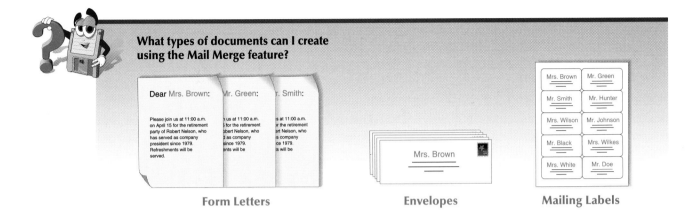

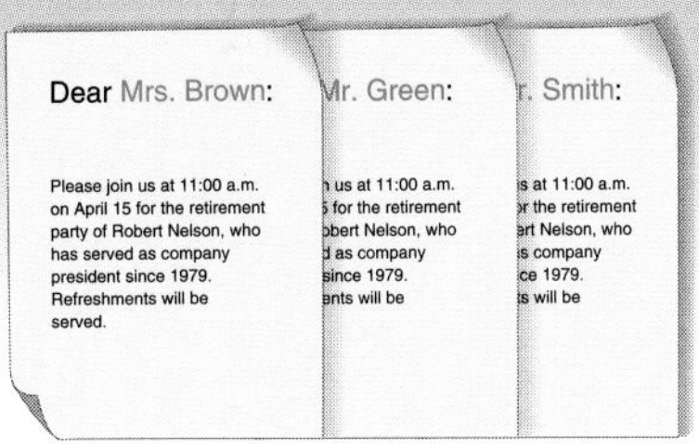
Dear Mrs. Brown:
Please join us at 11:00 a.m. on April 15 for the retirement party of Robert Nelson, who has served as company president since 1979. Refreshments will be served.
Mr. Green:
r. Smith:

Form Letters

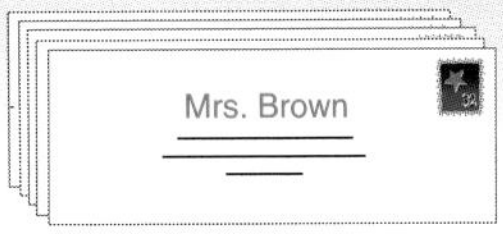
Mrs. Brown

Envelopes

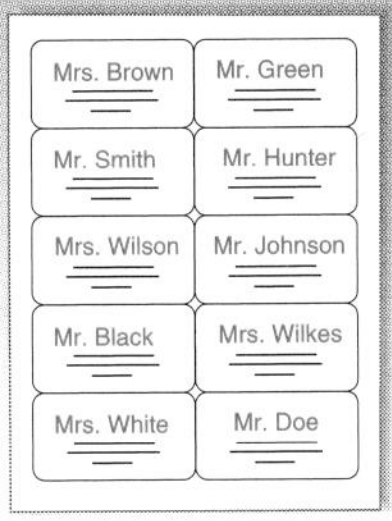
Mrs. Brown
Mr. Green
Mr. Smith
Mr. Hunter
Mrs. Wilson
Mr. Johnson
Mr. Black
Mrs. Wilkes
Mrs. White
Mr. Doe

Mailing Labels

STEP THREE

Complete the Main Document

You must insert special instructions into the main document. These instructions tell Word where to place the personalized information from the data source.

ABC Inc.
March 20, 1997
{{FirstName}} {{LastName}}
{{Address1}}
{{City}}, {{State}} {{PostalCode}}
Dear {{Greeting}}:
Please join us at 11:00 a.m. on April 15 for the retirement party of Robert Nelson, who has served as company president since 1979. Refreshments will be served.
Sincerely,
Linda Campbell
Vice-president
{{FirstName}} {{LastName}}
{{Address1}}
{{City}}, {{State}} {{PostalCode}}
{{Greeting}}

STEP FOUR

Merge the Main Document and Data Source

You combine, or merge, the main document and the data source to create a personalized letter for each customer on your mailing list.

Word replaces the special instructions in the main document with the personalized information from the data source.

CREATE A MAIN DOCUMENT

The main document contains the text that remains the same in each letter.
March 20, 1997
Dear ______:
Please join us at 11:00 a.m. on April 15 for the retirement party of Robert Nelson, who has served as company president since 1979. Refreshments will be served.
Sincerely,

A main document can be a new document or a document you previously created.

CREATE A MAIN DOCUMENT

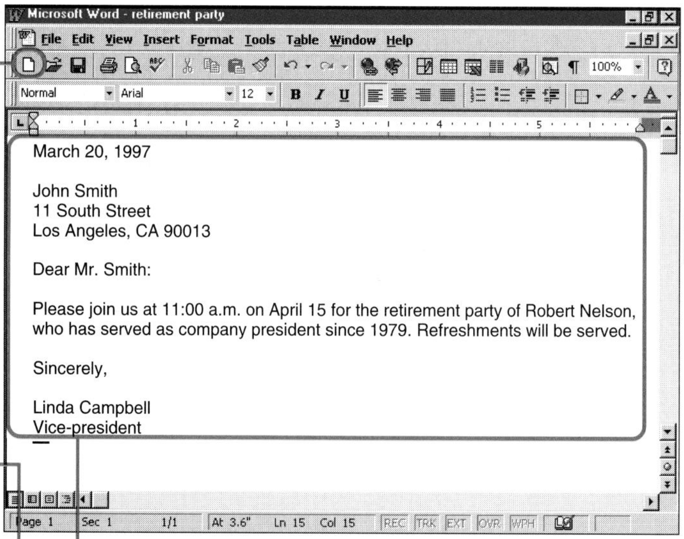

Microsoft Word - retirement party
File Edit View Insert Format Tools Table Window Help
March 20, 1997
John Smith
11 South Street
Los Angeles, CA 90013
Dear Mr. Smith:
Please join us at 11:00 a.m. on April 15 for the retirement party of Robert Nelson, who has served as company president since 1979. Refreshments will be served.
Sincerely,
Linda Campbell
Vice-president

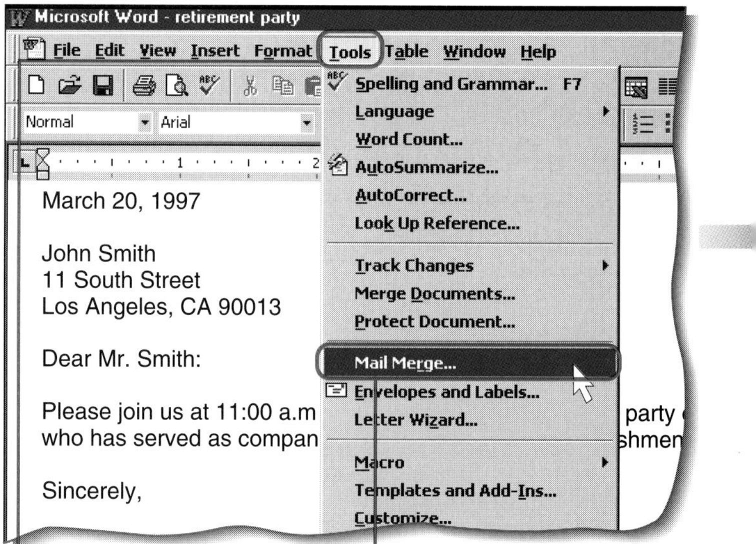

Microsoft Word - retirement party
File Edit View Insert Format Tools Table Window Help
Spelling and Grammar... F7
Language
Word Count...
AutoSummarize...
AutoCorrect...
Look Up Reference...
Track Changes
Merge Documents...
Protect Document...
Mail Merge...
Envelopes and Labels...
Letter Wizard...
Macro
Templates and Add-Ins...
Customize...

1 To create a new document, move the mouse over ▢ and then press the left mouse button.

2 Type the letter you want to send to each customer on your mailing list. Include the personalized information for one customer.

3 Save the document. To save a document, refer to page 20.

*Note: In this example, the document was named **retirement party**.*

4 Move the mouse over **Tools** and then press the left mouse button.

5 Move the mouse over **Mail Merge** and then press the left mouse button.

When should I check my main document for errors?

Make sure you carefully review the text in your main document right after you type the document. Check for spelling and grammar errors and review the layout and formatting of the document. Remember that the document will be read by every person on your mailing list.

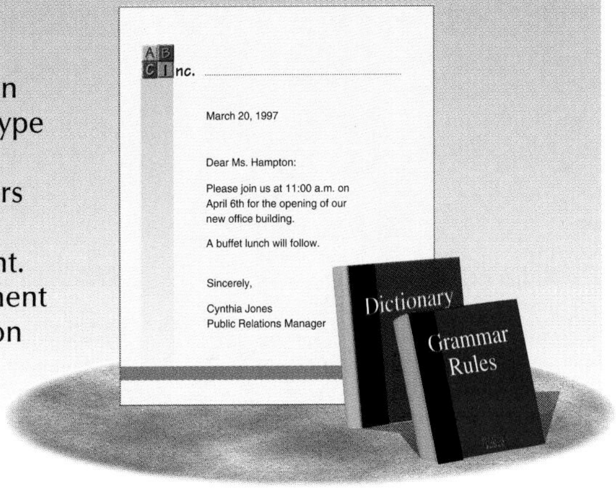
March 20, 1997
Dear Ms. Hampton:
Please join us at 11:00 a.m. on April 6th for the opening of our new office building.
A buffet lunch will follow.
Sincerely,
Cynthia Jones
Public Relations Manager
Dictionary
Grammar Rules

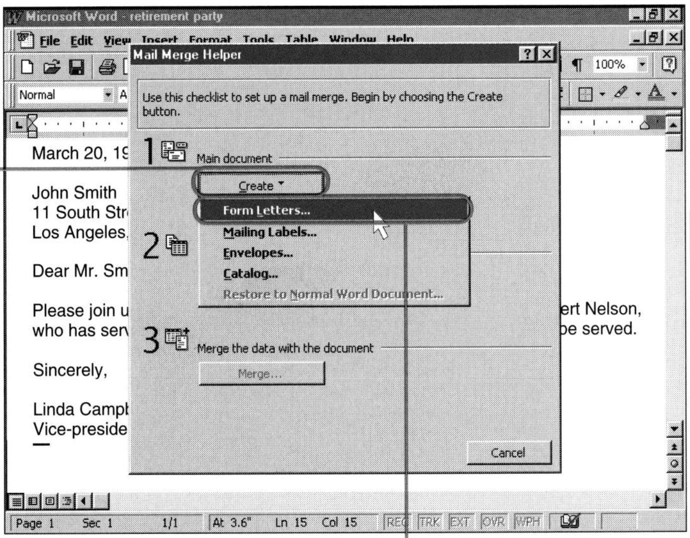
Microsoft Word - retirement party
Mail Merge Helper
Use this checklist to set up a mail merge. Begin by choosing the Create button.
Main document
Create
Form Letters...
Mailing Labels...
Envelopes...
Catalog...
Restore to Normal Word Document...
Merge the data with the document
Merge...
Cancel

■ The **Mail Merge Helper** dialog box appears.

6 To select the type of main document you want to create, move the mouse over **Create** and then press the left mouse button.

7 Move the mouse over **Form Letters** and then press the left mouse button.

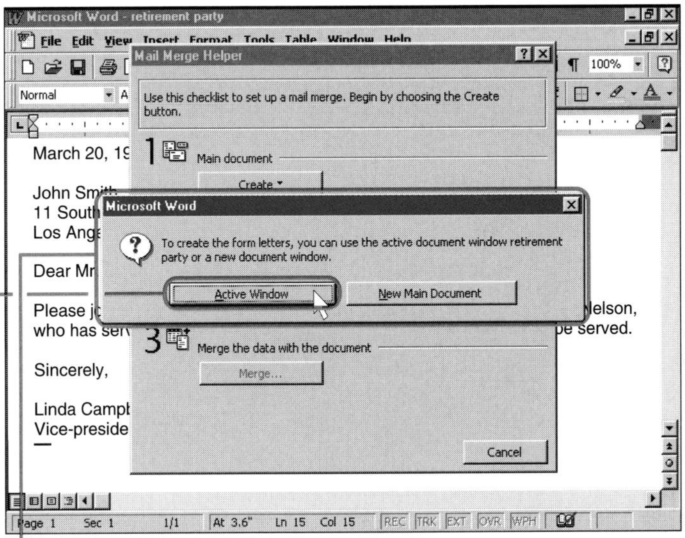
Microsoft Word - retirement party
Mail Merge Helper
Microsoft Word
To create the form letters, you can use the active document window retirement party or a new document window.
Active Window
New Main Document
Merge the data with the document
Merge...
Cancel

■ A dialog box appears.

8 To make the document displayed on your screen the main document, move the mouse over **Active Window** and then press the left mouse button.

■ To continue, you must create a data source or open an existing data source. To create a data source, refer to page 186. To open an existing data source, refer to page 192.

CREATE A DATA SOURCE

You only need to create a data source once. To use an existing data source, refer to page 192.

CREATE A DATA SOURCE

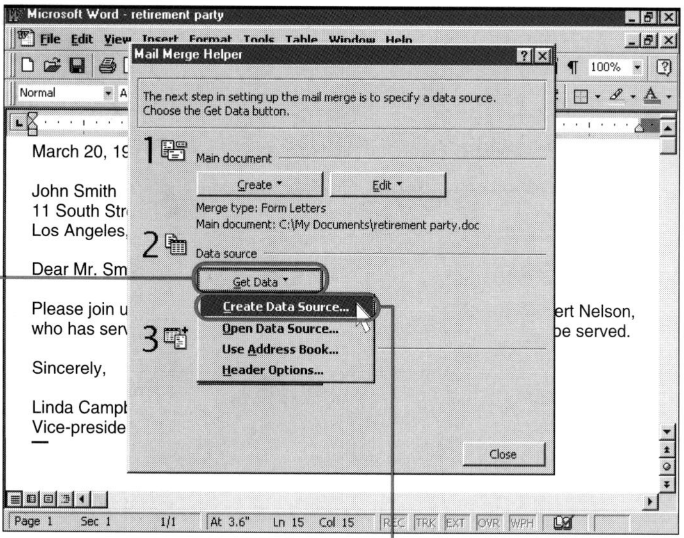

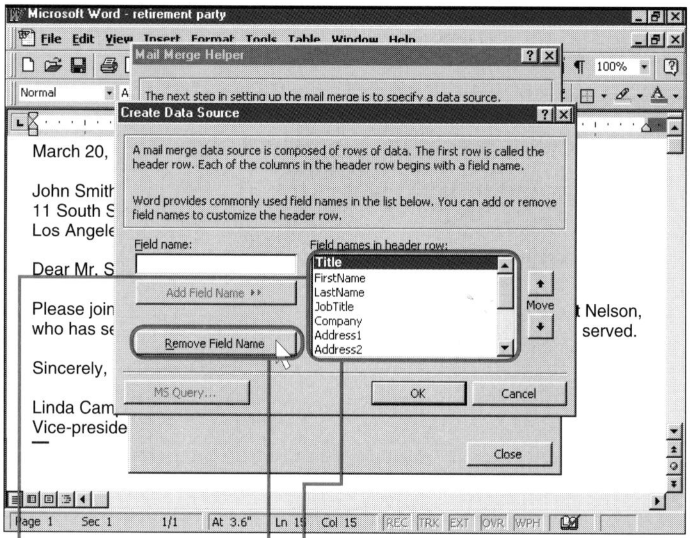

■ Before creating a data source, you must create a main document. To create a main document, refer to page 184.

1 Move the mouse over **Get Data** and then press the left mouse button.

2 Move the mouse over **Create Data Source** and then press the left mouse button.

■ The **Create Data Source** dialog box appears.

■ Word provides a list of commonly used field names.

REMOVE A FIELD NAME

3 To remove a field name you do not need, move the mouse over the field name and then press the left mouse button.

4 Move the mouse over **Remove Field Name** and then press the left mouse button.

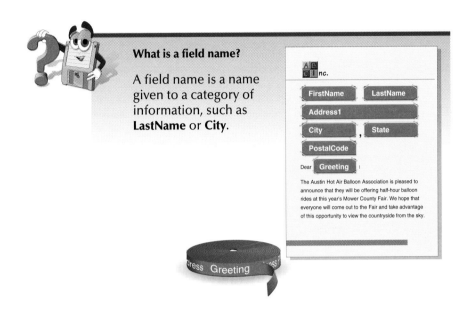

What is a field name?

A field name is a name given to a category of information, such as **LastName** or **City**.

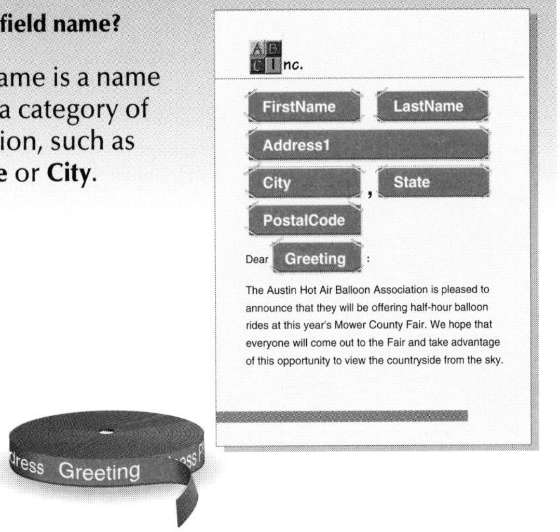
FirstName
LastName
Address1
City
State
PostalCode
Dear Greeting :
The Austin Hot Air Balloon Association is pleased to announce that they will be offering half-hour balloon rides at this year's Mower County Fair. We hope that everyone will come out to the Fair and take advantage of this opportunity to view the countryside from the sky.
Greeting

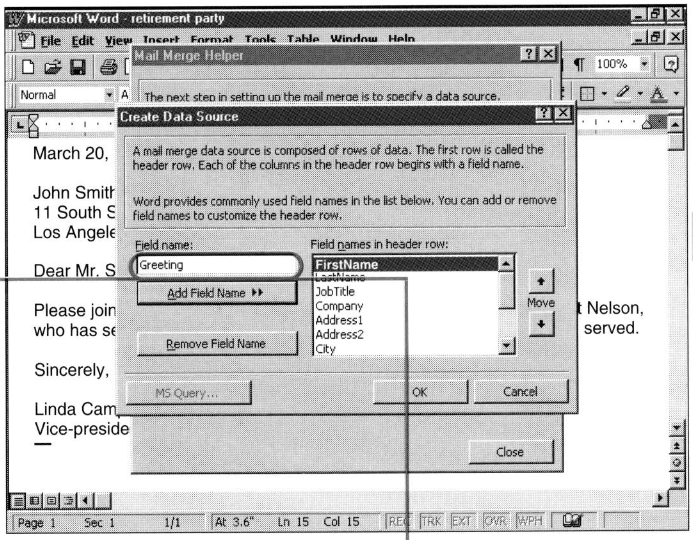
Microsoft Word - retirement party
Mail Merge Helper
Create Data Source
A mail merge data source is composed of rows of data. The first row is called the header row. Each of the columns in the header row begins with a field name.
Word provides commonly used field names in the list below. You can add or remove field names to customize the header row.
Field name:
Greeting
Field names in header row:
FirstName
JobTitle
Company
Address1
Address2
City
Add Field Name
Remove Field Name
Move
MS Query...
OK
Cancel
Close

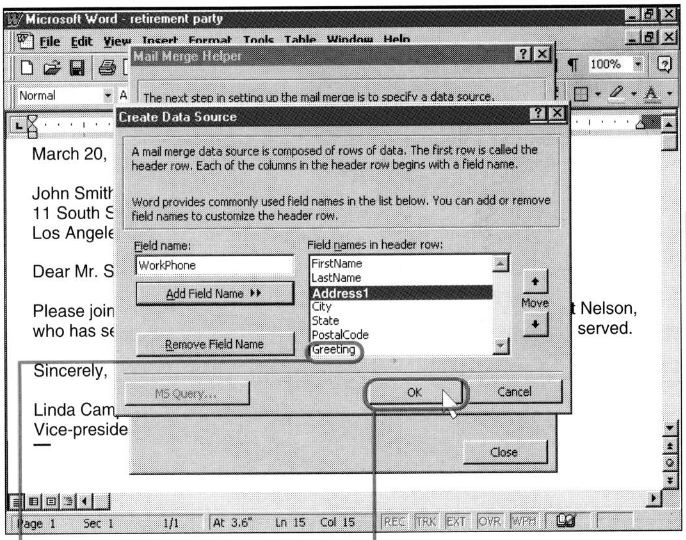
Microsoft Word - retirement party
Mail Merge Helper
Create Data Source
Field name:
WorkPhone
Field names in header row:
FirstName
LastName
Address1
City
State
PostalCode
Greeting
Add Field Name
Remove Field Name
Move
MS Query...
OK
Cancel
Close

ADD A FIELD NAME

5 To add a field name to the list, move the mouse over this area and then press the left mouse button.

Note: If there is text in the area, press **Delete** *or* **←Backspace** *on your keyboard until you have removed all the text.*

6 Type the field name and then press **Enter** on your keyboard.

Note: The field name cannot contain spaces and must begin with a letter.

■ The field name appears in the list.

7 Remove and add field names until the list displays the field names you need.

8 Move the mouse over **OK** and then press the left mouse button.

CONTINUED

After you save the data source, you can enter the information for each customer.

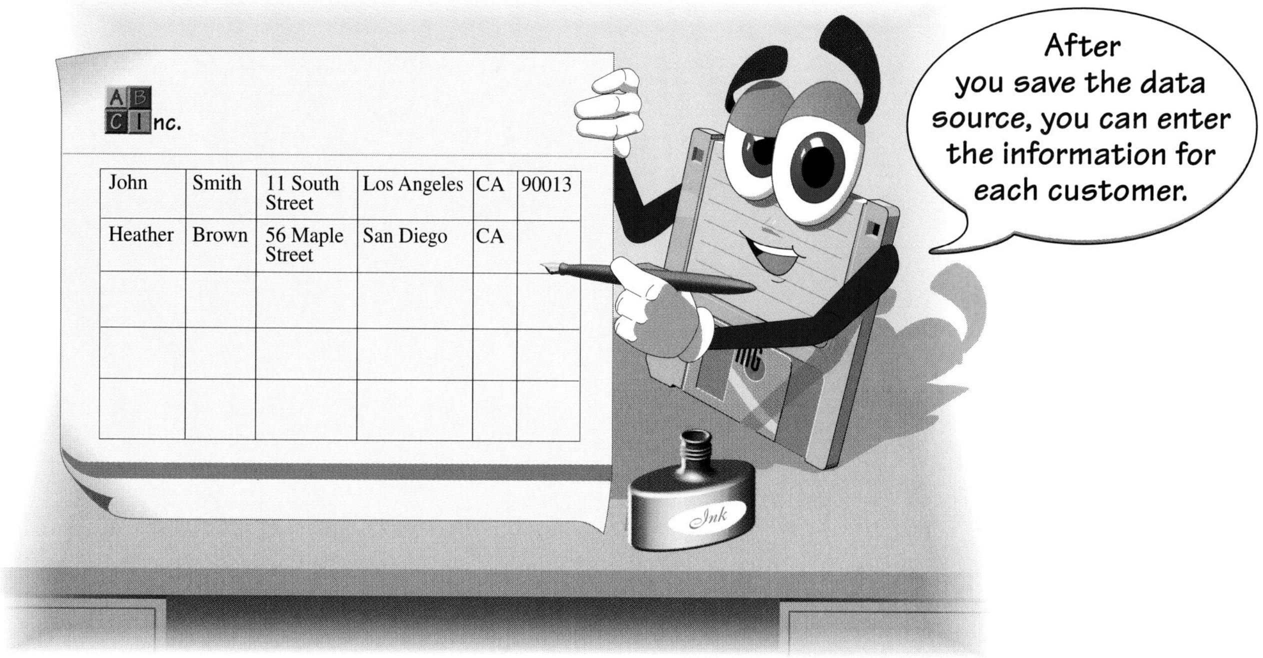

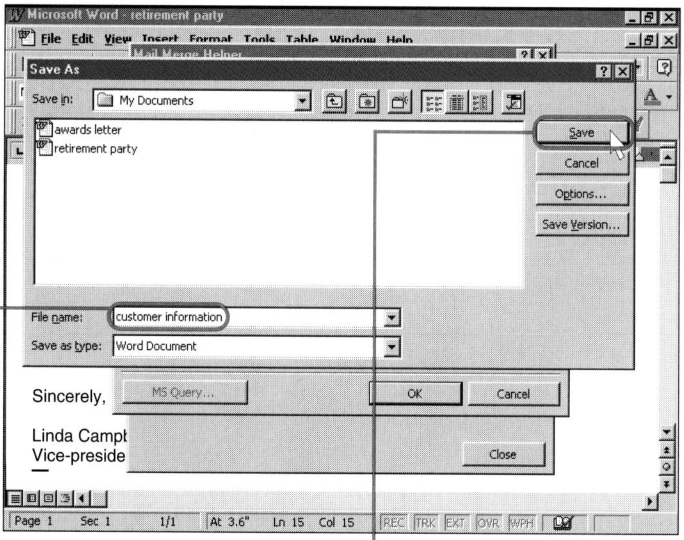

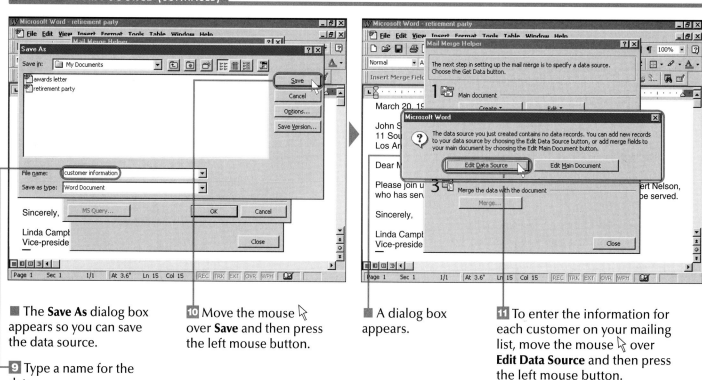

■ The **Save As** dialog box appears so you can save the data source.

9 Type a name for the data source.

10 Move the mouse ⌖ over **Save** and then press the left mouse button.

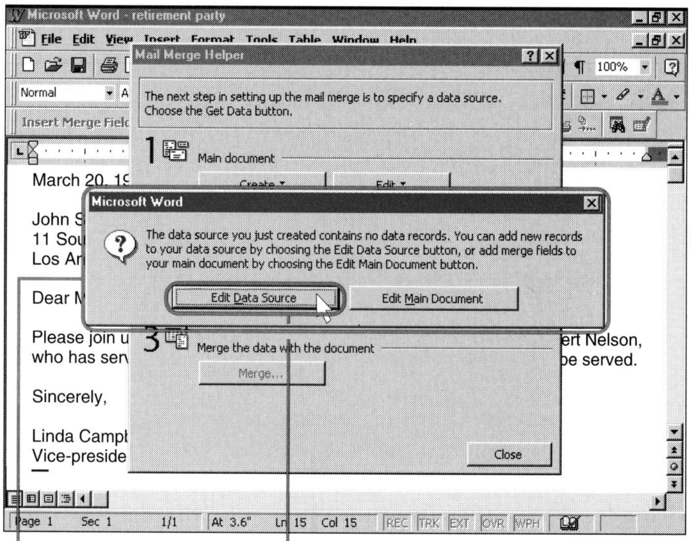

■ A dialog box appears.

11 To enter the information for each customer on your mailing list, move the mouse ⌖ over **Edit Data Source** and then press the left mouse button.

How can I browse through the customer information I have entered?

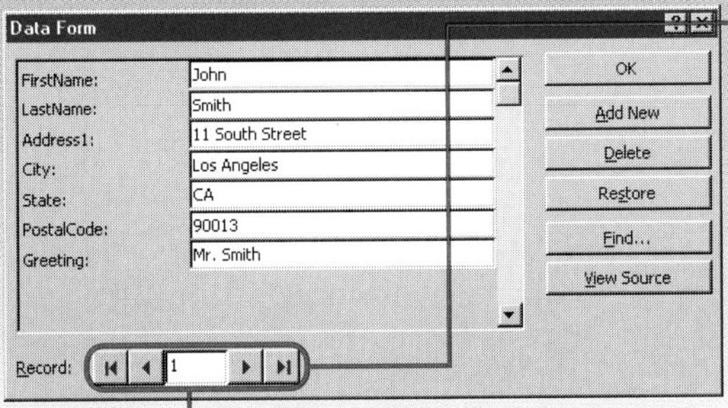

■ This area displays the number of the customer that is currently displayed.

1 To browse through the customers, move the mouse over one of the following options and then press the left mouse button.

- Display the first customer.
- Display the previous customer.
- Display the next customer.
- Display the last customer.

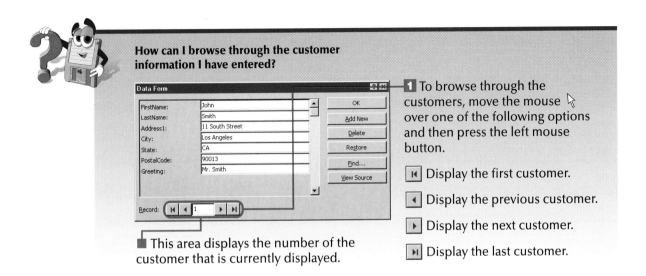

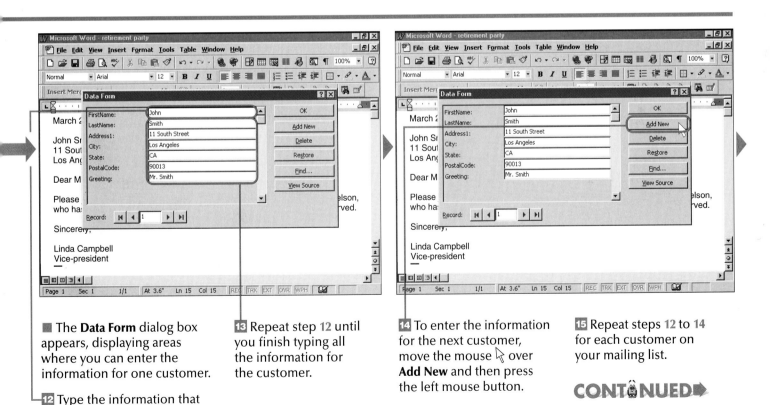

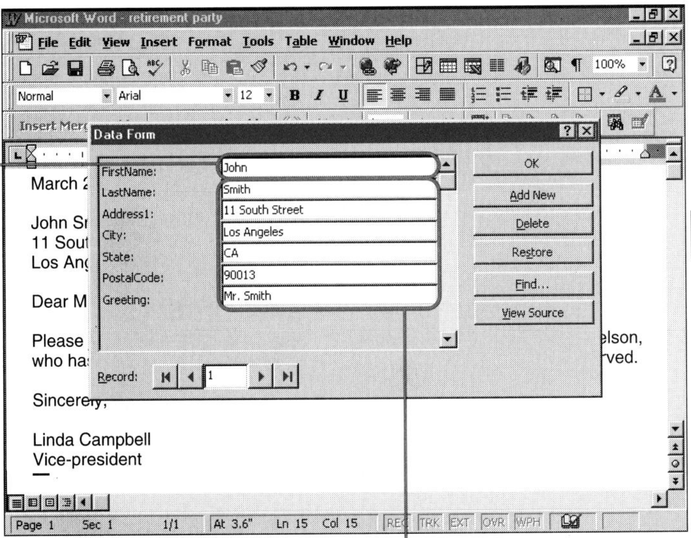

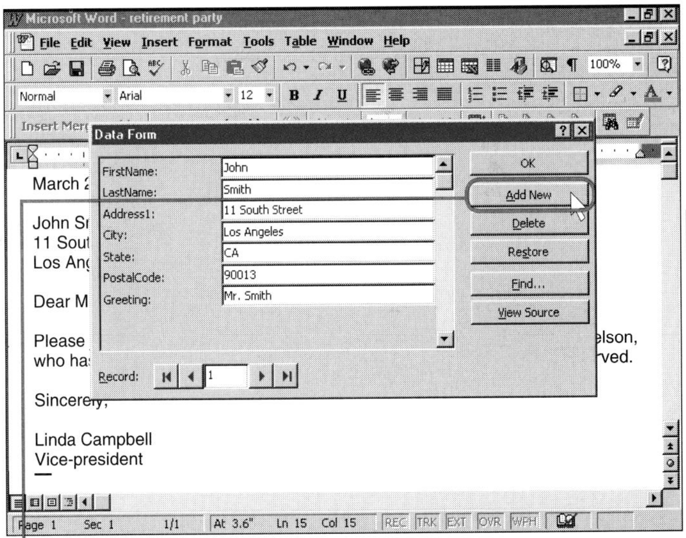

■ The **Data Form** dialog box appears, displaying areas where you can enter the information for one customer.

12 Type the information that corresponds to the first area. To move to the next area, press Tab on your keyboard.

13 Repeat step 12 until you finish typing all the information for the customer.

14 To enter the information for the next customer, move the mouse over **Add New** and then press the left mouse button.

15 Repeat steps 12 to 14 for each customer on your mailing list.

CONTINUED

You can have Word display a table containing all the customer information you have entered.

CREATE A DATA SOURCE (CONTINUED)

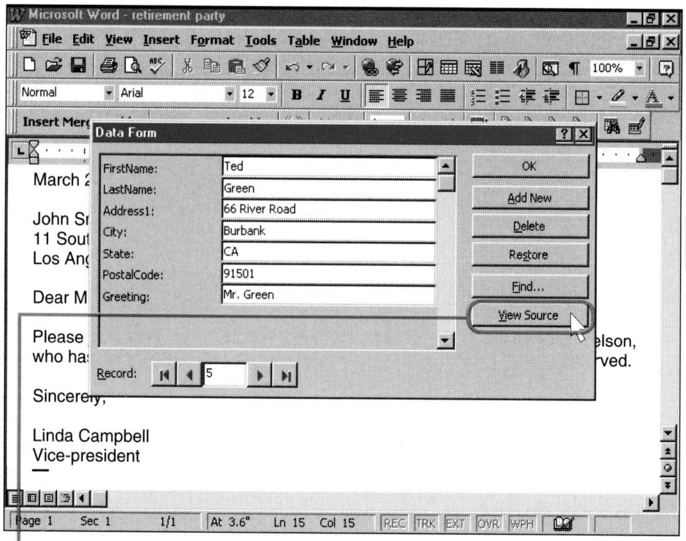

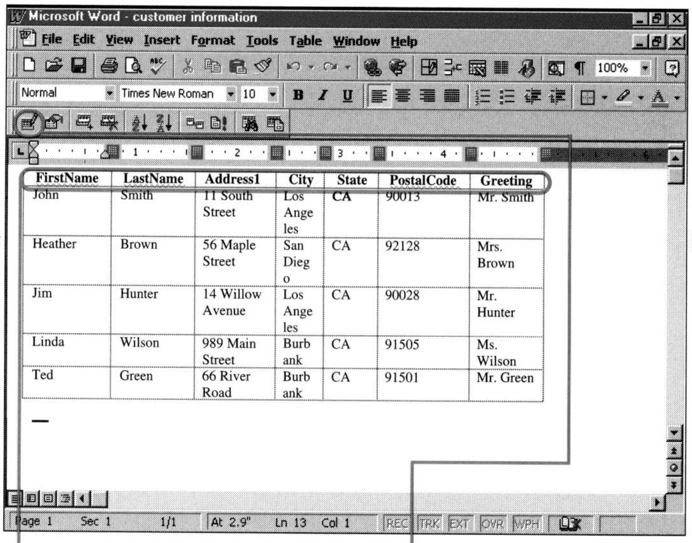

16 When you have entered the information for all your customers, move the mouse over **View Source** and then press the left mouse button.

■ The information you entered appears in a table.

■ The first row in the table contains the field names. Each of the following rows contains the information for one customer.

Note: Text that does not fit on one line in the table will appear on one line when you print the letters.

■ If you want to add or change customer information, move the mouse over and then press the left mouse button to display the **Data Form** dialog box.

Can I use the data source with other letters?

Once you create a data source, you can use the data source for any future mailings.

Before using a data source with a new letter, you may want to update your customer information. You can open, edit and save a data source as you would any document.

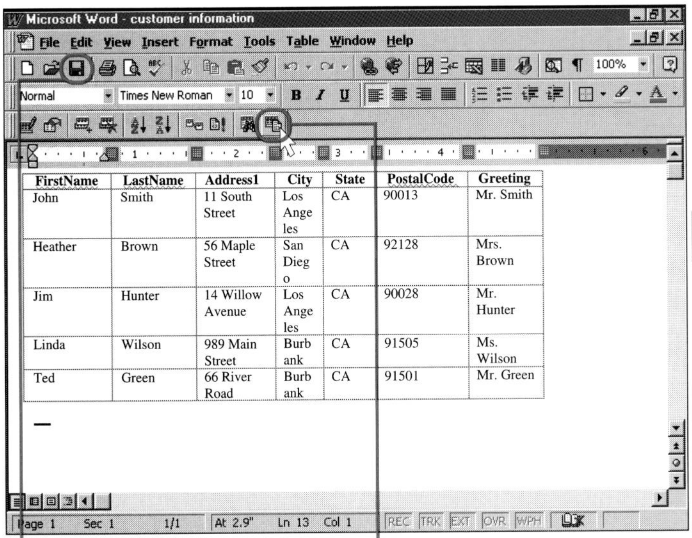

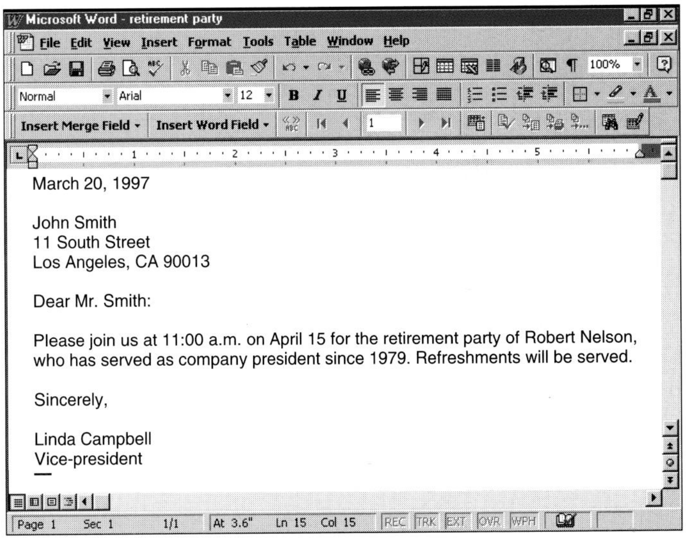

17 To save the information you entered, move the mouse over 💾 and then press the left mouse button.

18 To return to the main document, move the mouse over the Mail Merge Main Document button and then press the left mouse button.

■ The main document appears on your screen.

■ To continue, you must complete the main document. To complete the main document, refer to page 194.

OPEN AN EXISTING DATA SOURCE

OPEN AN EXISTING DATA SOURCE

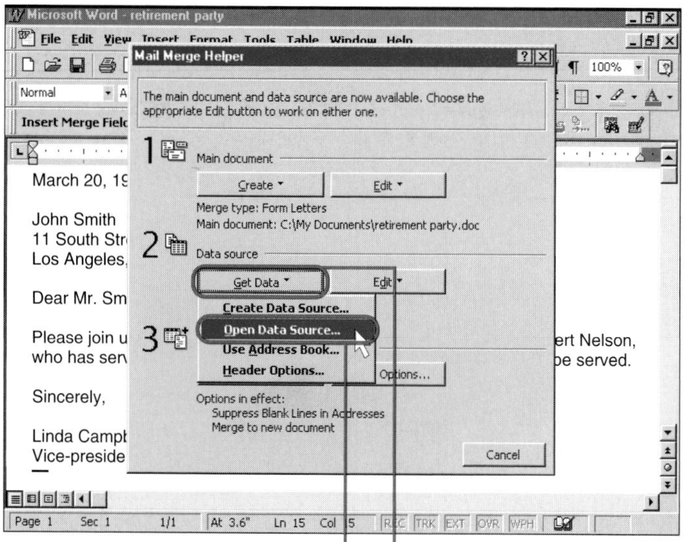

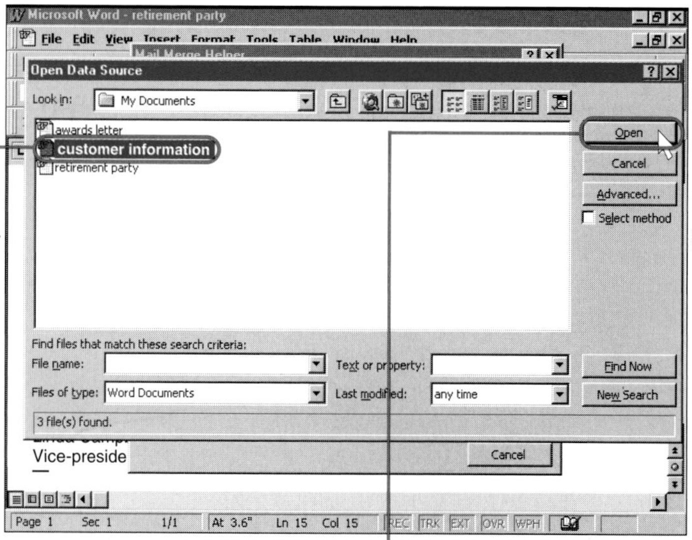

■ Before opening an existing data source, you must create a main document. To create a main document, refer to page 184.

1 Move the mouse over **Get Data** and then press the left mouse button.

2 Move the mouse over **Open Data Source** and then press the left mouse button.

■ The **Open Data Source** dialog box appears.

3 Move the mouse over the name of the data source you want to open and then press the left mouse button.

4 Move the mouse over **Open** and then press the left mouse button.

Can Word help me find a data source I previously created?

If you cannot find your data source, you can have Word search for the data source. To find a document, refer to page 26.

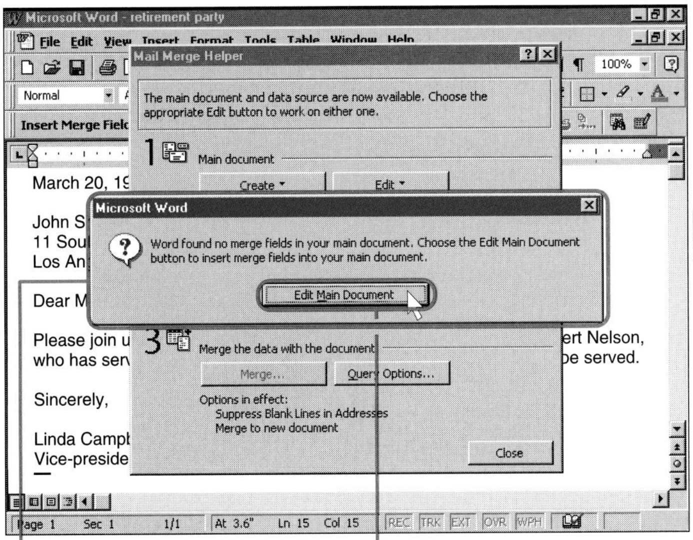
Microsoft Word - retirement party
Mail Merge Helper
The main document and data source are now available. Choose the appropriate Edit button to work on either one.
Main document
Create
Edit
Microsoft Word
Word found no merge fields in your main document. Choose the Edit Main Document button to insert merge fields into your main document.
Edit Main Document
Merge the data with the document
Merge...
Query Options...
Options in effect:
Suppress Blank Lines in Addresses
Merge to new document
Close

■ A dialog box appears.

5 To return to the main document, move the mouse over **Edit Main Document** and then press the left mouse button.

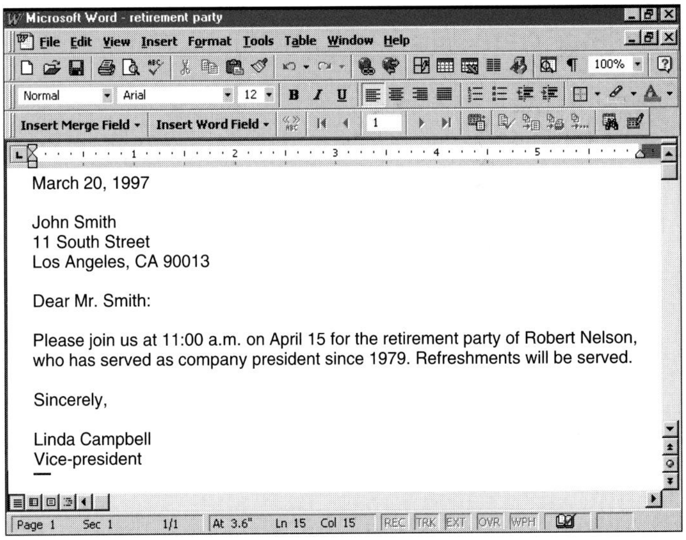
Microsoft Word - retirement party
March 20, 1997
John Smith
11 South Street
Los Angeles, CA 90013
Dear Mr. Smith:
Please join us at 11:00 a.m. on April 15 for the retirement party of Robert Nelson, who has served as company president since 1979. Refreshments will be served.
Sincerely,
Linda Campbell
Vice-president

■ The main document appears on your screen.

■ To continue, you must complete the main document. To complete the main document, refer to page 194.

COMPLETE THE MAIN DOCUMENT

You must insert special instructions to complete the main document. These instructions tell Word where to place the personalized information that changes for each customer.
Inc.
FirstName
LastName
Address1
City
State
PostalCode
Greeting
Dear
The Austin Hot Air Balloon Association is pleased to announce that they will be offering half-hour balloon rides at this year's Mower County Fair. We hope that everyone will come out to the Fair and take advantage of this opportunity to view the countryside from the sky.

COMPLETE THE MAIN DOCUMENT

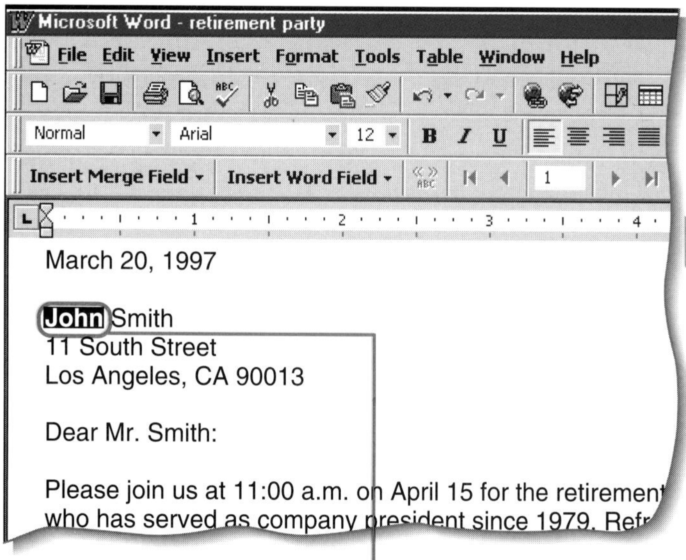

Microsoft Word - retirement party
File Edit View Insert Format Tools Table Window Help
Normal
Arial
12
Insert Merge Field
Insert Word Field
March 20, 1997
John Smith
11 South Street
Los Angeles, CA 90013
Dear Mr. Smith:
Please join us at 11:00 a.m. on April 15 for the retirement
who has served as company president since 1979. Ref

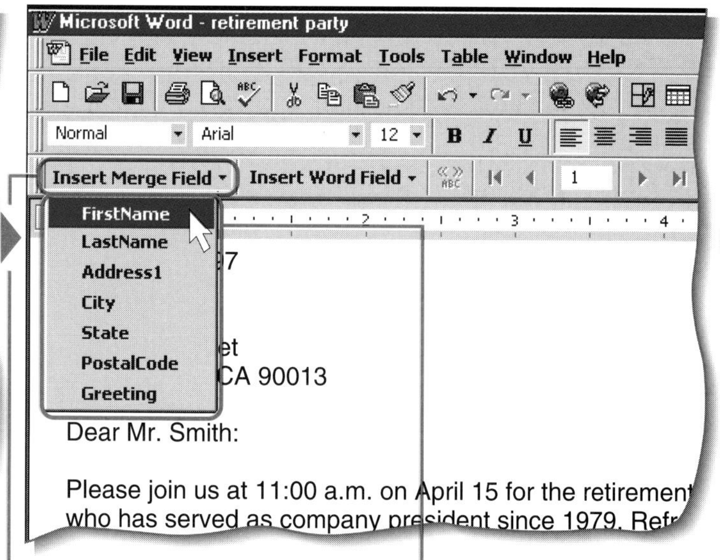

Microsoft Word - retirement party
File Edit View Insert Format Tools Table Window Help
Normal
Arial
12
Insert Merge Field
Insert Word Field
FirstName
LastName
Address1
City
State
PostalCode
Greeting
Dear Mr. Smith:
Please join us at 11:00 a.m. on April 15 for the retirement
who has served as company president since 1979. Ref

■ Before completing the main document, you must create a main document. To create a main document, refer to page 184.

1 Select the first area of text that you want to change in each letter. Do not select any spaces before or after the text. To select text, refer to page 12.

2 To display a list of field names, move the mouse over **Insert Merge Field** and then press the left mouse button.

Note: The field names that appear depend on the field names you specified when you created the data source.

3 Move the mouse over the field name that corresponds to the text you selected in step 1 and then press the left mouse button.

After I complete the main document, can I see an example of how my letters will look?

You can temporarily replace the field names in the main document with the information for one customer.

1 Move the mouse over «» ABC and then press the left mouse button.

■ To view the field names again, repeat step **1**.

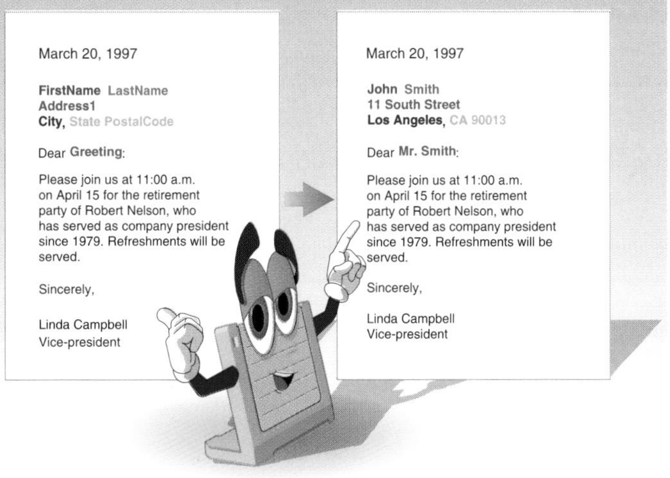
March 20, 1997
FirstName LastName
Address1
City, State PostalCode
Dear Greeting:
Please join us at 11:00 a.m. on April 15 for the retirement party of Robert Nelson, who has served as company president since 1979. Refreshments will be served.
Sincerely,
Linda Campbell
Vice-president
March 20, 1997
John Smith
11 South Street
Los Angeles, CA 90013
Dear Mr. Smith:
Please join us at 11:00 a.m. on April 15 for the retirement party of Robert Nelson, who has served as company president since 1979. Refreshments will be served.
Sincerely,
Linda Campbell
Vice-president

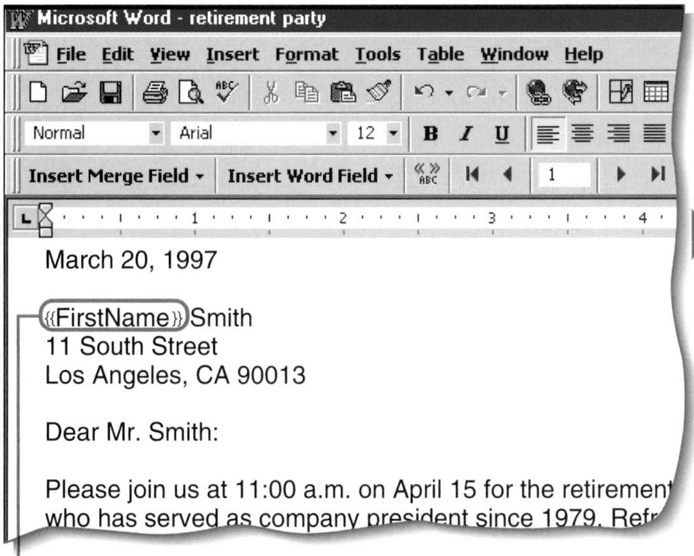
Microsoft Word - retirement party
File Edit View Insert Format Tools Table Window Help
Normal
Arial
12
Insert Merge Field
Insert Word Field
March 20, 1997
«FirstName» Smith
11 South Street
Los Angeles, CA 90013
Dear Mr. Smith:
Please join us at 11:00 a.m. on April 15 for the retiremen
who has served as company president since 1979. Refr

■ The field name replaces the text you selected.

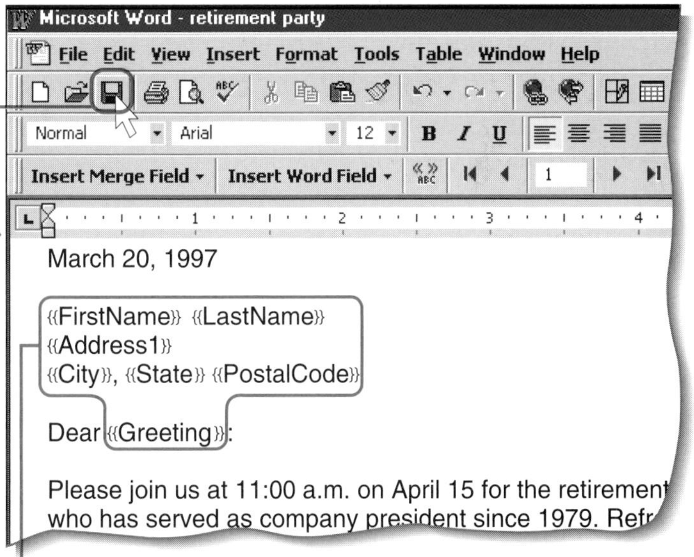
Microsoft Word - retirement party
File Edit View Insert Format Tools Table Window Help
Normal
Arial
12
Insert Merge Field
Insert Word Field
March 20, 1997
«FirstName» «LastName»
«Address1»
«City», «State» «PostalCode»
Dear «Greeting»:
Please join us at 11:00 a.m. on April 15 for the retiremen
who has served as company president since 1979. Refr

4 Repeat steps **1** to **3** for all the text you want to change in each letter.

5 To save the document, move the mouse over the save button and then press the left mouse button.

■ To continue, you must merge the main document and the data source. To merge the main document and the data source, refer to page 196.

MERGE MAIN DOCUMENT AND DATA SOURCE

You can combine the main document and the data source to create a personalized letter for each customer on your mailing list.

MERGE MAIN DOCUMENT AND DATA SOURCE

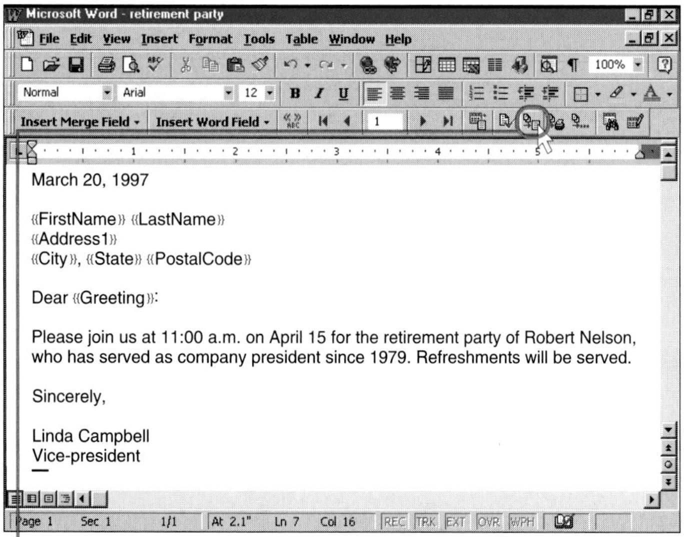
Microsoft Word - retirement party
File Edit View Insert Format Tools Table Window Help
Insert Merge Field
Insert Word Field
March 20, 1997
«FirstName» «LastName»
«Address1»
«City», «State» «PostalCode»
Dear «Greeting»:
Please join us at 11:00 a.m. on April 15 for the retirement party of Robert Nelson, who has served as company president since 1979. Refreshments will be served.
Sincerely,
Linda Campbell
Vice-president
Page 1 Sec 1 1/1 At 2.1" Ln 7 Col 16

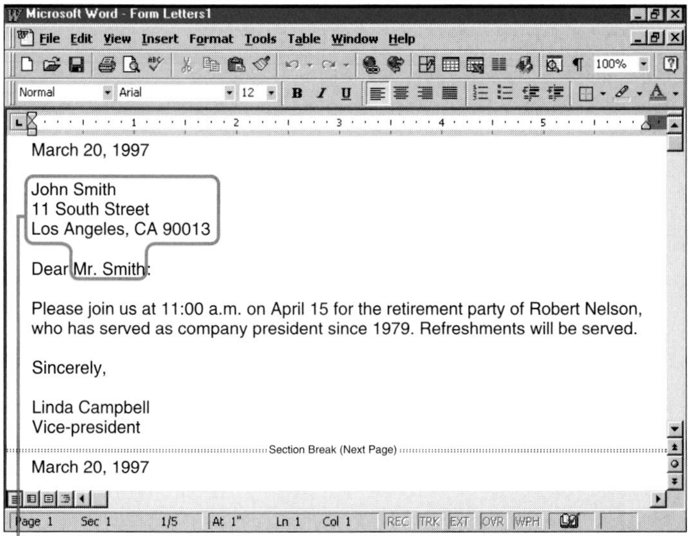
Microsoft Word - Form Letters1
File Edit View Insert Format Tools Table Window Help
March 20, 1997
John Smith
11 South Street
Los Angeles, CA 90013
Dear Mr. Smith:
Please join us at 11:00 a.m. on April 15 for the retirement party of Robert Nelson, who has served as company president since 1979. Refreshments will be served.
Sincerely,
Linda Campbell
Vice-president
Section Break (Next Page)
March 20, 1997
Page 1 Sec 1 1/5 At 1" Ln 1 Col 1

1 To merge the main document and the data source, move the mouse over the merge button and then press the left mouse button.

■ Word replaces the field names in the main document with the corresponding information from the data source. This creates a personalized letter for each customer.

Note: You can edit the letters as you would edit any document. You may wish to add personalized comments to some letters.

Should I save the merged document?

To conserve hard drive space, do not save the merged document. You can easily recreate the merged document at any time by opening the main document and then performing step 1 on page 196.

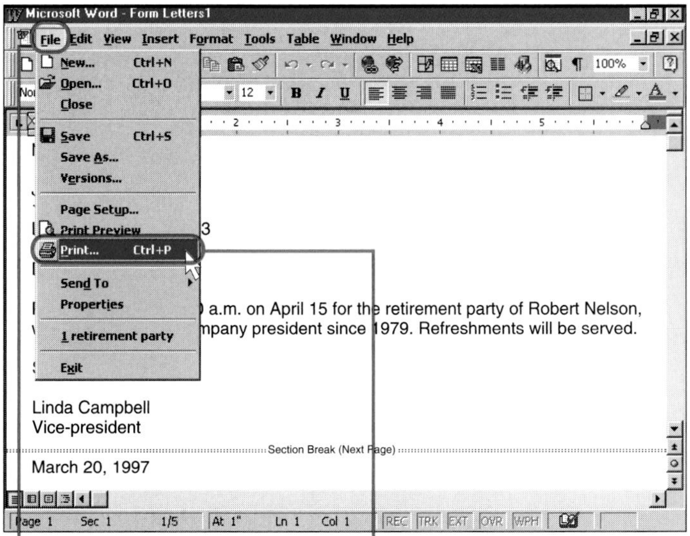

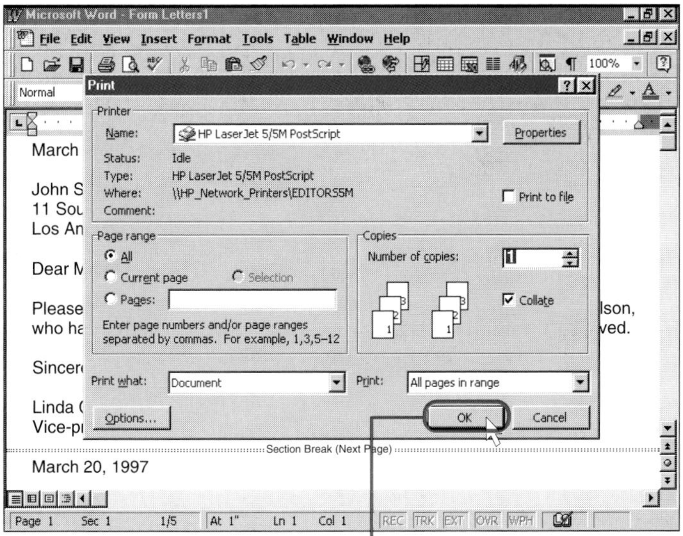

2 To print the letters, move the mouse over **File** and then press the left mouse button.

3 Move the mouse over **Print** and then press the left mouse button.

■ The **Print** dialog box appears.

4 Move the mouse over **OK** and then press the left mouse button.

USING MAIL MERGE TO PRINT LABELS

You can use the Mail Merge feature to print a mailing label for every customer on your mailing list.
John Smith
11 South Street
Los Angeles, CA 90013

USING MAIL MERGE TO PRINT LABELS

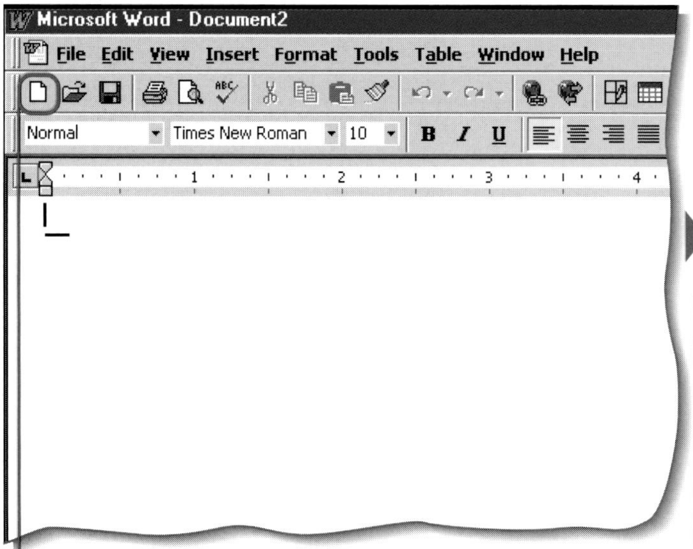
Microsoft Word - Document2
File Edit View Insert Format Tools Table Window Help
Normal
Times New Roman
10

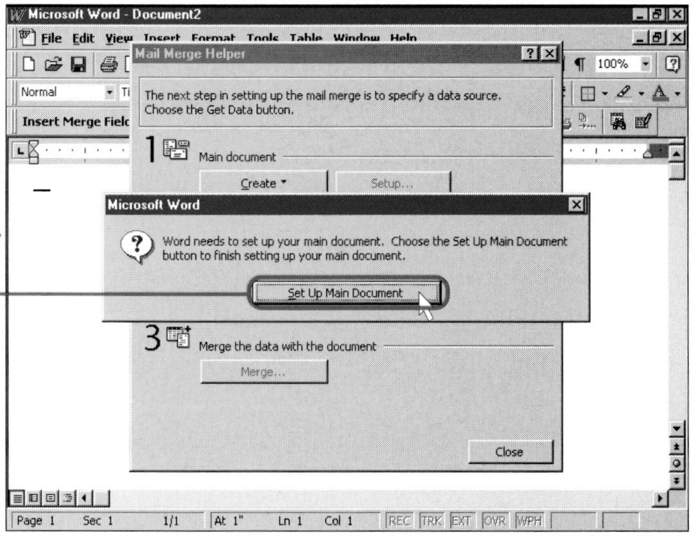
Microsoft Word - Document2
Mail Merge Helper
The next step in setting up the mail merge is to specify a data source. Choose the Get Data button.
Main document
Create
Setup...
Microsoft Word
Word needs to set up your main document. Choose the Set Up Main Document button to finish setting up your main document.
Set Up Main Document
Merge the data with the document
Merge...
Close

1 To create a new document, move the mouse over and then press the left mouse button.

2 To tell Word that you want to create mailing labels, perform steps **4** to **8** starting on page 184, selecting **Mailing Labels** in step **7**.

3 To open an existing data source, perform steps **1** to **4** on page 192.

4 To set up the labels, move the mouse over **Set Up Main Document** and then press the left mouse button.

■ The **Label Options** dialog box appears.

How can I tell which label product I am using?

You can check your label packaging to determine which label product to select in step 6 below.

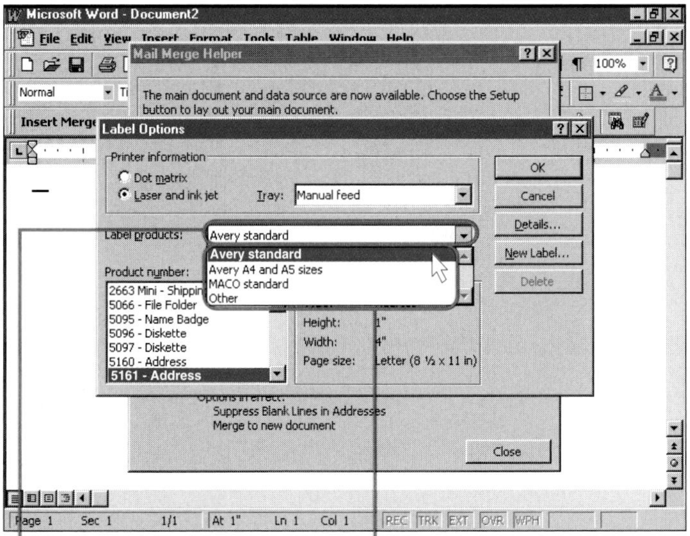

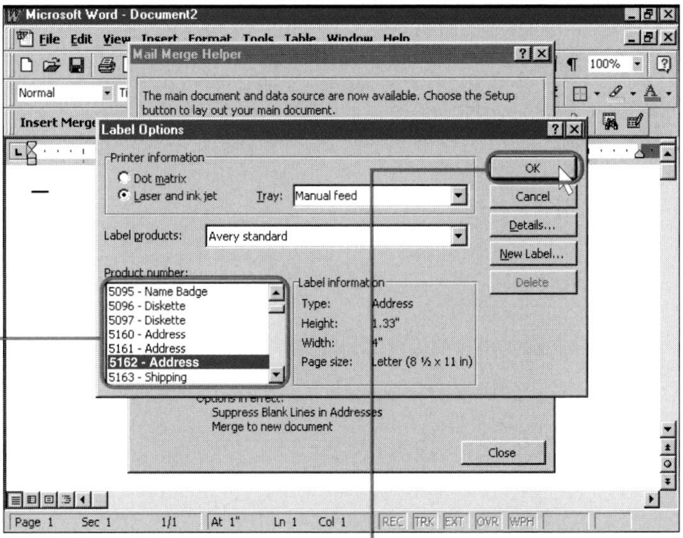

5 To display a list of label products, move the mouse over this area and then press the left mouse button.

6 Move the mouse over the label product you want to use and then press the left mouse button.

■ This area displays the types of labels for the product you selected.

7 Move the mouse over the type of label you want to use and then press the left mouse button.

8 Move the mouse over **OK** and then press the left mouse button.

CONTINUED

USING MAIL MERGE TO PRINT LABELS

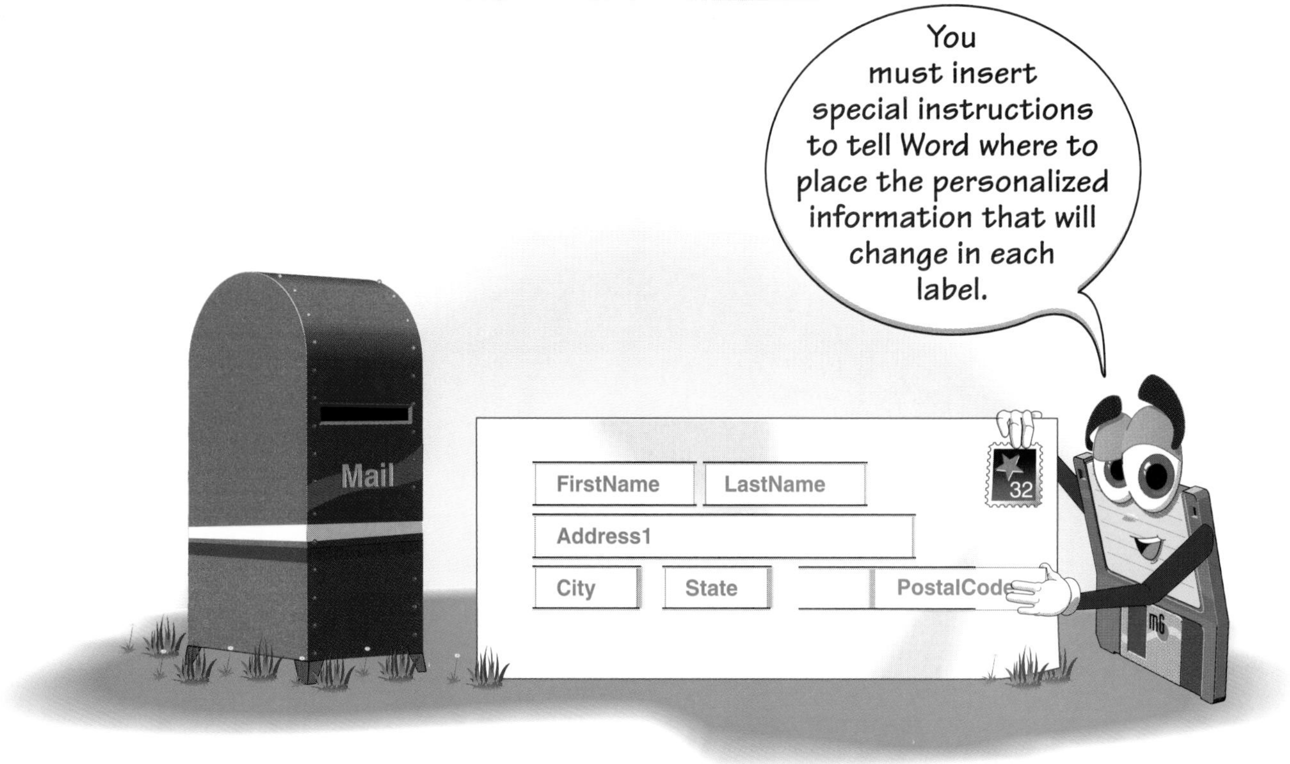

USING MAIL MERGE TO PRINT LABELS (CONTINUED)

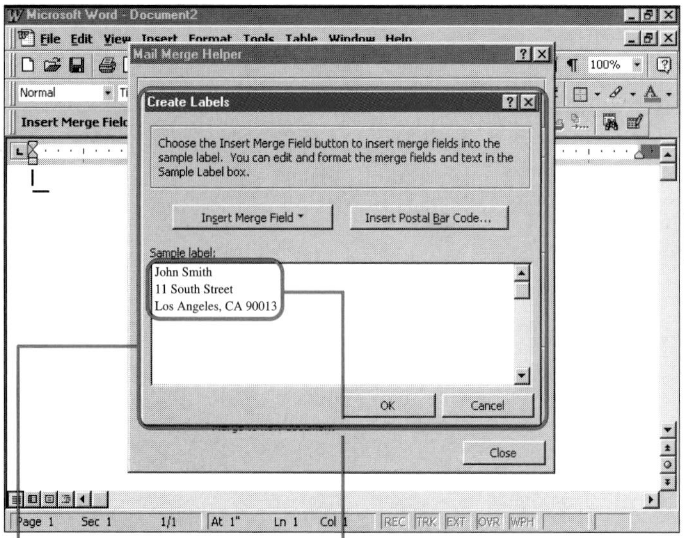

■ The **Create Labels** dialog box appears.

9 Type a label for one of the customers on your mailing list.

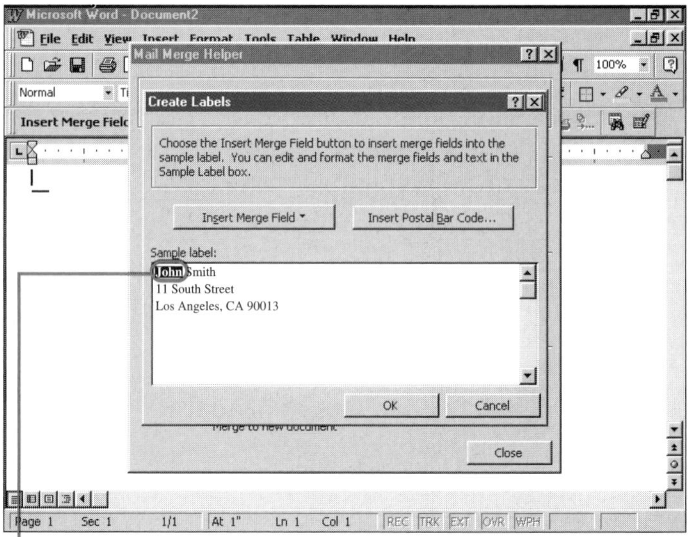

10 Select the first area of text that you want to change in each label. Do not select any spaces before or after the text. To select text, refer to page 12.

How can I use the labels that I print using the Mail Merge feature?

You can use the labels for items such as envelopes, packages, file folders and name tags.

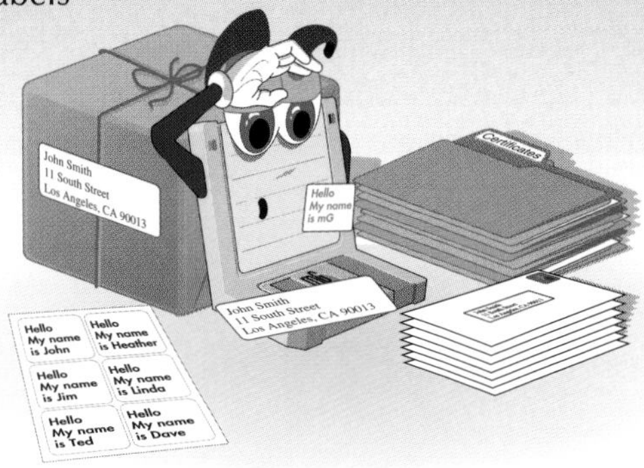

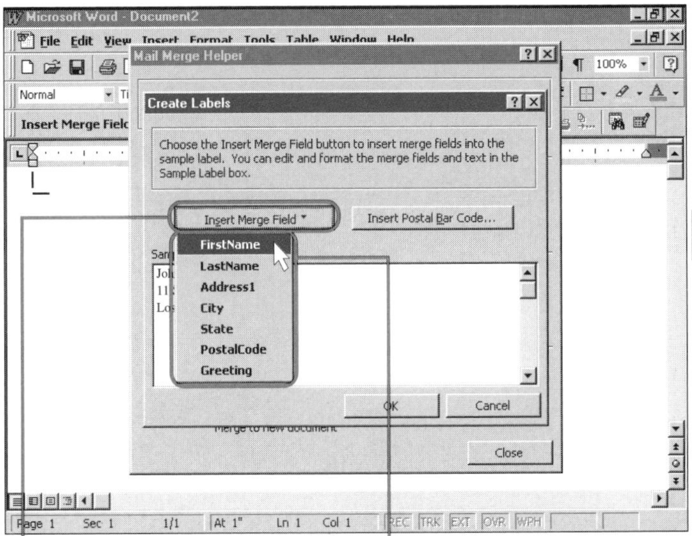

11 To display a list of field names, move the mouse over **Insert Merge Field** and then press the left mouse button.

Note: The field names that appear depend on the field names you specified when you created the data source.

12 Move the mouse over the field name that corresponds to the text you selected in step 10 and then press the left mouse button.

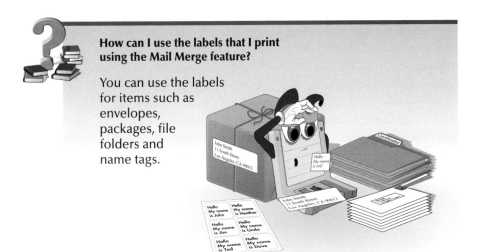

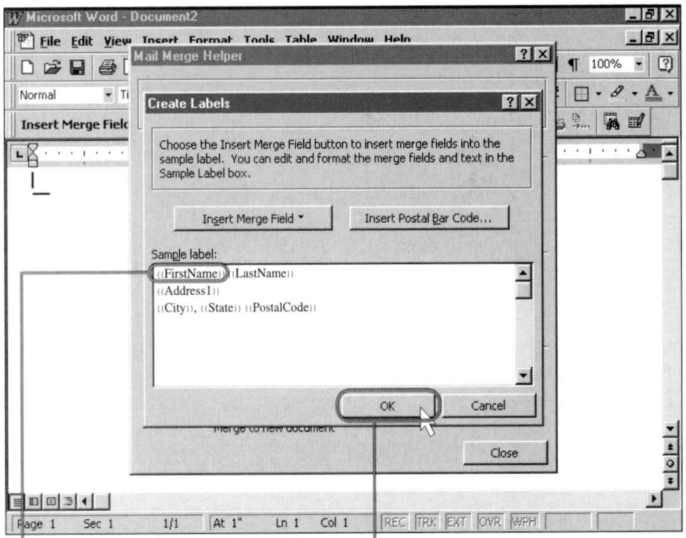

■ The field name replaces the text you selected.

13 Repeat steps 10 to 12 for all the text you want to change in each label.

14 Move the mouse over **OK** and then press the left mouse button.

CONTINUED

USING MAIL MERGE TO PRINT LABELS

After you merge the labels and the data source, you can print the labels.

USING MAIL MERGE TO PRINT LABELS (CONTINUED)

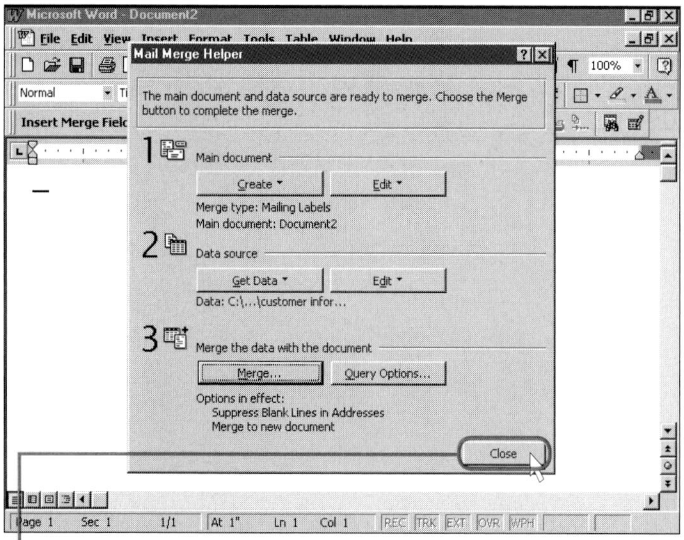

15 To close the **Mail Merge Helper** dialog box, move the mouse over **Close** and then press the left mouse button.

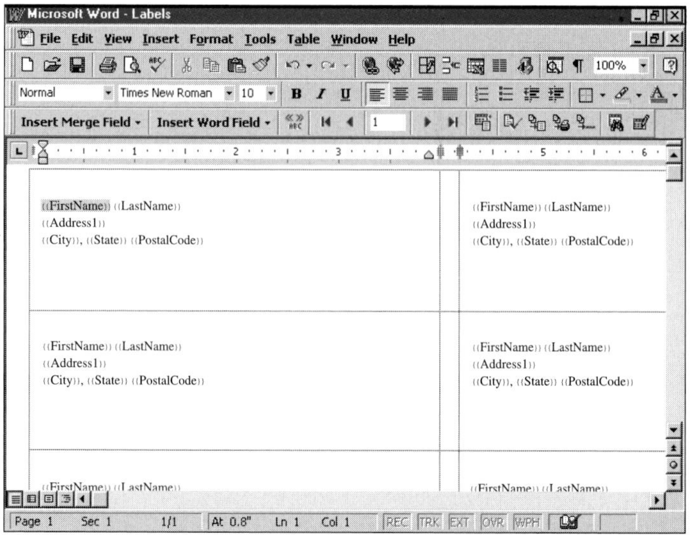

■ The labels appear, displaying the field names you selected.

16 Save the document. To save a document, refer to page 20.

Note: In this example, the document was named ***Labels****.*

Should I save the merged labels?

To conserve hard drive space, do not save the merged labels. You can easily recreate the merged labels at any time. To do so, open the label document you saved in step **16** on page 202. Then perform step **17** below.

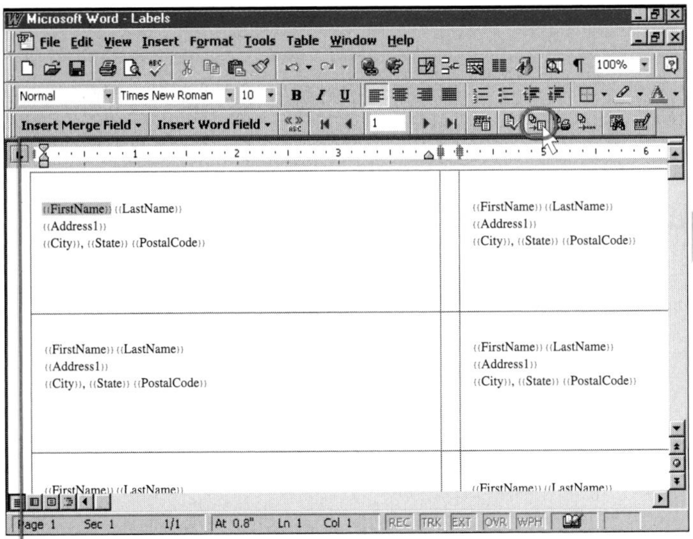

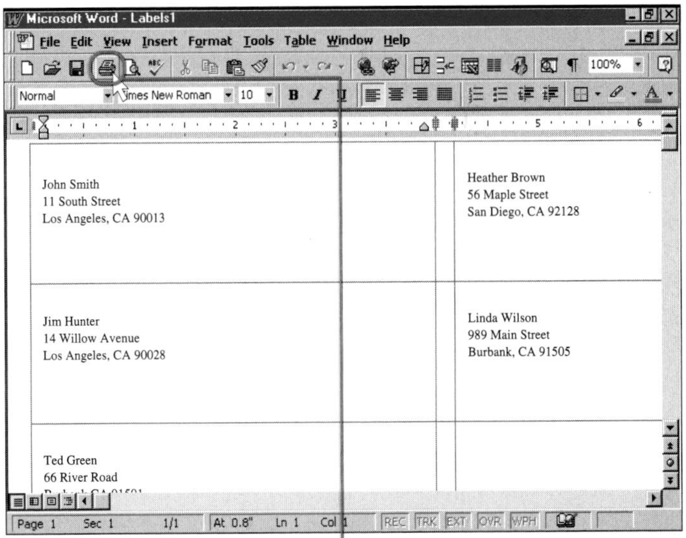

17 To merge the labels and the data source, move the mouse over the merge button and then press the left mouse button.

■ Word creates a personalized label for each customer.

18 To print the labels, move the mouse over the print button and then press the left mouse button.

Microsoft Word - Product Listing
File Edit View Insert Format Tools Table Window Help
EARTH WISE ENTERPRISES
We care about the environment.
All products created and marketed by Earth Wise Enterprises are designed to increase awareness of environmental issues around the world.
A list of our main types of products is presented below. To find out more about the products in any category, select the category name.
Tree planting kits
Recycle bins
Compost kits
PRESS
ADS

CHAPTER 12

WORD AND THE INTERNET

How can Word help me take advantage of the Internet? Learn how to create hyperlinks, use the Favorites feature, save a document as a Web page and more.

CREATE A HYPERLINK

A hyperlink is a word or phrase that connects one document to another document. You can easily create a hyperlink in your document.

CREATE A HYPERLINK

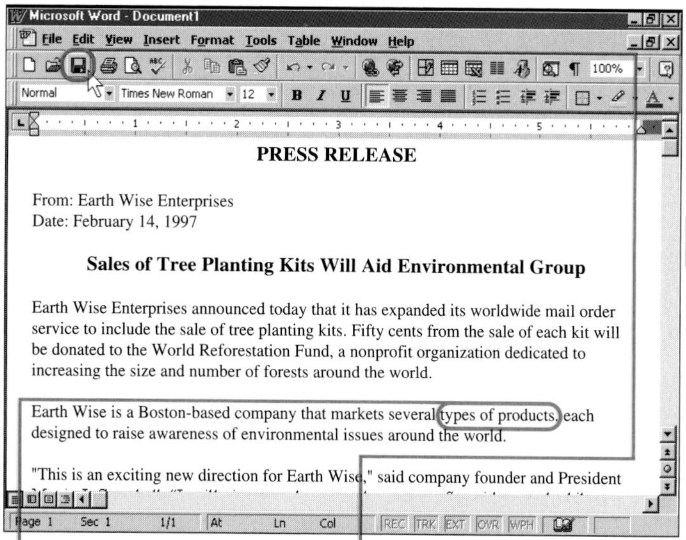

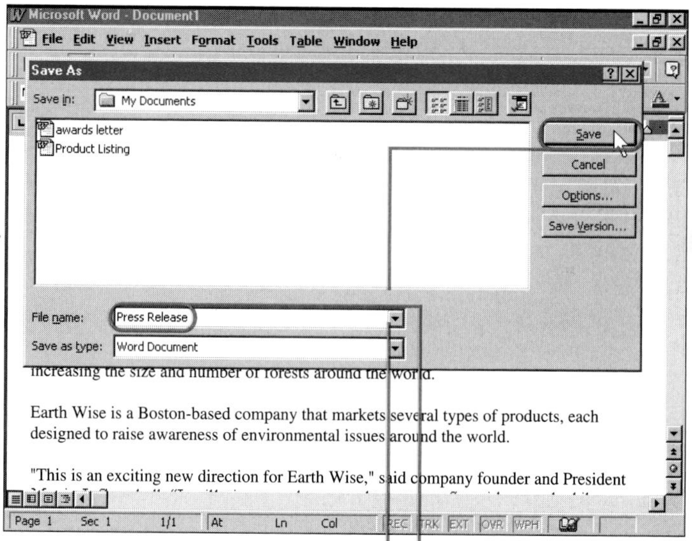

1 Type the text you want to link to another document.

2 To save the document, move the mouse over 💾 and then press the left mouse button.

■ The **Save As** dialog box appears.

*Note: If you previously saved the document, the **Save As** dialog box will not appear since you have already named the document.*

3 Type a name for the document.

4 Move the mouse over **Save** and then press the left mouse button.

Where can a hyperlink take me?

You can create a hyperlink that takes you to another document on your computer, network, corporate intranet or the Internet.

types of products

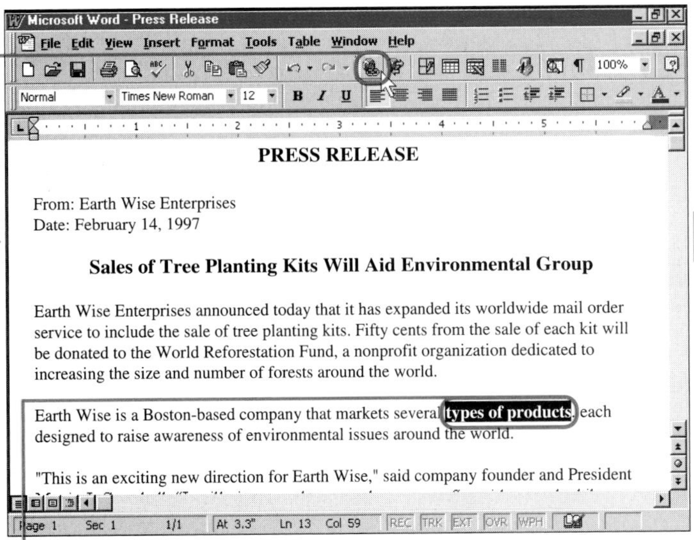
Microsoft Word - Press Release
File Edit View Insert Format Tools Table Window Help
Normal
Times New Roman
12
PRESS RELEASE
From: Earth Wise Enterprises
Date: February 14, 1997
Sales of Tree Planting Kits Will Aid Environmental Group
Earth Wise Enterprises announced today that it has expanded its worldwide mail order service to include the sale of tree planting kits. Fifty cents from the sale of each kit will be donated to the World Reforestation Fund, a nonprofit organization dedicated to increasing the size and number of forests around the world.
Earth Wise is a Boston-based company that markets several types of products, each designed to raise awareness of environmental issues around the world.
"This is an exciting new direction for Earth Wise," said company founder and President
Page 1 Sec 1 1/1 At 3.3" Ln 13 Col 59 REC TRK EXT OVR WPH

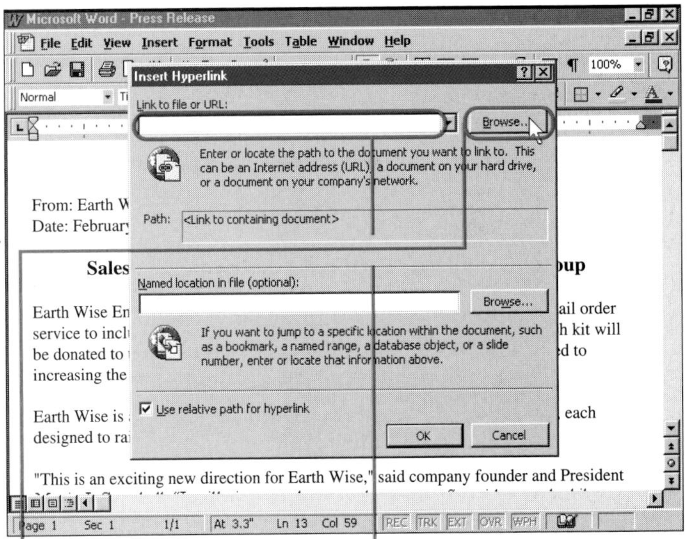
Microsoft Word - Press Release
File Edit View Insert Format Tools Table Window Help
Insert Hyperlink
Link to file or URL:
Browse...
Enter or locate the path to the document you want to link to. This can be an Internet address (URL), a document on your hard drive, or a document on your company's network.
Path: <Link to containing document>
Named location in file (optional):
Browse...
If you want to jump to a specific location within the document, such as a bookmark, a named range, a database object, or a slide number, enter or locate that information above.
Use relative path for hyperlink
OK
Cancel
Page 1 Sec 1 1/1 At 3.3" Ln 13 Col 59 REC TRK EXT OVR WPH

5 Select the text you typed in step **1**. To select text, refer to page 12.

6 Move the mouse over (hyperlink button) and then press the left mouse button.

■ The **Insert Hyperlink** dialog box appears.

7 To link the text to a document on your computer or network, move the mouse over **Browse** and then press the left mouse button.

■ To link the text to a Web page, type the address of the Web page (example: http://www.maran.com). Then skip to step **10** on page 208.

CONTINUED

CREATE A HYPERLINK

EARTH WISE ENTERPRISES
We care about the environment.
All products created and marketed by Earth Wise Enterprises are designed to increase awareness of environmental issues around the world.
A list of our main types of products is presented below. To find out more about the products in any category, select the category name.
Tree planting kits
Recycle bins
Compost kits
You can easily see hyperlinks in a document. Hyperlinks appear underlined and in color.

CREATE A HYPERLINK (CONTINUED)

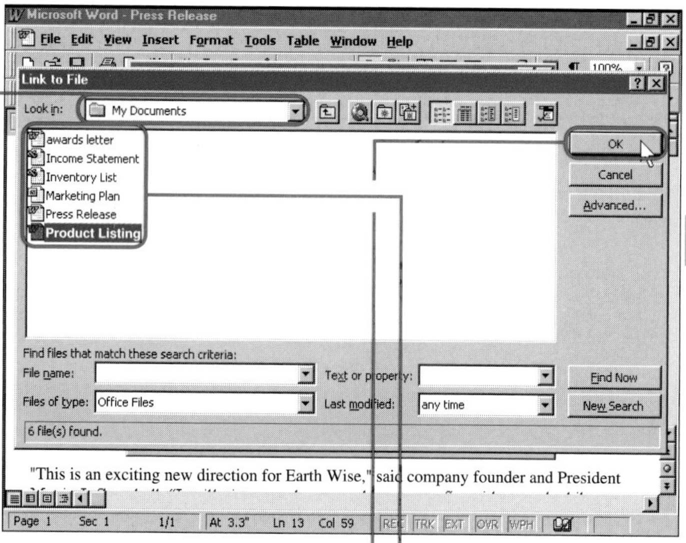

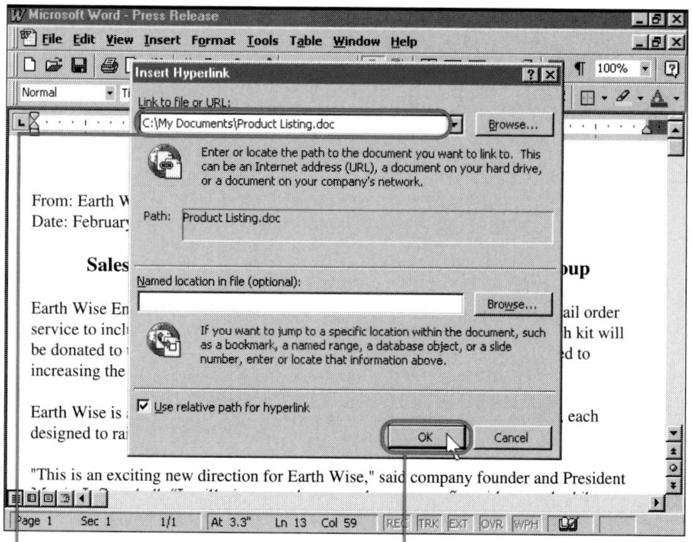

■ The **Link to File** dialog box appears.

■ This area displays the location of the documents listed in the dialog box.

8 Move the mouse over the document you want to link to and then press the left mouse button.

9 Move the mouse over **OK** and then press the left mouse button.

■ The address of the document appears in this area.

10 Move the mouse over **OK** and then press the left mouse button.

Can Word automatically create hyperlinks for me?

When you type the address of a document located on a network or the Internet, Word automatically changes the address to a hyperlink.

http://www.maran.com

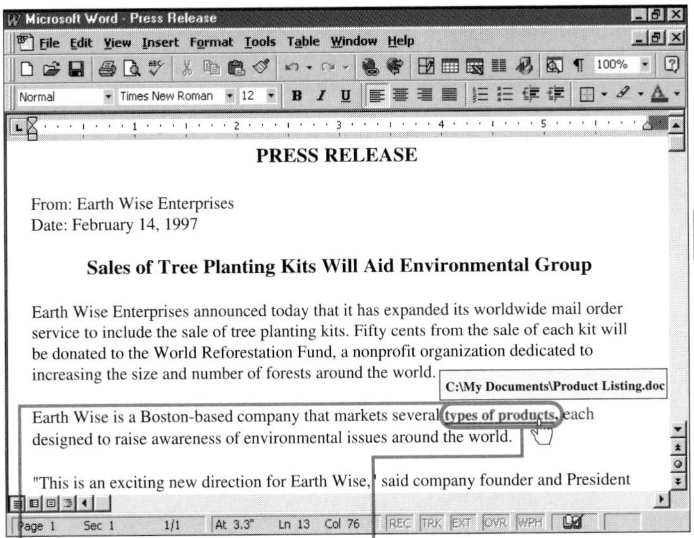
Microsoft Word - Press Release
File Edit View Insert Format Tools Table Window Help
PRESS RELEASE
From: Earth Wise Enterprises
Date: February 14, 1997
Sales of Tree Planting Kits Will Aid Environmental Group
Earth Wise Enterprises announced today that it has expanded its worldwide mail order service to include the sale of tree planting kits. Fifty cents from the sale of each kit will be donated to the World Reforestation Fund, a nonprofit organization dedicated to increasing the size and number of forests around the world.
C:\My Documents\Product Listing.doc
Earth Wise is a Boston-based company that markets several types of products, each designed to raise awareness of environmental issues around the world.
"This is an exciting new direction for Earth Wise," said company founder and President
Page 1 Sec 1 1/1 At 3.3" Ln 13 Col 76

■ The text you selected in step 5 appears as a hyperlink.

11 To display the destination address of the hyperlink, move the mouse over the hyperlink (changes to). After a few seconds, the address appears.

SELECT A HYPERLINK

1 To select a hyperlink, move the mouse over the hyperlink (changes to) and then press the left mouse button.

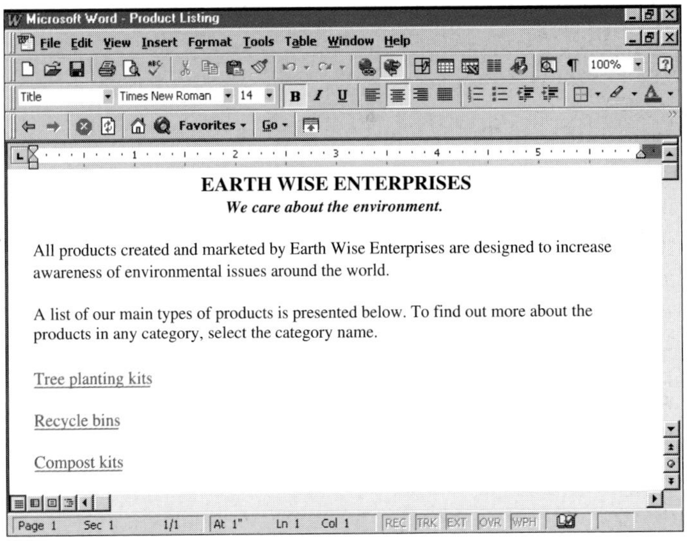
Microsoft Word - Product Listing
File Edit View Insert Format Tools Table Window Help
Favorites Go
EARTH WISE ENTERPRISES
We care about the environment.
All products created and marketed by Earth Wise Enterprises are designed to increase awareness of environmental issues around the world.
A list of our main types of products is presented below. To find out more about the products in any category, select the category name.
Tree planting kits
Recycle bins
Compost kits
Page 1 Sec 1 1/1 At 1" Ln 1 Col 1

■ The document connected to the hyperlink appears.

■ If the hyperlink is connected to a Web page, your Web browser opens and displays the Web page.

DISPLAY THE WEB TOOLBAR

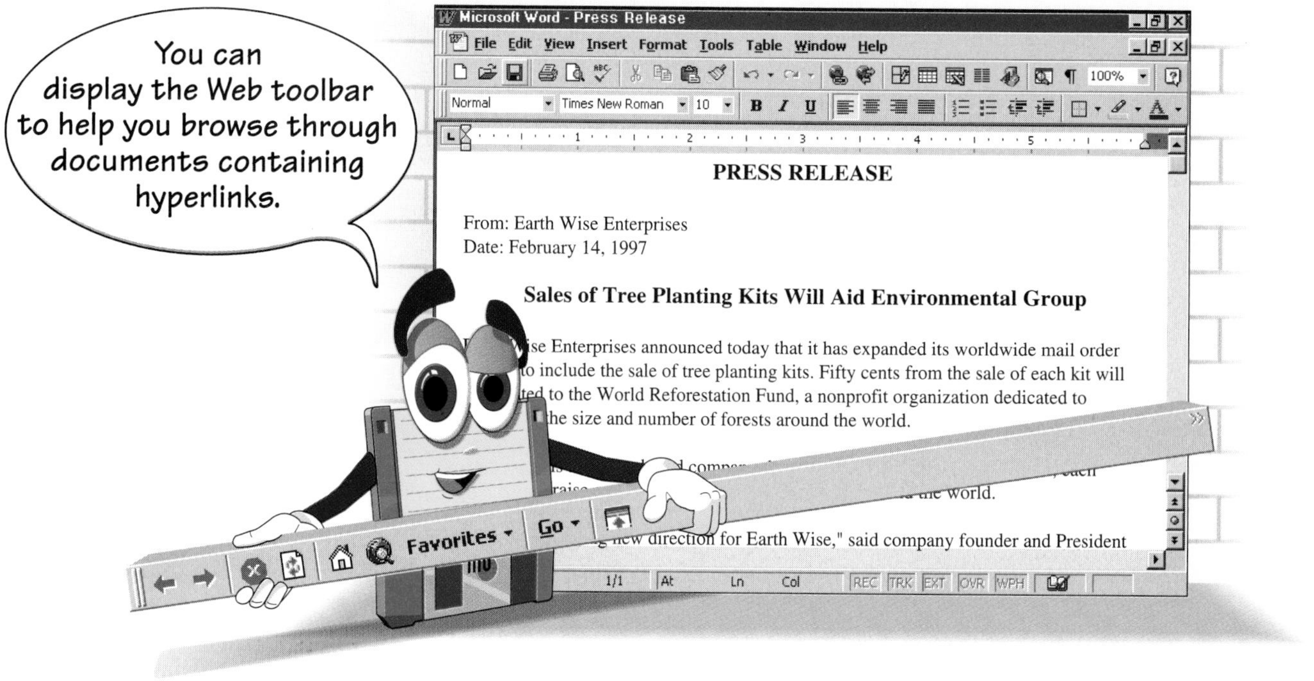
You can display the Web toolbar to help you browse through documents containing hyperlinks.
Microsoft Word - Press Release
PRESS RELEASE
From: Earth Wise Enterprises
Date: February 14, 1997
Sales of Tree Planting Kits Will Aid Environmental Group
Favorites
Go

DISPLAY THE WEB TOOLBAR

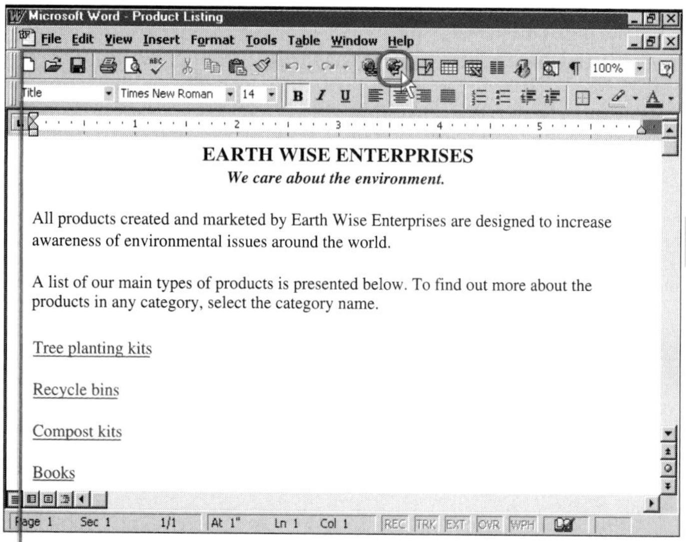
Microsoft Word - Product Listing
EARTH WISE ENTERPRISES
We care about the environment.
All products created and marketed by Earth Wise Enterprises are designed to increase awareness of environmental issues around the world.
A list of our main types of products is presented below. To find out more about the products in any category, select the category name.
Tree planting kits
Recycle bins
Compost kits
Books

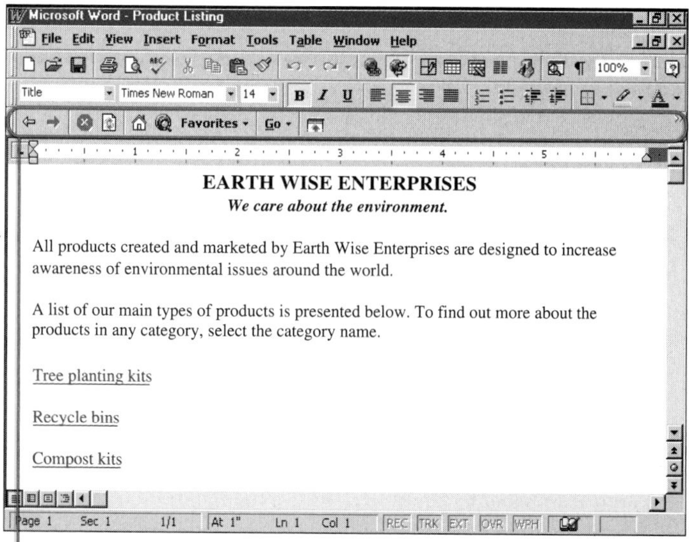
Microsoft Word - Product Listing
Favorites
Go
EARTH WISE ENTERPRISES
We care about the environment.
All products created and marketed by Earth Wise Enterprises are designed to increase awareness of environmental issues around the world.
A list of our main types of products is presented below. To find out more about the products in any category, select the category name.
Tree planting kits
Recycle bins
Compost kits

1 Move the mouse over and then press the left mouse button.

■ The **Web** toolbar appears.

■ To hide the **Web** toolbar, repeat step 1.

MOVE BETWEEN DOCUMENTS

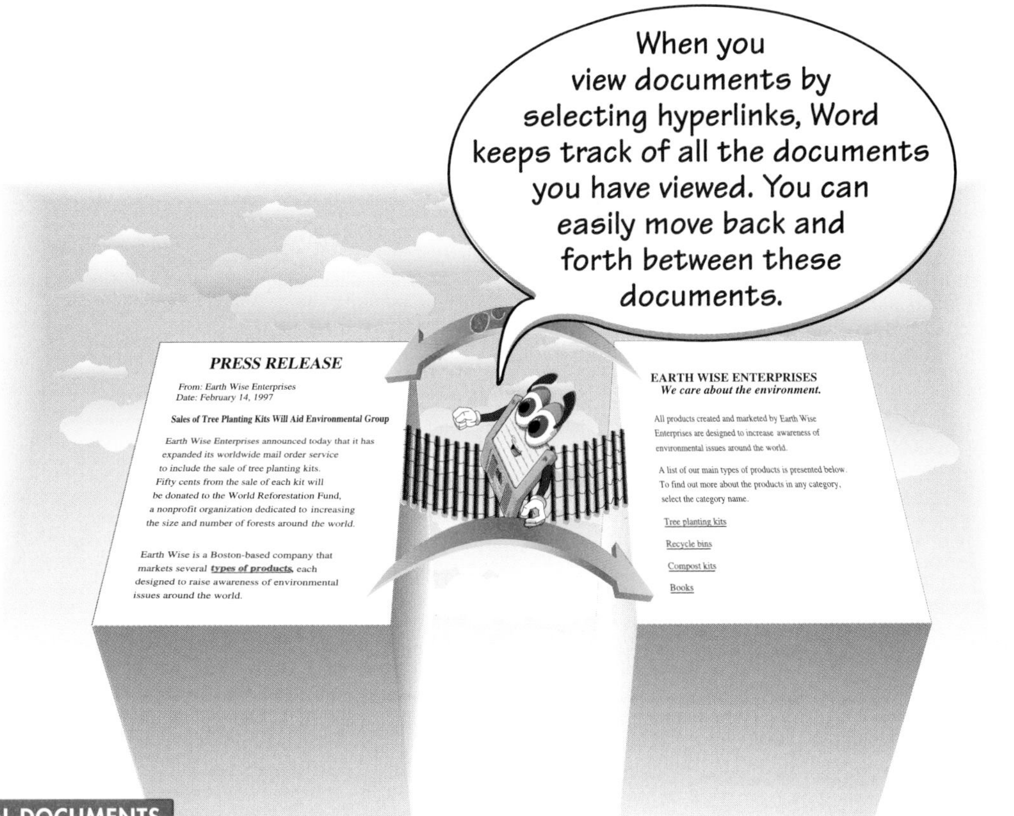
When you view documents by selecting hyperlinks, Word keeps track of all the documents you have viewed. You can easily move back and forth between these documents.
PRESS RELEASE
EARTH WISE ENTERPRISES
We care about the environment.

MOVE BETWEEN DOCUMENTS

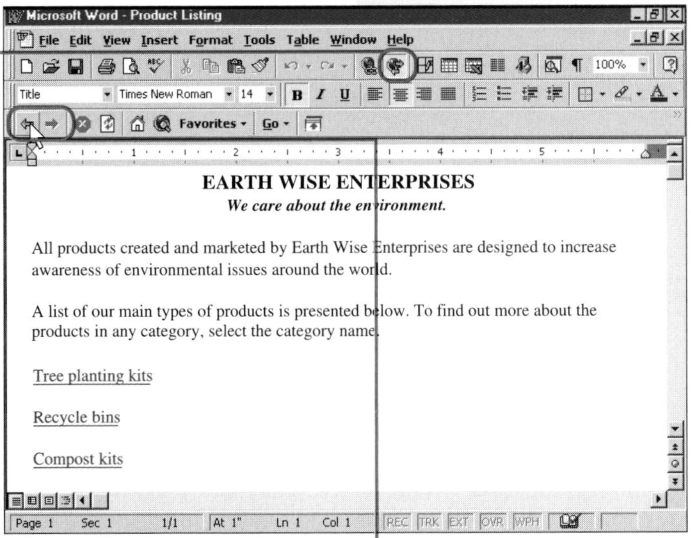
Microsoft Word - Product Listing
File Edit View Insert Format Tools Table Window Help
Favorites Go
EARTH WISE ENTERPRISES
We care about the environment.
All products created and marketed by Earth Wise Enterprises are designed to increase awareness of environmental issues around the world.
A list of our main types of products is presented below. To find out more about the products in any category, select the category name.
Tree planting kits
Recycle bins
Compost kits

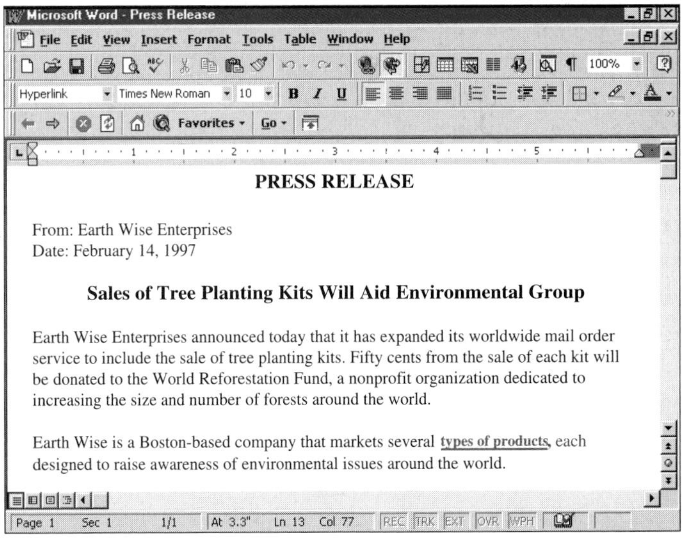
Microsoft Word - Press Release
File Edit View Insert Format Tools Table Window Help
Favorites Go
PRESS RELEASE
From: Earth Wise Enterprises
Date: February 14, 1997
Sales of Tree Planting Kits Will Aid Environmental Group
Earth Wise Enterprises announced today that it has expanded its worldwide mail order service to include the sale of tree planting kits. Fifty cents from the sale of each kit will be donated to the World Reforestation Fund, a nonprofit organization dedicated to increasing the size and number of forests around the world.
Earth Wise is a Boston-based company that markets several types of products, each designed to raise awareness of environmental issues around the world.

■ To display the **Web** toolbar, move the mouse over the Web toolbar button and then press the left mouse button.

1 Move the mouse over one of the following options and then press the left mouse button.

⇦ Move back

⇨ Move forward

■ The document you selected appears.

OPEN A DOCUMENT

You can quickly open a document that is on your computer, network, corporate intranet or the Internet.

OPEN A DOCUMENT

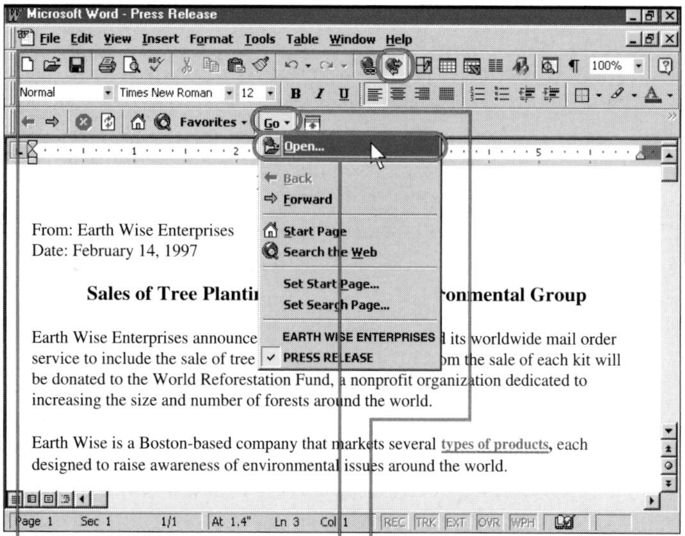

■ To display the **Web** toolbar, move the mouse over [button] and then press the left mouse button.

1 To open a document, move the mouse over **Go** and then press the left mouse button.

2 Move the mouse over **Open** and then press the left mouse button.

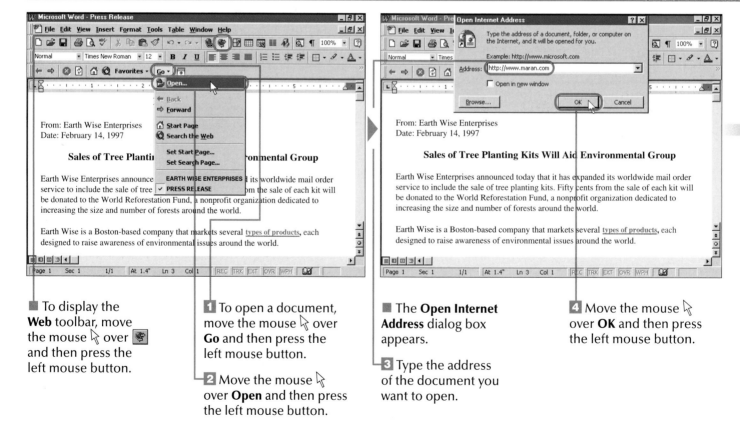

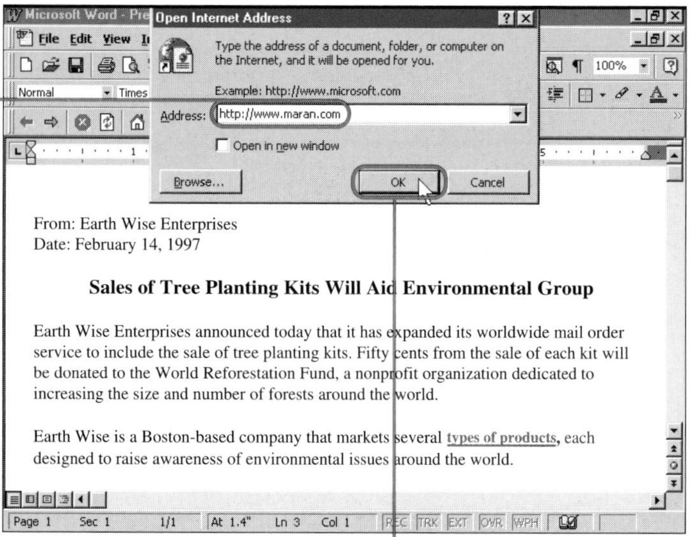

■ The **Open Internet Address** dialog box appears.

3 Type the address of the document you want to open.

4 Move the mouse over **OK** and then press the left mouse button.

STOP THE CONNECTION

If a Web page is taking a long time to appear, you can stop the transfer of information.
STOP

■ The document appears.

■ If you typed a Web page address in step 3, your Web browser opens and displays the Web page.

STOP THE CONNECTION

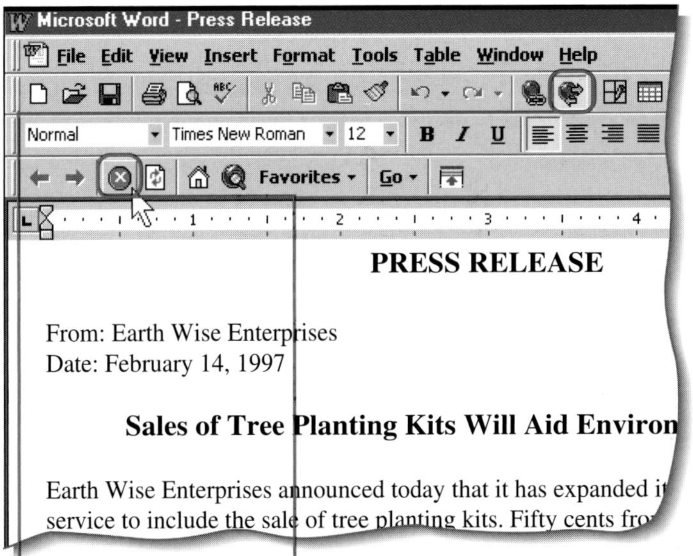

■ To display the **Web** toolbar, move the mouse over and then press the left mouse button.

■ The **Stop** button is red ( ) when information is transferring to your computer.

1 To stop the transfer of information, move the mouse over and then press the left mouse button (changes to).

DISPLAY THE START PAGE

The start page is the first page that appears when you start a Web browser.
START

The start page includes instructions and hyperlinks that let you quickly connect to interesting documents.

DISPLAY THE START PAGE

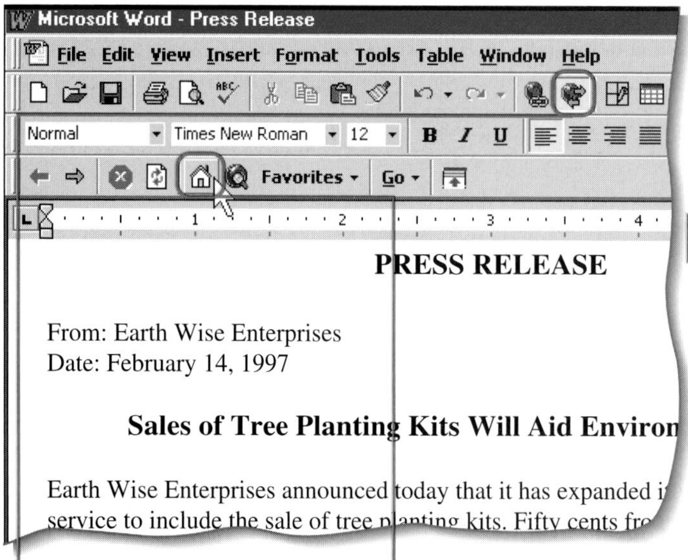

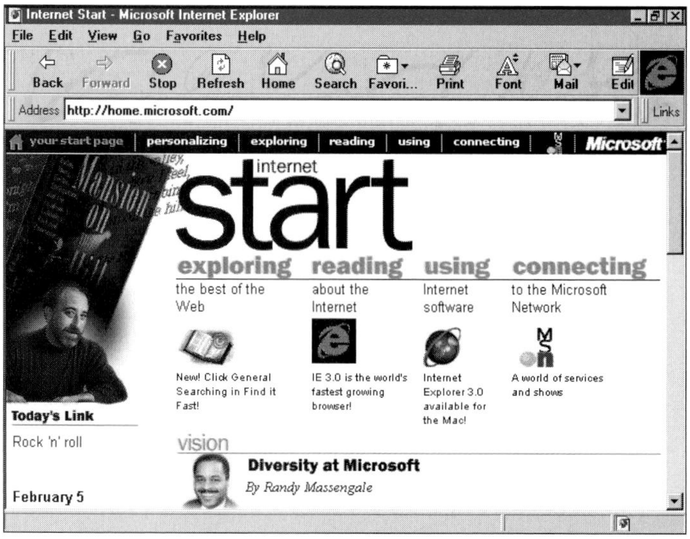

■ To display the **Web** toolbar, move the mouse over the Web toolbar button and then press the left mouse button.

1 To display the start page, move the mouse over the Home button and then press the left mouse button.

■ Your Web browser opens and displays the start page.

■ This page is automatically set as your start page.

DISPLAY THE SEARCH PAGE

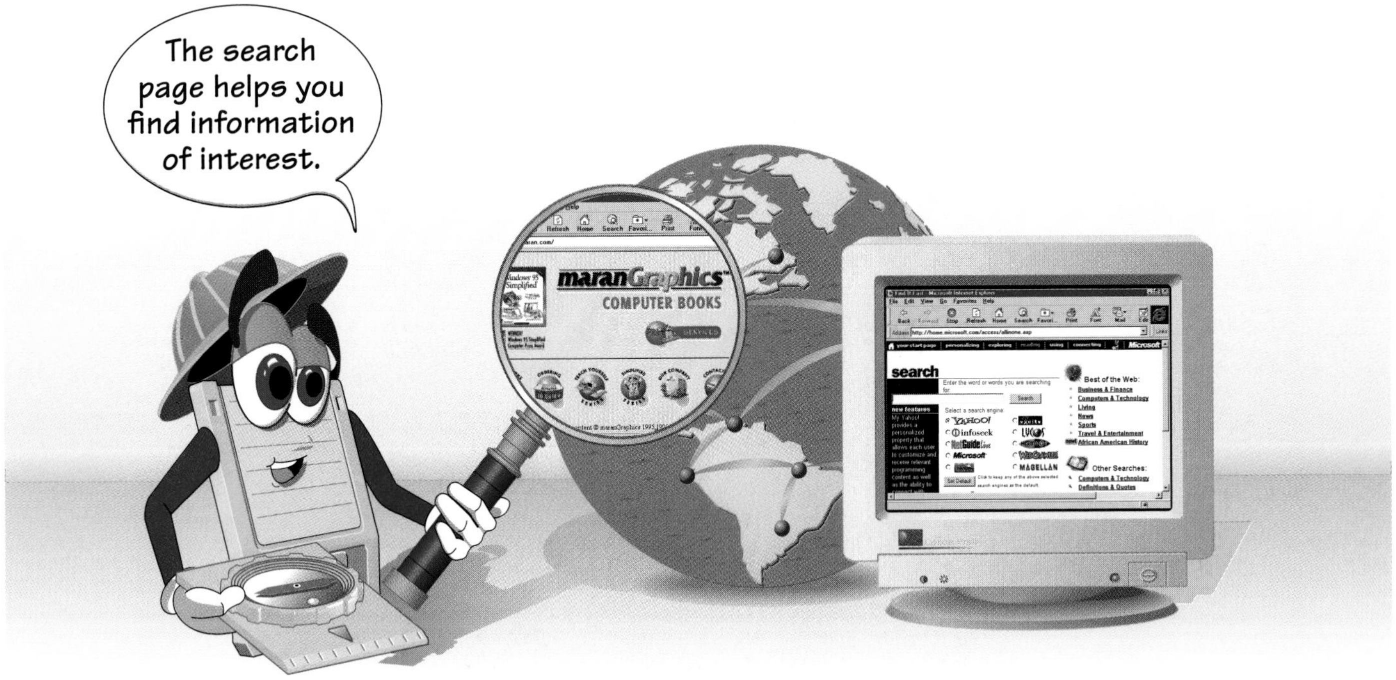
The search page helps you find information of interest.
maranGraphics
COMPUTER BOOKS
search
Best of the Web:

DISPLAY THE SEARCH PAGE

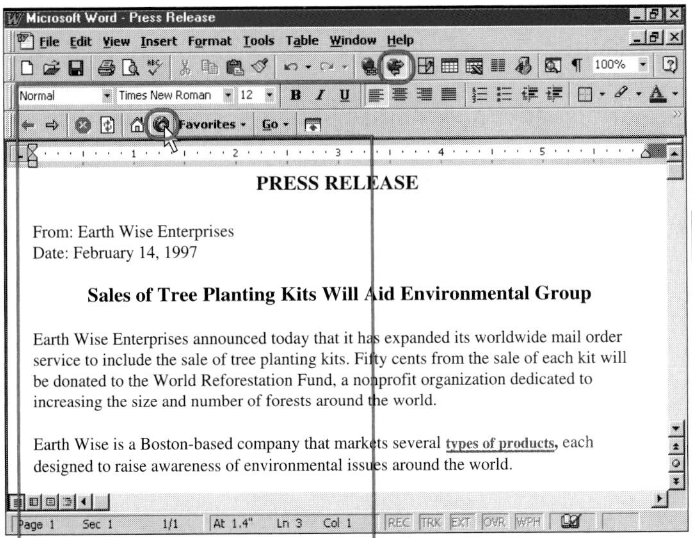
Microsoft Word - Press Release
File Edit View Insert Format Tools Table Window Help
Normal
Times New Roman
12
100%
Favorites
Go
PRESS RELEASE
From: Earth Wise Enterprises
Date: February 14, 1997
Sales of Tree Planting Kits Will Aid Environmental Group
Earth Wise Enterprises announced today that it has expanded its worldwide mail order service to include the sale of tree planting kits. Fifty cents from the sale of each kit will be donated to the World Reforestation Fund, a nonprofit organization dedicated to increasing the size and number of forests around the world.
Earth Wise is a Boston-based company that markets several types of products, each designed to raise awareness of environmental issues around the world.
Page 1 Sec 1 1/1 At 1.4" Ln 3 Col 1 REC TRK EXT OVR WPH

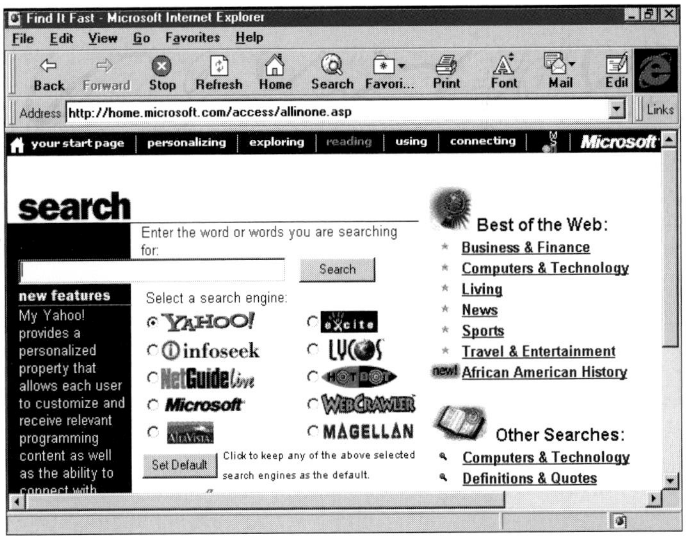
Find It Fast - Microsoft Internet Explorer
File Edit View Go Favorites Help
Back Forward Stop Refresh Home Search Favori... Print Font Mail Edit
Address http://home.microsoft.com/access/allinone.asp
Links
your start page personalizing exploring reading using connecting Microsoft
search
Enter the word or words you are searching for:
Search
new features
My Yahoo! provides a personalized property that allows each user to customize and receive relevant programming content as well as the ability to connect with
Select a search engine:
YAHOO!
infoseek
NetGuide Live
Microsoft
excite
LYCOS
HOTBOT
WEBCRAWLER
MAGELLAN
Set Default
Click to keep any of the above selected search engines as the default.
Best of the Web:
Business & Finance
Computers & Technology
Living
News
Sports
Travel & Entertainment
new! African American History
Other Searches:
Computers & Technology
Definitions & Quotes

■ To display the **Web** toolbar, move the mouse over the Web toolbar button and then press the left mouse button.

1 To display the search page, move the mouse over the search button and then press the left mouse button.

■ Your Web browser opens and displays the search page.

■ This page is automatically set as your search page.

ADD A DOCUMENT TO FAVORITES

You can add documents you frequently use to the Favorites folder. This lets you quickly open these documents at any time.
PRODUCT LIST
AWARDS LETTER
PRESS RELEASE
FAVORITES

ADD A DOCUMENT TO FAVORITES

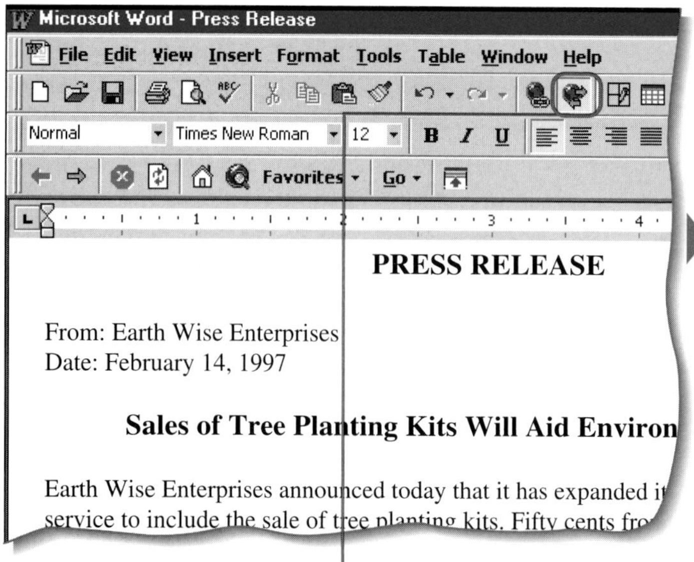
Microsoft Word - Press Release
File Edit View Insert Format Tools Table Window Help
Normal
Times New Roman
12
Favorites
Go
PRESS RELEASE
From: Earth Wise Enterprises
Date: February 14, 1997
Sales of Tree Planting Kits Will Aid Environ
Earth Wise Enterprises announced today that it has expanded i

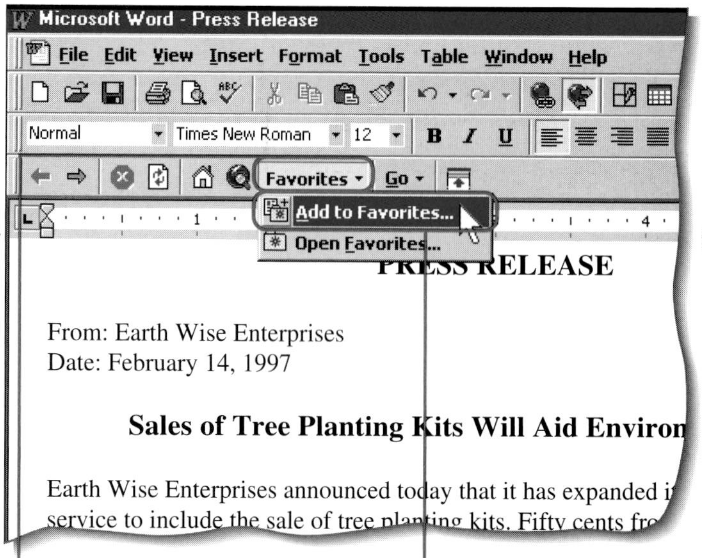
Microsoft Word - Press Release
File Edit View Insert Format Tools Table Window Help
Normal
Times New Roman
12
Favorites
Go
Add to Favorites...
Open Favorites...
From: Earth Wise Enterprises
Date: February 14, 1997
Sales of Tree Planting Kits Will Aid Environ
Earth Wise Enterprises announced today that it has expanded i

1 Open the document you want to add to the Favorites folder. To open a document, refer to page 24.

■ To display the **Web** toolbar, move the mouse over and then press the left mouse button.

2 Move the mouse over **Favorites** and then press the left mouse button.

3 Move the mouse over **Add to Favorites** and then press the left mouse button.

When I add a document to the Favorites folder, does the document change location?

When you add a document to the Favorites folder, you create a shortcut to the original document. The original document does not change its location on your computer.

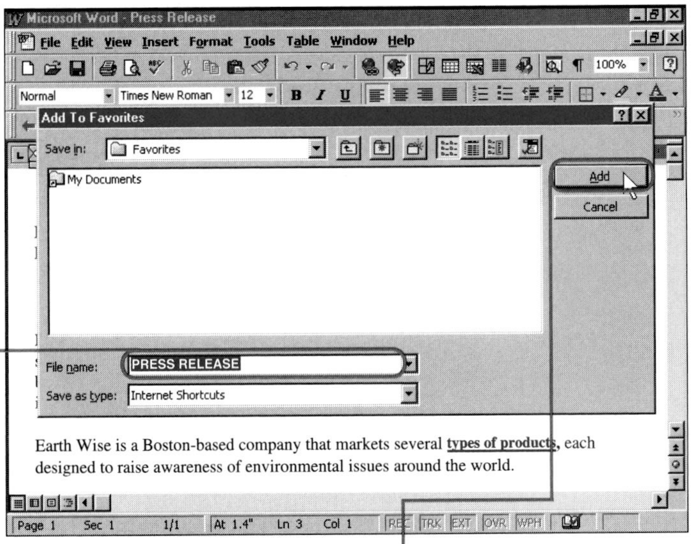

■ The **Add To Favorites** dialog box appears.

■ This area displays a name for the document. To change the name, type a new name.

4 Move the mouse over **Add** and then press the left mouse button.

OPEN A DOCUMENT IN FAVORITES

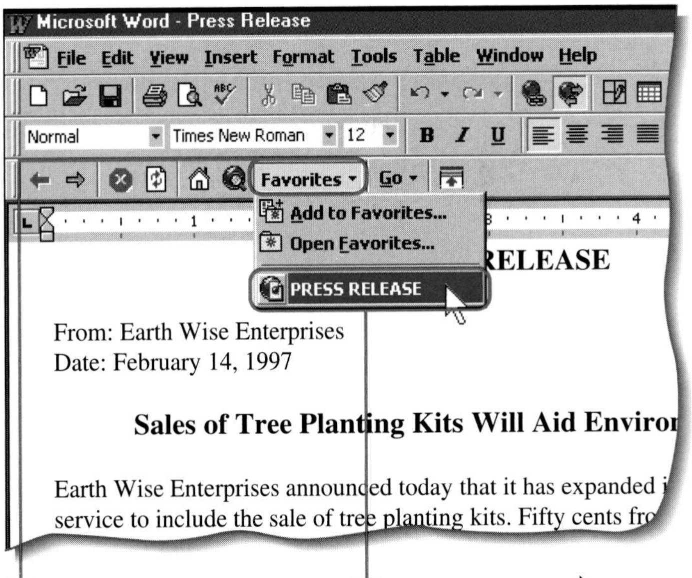

1 To open a document in the Favorites folder, move the mouse over **Favorites** and then press the left mouse button.

2 Move the mouse over the name of the document you want to open and then press the left mouse button.

SAVE A DOCUMENT AS A WEB PAGE

SAVE A DOCUMENT AS A WEB PAGE

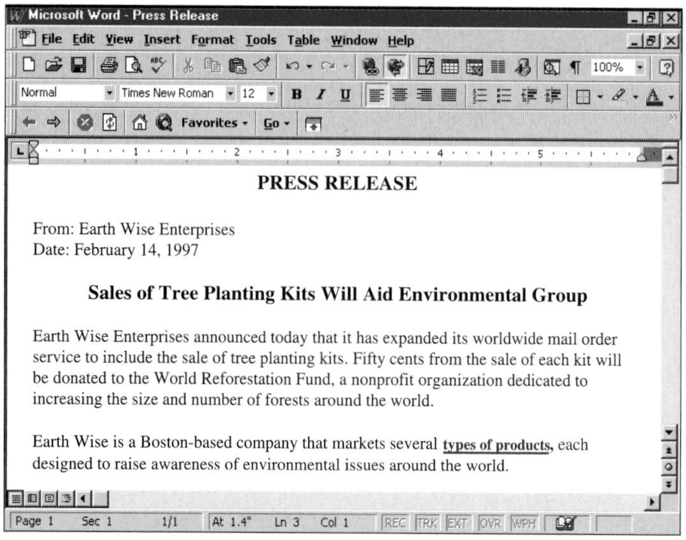

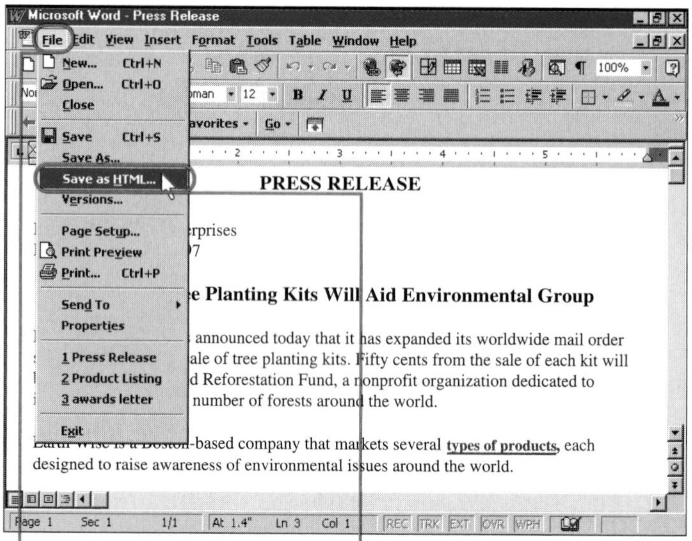

1 Open the document you want to save as a Web page. To open a document, refer to page 24.

2 Move the mouse over **File** and then press the left mouse button.

3 Move the mouse over **Save as HTML** and then press the left mouse button.

*Note: If the **Save as HTML** command is not available, you need to add the Web Page Authoring (HTML) component from the Microsoft Word or Microsoft Office CD-ROM disc.*

Can Word help me create a new Web page?

You can use a template or wizard to help you create a new Web page. Templates and wizards complete the layout and formatting of a document so you can concentrate on the content. For information on using templates and wizards, refer to page 148.

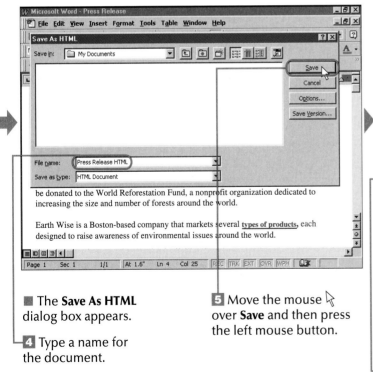

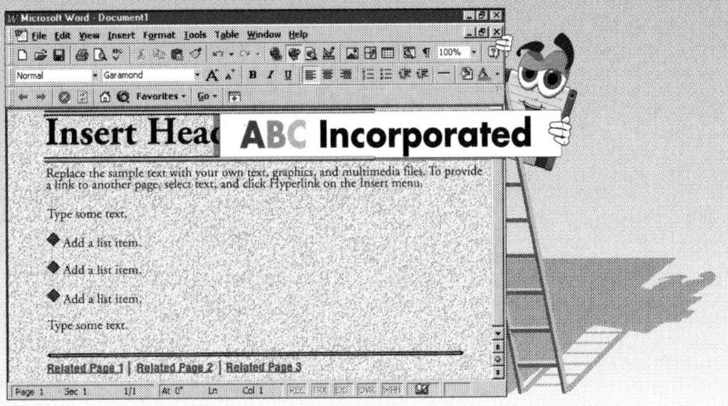
Insert Heading
ABC Incorporated
Replace the sample text with your own text, graphics, and multimedia files. To provide a link to another page, select text, and click Hyperlink on the Insert menu.
Type some text.
Add a list item.
Add a list item.
Add a list item.
Type some text.
Related Page 1 | Related Page 2 | Related Page 3

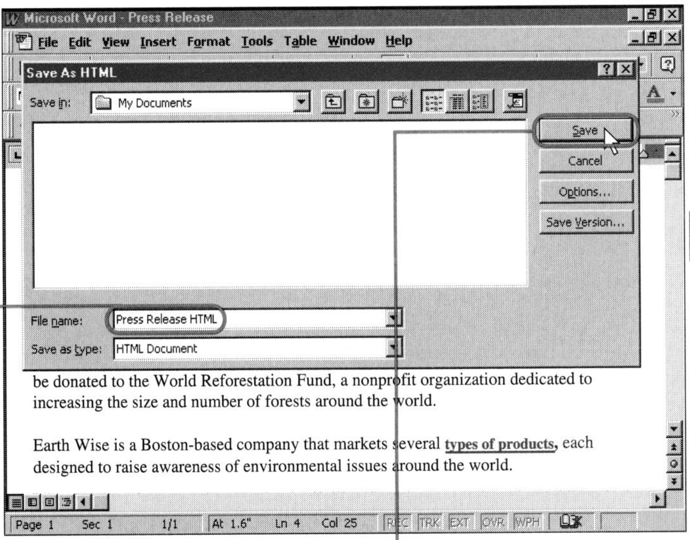
Microsoft Word - Press Release
Save As HTML
Save in: My Documents
Save
Cancel
Options...
Save Version...
File name: Press Release HTML
Save as type: HTML Document
be donated to the World Reforestation Fund, a nonprofit organization dedicated to increasing the size and number of forests around the world.
Earth Wise is a Boston-based company that markets several types of products, each designed to raise awareness of environmental issues around the world.

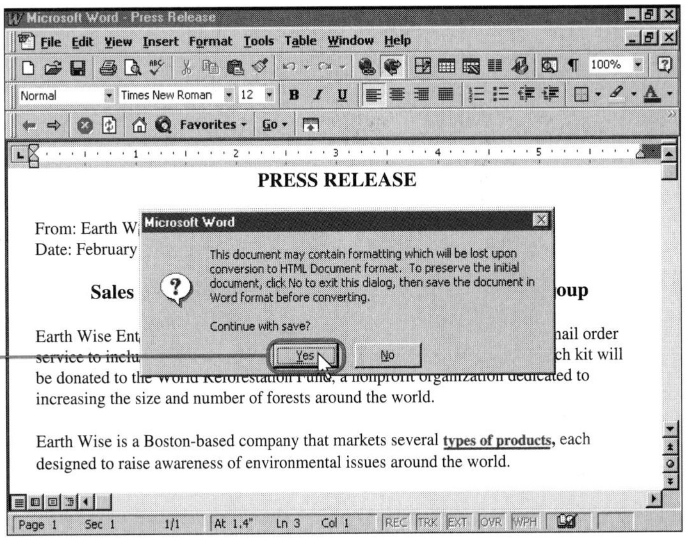
Microsoft Word - Press Release
PRESS RELEASE
Microsoft Word
This document may contain formatting which will be lost upon conversion to HTML Document format. To preserve the initial document, click No to exit this dialog, then save the document in Word format before converting.
Continue with save?
Yes
No
increasing the size and number of forests around the world.
Earth Wise is a Boston-based company that markets several types of products, each designed to raise awareness of environmental issues around the world.

■ The **Save As HTML** dialog box appears.

4 Type a name for the document.

5 Move the mouse over **Save** and then press the left mouse button.

■ A dialog box may appear, warning you that your document may contain formatting that will be lost.

6 To save the document as a Web page, move the mouse over **Yes** and then press the left mouse button.

■ You can now place the document on a corporate intranet or the Web for others to view.

INDEX

E

INDEX

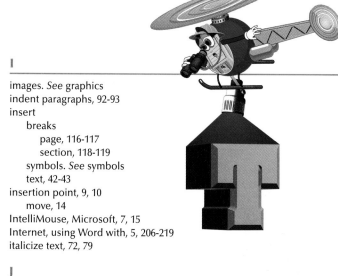

INDEX

U

V

W

Z

The fun & easy way to learn about computers and more!

SUPER STAR

Windows 3.1 For Dummies,™ 2nd Edition
by Andy Rathbone

ISBN: 1-56884-182-5
$16.95 USA/$22.95 Canada

SUPER STAR

MORE Windows For Dummies™
by Andy Rathbone

ISBN: 1-56884-048-9
$19.95 USA/$26.95 Canada

SUPER STAR

DOS For Dummies,® 2nd Edition
by Dan Gookin

ISBN: 1-878058-75-4
$16.95 USA/$22.95 Canada

IX FINALIST *Ninth Annual Computer Press Awards 1993*

The Internet For Dummies™
by John Levine & Carol Baroudi

ISBN: 1-56884-024-1
$19.95 USA/$26.95 Canada

NATIONAL BESTSELLER!

Personal Finance For Dummies™
by Eric Tyson

ISBN: 1-56884-150-7
$16.95 USA/$22.95 Canada

VIII FINALIST *Eighth Annual Computer Press Awards 1992*

PCs For Dummies,™ 2nd Edition
by Dan Gookin & Andy Rathbone

ISBN: 1-56884-078-0
$16.95 USA/$22.95 Canada

SUPER STAR

Macs For Dummies,™ 2nd Edition
by David Pogue

ISBN: 1-56884-051-9
$19.95 USA/$26.95 Canada

Here's a complete listing of IDG's...*For Dummies* Titles

Title	Author	ISBN #	Price
DATABASE			
Access 2 For Dummies™	by Scott Palmer	ISBN: 1-56884-090-X	$19.95 USA/$26.95 Canada
Access Programming For Dummies™	by Rob Krumm	ISBN: 1-56884-091-8	$19.95 USA/$26.95 Canada
Approach 3 For Windows For Dummies™	by Doug Lowe	ISBN: 1-56884-233-3	$19.99 USA/$26.99 Canada
dBASE For DOS For Dummies™	by Scott Palmer & Michael Stabler	ISBN: 1-56884-188-4	$19.95 USA/$26.95 Canada
dBASE For Windows For Dummies™	by Scott Palmer	ISBN: 1-56884-179-5	$19.95 USA/$26.95 Canada
dBASE 5 For Windows Programming For Dummies™	by Ted Coombs & Jason Coombs	ISBN: 1-56884-215-5	$19.99 USA/$26.99 Canada
FoxPro 2.6 For Windows For Dummies™	by John Kaufeld	ISBN: 1-56884-187-6	$19.95 USA/$26.95 Canada
Paradox 5 For Windows For Dummies™	by John Kaufeld	ISBN: 1-56884-185-X	$19.95 USA/$26.95 Canada
DESKTOP PUBLISHING/ILLUSTRATION/GRAPHICS			
CorelDRAW! 5 For Dummies™	by Deke McClelland	ISBN: 1-56884-157-4	$19.95 USA/$26.95 Canada
CorelDRAW! For Dummies™	by Deke McClelland	ISBN: 1-56884-042-X	$19.95 USA/$26.95 Canada
Harvard Graphics 2 For Windows For Dummies™	by Roger C. Parker	ISBN: 1-56884-092-6	$19.95 USA/$26.95 Canada
PageMaker 5 For Macs For Dummies™	by Galen Gruman & Deke McClelland	ISBN: 1-56884-178-7	$19.95 USA/$26.95 Canada
PageMaker 5 For Windows For Dummies™	by Deke McClelland & Galen Gruman	ISBN: 1-56884-160-4	$19.95 USA/$26.95 Canada
QuarkXPress 3.3 For Dummies™	by Galen Gruman & Barbara Assadi	ISBN: 1-56884-217-1	$19.99 USA/$26.99 Canada
FINANCE/PERSONAL FINANCE/TEST TAKING REFERENCE			
QuickBooks "X" For Dummies™	by Stephen L. Nelson	ISBN: 1-56884-227-9	$19.99 USA/$26.99 Canada
Quicken "X" For DOS For Dummies™, 2nd Edition	by Stephen L. Nelson	ISBN: 1-56884-210-4	$19.95 USA/$26.95 Canada
Quicken "X" For Macs For Dummies™	by Stephen L. Nelson	ISBN: 1-56884-211-2	$19.95 USA/$26.95 Canada
Quicken "X" For Windows For Dummies™, 2nd Edition	by Stephen L. Nelson	ISBN: 1-56884-209-0	$19.95 USA/$26.95 Canada
The SAT I For Dummies™	by Suzee Vlk	ISBN: 1-56884-213-9	$14.99 USA/$20.99 Canada
TurboTax For Windows For Dummies™	by Gail A. Perry, CPA	ISBN: 1-56884-228-7	$19.99 USA/$26.99 Canada
GROUPWARE/INTEGRATED			
Lotus Notes 3.0/3.1 For Dummies™	by Paul Freeland & Stephen Londergan	ISBN: 1-56884-212-0	$19.95 USA/$26.95 Canada
Microsoft Office 4 For Windows For Dummies™	by Roger C. Parker	ISBN: 1-56884-183-3	$19.95 USA/$26.95 Canada
Microsoft Works For Windows 3 For Dummies™	by David C. Kay	ISBN: 1-56884-214-7	$19.99 USA/$26.99 Canada

FOR MORE INFO OR TO ORDER, PLEASE CALL ▸ 800 762 2974 For volume discounts & special orders please call Tony Real, Special Sales, at 415. 312. 0644

Title	Author	ISBN #	Price
INTERNET/COMMUNICATIONS/NETWORKING			
CompuServe For Dummies™	by Wallace Wang	ISBN: 1-56884-181-7	$19.95 USA/$26.95 Canada
Modems For Dummies™, 2nd Edition	by Tina Rathbone	ISBN: 1-56884-223-6	$19.99 USA/$26.99 Canada
Modems For Dummies™	by Tina Rathbone	ISBN: 1-56884-001-2	$19.95 USA/$26.95 Canada
MORE Internet For Dummies™	by John Levine & Margaret Levine Young	ISBN: 1-56884-164-7	$19.95 USA/$26.95 Canada
NetWare For Dummies™	by Ed Tittel & Deni Connor	ISBN: 1-56884-003-9	$19.95 USA/$26.95 Canada
Networking For Dummies™	by Doug Lowe	ISBN: 1-56884-079-9	$19.95 USA/$26.95 Canada
ProComm Plus 2 For Windows For Dummies™	by Wallace Wang	ISBN: 1-56884-219-8	$19.99 USA/$26.99 Canada
The Internet Help Desk For Dummies™	by John Kaufeld	ISBN: 1-56884-238-4	$16.99 USA/$22.99 Canada
The3 Internet For Dummies™, 2nd Edition	by John Levine & Carol Baroudi	ISBN: 1-56884-222-8	$19.99 USA/$26.99 Canada
The Internet For Macs For Dummies™	by Charles Seiter	ISBN: 1-56884-184-1	$19.95 USA/$26.95 Canada
MACINTOSH			
Mac Programming For Dummies™	by Dan Parks Sydow	ISBN: 1-56884-173-6	$19.95 USA/$26.95 Canada
Macintosh System 7.5 For Dummies™	by Bob LeVitus	ISBN: 1-56884-197-3	$19.95 USA/$26.95 Canada
MORE Macs For Dummies™	by David Pogue	ISBN: 1-56884-087-X	$19.95 USA/$26.95 Canada
PageMaker 5 For Macs For Dummies™	by Galen Gruman & Deke McClelland	ISBN: 1-56884-178-7	$19.95 USA/$26.95 Canada
QuarkXPress 3.3 For Dummies™	by Galen Gruman & Barbara Assadi	ISBN: 1-56884-217-1	$19.99 USA/$26.99 Canada
Upgrading and Fixing Macs For Dummies™	by Kearney Rietmann & Frank Higgins	ISBN: 1-56884-189-2	$19.95 USA/$26.95 Canada
MULTIMEDIA			
Multimedia & CD-ROMs For Dummies™, Interactive Multimedia Value Pack	by Andy Rathbone	ISBN: 1-56884-225-2	$29.95 USA/$39.95 Canada
Multimedia & CD-ROMs For Dummies™	by Andy Rathbone	ISBN: 1-56884-089-6	$19.95 USA/$26.95 Canada
OPERATING SYSTEMS/DOS			
MORE DOS For Dummies™	by Dan Gookin	ISBN: 1-56884-046-2	$19.95 USA/$26.95 Canada
S.O.S. For DOS™	by Katherine Murray	ISBN: 1-56884-043-8	$12.95 USA/$16.95 Canada
OS/2 For Dummies™	by Andy Rathbone	ISBN: 1-878058-76-2	$19.95 USA/$26.95 Canada
UNIX			
UNIX For Dummies™	by John Levine & Margaret Levine Young	ISBN: 1-878058-58-4	$19.95 USA/$26.95 Canada
WINDOWS			
S.O.S. For Windows™	by Katherine Murray	ISBN: 1-56884-045-4	$12.95 USA/$16.95 Canada
Windows "X" For Dummies™, 3rd Edition	by Andy Rathbone	ISBN: 1-56884-240-6	$19.99 USA/$26.99 Canada
PCS/HARDWARE			
Illustrated Computer Dictionary For Dummies™	by Dan Gookin, Wally Wang, & Chris Van Buren	ISBN: 1-56884-004-7	$12.95 USA/$16.95 Canada
Upgrading and Fixing PCs For Dummies™	by Andy Rathbone	ISBN: 1-56884-002-0	$19.95 USA/$26.95 Canada
PRESENTATION/AUTOCAD			
AutoCAD For Dummies™	by Bud Smith	ISBN: 1-56884-191-4	$19.95 USA/$26.95 Canada
PowerPoint 4 For Windows For Dummies™	by Doug Lowe	ISBN: 1-56884-161-2	$16.95 USA/$22.95 Canada
PROGRAMMING			
Borland C++ For Dummies™	by Michael Hyman	ISBN: 1-56884-162-0	$19.95 USA/$26.95 Canada
"Borland's New Language Product" For Dummies™	by Neil Rubenking	ISBN: 1-56884-200-7	$19.95 USA/$26.95 Canada
C For Dummies™	by Dan Gookin	ISBN: 1-878058-78-9	$19.95 USA/$26.95 Canada
C++ For Dummies™	by S. Randy Davis	ISBN: 1-56884-163-9	$19.95 USA/$26.95 Canada
Mac Programming For Dummies™	by Dan Parks Sydow	ISBN: 1-56884-173-6	$19.95 USA/$26.95 Canada
QBasic Programming For Dummies™	by Douglas Hergert	ISBN: 1-56884-093-4	$19.95 USA/$26.95 Canada
Visual Basic "X" For Dummies™, 2nd Edition	by Wallace Wang	ISBN: 1-56884-230-9	$19.99 USA/$26.99 Canada
Visual Basic 3 For Dummies™	by Wallace Wang	ISBN: 1-56884-076-4	$19.95 USA/$26.95 Canada
SPREADSHEET			
1-2-3 For Dummies™	by Greg Harvey	ISBN: 1-878058-60-6	$16.95 USA/$22.95 Canada
1-2-3 For Windows 5 For Dummies™, 2nd Edition	by John Walkenbach	ISBN: 1-56884-216-3	$16.95 USA/$22.95 Canada
1-2-3 For Windows For Dummies™	by John Walkenbach	ISBN: 1-56884-052-7	$16.95 USA/$22.95 Canada
Excel 5 For Macs For Dummies™	by Greg Harvey	ISBN: 1-56884-186-8	$19.95 USA/$26.95 Canada
Excel For Dummies™, 2nd Edition	by Greg Harvey	ISBN: 1-56884-050-0	$16.95 USA/$22.95 Canada
MORE Excel 5 For Windows For Dummies™	by Greg Harvey	ISBN: 1-56884-207-4	$19.95 USA/$26.95 Canada
Quattro Pro 6 For Windows For Dummies™	by John Walkenbach	ISBN: 1-56884-174-4	$19.95 USA/$26.95 Canada
Quattro Pro For DOS For Dummies™	by John Walkenbach	ISBN: 1-56884-023-3	$16.95 USA/$22.95 Canada
UTILITIES			
Norton Utilities 8 For Dummies™	by Beth Slick	ISBN: 1-56884-166-3	$19.95 USA/$26.95 Canada
VCRS/CAMCORDERS			
VCRs & Camcorders For Dummies™	by Andy Rathbone & Gordon McComb	ISBN: 1-56884-229-5	$14.99 USA/$20.99 Canada
WORD PROCESSING			
Ami Pro For Dummies™	by Jim Meade	ISBN: 1-56884-049-7	$19.95 USA/$26.95 Canada
More Word For Windows 6 For Dummies™	by Doug Lowe	ISBN: 1-56884-165-5	$19.95 USA/$26.95 Canada
MORE WordPerfect 6 For Windows For Dummies™	by Margaret Levine Young & David C. Kay	ISBN: 1-56884-206-6	$19.95 USA/$26.95 Canada
MORE WordPerfect 6 For DOS For Dummies™	by Wallace Wang, edited by Dan Gookin	ISBN: 1-56884-047-0	$19.95 USA/$26.95 Canada
S.O.S. For WordPerfect™	by Katherine Murray	ISBN: 1-56884-053-5	$12.95 USA/$16.95 Canada
Word 6 For Macs For Dummies™	by Dan Gookin	ISBN: 1-56884-190-6	$19.95 USA/$26.95 Canada
Word For Windows 6 For Dummies™	by Dan Gookin	ISBN: 1-56884-075-6	$16.95 USA/$22.95 Canada
Word For Windows 2 For Dummies™	by Dan Gookin	ISBN: 1-878058-86-X	$16.95 USA/$22.95 Canada
WordPerfect 6 For Dummies™	by Dan Gookin	ISBN: 1-878058-77-0	$16.95 USA/$22.95 Canada
WordPerfect For Dummies™	by Dan Gookin	ISBN: 1-878058-52-5	$16.95 USA/$22.95 Canada
WordPerfect For Windows For Dummies™	by Margaret Levine Young & David C. Kay	ISBN: 1-56884-032-2	$16.95 USA/$22.95 Canada

IDG BOOKS®

TRADE & INDIVIDUAL ORDERS

Phone: **(800) 762-2974**
or **(317) 895-5200**
(8 a.m.–6 p.m., CST, weekdays)
FAX : **(317) 895-5298**

EDUCATIONAL ORDERS & DISCOUNTS

Phone: **(800) 434-2086**
(8:30 a.m.–5:00 p.m., CST, weekdays)
FAX : **(817) 251-8174**

CORPORATE ORDERS FOR 3-D VISUAL™ SERIES

Phone: **(800) 469-6616**
(8 a.m.–5 p.m., EST, weekdays)
FAX : **(905) 890-9434**

Qty	ISBN	Title	Price	Total

Shipping & Handling Charges

	Description	First book	Each add'l. book	Total
Domestic	Normal	$4.50	$1.50	$
	Two Day Air	$8.50	$2.50	$
	Overnight	$18.00	$3.00	$
International	Surface	$8.00	$8.00	$
	Airmail	$16.00	$16.00	$
	DHL Air	$17.00	$17.00	$

Subtotal ______________

CA residents add applicable sales tax ______________

IN, MA and MD residents add 5% sales tax ______________

IL residents add 6.25% sales tax ______________

RI residents add 7% sales tax ______________

TX residents add 8.25% sales tax ______________

Shipping ______________

Total ______________

Ship to:

Name ______________________________

Address ______________________________

Company ______________________________

City/State/Zip ______________________________

Daytime Phone ______________________________

Payment: □ Check to IDG Books (US Funds Only)
□ Visa □ Mastercard □ American Express

Card # ______________ Exp. __________ Signature ______________

maranGraphics™